Object-Oriented Programming with. Visual C++™ 1.5

Jack Tackett, Jr.
Ed Mitchell

Object-Oriented Programming with Visual C++™ 1.5

Copyright © 1994 by Que® Corporation

Library of Congress Catalog No.: 94-65881

ISBN: 1-56529-686-9

96 95 94   4 3 2 1

Interpretation of the printing code: the rightmost double-digit number is the year of the book's printing; the rightmost single- digit number is the number of the book's printing. For example, a printing code of 94-1 shows that the first printing of the book occurred in 1994.

Screens reproduced in this book were created with Collage Complete from Inner Media, Inc., Hollis, NH.

Publisher: David P. Ewing

Associate Publisher: Michael Miller

Managing Editor: Michael Cunningham

Product Marketing Manager: Ray Robinson

Dedication

To my wife, Peggy.
I love you!

Credits

Publishing Manager
Joseph B. Wikert

Product Director
Bryan Gambrel

Production Editor
Virginia Noble

Editors
Jeanne Lemen
Elsa Bell
Lori Cates
Jodi Jensen
Linda Seifert

Technical Editor
Bob Zigon

Book Designer
Amy Peppler-Adams

Cover Designer
Jay Corpus

Production Team
Angela Bannan
Stephen Adams
Cameron Booker
Carla Hall
William J. Hartmann
Aren Munk

Indexer
Jennifer Eberhardt

Editorial Assistant
Michelle Williams

Composed in *Stone Serif* and *MCP Digital*
by Que Corporation

About the Authors

Formerly a software engineer at the Oak Ridge National Lab, **Jack Tackett, Jr.**, helped designed and implement user interfaces for corporate information centers, moving legacy systems from the lab's aging mainframes to its desktop PCs.

Currently, Jack works for Wandel and Goltermann Technologies, located in Research Triangle Park, North Carolina. W&G is a leader in the design and development of advance network and telecom analyzers. Jack is the lead software engineer for the user interface of W&G's Asynchronous Transfer Mode (ATM) protocol analyzer.

During his spare time, Jack enjoys writing, reading, building his family's new home, and chasing his family's two dogs and two cats around a very small apartment.

Formerly a project manager at Software Publishing Corporation, **Ed Mitchell** created and coauthored the award-winning, best-selling PFS:First Choice integrated software package for DOS. At SPC, he also coauthored one of the first word processors for the IBM PC, PFS:Write (now known as Professional Write). In the early days of the PC, PFS:Write was the best-selling word processing software for the IBM PC and compatible computers.

Mr. Mitchell now writes computer books full-time. In addition to writing *Object-Oriented Programming from Square One*, he is principal author of several books, including *Secrets of the Borland C++ Masters* (Sams Publishing, 1992); coauthor of *Using Microsoft C/C++ 7* (Que, 1992); and author of *Borland Pascal Developer's Guide* (Que, 1993). Mr. Mitchell has also written magazine articles.

Acknowledgments

I would like to thank Joe Wikert, Bryan Gambrel, Ginny Noble, and the entire crew at Que for their help and guidance throughout this project. This book is truly a team effort, and I have nothing but praise for the people at the Que continuum.

So many people helped in the production of this book that it would be difficult to thank everyone, but I would like to say thank you to Ed Mitchell, who wrote the first version of this book, *Object-Oriented Programming from Square One*. Special thanks to my friend and cohort Keith Bugg, thanks for the help Skipper! Special thanks also goes to Jim Ross, a fellow Que author, for his help with the QuickWin/MFC issues I encountered.

To my friends Paul Barrett, Keith Bugg, Gregg Field, Dave and Lola Gunter, Dianna Smith, Bill Tackett, Jr., Joe Williams, and Kell Wilson, thanks for the memories! The same goes to my coworkers at Wandel and Goltermann Technologies; thanks for putting up with me those last few days as I finished the manuscript.

Finally, using up the last of my 15 minutes of fame, I'd like to thank two of the best instructors in the world, Dr. Joe Daugherty of UNC-Asheville and Myrtice Trent of the Blue Ridge Technical Community College; thanks for the help and encouragement you both provided.

And thanks to you too, Peggy.

Jack Tackett, Jr., February, 1994.
CompuServe 70312,132

Trademarks

We'd Like to Hear from You!

In a continuing effort to produce the highest-quality books possible, Que would like to hear your comments. As radical as this may sound for a publishing company, we really want you, the reader and user, to let us know what you like and dislike about this book, and what we can do to improve this book and future books.

In order to provide the most service to you, Prentice Hall Computer Publishing now has a forum on CompuServe (type **GO QUEBOOKS** at any prompt) through which our staff and authors are available for questions and comments. In addition to visiting our forum, feel free to contact me personally on CompuServe at 70714,1516. Or send your comments, ideas, or corrections to me by fax at (317) 581-4663, or write to me at the address below. Your comments will help us to continue publishing the best books on the market.

Bryan Gambrel
Product Development Specialist
Que
201 W. 103rd Street
Indianapolis, IN 46290

Contents at a Glance

Contents

8 Classes   305

12 Debugging Visual C++ Programs   435

13 Graphics Programming with QuickWin   459

14 The MFC General-Purpose Classes and Collection Classes — 493

Introduction

Welcome to *Object-Oriented Programming with Visual C++ 1.5*. This book is a complete tutorial for understanding and programming in Microsoft's Visual C++. The C++ programming language has become the standard development language for professional software developers. Many see C++ becoming the standard programming language for programmers who want to develop powerful software that executes efficiently on personal computers.

Most C++ programming books begin by teaching you the C programming language and then teach C++ as a superset of C. However, C++ is a distinct language. To become a proficient C++ programmer, you don't need to learn C. From the beginning, *Object-Oriented Programming with Visual C++ 1.5* shows you how to program in C++ and introduces the concept of object-oriented programming. This approach, teaching C++ rather than C, helps you think
in terms of objects and C++ features from the beginning and eliminates the need to learn obsolete features of C.

You will find *Object-Oriented Programming with Visual C++ 1.5* to be the easiest C++ book for you to understand. With it, you will quickly master C++.

Who Should Use This Book?

Object-Oriented Programming with Visual C++ 1.5 is targeted to those who want to learn how to program in C++. Previous programming experience in any language—such as BASIC, FORTRAN, Visual Basic, or especially C—is very helpful, but not necessary. You do need to know how to navigate through Microsoft Windows. You don't need to be an expert, but you should be comfortable with using a mouse and making selections from dialog boxes and menus.

Although beginners can benefit from this book, it is not intended to be a beginner's tool. You should also examine *Visual C++ By Example* (Que, 1994) for a beginner's guide to examples of programming in Visual C++. Que also offers a midlevel, comprehensive reference book, *Using Visual C++* (Que, 1994). This book is appropriate for learning C++ at the college level in a classroom setting, or you can use the book to learn C++ through self-study. The text covers all the major aspects of C++ programming, in a step-by-step manner, from square one. You will be surprised at how quickly you will be programming your own applications in Visual C++.

Why C++?

Dennis Ritchie, a researcher at Bell Laboratories, developed the C language as the programming language of choice for computers using the UNIX operating system. Since the introduction of C, the language has been widely adopted for programming all types of computers, from microcomputers to mainframes.

In the 1980s, a programming technique known as *object-oriented programming*, or *OOP*, began generating widespread interest in the programming community (although the basic concepts of OOP had been around for at least two decades). Bjarne Stroustrup, also of AT&T Bell Laboratories, developed C++ as an object-oriented programming language incorporating all the elements of the popular C programming language. Many people have viewed C++ as an extension or superset of C. Nevertheless, C++ is truly a complete programming language by itself (albeit with some similarities to C).

Because of this heritage, most books on C++ start by teaching you the C programming language and then describe C++ as a separate set of features added to C. This approach, as noted earlier, made sense when most programmers learning C++ were already proficient at C programming. But today, as new programmers start learning C++ from the beginning, it is not necessary to learn the idiosyncrasies of C, particularly with respect to C's input and output routines and other library features. These features are implemented in C++ using an object-oriented approach that is fundamentally different from that used in C.

For example, if you already program in C, you might be surprised to learn that `printf()` and `scanf()` are not used for input and output in this book. You learn to use the cout and cin streams instead, which are easier and less confusing than the C library functions.

How to Use This Book

Microsoft provides two versions of Visual C++: a Standard Edition and a Professional Edition. You can use either version with this book. Both provide a rich environment including not only a programming language but also a Visual Workbench, or VWB. The Visual Workbench offers a variety of features, including a program text editor for typing and editing your C++ programs, a built-in compiler and linker, and a special debugger to help you find and fix program errors.

Visual C++ is an environment hosted by Microsoft Windows. Although Windows has become one of the most popular operating systems in the world, it is not an easy platform on which to learn C++ programming. Fortunately, you do not need to learn C, C++, *and* Windows programming all at the same time. For this book, you will write your programs as if they were to be executed under MS-DOS, but instead, they will run under Windows (without your having to learn to write Windows code). This magic is accomplished by a library that Microsoft supplies with Visual C++, called QuickWin. You learn how to write C++ programs in this environment in Chapter 1.

Chapter 1, "The Fundamentals of C++ Programming," introduces you to the use of the Visual Workbench for typing and editing programs. You see your first C++ programs and a number of C++ programming statements, and you learn the basic concepts of variables. You learn also how to produce output to the screen and how to accept input from the keyboard. By the time you finish Chapter 1, you will know how to write a simple C++ program and how to use the Visual Workbench to type, compile, and execute your program.

Computer programs have been described as a collection of program instructions (or statements) that include data. In Chapter 2, "C++ Data Types and Expressions," you learn the fundamental C++ data types used to store and manipulate different types of numbers, characters, and text. You learn also about the types of arithmetic expressions (or equations) you can use in the C++ language.

Chapter 3, "C++ Advanced Data Types," continues the discussion of C++ data storage techniques by introducing the array, the structure, and the union.

This chapter also presents objects, which are the core of object-oriented programming.

You take your first in-depth look at C++ programming statements in Chapter 4, "Selection and Loop Statements." In this chapter, you learn more about the `if` statement for conditionally executing sections of your programs. You learn also about the `switch` statement, used to select one alternative from many possible outcomes. The three C++ looping instructions, each of which is used to repeatedly execute a section of program, are also covered.

All of Chapter 5, "Pointers," is devoted to the C++ pointer type. A pointer, as the name suggests, stores a pointer to items located elsewhere in memory. The concept of a pointer is difficult to master, so an entire chapter is devoted to this data type. Using the pointer type is essential to advanced C++ programming, so it is important to understand the essence of pointers and how they may be used in your C++ programs.

Programs written in C++, especially for all but very small programs, are split into smaller sections called functions. Most C++ programs consist of many functions rather than one large `main()` function. With your code separated into functions, it becomes reusable in your program and in other programs. You learn how to design and implement functions in Chapter 6, "Functions and Macros."

As your programs grow in size, you find that splitting large programs into multiple source files makes editing and compiling easier. A program split into several files is collectively referred to as a project. Visual C++ provides special tools to help you manage projects that contain multiple source files and object modules. You learn in Chapter 7, "Projects," how to split your program into multiple files and how to manage the compilation and linkage process by using the Visual Workbench's project features. You learn also how to use the external tools provided with Microsoft Visual C++ (MSVC) to build projects external to the Workbench.

Chapter 8, "Classes," expands on the object concept and teaches you how to define objects by using the class declaration. You learn about constructor and destructor functions, friend functions, and passing objects as parameters to functions.

The discussion of classes and object-oriented programming is continued in Chapter 9, "The Power of Inheritance." You learn how to *derive* a new class from a previously defined class so that you can *inherit* and thus reuse code instead of having to rewrite code.

Chapter 10, "Virtual Functions and Polymorphism," expands on the concept of inheritance. In this chapter, you explore one of the most powerful aspects of object-oriented programming: polymorphism. You learn how to use inheritance and virtual functions to achieve polymorphism.

At the beginning of the book, you learn that C++ input and output operations are handled through C++ streams. In Chapter 11, "C++ Input and Output," you learn more techniques for performing and formatting your output, including positioning text on the screen and selecting colors. You learn also how to use disk files for long-term storage of data.

Chapter 12, "Debugging Visual C++ Programs," introduces you to the different types of errors you are likely to encounter. You learn how to use the integrated debugger to find program errors. This chapter shows you how to prepare your program for debugging and then how to use the debugger to track down and eliminate those pesky bugs.

Chapter 13, "Graphics Programming with QuickWin," introduces you to the drawing features of QuickWin and shows you how to access and link in the graphics library. Visual C++ provides extensive two-dimensional computer graphics support in an easy-to-use graphics library for QuickWin-based applications. The library contains routines for basic drawing (lines, rectangles, circles, ellipses, polygons, and more), as well as multiple text fonts, text output routines, and special-purpose routines for creating various graphs.

The power of object-oriented programming comes when you can build on the work of others and can inherit features from predesigned classes. Visual C++ provides various general-purpose classes, including a collection class library that gives you a variety of routines for handling the storage and retrieval of data. Considering that all programs rely on data of one type or another, the classes provided in the collection library can reduce the time it takes to build your application. You learn about the collection class library and many of the collection classes in Chapter 14, "The MFC General-Purpose Classes and Collection Classes."

Chapter 15, "Windows Programming with MFC," introduces you to true Microsoft Windows programming with the Microsoft Foundation Class library, or MFC. MFC simplifies the complicated programming interface that you must otherwise use when developing Windows-compatible applications.

Appendix A, "ASCII and Extended ASCII Codes," provides a list of the ASCII characters available on most IBM-compatible PCs running MS-Windows. This chart provides you with the character and the numeric value used by the computer to represent the character.

To Learn C++, You Must Program in C++

The only way to learn programming is to write programs. To make the best use of this book, you should use the review questions at the end of each chapter to ensure that you are learning the topics covered in the chapter. A number of exercises are also included at the end of each chapter to help you sharpen your C++ programming skills. You should use these exercises, or construct your own, to give yourself as much programming practice as possible. Experiment as much as you want with Visual C++. As you build your confidence and skills, you should write software that solves your own problems. Each new program that you write helps you further develop and refine your programming skills.

Conventions Used in This Book

Italic type is used to emphasize an important word or phrase or a new term. **Bold** type is used to indicate text you should type. Program statements, function names, and keywords such as main(), if, and while appear in a special typeface. All program listings appear also in this special typeface.

Items that appear in both italic and the special typeface are to be replaced with other values (depending on the context). For example, in the statement

```
if (expression) statement1;
```

expression indicates an item that can be replaced by a C++ arithmetic expression. *statement1* is to be replaced by a valid C++ statement.

In sections of C++ statements, you sometimes see the vertical ellipsis, used to denote an arbitrary number of program lines. For example, in the lines

```
void main(void)
{
   .
   .
   .
}
```

the ellipsis indicates that zero or more unspecified lines might appear in this section. This ellipsis is not a C++ statement.

Visual C++ menu selections are indicated as **F**ile or **F**ile **N**ew. The bold letters are hot keys that you can use to access the menu item. By pressing and holding down the Alt key and then pressing F, you access the **F**ile menu.

You will also see such key combinations as Ctrl+F3 in the text. This means that you should press and hold down the Ctrl key and then press the F3 function key. In Chapter 2, you learn a few Visual C++ commands that use this type of key combination. You might also see such commands as Alt+F, X. In this case, you press Alt+F and then press X. You do not need to hold down the Alt key when pressing the second letter (X in this example).

About the Sample Programs

The sample programs contained in this book are believed to be accurate. However, the usual disclaimers must apply. No warranties are implied or provided.

> **Note**
>
> These programs have been designed solely to illustrate programming techniques. They have not undergone the rigorous software testing of a professional software quality-assurance organization.

You are welcome to use the sample programs provided in this book to build your own applications. When using these routines in your programs, be sure to test them, both individually and as they are integrated into your software. There is no guarantee that the provided source code works as expected in your application.

The sample programs printed in this book contain line numbers at the left. These numbers are present so that the text can refer to specific lines of code. Do not type the line numbers when you type the programs in this book.

How to Obtain the Source Code Disk

To save yourself the time and trouble of typing the sample programs, you can obtain a supplementary program disk containing all the book's sample programs (those printed in the book with line numbers) for an additional charge. To order the disk, see the "Order Your Program Disk Today" page at the back of this book.

How to Contact the Author

I welcome your thoughts, criticisms, and general feedback. Please send your comments by electronic mail to

CompuServe: 70312,132

Internet addresses: 70312,132@compuserve.com

tackett@wg.com

I will try to read all comments that I receive, but I may not be able to provide a personal reply to each inquiry.

Chapter 1

The Fundamentals of C++ Programming

Before you can begin writing C++ programs, you need to familiarize yourself with the Visual C++ programming environment. You use Visual C++ to edit, compile, and debug your programs. In the edit stage, you use Visual C++ to type or modify your C++ program text. The *compile* stage translates your source program into an object file, and then the *link* phase combines the object file with startup code and library code to create an executable .EXE application. Visual C++ also has a number of tools, including a built-in debugging tool, to make your programming efforts as productive as possible.

This chapter introduces you to the Visual C++ *Visual Workbench*, which is the name Microsoft gives to the set of editing and program development tools in Visual C++. Then you are introduced to your first C++ program and the common components of C++ programs, including a number of C++ statements. After you read this chapter, you should be able to edit and compile simple C++ programs. You should understand also the basic concept of a variable, the use of cin and cout streams to perform input and output, and the use of if and for loop statements to control execution of your program.

Using Microsoft Windows

Because Visual C++ is an environment hosted by Microsoft Windows, you will need to be familiar with navigating through the Windows user interface. The next few paragraphs give you a quick introduction to using Windows. You can skip to the section on installing Visual C++ if you already feel comfortable using Windows.

Microsoft Windows is a *graphical user interface*, or *GUI*, that makes using computers easier. Instead of interacting with a computer through a system of typed, hard-to-remember commands, a GUI enables a user to interact graphically with the computer by selecting graphic representations of buttons and pictures (called icons). Figure 1.1 shows you a sample screen from Windows.

> **Note**
>
> Please note for this book that the term Windows (with a capital W) refers to the Microsoft product known as Microsoft Windows. The term *window* or *windows* refers to a generic window.

Fig. 1.1
A typical Microsoft Windows window.

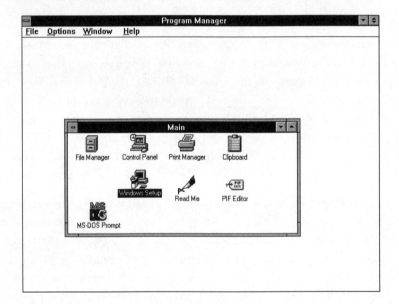

You interact with Windows through the keyboard and a tool called a mouse. The mouse allows you to move a cursor, usually an arrow-shaped pointer, around the screen to choose and execute commands. To choose an item, you need to use the mouse to move the cursor to the item, and then click once with the left mouse button. A *click* merely means that you press down and let go of the left mouse button. To activate a command, you normally double-click the item. A *double-click* means that you press and release the mouse button two times in quick succession. You should spend a few minutes getting comfortable with these techniques for navigating through Windows.

Defining a Generic Window

Windows are areas on the screen that enable you to interact with various parts of the user interface. This type of user interface was first developed by Xerox and made popular by the Apple MacIntosh. Figure 1.1 displayed a typical window along with its various components.

Defining a Dialog Box

Dialog boxes are another item used throughout Windows for controlling options. Figure 1.2 shows a sample dialog box.

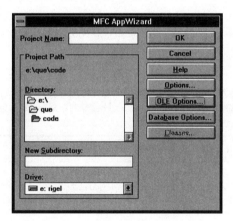

Fig. 1.2
An example of the dialog boxes used in the Visual Workbench to obtain user input.

Most dialog boxes are *modal dialog boxes*. This means that while the modal dialog box is on the screen, you cannot perform any other function until you complete the dialog box. When the dialog box is first displayed, the cursor is visible in an input field, or some other highlight is used to indicate the location of your input within the dialog box. The dialog box contains several types of input controls, including the following:

- Input or edit fields for typing text responses

- Radio buttons for selecting one item from a group

- Check boxes for enabling or disabling a large number of options

- Lists for displaying, selecting, and scrolling through information

- Buttons, such as OK and Cancel

To move among dialog box controls, press the Tab key or use the mouse to click a particular selection. This movement is called *changing the input focus*. The control that has the current input focus is the only control you can activate/deactivate. Sometimes groups of radio buttons and check boxes are treated as a single control: you press the Tab key while within a group to move to the next control rather than the next selection within the group. Hence, you use the arrow keys to move the input focus within a group of radio buttons or check boxes, and you use the Tab key to move from one control or group to another. Table 1.1 summarizes the navigation keys you can use inside dialog boxes. Table 1.2 shows a list of the dialog box controls, along with explanations of their uses. You do not need to memorize most of the information in these tables—just remember to use the Tab key to move from one control to another, the arrow keys to move among selections in groups of radio buttons or check boxes, and the space bar to select or deselect a button or check box.

Table 1.1 Summary of Navigation Keys Used in Dialog Boxes

Key(s)	Action
Tab key	Moves forward to next control in sequence.
Shift+Tab	Moves backward to previous control in sequence.
Arrow keys	Moves among selections in check boxes and radio buttons.
Space bar	Selects or deselects a radio button or check box item.
Enter key	Selects a button control.
Mouse click	Enables or disables radio button and check box items, selects button controls, moves the current focus to the item clicked.
Alt+underlined key	Selects the item containing the underlined key. This action also moves the current input focus to the selected item.

Table 1.2 The Types of Controls Found in a Dialog Box

Controls	Uses
Radio buttons	Radio buttons allow only one item to be selected from a group of items. Each button is represented by the symbol ( ) in front of a selection. You select a radio button by pressing the space bar, clicking with the mouse, or pressing the item's highlighted letter. Within each group, you can select only one button at a time, much like the "preset" quick-selection buttons on an automobile radio. When you select one button, any other selected radio button in the same group becomes deselected. Figure 1.3 shows an example of radio buttons.

Controls	**Uses**
Check boxes	Check boxes provide for enabling or disabling any number of items. The check boxes are usually grouped together. You can use the arrow keys to move among them. Press the space bar to select a check box item or, if it is already selected, to clear it.
Input fields	Input fields allow you to enter arbitrary text information. You use the left- and right-arrow keys to move within the text, the Backspace and Del keys to delete text, the Home key to move to the beginning of the field, and the End key to move to the end of the field. Many of the fields provide horizontal scrolling, enabling you to type text wider than the displayed input field. When you scroll, either or both ends of the input field display left and right arrows to show that more text exists on either side of the input area. Use the left- and right-arrow keys to scroll through the text, or click the mouse pointer on the arrows.
List boxes	List boxes enable you to select from a large list of items. If there are more items than fit in the list box, a scroll bar appears on the right side of the list box. Use the Tab key to move the cursor to the list box, or use the mouse to click an item in the box. When the cursor is inside the list box, you can use the standard keyboard navigation keys to move around: the arrow keys, PgUp, PgDn, Home, and End. You can often find an item you want by pressing a single letter. Many list boxes automatically scroll to the first item beginning with the letter you pressed. When the cursor is positioned on the correct item in the list box, you can select the item by pressing the Enter key. See figure 1.3 for an example of a list box.
Combo boxes	Combo boxes combine input fields with list boxes. Combo boxes enable you either to select from a large list of items or to type your choice in the input box. The input portion of such a control can also be made read-only and thus merely display your choice rather than allow you to edit it. Figure 1.3 shows an example of a combo box. Some combo boxes do not allow you to type a choice, but require you to select an item from the list box.

Installing Visual C++

To use Visual C++, you must have a 80386 or newer microprocessor (80486, Pentium, and so on), 640K of RAM or more, and at least 4M of extended memory. You must be running Microsoft Windows Version 3.1 or later. You must also have a hard disk with at least 75M of free space. The default installation installs all the options provided with Visual C++ and will require 75M of disk space. You can customize the installation by carefully choosing these options.

Fig. 1.3
Examples of
dialog box
controls.

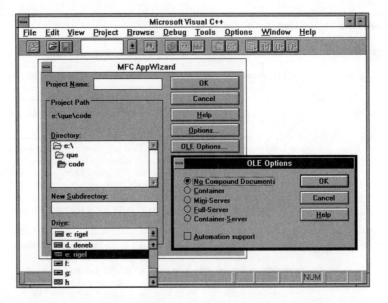

Note

Microsoft markets two versions of Visual C++: a Standard Edition (Version 1.0) and a Professional Edition (Version 1.5). If you are just starting to learn C++ programming, the less-expensive Standard Edition will fit your needs nicely. The Professional Edition is for more serious Windows and DOS development. The Professional Edition was used for the programs in this book, but you will have no problems using the Standard Edition.

For this book, you will not need to learn Windows programming, although a simple program is demonstrated in Chapter 15, "Windows Programming with Visual C++." Instead, the focus is on learning C++. To facilitate this quest, you will use a library, called QuickWin, which allows you to write MS-DOS programs that behave like Windows applications.

To install Visual C++ on your hard disk, use Microsoft's automated Setup program. This program is a Windows-hosted application; in fact, you cannot install the product from DOS. Follow the directions provided by Microsoft to run Setup. The installation process is straightforward: just answer the questions that the Visual C++ installation program asks.

Using Visual C++

After the system is installed, the Setup program creates a Program Manager group containing icons for all the Visual C++ programs and support files. You will use Visual C++'s integrated environment, called the Visual Workbench. This integrated environment features a text editor, C++ compiler, linker, and debugging system—all within a convenient and efficient framework for program development. Most programmers find that the Visual Workbench is easy to learn and makes program development much simpler than using your own editor and the stand-alone Visual C++ compiler. For all the examples in this book, therefore, it is assumed that you are using the Visual Workbench. You should also create your own DOS directory to hold the sample programs you create while using this book.

To begin using Visual C++, just double-click the Visual C++ icon, (see fig. 1.4). The Visual Workbench displays a menu bar and a toolbar across the top of the window, and a status bar at the bottom of the window (see fig. 1.5).

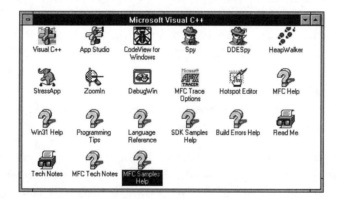

Fig. 1.4
The Visual C++ group.

Using the Visual Workbench

The Visual Workbench provides you with a wealth of program development features. At first, you use the text editor for typing new programs and modifying existing ones. After you type your program, you can compile, link, and run it by using the Visual Workbench.

When this integrated environment begins running, it displays the various windows you left opened during your last session. If this is your first time,

Fig. 1.5

The Visual C++ Visual Work-bench.

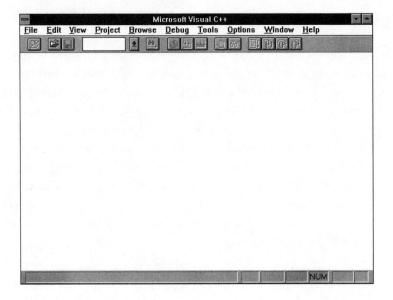

the screen will be blank. The uppermost line on the screen is called the *title bar*. It contains the name of the application and the name of the project. The next bar in the window is the main menu. When you choose options from the main menu, another menu drops down (sometimes called a pull-down or drop-down menu). To begin editing a new file, you need to pull down the File menu and choose the New command, as shown in figure 1.6. This opens a new window in which you can enter a program. First, however, you may want to explore the other pull-down menus.

You can select items from the menu bar in several ways. The easiest is to use the mouse. Just move the mouse pointer to the item you want to select, and then click the left mouse button. A pull-down menu appears, and you can *drag* the mouse (by holding down the left mouse button) to whichever selection you want. When you let go of the mouse button, your selection is invoked. (You can also move the mouse pointer, without holding down any buttons, and then click once on the appropriate selection.)

If you do not have a mouse, you can make menu selections with the keyboard. To access a pull-down menu with this method, press the Alt key and, while holding it down, press the highlighted letter of the menu item. For example, to access the File menu, press Alt+F. You can choose individual items from the menu by using the Alt key and the highlighted letter of the menu item you want, or you can use the arrow keys to move the cursor up or down in the list of items. Then you press the Enter key to select the

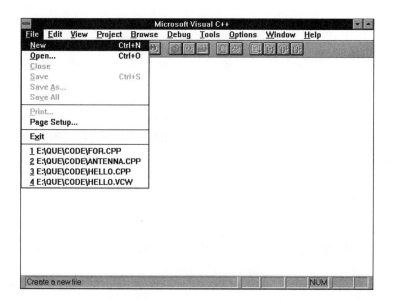

Fig. 1.6
The Visual
Workbench File
menu.

highlighted item on the pull-down menu. Using shortcut keys is another
method of accessing menu items. Shortcut keys allow you to choose a menu
item from the keyboard without using the mouse, arrow keys, or Alt+key
method. Not all menu items have shortcut keys, however, so you still need to
be familiar with the other methods for choosing menu items. Each menu
item that does have a shortcut shows the keys to the right of the menu entry.
For example, in the **F**ile menu item shown in figure 1.6, you can open a file
by using the shortcut Ctrl+O without pulling down the **F**ile menu and choosing the **O**pen option.

The Visual Workbench Toolbar

You will find a toolbar located below the main menu. This bar contains buttons that give you access to many of the same menu commands without
having to pull down the menu and chose the command. You will need a
mouse in order to use the toolbar. Figure 1.7 displays the toolbar.

The first toolbar button provides a drop-down list, giving you access to all the
files in your project. Projects are briefly explained later in this chapter and
also in Chapter 7, "Projects." The second button enables you to open any file
into the Visual Workbench editor. This button performs the same action as
the **F**ile **O**pen command. The third button allows you to save the current file
you are editing; this button performs the same action as the **F**ile **S**ave menu
item (note that this is not the same as the **F**ile Save **A**s command). The next
item on the toolbar is a combo box that enables you to search the current file

for the listed text; this combo box provides the same function as **Edit Find**. The next button, which looks like a pair of binoculars, allows you to find the next occurence of the text listed in the combo box; You can also use the F3 function key to perform this function. The next three buttons deal with compiling and building your project files. Their uses are covered later in this chapter. The rest of the buttons deal with a Visual Workbench tool called the *integrated debugger*, which is explained in Chapter 12, "Debugging Visual C++ Programs." Table 1.3 lists all the toolbar items, shown in figure 1.7, and briefly explains the action of each.

Fig. 1.7
The Visual
Workbench
toolbar.

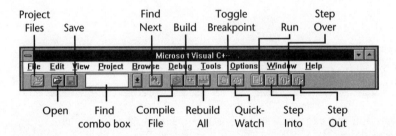

Table 1.3 The Visual Workbench Toolbar Items	
Toolbar Item	**Action**
Project Files	Allows you to open any file in your current project
Open	Allows you to open any file
Save	Enables you to save the current file
Find combo box	Enables you to enter search text to search for in the current file
Find Next	Allows you to repeat the last find text operation
Compile File	Compiles the current source file
Build	Compiles only the source files that have changed in your project, and then links them into an executable file
Rebuild All	Compiles every file in your project and links them to form an executable file
Toggle Breakpoint	Allows you to toggle on and off a breakpoint at the current line in the source file
QuickWatch	Enables you to view a variable's value
Run	Activates the current program for debugging

Toolbar Item	Action
Step Into	Allows you to step into a function during debugging
Step Over	Allows you to step over a function during debugging
Step Out	Allows you to step out of a function during debugging

Take a moment to display the menus and become familiar with menu item selection. You can cancel unintended operations by pressing the Esc (Escape) key on your keyboard.

The Visual Workbench Help System

The Visual Workbench provides a convenient on-line help system that uses the standard Windows help engine. This system gives you fully indexed help for the Visual Workbench, the C/C++ programming languages, and Windows programming. The Visual Workbench's help system is *context-sensitive*, which means that you can select help for the current menu or dialog box selection, or even look up a C++ keyword by placing the cursor on the keyword and pressing F1. The Workbench also displays a help mnemonic for menu items in the first pane of the status bar. The Workbench gives you a short memory jog as to what action the menu command executes, as you move across the menu items.

To use the help system, press Alt+H or choose the **H**elp item from the menu bar. The Windows help program is displayed (see fig. 1.8).

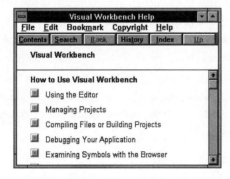

Fig. 1.8
The Windows help program for Visual C++.

From this program, you can search through a linked system of help topics to find the answers to your questions. Within a help topic, you will see items in a different color (usually green), indicating a linked topic. You will also see the cursor change from an arrow to a hand. When you click a word, the WinHelp program "jumps" you to the specified topic.

Searching for a Help Topic. WinHelp also lets you search for information on a given topic. You start a search for a topic by displaying the WinHelp window and clicking the Search button. The Search dialog box is displayed, as shown in figure 1.9. As you type a word or phrase in the first input field (also known as an edit box), the program searches its list of topics, trying to match one to the word(s) you entered. When you find an appropriate topic, you can double-click the item to display the help file.

Fig. 1.9
Searching for
help.

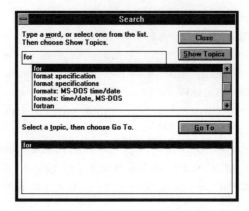

Copying WinHelp Information. If you find a topic of interest or an interesting piece of sample code, you can use WinHelp's Copy command on the Edit menu to copy the text into your current file. When you use this menu command, you see a dialog box much like the one shown in figure 1.10. From this dialog box, you can highlight the section of text you want to copy. You then need to copy that text to the Windows Clipboard, using either the Copy button or the shortcut keys. Next, return to your file, place the cursor in the position you want the text pasted, and paste the text from the Clipboard into your program. You learn in the next section exactly how to copy and paste text to and from various sources.

Exiting the Visual Workbench

To exit from Visual C++, choose the Exit option or press the Alt+F+X key combination. You can also use Windows' exit key combination, Alt+F4. If you have not saved any of the files you have modified, Visual C++ prompts you, asking whether you want to save them before exiting the program.

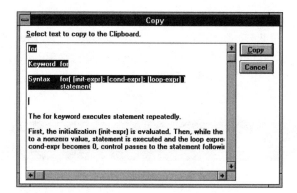

Fig. 1.10
Copying text
from the
Windows help
system.

Using the Visual Workbench Editor

The Visual Workbench's editor is where you spend most of your time: typing
new code, editing existing programs, and fixing program defects. You access
the editor by choosing **N**ew from the **F**ile menu, or choosing **O**pen from the
File menu to open an existing file.

A variety of keyboard commands, mouse movements, and menu selections
provide a full-featured editing system. As you type text in the text edit window, the cursor moves across the screen to the right. Press the Enter key
when you have reached the end of the code line.

Text entry can occur in either *insert mode* or *overstrike mode*. In insert mode,
new text is placed in front of existing text, pushing it further along the line.
In overstrike mode, new text that you type replaces any other text at the
cursor's location. You can toggle between these modes by pressing the Ins
(Insert) key. The state of the current mode is displayed in the status bar at the
bottom of the Workbench. The status bar displays also the state of the Num
Lock and Caps Lock keys, as shown in figure 1.11, as well as the cursor's position in your text file.

Navigating in the Editor
In the editor, a horizontal scroll bar at the bottom of the screen displays the
current position of the cursor, relative to the beginning and end of the line
on which the cursor is located. A vertical scroll bar displays the current position of the cursor in the file you are editing, relative to the first and last lines
of the file. Each scroll bar displays a square marker (called the scroll box),
which you can drag with the mouse to move rapidly to other locations in the
file. To move line by line, press the up- or down-arrow key, or click the up- or

down-arrow icon inside the scroll bar. To page through the file screen by screen, press the PgUp or PgDn key, or click the mouse on the empty space between the scroll bar marker and the top or bottom of the scroll bar (or between the left and right sides if you are clicking on the horizontal scroll bar).

Fig. 1.11
The status bar at the bottom of the screen.

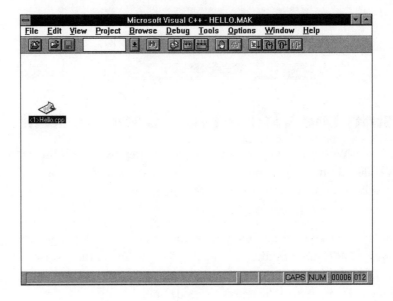

Table 1.4 summarizes the various keyboard commands.

Table 1.4 The Workbench Editor Commands	
To Do This	**Press**
Move one character left	Left arrow
Move one word left	Ctrl+left arrow
Move one character right	Right arrow
Move one word right	Ctrl+right arrow
Move one line up	Up arrow
Move one line down	Down arrow
Move to the first indentation of current line	Home
Move to the beginning of current line	Home, Home
Move to the end of line	End

To Do This	Press
Move to the beginning of file	Ctrl+Home
Move to the end of file	Ctrl+End
Delete one character to the left	Backspace
Delete one character to the right	Del
Delete selected text and copy to Clipboard	Ctrl+X, Shift+Del
Turn keyboard insert mode on or off	Ins
Copy selected text to Clipboard, keeping it	Ctrl+C, Ctrl+Ins
Insert contents of Clipboard	Ctrl+V, Shift+Ins
Copy current line to Clipboard, deleting it	Ctrl+Y
Undo the last edit	Ctrl+Z, Alt+Backspace
With multiple lines selected, move lines one tab stop to the right	Tab
With multiple lines selected, move lines one tab stop to the left	Shift+Tab
Scroll up one line at a time	Up arrow
Scroll down one line at a time	Down arrow
Scroll up one page at a time	PgUp
Scroll down one page at a time	PgDn
Open the Find dialog box	Alt+F3
Find the selected text	Ctrl+F3
Find next selected text in forward direction	F3
Find next selected text in backward direction	Shift+F3
Find matching brace	Ctrl+]
Set a bookmark	Ctrl+F2
Jump to next bookmark	F2

Selecting Text and Performing Text-Block Operations

By selecting text, you can perform such operations as cut and copy on entire text blocks. If you have used any modern word processing or spreadsheet programs, you are familiar with the processes of selecting, cutting or copying, and pasting text.

To select text with the mouse, move the mouse pointer to the beginning of the text to be selected. While holding down the left mouse button, drag the mouse to the end of the text block you want to select. The text is highlighted as you drag the mouse.

Using the keyboard, you select text by pressing and holding down the Shift key and then pressing the navigation keys, including the arrow keys, PgUp, and PgDn. As you move the cursor with the Shift key pressed, your selection is highlighted.

Windows maintains a Clipboard to which selected text can be cut or copied. When an item is *cut*, it is deleted from the current file and placed on the Clipboard. An item that is *copied* remains in the current file, and a copy of the selection is placed on the Clipboard. Use Cu**t** from the **E**dit menu to delete text blocks or to move them temporarily to the Clipboard for later pasting to another location. Use **C**opy (also on the **E**dit menu) to duplicate text without deleting it. You can access these functions also by using the shortcut keys shown to the right of the **E**dit menu selections: Ctrl+X to cut the text and Ctrl+C to copy the text to the Clipboard.

You can paste the contents of the Clipboard to a new location or even to another file by choosing the **P**aste command from the **E**dit menu or by pressing Ctrl+V.

If you want to cut a section of marked text without copying it to the Clipboard, choose the **D**elete command from the **E**dit menu or press the Del key on the keyboard.

Warning

After you delete a text selection, that text is gone forever. You cannot recall deleted text with the **P**aste command. However, you can correct your mistakes (up to a certain point) by using the **U**ndo command (Ctrl+Z) from the **E**dit menu. You can also use the key combination Alt+Backspace.

Opening an Existing File

To open an existing file, use the **O**pen command from the **F**ile menu. The **O**pen command displays a standard file dialog box, showing matching files

in the current directory and providing a prompt line where you can enter
a new file name. You can also click the Open button on the toolbar (the
second toolbar item shown in fig. 1.7). Figure 1.12 shows the Open File
dialog box.

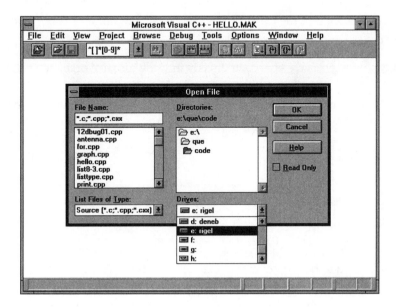

Fig. 1.12
The Open File
dialog box.

As with most dialog boxes, you can use the mouse to click a particular control, or you can use the Tab key to move from one control to the next. Usually, you type the name of the file you want to open, or press Tab to move to
the File **N**ame list box. In the list box, you can use the arrow keys or the
mouse to point to a specific file; then you can choose the OK button to open
the file. To move quickly through the File **N**ame list box, use the PgDn or
PgUp key or click the mouse on the scroll bar.

When you choose OK, the Visual Workbench creates a new edit window and
then reads the file into this new window. You can open files located in other
DOS directories by tabbing to the **D**irectories list box in the Open File dialog
box and selecting from the list the directory you want. If you need to change
drives, you can use the Dri**v**es combo box to select a new drive. The Visual
Workbench enables you to open multiple edit windows simultaneously, from
which you can cut and paste source text from one program to another.

Creating Your First C++ Program

You can begin typing your first program when you have an empty edit window. (You can create a new edit window by choosing the **N**ew command from the **F**ile menu.) An empty window appears on the screen, with the title *untitled.1* centered in the title bar. The text cursor appears at the upper-left corner of the window.

You can now type a C++ program directly into the Visual Workbench editor. Because it has become a tradition to learn a new computer language by writing a Hello World program, that is your first task. Type the following into the Visual Workbench (don't worry about the specific details of C++ yet):

```
#include <iostream.h>
void main(void)
{
  cout << "Hello World" << endl;
  cout << "Press Enter to Continue.";
  cin.get();
}
```

If you make a mistake while typing, you can use the Backspace key (←) on your keyboard to back up over the text you have typed. To move around in the editor, use the arrow keys on your keyboard's keypad. (To use the arrow keys, you must have the Num Lock feature of your keyboard disabled. Press the Num Lock key if the arrow keys are not working; then try using the arrow keys again.) Another way to make a change is to move the cursor, using the arrow keys, to the character you want to change. Then press the Del key to delete the character where the cursor is located.

As you type, you will notice that certain words change color. The Workbench distinguishes various C++ keywords and compiler directives with a different color, a process Microsoft calls *syntax coloring*. The **C**olor option on the **O**ptions menu displays the Color dialog box shown in figure 1.13. You can use this dialog box to control the color that the Visual Workbench uses for syntax coloring. You can control also what type of language the Workbench processes from the **S**yntax Coloring choice on the **V**iew menu. You can choose C, C++, or no language processing.

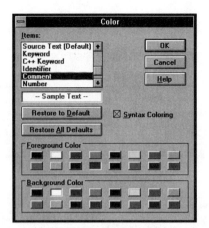

Fig. 1.13
The Color
dialog box.

> **Note**
>
> *Keywords* designate words that programming languages reserve for their own use.
> You use these keywords to build programs. The syntax coloring feature will display
> these words, as well as other language features, in a specified color in order to distin-
> guish them from other words. *Compiler directives* are commands that you give to the
> compiler to tell it to do certain things. Don't worry about this at the moment, as
> these terms are covered later in the chapter. For now, just realize that the Visual
> Workbench provides this syntax coloring feature to help you learn C++.

After typing this program in the editor, you can save the program by choosing the Save **A**s command from the **F**ile menu or by clicking the Save button
on the toolbar. A dialog box appears, asking you to enter the name of the file
in which this program should be saved. Type a program file name, such as
HELLO, and add the .CPP extension. This extension indicates that this file is
a C++ program source file. You should also make sure that the correct drive
and directory are listed in the dialog box. After you have added the .CPP
extension and checked the drive/directory listings, move the cursor to the OK
button and press Enter. Alternatively, you can use the mouse to click the OK
button. The result is the same with either method: your newly entered program is saved to a disk file.

Creating a Project File

Before you can execute the program you typed in the editor, you must construct a Visual C++ project file. This project file will guide the Workbench as
it compiles, links, and executes your program.

> **Note**
>
> Project files make program development a less time-consuming task by keeping track of various housekeeping details. You learn more about Visual C++ projects in Chapter 7, "Projects." For now, just follow along with these instructions.

You will interact often with the **P**roject menu, shown in figure 1.14, and with the toolbar both to create your program executables and to run them. You should take a few moments to become familiar with these items.

Fig. 1.14
The Project menu.

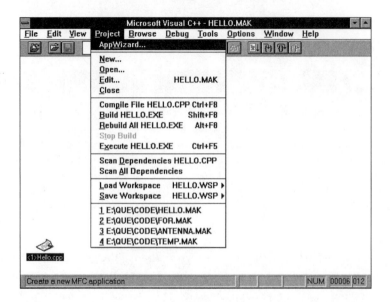

First choose the **N**ew command from the **P**roject menu, which brings up the New Project dialog box, as shown in figure 1.15. You need to enter a project name and a project type. You can enter the file name, without the .CPP extension, as the project name. This helps you keep track of your projects in the future. The project type allows you to choose what type of program to build; for most of the examples in this book, that type is a QuickWin .EXE. Also deselect (uncheck) the **U**se Microsoft Foundation Classes check box; you do not require this feature yet. Click the OK button and watch as the Visual Workbench creates a project file for you.

Fig. 1.15
The New Project dialog box.

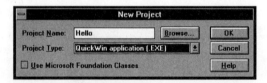

After you create the project file, the Workbench displays the Edit -<project name> dialog box, as shown in figure 1.16. You need to add to the project your source code file that you previously saved (HELLO.CPP). This file should be listed in the File **N**ame list box. You can double-click HELLO.CPP to add it to the project file, or you can highlight the name and click the **A**dd button. The Workbench then updates the project to include this file. You must then click the Cl**o**se button to finish editing your project file.

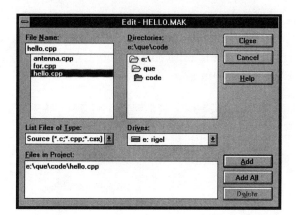

Fig. 1.16
The Edit -
<project name>
dialog box.

Compiling Your Program

You can now tell the Workbench to build your application. You can do this in one of three ways: choosing the **B**uild <project name> command from the **P**roject menu, using the build shortcut Shift+F8, or using the mouse to click the Build toolbar button (the sixth button on the toolbar shown in fig. 1.7). All these methods cause the Workbench to compile and link your program, thus creating an executable file you can run. As the Workbench processes your file, it displays a list of results in an output window called Output. Figure 1.17 displays the results of building your first sample program.

Fig. 1.17
Output results
from
HELLO.CPP.

> **Note**
>
> Compiling and building are normally considered different actions in software engineering, but in Visual C++ the two actions are almost always done together, because *building* means both to compile and then to link the project. These are separate steps in the DOS world, but the Workbench does not provide a way to separately invoke the linker—it is always part of the build process.

Running Your Program

Running your program is now just a matter of choosing the E**x**ecute <project name> command from the **P**roject menu or using the shortcut Ctrl+F5. Figure 1.18 displays the output from the Hello World program.

Fig. 1.18
The Hello World program.

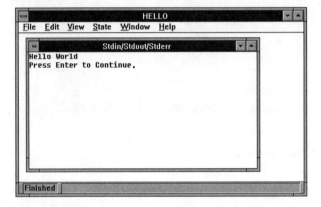

The QuickWin Library

Figure 1.18 displays your program within a framework created by the QuickWin library. A QuickWin program places a window and a menu on the screen with little else. This library allows you to create an MS-DOS program that controls the window much like a terminal screen. You will be able to display text in a window and receive keyboard input from a user with this window. The QuickWin library allows you to do this without climbing the large learning curve associated with writing Windows programs.

The window shown in figure 1.18 contains the title `Stdin/Stdout/Stderr`. This window is analogous to the normal screen presented by DOS programs. All of your program's textual input and output statements will use this window. Chapter 13, "Graphics Programming with QuickWin," provides more details on using the QuickWin library.

A Sample C++ Program

To begin understanding the C++ programming language, look at the small
sample program presented in this section. You learn about a simple C++ program used to perform a calculation for designing a half-wave dipole antenna
used for radio communications. This program demonstrates several features
of C++, including how to create variables for storing data, read keystroke
input from the keyboard, and write messages to the screen. When you run
the program, it asks for an input frequency, calculates the length of the
halves of the dipole antenna, and displays the result. The source code for the
sample program is in listing 1.1. The output follows the listing.

Note

The line numbers to the left of each line are for reference only. Do *not* include them
when you type this program into the Visual Workbench's editor.

Listing 1.1 A Sample Program Written in C++

```
1   // ANTENNA.CPP
2   // This program calculates the length of a
3   // half-wave dipole antenna.
4   #include <iostream.h>
5
6   void main(void) {
7     float frequency;
8
9     cout << "Antenna half-wave dipole calculator"
10         << endl << endl;
11
12    // Display prompt for frequency.
13    cout << "Enter frequency, in MHz (such as 7.050 Mhz):   ";
14
15    // Read keyboard input.
16    cin >> frequency;
17
18    // Display the calculated result.
19    cout << endl << "Half-wave dipole length is "
20         << 468.0/frequency << " feet." << endl << endl;
21
22    cout << "Each dipole half section is " << (468.0/frequency)/2
23         << " feet." << endl << endl;
24
25    cout << "Press Enter to continue." << endl;
26    cin.ignore(1); // Ignore leftover Enter key.
27    cin.get();
28  } // main
```

Figure 1.19 displays the output from listing 1.1. The highlighted text indicates what the user typed in response to the prompt Enter frequency, in MHz (such as 7.050 Mhz):.

Fig. 1.19
The output generated by listing 1.1.

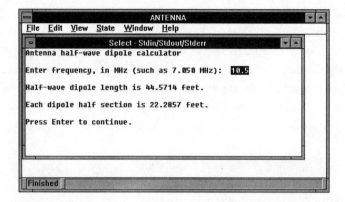

The sample program ANTENNA.CPP illustrates several parts of a typical C++ program. First note that the name of the source file ends in .CPP to indicate that this is a "C Plus Plus" program.

The first three lines of the program begin with two slash characters, //. The slash characters mark the beginning of a *comment* that is not part of the program code. The compiler ignores the text that follows the // characters, so you can use the characters that follow to provide explanatory information about your program. Comments can begin anywhere on a line. In this program, most of the comments start at the beginning of lines, but you can place the comments after statements, as shown in line 26. When you place the comment on a line that contains C++ code, remember that the comment section remains in effect through the end of the line. Therefore, you cannot start a line with // and expect to add code to the right of the // characters; the compiler ignores the code that follows the slash characters. The Workbench will indicate commented text in a different color, usually green, as part of its syntax coloring.

Line 4 contains #include <iostream.h>. #include is a *compiler directive* that tells the compiler to include some information that is stored in another file named IOSTREAM.H. The IOSTREAM.H file tells the compiler how to use the cin and cout symbols shown in lines 9, 13, 16, 19, 22, 25, 26, and 27. Most programs you write in C++ use the #include compiler directive to access features of the C++ development environment. The Workbench will display these directives in blue. You learn more about the other features of C++ as you progress through this book.

Line 6 begins the definition of a *function* named main(). All C++ programs (except those written for Microsoft Windows) have a main() function. When you begin execution of your program from within Visual C++, the PC starts the program by *calling*, or jumping, to the location named by main(). In line 6, the main() function contains an empty parameter list, denoted by the keyword void. All C++ functions are designed to return a result to the caller. However, because there is no need for main() to return a value, its return result is set to type void.

At the end of line 6, you see a left brace ({) symbol. All the program statements from this left brace down to the concluding right brace (}) in line 28 are contained within the main() function. The statements between the braces define the actions the main() function undertakes.

Line 7 defines a single *variable* named frequency. This variable is defined using the float type so that the compiler knows that frequency contains *floating-point* numbers (numbers that contain a decimal point, such as 3.14). When the compiler translates your source program into machine instructions, the compiler sets aside an area of memory to store the value of this variable. The amount of memory the compiler sets aside is determined by the type of variable you use. You learn about variables and their memory requirements in Chapter 2, "C++ Data Types and Expressions."

The compiler can work also with other types of numbers, such as integers (numbers that do not contain a decimal point, such as 100, 10234, and 55). Also note that the floating-point declaration statement ends with a single semicolon (;). All C++ statements end with a semicolon, so you should become familiar with this notation. When you look through the rest of listing 1.1, you see that each of the C++ statements ends with a semicolon.

The *cout* and *cin* Streams

The most interesting part of this program is its use of the cout and cin identifiers to display information and to get keyboard input, respectively. cout stands for *console output*, and cin stands for *console input*. In lines 9 and 10, the text string "Antenna half-wave dipole calculator" is written to the display by inserting the text into the output stream that is being written to cout. The easiest way to understand this is to think of the << characters as forming a left-pointing arrow. The << characters show that "Antenna half-wave dipole

calculator" is being directed to the cout stream. The special symbol endl is
an end-of-line marker; you can think of endl as being equivalent to pressing
the Enter key at the end of a line. Without endl in the output statement,
subsequent output would appear immediately following the text. cout uses
endl twice: first to display the output string and then to display a blank line.

The symbol << is called the *insertion operator* because it inserts data into the
output stream. You can use this symbol repeatedly to display several items in
a single statement, as in lines 19 and 20 of listing 1.1. When the insertion
operator is used several times in one statement, C++ programmers say that
the operator is *cascaded*.

Another interesting feature of lines 9 and 10 is that the instruction to send
output to cout is split across two lines. This enables you to write statements
that may not conveniently fit on a single line. The actual end of the cout
statement is the semicolon at the end of line 10. All C++ statements can be
split across lines, if needed. The only restriction is that the line split should
occur between symbols or in blank spaces in the line. You should not split a
line in the middle of text string, such as "Antenna half-wave dipole calculator". You do not have to split statements across more than one line; the
statements in listing 1.1 are split so that each line fits conveniently on the
printed pages of this book.

In some instances, you might find that a text string does not fit on a single
line. You can split a text string into more than one line by placing a
backslash (\) in the text string, as in the following:

```
cout << "Antenna half-wave dipole \
        "calculator"
```

Internally, the C++ compiler combines this split text string into a single text
string.

Line 13 displays a prompt asking for the antenna's input frequency. Because
this use of cout does not include the endl symbol, the on-screen cursor remains at the end of the output text, enabling you to type an answer at the
end of the prompt line.

Line 16 reads your keystroke input from cin and extracts your data, storing it
in the variable frequency. Note carefully the use of the cin >> *extraction operator*. You can think of the extraction operator as a right-pointing arrow. In line
16, the >> says to store the console input in the variable on the right. You can

also cascade the extraction operator. For example, if you have two integer variables named A and B and you wrote the statement

```
cin >> A >> B;
```

the cin stream expects you to type two integer numbers, separated by one or more blanks. If you type

```
100 200
```

100 is assigned to A, and 200 is assigned to B.

Finally, lines 19 through 23 calculate and display the result. The length of the dipole antenna is calculated from the following formula:

```
                      468.0
Length in feet =  ───────────
                     f (MHz)
```

In C++, this equation is expressed as

```
468.0/frequency
```

in which / is the division operator and frequency is the variable that holds the radio frequency, in megahertz.

Line 25 displays the prompt

```
Press Enter to continue
```

and waits for you to press the Enter key before terminating the program. In line 27, the statement

```
cin.get();
```

waits for the program's user to press any key. cin.get() is a special function defined as part of the cin stream. Note that you do not use the >> extraction operator when you call the cin.get() function.

The cin.ignore(1) function is called in line 26 to discard the Enter key left over from the previous cin input statement in line 16. When Visual C++ processes the cin >> frequency statement, it scans the input until it finds the first nonnumeric value. This causes the >> extraction operator to stop scanning at the end-of-line keystroke, leaving the end-of-line character available for the next input operation. The cin.ignore(1) tells the cin input stream to ignore or discard the next character in the input, which is the leftover end-of-line keystroke. If the program did not throw away the leftover Enter key, the cin.get() operation in line 27 would read it without stopping to wait for the user to press the Enter key again.

Compiling and Running Your Program

Just as with the Hello World program, you need to create a project file in order to compile, link, and run the program in listing 1.1. Here's a brief outline of what you need to do:

1. *Create the source file.* Type the program shown in listing 1.1 and save it to a file.

2. *Create a new project file.* Choose the **N**ew option from the **P**roject menu. Enter the project file's name (antenna) and make sure to choose QuickWin.EXE for the program type.

3. *Add the source file to the project.* Select the file you saved in step 1 and add it to the project file. You can add the file by double-clicking the file name, or by highlighting the file and clicking the **A**dd button. Then click the Cl**o**se button to update your project file.

4. *Compile the program.* You can do this by choosing the **B**uild <project name> option from the **P**roject menu, pressing the shortcut Shift+F8, or clicking the Build toolbar button. This causes the C++ compiler and linker to generate an executable file you can run.

5. *Run the program.* To run the program, choose the E**x**ecute <project name> command from the **P**roject menu or use the shortcut Ctrl+F5. If the program has not been compiled or if the source file has been changed since the last compilation, Visual C++ will alert you to this fact and ask whether you want to rebuild the program. The Visual Workbench displays the dialog box shown in figure 1.20.

Fig. 1.20
The Visual Workbench out-of-date alert dialog box.

6. *Dismiss the QuickWin program.* When your program is finished, QuickWin displays the word Finished in its status bar. You can then use the QuickWin E**x**it command from the **F**ile menu to finish the program and return to the Visual C++ Workbench.

The compilation step (4) invokes the compiler to convert your source code into an internal machine code format known as an *object module*. The object module is a nonexecutable file stored in a disk file, which Visual C++ has given the .OBJ file extension. Before an object module can be made capable of execution, it must be linked with other object modules and routines stored in libraries. When you choose the **R**ebuild All <project name> command (Alt+F8), Visual C++ takes care of both the compilation and the link steps for you. You can also invoke this mode with the Rebuild All toolbar button.

During the link step, your compiled object module is combined with routines stored in Visual C++ libraries. For instance, the code to implement the cin and cout input/output functions is stored in a library file. The link step combines or links these components together to produce an executable .EXE file. Figure 1.21 illustrates the process of editing, compiling, linking, and running your program.

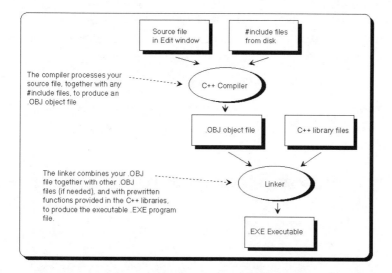

Fig. 1.21
An overview of the edit, compile, link, and execution phases of program development.

You can also compile the program without executing it, by selecting Com**p**ile File from the **P**roject menu. Or you can use the Compile File toolbar button. This command compiles your source code and creates an object module. It does not link your program to produce an executable .EXE file. This command is useful when you want to see whether the changes you made to your program can be successfully compiled. If the compiler detects errors, it reports the problems to you.

Choosing a Memory Model

For most applications, you should select a *memory model* before compiling your program. The choice of memory model affects how the compiler translates your source code into machine instructions to be processed by your computer's microprocessor. For now, you need to know only that Visual C++ supports six different memory model configurations: Tiny, Small, Medium, Compact, Large, and Huge. Your choice of which memory model to use when compiling your program is determined by the size of your program, the amount of data it needs to process, and which C++ libraries you chose to create when you ran the Visual C++ installation program. For the sample programs presented in the first few chapters of this book, any of the memory model choices work. You should probably choose the Medium memory model for the examples you work with in the first few chapters. You learn more about memory model choices in Chapter 7, "Projects."

Compiler, Linker, and Syntax Errors

During the compilation process, the compiler may encounter problems. Suppose that you forget to include the declaration of the frequency variable shown in line 7. When the compiler encounters the undeclared and unexpected variable in line 16, it issues the following message:

```
Error ANTENNA.CPP 16: Undefined symbol 'frequency'
```

Error messages such as this one appear in the Output window, illustrated in figure 1.22. The linker also displays its messages, including errors, in the Output window.

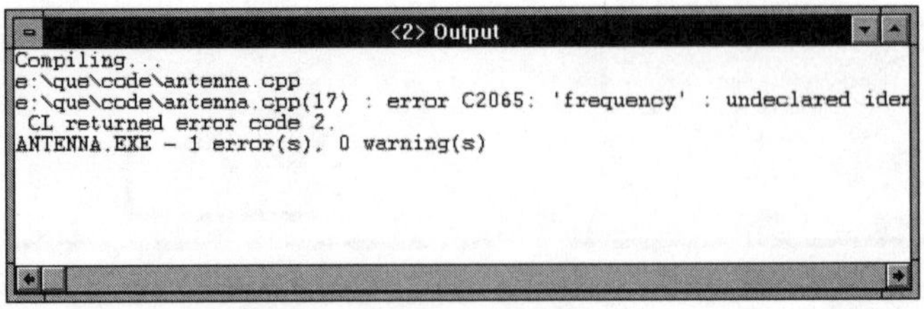

Fig. 1.22

The message window displaying information about the compilation and linking process.

```
<2> Output
Compiling...
e:\que\code\antenna.cpp
e:\que\code\antenna.cpp(17) : error C2065: 'frequency' : undeclared ider
 CL returned error code 2.
ANTENNA.EXE - 1 error(s), 0 warning(s)
```

If you need additional information about the error, place the cursor on the error line and press F1 to view the on-line help text about the error, as illustrated in figure 1.23. If you want to see the line in your source code file that caused this error, you can double-click anywhere on the error line. This automatically opens an edit window containing the source file and moves you to the offending line.

You can use the on-line help system to learn more about the meaning of errors you encounter. You can also consult your Visual C++ documentation.

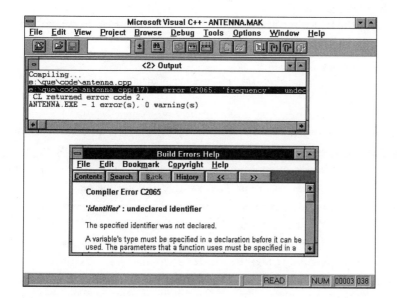

Fig. 1.23
If you press F1 while viewing an error message, you see additional information about the possible causes of the error.

The Components of a C++ Program

The sample program in listing 1.1 illustrates the basic components of a C++ program. Most C++ programs that you write use the #include directive and the main() function. They use cin and cout for input and output, and they declare and use variables to perform calculations. These components are essential to nearly all C++ programs; you will use them in nearly all your application software.

Comments

It is useful to add explanatory notes to the program text that you write. These notes can explain program operation, provide information about special techniques used, or act as reminders of how you constructed tricky sections of code.

You have already seen the // symbol used to mark the beginning of a single-line comment. This type of comment is used frequently in C++ programs. Another type of comment enables you to write multiline comments. To write a multiline comment, mark the beginning of the comment text by typing /* and then mark the end by typing */. For example, instead of using the //

symbol for the first three lines of the ANTENNA.CPP program shown in listing 1.1, you may want to write this comment as a multiline comment:

```
/*  ANTENNA.CPP
    This program calculates the length of a
    half-wave dipole antenna.
*/
```

For short one- or two-line comments, the // comment is quick to type and easy to use. For lengthy comments, however, you may want to use the /* and */ characters. When your comment needs editing, the multiline characters simplify problems that can occur. For example, if you type new text and your single-line comment needs to be split into two or more lines, you must manually reinsert // symbols on subsequent lines. If you use the /* and */ characters, you don't have to type new // characters for each new comment line; you just keep adding text between the two markers. As with the // symbol, the Workbench will color everything between the /* and */ characters green.

C++ Input and Output

The programs throughout this book use cin and cout, together with the << insertion and >> extraction operators, to perform input and output. In Chapter 11, "C++ Input and Output," you learn additional input and output instructions that make use of C++ streams. You use these additional instructions to produce formatted stream output. You learn also how to use streams to write data to and read data from disk files.

C++ Functions

All programs (except programs written for Microsoft Windows) must have a main() function. Most programs that you write also declare and use additional functions. Your programs may also use prewritten functions that have been precompiled and stored in libraries. Visual C++ provides many predefined functions for use in your programs. You learn how to use these libraries later.

Variables

Most programs also declare and use variables. You have already seen the use of a variable for storing floating-point numbers. C++ includes special types for storing integers and text characters, plus a variety of additional floating-point types for compatibility with the floating-point coprocessor. You can combine these basic types to form additional data types, such as strings of characters or complex numbers.

One variable type that you use frequently is the *integer*. An integer stores whole numbers over a range of –32768 to +32767. (This is the range used by Visual C++, but the range may vary if you are using a different C++ compiler.) You declare an integer variable by using the keyword `int` followed by a variable identifier. For example, the line

```
int number_of_dogs;
```

declares `number_of_dogs` as a variable that will store integer values. You can assign a value to `number_of_dogs` by writing

```
number_of_dogs = 5;
```

Keep in mind that integer variables store only whole numbers, not fractional numbers. Use a floating-point variable to store numbers that contain decimal points.

You can declare multiple variables, all having the same type, in a single declaration:

```
int a, b, c, d;
```

This creates four separate variables named `a`, `b`, `c`, and `d`, each of which is declared to hold integer values. You learn more about the basic data types and their declarations in Chapter 2, "C++ Data Types and Expressions."

Symbolic Constants

Another special symbol in C++ is the *symbolic constant*. A constant value, such as 10, is a value that does not change during execution of your program. When you use a constant value, you will probably want to use a symbolic constant to improve the program's readability and to make it easier to modify the program in the future.

Consider a program to convert miles to kilometers. To perform the conversion to kilometers, you divide the number of miles by 1.609344 (there are 1.609344 kilometers per mile). Listing 1.2 contains a program to perform this conversion.

Listing 1.2 A Simple C++ Program to Convert Miles into Kilometers

```
1   // METRIC1.CPP
2   // METRIC1.CPP converts a measurement in miles
3   // into a measurement in kilometers and meters.
4   #include <iostream.h>
5
```

(continues)

Listing 1.2 Continued

```
 6  void main(void) {
 7    float miles;
 8
 9    cout << "English to metric conversion calculator."
10        << endl << endl;
11
12    // Display prompt for number of miles.
13    cout << "Enter number of miles:  ";
14
15    // Read keyboard input.
16    cin >> miles;
17
18    // Display the calculated result.
19    cout << endl << miles << " converts to " << miles*1.609344
20        << " kilometers." << endl << endl;
21
22    cout << "Or, " <<  (miles*1.609344)/1000  << " meters."
23        << endl << endl;
24
25    cout << "Press Enter to continue." << endl;
26    cin.ignore(1);  // Ignore leftover Enter key.
27    cin.get();
28
29  } // main
```

When you read the program source code for the miles-to-kilometers converter, note the use of the constant 1.609344 in lines 19 and 22. This is a small program, and the reference to this constant is obvious; however, imagine the difficulty you might have if you encountered this strange constant while perusing a program consisting of thousands of lines of code.

You can make this program more readable by creating a symbolic constant with a name such as KILOMETERS_PER_MILE. A symbolic name such as this is easier to understand because it is meaningful to both you and another programmer. Also, if you decide to change the operation of your program (perhaps to reduce the number of digits of accuracy from seven to two), you can easily redefine the value of the KILOMETERS_PER_MILE constant to 1.6.

You define a symbolic constant by using the const modifier before the type:

```
const float KILOMETERS_PER_MILE = 1.609344;
```

The const keyword tells the C++ compiler that the variable named KILOMETERS_PER_MILE cannot be altered during program execution. In this example, KILOMETERS_PER_MILE is set to 1.609344. At this point, wherever you need to use the value 1.609344, you can substitute KILOMETERS_PER_MILE.

Listing 1.3 shows the metric calculator program from listing 1.2 but modified to use the symbolic constant KILOMETERS_PER_MILE in place of the floating-point constant.

Listing 1.3 A Sample Program That Uses a Symbolic Constant

```
1   // METRIC2.CPP
2   // METRIC2.CPP uses a symbolic constant to
3   // improve readability of the program.
4   #include <iostream.h>
5
6   void main(void) {
7     float miles;
8     const float KILOMETERS_PER_MILE = 1.609344;
9
10    cout << "English to metric conversion calculator."
11        << endl << endl;
12
13    // Display prompt for number of miles.
14    cout << "Enter number of miles:  ";
15
16    // Read keyboard input.
17    cin >> miles;
18
19    // Display the calculated result.
20    cout << endl << miles << " converts to "
21        << miles*KILOMETERS_PER_MILE
22        << " kilometers." << endl << endl;
23
24    cout << "Or, " <<  (miles*KILOMETERS_PER_MILE)/1000
25        << " meters." << endl << endl;
26
27    cout << "Press Enter to continue." << endl;
28    cin.ignore(1);  // Ignore leftover Enter key.
29    cin.get();
30
31  } // main
```

In Chapter 2, "C++ Data Types and Expressions," you learn about the #define directive, which provides an alternative method of defining a constant symbol. In general, it is good programming practice to use symbolic constants in place of fixed constants. Symbolic constants greatly improve the readability of your program. If you need to change the value represented by the symbolic constant, you need only change the definition of the symbolic constant. If you do not use a symbolic constant, you will be forced to manually search your entire program source code and find and replace each occurrence of your fixed constant. Clearly, the use of symbolic constants improves readability and maintainability of your software.

Expressions

Data is useful only when you manipulate and perform operations on it.
In C++, you can write arithmetic expressions to calculate new values. For
example, where `number_of_dogs` is an `int` type variable, you may write the
following:

```
number_of_dogs = 5;
   .
   .
   .
number_of_dogs = number_of_dogs + 10;
```

The last statement adds 10 to 5, the current value of `number_of_dogs`, producing the new value 15. The calculated value is then assigned or stored to
`number_of_dogs`. You perform subtraction with the - operator:

```
number_of_dogs = number_of_dogs - 4;
```

A frequent arithmetic operation involving integers is to increment or decrement the value of a variable by 1. This operation is so frequently needed that
C++ has a special shorthand notation for it. For the increment operation, you
may write

```
number_of_dogs++;
```

This is equivalent to writing

```
number_of_dogs = number_of_dogs + 1;
```

The decrement operation is performed by writing

```
number_of_dogs--;
```

This is equivalent to writing

```
number_of_dogs = number_of_dogs - 1;
```

You will see the increment and decrement operators used frequently in C++
code, so you should commit them to memory.

You can also multiply and divide values in C++ using the * and / operators,
respectively. For example, to multiply `number_of_dogs` by 100, you write

```
number_of_dogs = number_of_dogs * 100;
```

To divide the value of the frequency variable by 10, write

```
frequency = frequency / 10.0;
```

In Chapter 2, "C++ Data Types and Expressions," you learn about more
operators and the various ways to use them in C++.

Statements

Programs consist of data, such as variables, constants, and statements. Program *statements* instruct the computer to manipulate the data and to control the flow of execution. Each statement in C++ is terminated by the semicolon character. You can see the use of the semicolon as a statement terminator by closely examining the source code in listings 1.1, 1.2, and 1.3.

C++ has four basic statement types:

- The *assignment statement* assigns a value or the result of an expression to a variable.

- *Selector* or *conditional statements* selectively execute parts of a program.

- *Loop statements* repeatedly execute a sequence of statements.

- *Calls to functions* execute code located in another function. You can make function calls as part of an arithmetic expression evaluation or a stand-alone statement.

One of C++'s selectors is the `if` statement. You use an `if` statement when your program must make a decision. The `if` statement tests a condition. If the condition proves to be true, it selectively (hence, the name *selector*) executes one or more statements.

To describe the format of a C++ statement, such as the `if` statement, you often use a syntax description. The syntax of a language describes the order in which elements of grammar are assembled to form components of the language. The syntax of C++ describes the ordering of each statement. The syntax of the `if` statement is written as follows:

```
if (expression)
  statement1;
else
  statement2;
```

The `if` statement tests the value of the expression. If `expression` is nonzero, `statement1` is executed. If `expression` is zero, `statement2` is executed. In this way, you use the `if` statement to conditionally execute portions of your program. As an option, you can omit the `else` `statement2` part of the `if` statement. In some cases, you may need to test multiple conditions; you can do this by repeatedly adding `else` `if` as needed. Your `if` statement might resemble the following:

```
if (expression)
  statement1;
else if (expression)
  statement2;
else if (expression)
  statement3;
```

C++ supports many expressions suitable for use in an `if` statement. You have already seen an example of simple arithmetic expressions used to assign values to variables. Another type of expression is the *relational expression*, used to compare values to one another. For example, to test whether one value is equal to another, you may use the equality operator ==, as in the following example:

```
if (number_of_dogs == 1)
  cout << "There is 1 dog." << endl;
else
  cout << "There are " << number_of_dogs << " dogs." << endl;
```

To test whether one value is less than another, you should use the < operator:

```
if (frequency <= 5.0)
  cout << "Frequency must be greater than 5.0 MHz." << endl;
```

Table 1.5 shows the six relational operators you use when writing C++ programs. You can use these relational operators in `if` statements when your program must make a decision. You learn in Chapter 2, "C++ Data Types and Expressions," how to create powerful relational tests that use multiple conditions.

Table 1.5 The Equality and Relational Operators Used in C++

Operator	Purpose
a == b	Tests for a being equal to b
a != b	Tests for a not being equal to b
a < b	Tests for a being less than b
a <= b	Tests for a being less than or equal to b
a > b	Tests for a being greater than b
a >= b	Tests for a being greater than or equal to b

Compound Statements. Sometimes statements are grouped together by enclosing several of them in braces. This group of statements is called a *compound statement* or *block of statements*. Compound statements are used when, as the result of an if selection, several statements must be executed together. For example, in the metric calculator shown in listing 1.3, you might want to test for the condition when the number of miles entered is 0. If 0 miles are entered, the program can terminate immediately. To do this, you need to add an if statement and execute the following block of statements only when the miles are not equal to 0. The modified code section should look like the following:

```
// Read keyboard input.
cin >> miles;

if (miles != 0.0)
{
  // Display the calculated result.
  cout << endl << miles << " converts to "
       << miles*KILOMETERS_PER_MILE
       << " kilometers." << endl << endl;

  cout << "Or, " <<  (miles*KILOMETERS_PER_MILE)/1000
       << " meters." << endl << endl;
} // end if
```

The *for* Loop. The C++ language has three looping instructions known as the for, while, and do-while statements. This section introduces you to the for loop. All the looping statements are described in more detail in Chapter 4, "Selection and Loop Statements." Understanding the for loop enables you to write a number of interesting programs.

The for loop repeatedly executes a group of statements. (In some situations, however, you use the for loop when there are no statements!) The easiest way to understand use of the for loop is to see it in action. Listing 1.4 shows a for loop that is used to display the numbers from 0 to 10.

Listing 1.4 A Sample Program That Uses a *for* Loop

```
1   // FORLOOP1.CPP
2   // Uses a for loop to display numbers counting from
3   // 1 to 10.
4   #include <iostream.h>
5
6   void main(void) {
7     int count;
8
9     cout << "Demonstrates use of the for loop."
10         << endl << endl;
11
12    for (count=0; count <= 10; count++ )
13      cout << count << " ";
14
```

(continues)

Listing 1.4 Continued

```
15    cout << endl << "Press Enter to continue." << endl;
16    cin.get();
17
18  } // main
```

Figure 1.24 displays the output of the simple program shown in listing 1.4.

Fig. 1.24
The output
generated by
listing 1.4.

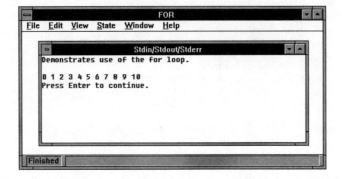

The for loop consists of four parts:

■ An initialization section

■ A conditional test to determine whether the loop should execute

■ An increment step

■ The set of statements to execute as part of the loop

Written in terms of the statement's syntax, the for loop looks like this:

```
for (initializer; conditional-test; increment-step)
   statement;
```

Look closely at the for loop in listing 1.4 and see whether you can spot the four parts:

```
for (count=0; count <= 10; count++ )
   cout << count << " ";
```

The first part, the *initializer*, is

```
count=0
```

and is executed once before entering the loop. In this example, the initialization sets count to 0.

The next part is the `conditional-test`

```
count <= 10
```

which specifies a stopping condition. As long as `count` is less than or equal to 10, the loop executes. If `count` is greater than 10, the loop terminates, and the next statement executed is the first statement after the loop.

The third part is the `increment-step`:

```
count++
```

This causes `count` to increment after each iteration of the loop's content.

To understand the operation of the `for` loop, you may want to manually follow this code through. At the beginning of the loop, `count` is set to 0 and is then compared to 10. Because `count` is less than 10, the statement part of the `for` loop is executed next.

The fourth part of the loop is the portion containing the statement to be executed repeatedly.

The statement part uses the `cout` stream to display the value of `count`. Then `count` is incremented, assigning `count` the value of 1. The loop continues to execute repeatedly until `count` is eventually incremented to 11. A value of 11 causes the loop to terminate. When the loop terminates, the statements in the `for` loop are no longer executed, and program execution jumps to the first statement after the end of the loop.

Often you want the `for` loop to execute many statements rather than just one. You can use the `for` loop to execute any number of statements by grouping them into a block. The following example uses a block to print the value of `count` and the value of `count` times 10:

```
for (count=0; count <= 10; count++ )
{
    cout << count << " ";
    cout << count * 10 << " ";
}
```

In this example, two statements are executed each time through the loop.

This concludes the brief introduction to the `for` loop. You learn about more of C++'s looping features in Chapter 4, "Selection and Loop Statements."

Functions

Most C++ programs have many functions defined in each program. You can use functions to split complex routines into several smaller and simpler routines. By splitting large functions into smaller ones, your program is easier to write, easier to repair when it does not work, and easier to modify when you want to make future changes.

To understand how you split a program into functions, consider splitting the simple miles-to-kilometers conversion program from listing 1.2 into two functions. You can use the existing main() function to display the prompt and to input the number of miles. Then you can easily place the actual conversion to kilometers into a function. Listing 1.5 shows the result of using a function.

Listing 1.5 A Program That Uses a Function

```
 1   // METRIC3.CPP
 2   // METRIC3.CPP shows an example use of a function.
 3   #include <iostream.h>
 4
 5   void convert_miles_to_km( float mileage )
 6   {
 7     const float KILOMETERS_PER_MILE = 1.609344;
 8
 9     // Display the calculated result.
10     cout << endl << mileage << " converts to "
11         << mileage*KILOMETERS_PER_MILE
12         << " kilometers." << endl << endl;
13
14     cout << "Or, " <<  (mileage*KILOMETERS_PER_MILE)/1000
15         << " meters." << endl << endl;
16   };
17
18   void main(void) {
19     float miles;
20
21     cout << "English to metric conversion calculator."
22         << endl << endl;
23
24     // Display prompt for number of miles.
25     cout << "Enter number of miles:  ";
26
27     // Read keyboard input.
28     cin >> miles;
29
30     convert_miles_to_km ( miles );
31
32     cout << "Press Enter to continue." << endl;
33     cin.ignore(1);   // Ignore leftover Enter key.
34     cin.get();
35   } // main
```

Lines 5 through 16 implement the new function, named `convert_miles_to_km()`. Programs that contain multiple functions still begin execution at the function named `main()`, whether `main()` is the first or last function in the program. In listing 1.5, `main()` displays a program title at line 21, prompts for a mileage figure to convert at line 25, and reads at line 28 the number of miles into the variable named `miles`. At line 30, `main()` invokes or calls the function named `convert_miles_to_km()`. The computer immediately begins executing the program code at line 5. `convert_miles_to_km()` performs the necessary conversion and displays the result on the screen. When it finishes executing, the computer returns to the `main()` function. Because there are no more statements in `main()` to execute, the program terminates.

The function `convert_miles_to_km()` contains a single parameter variable named `mileage`. This parameter is used to pass information—in this case, the mileage—to the function. Line 5 tells the compiler that `convert_miles_to_km()` expects this parameter to be a floating-point value. Within `convert_miles_to_km()`, the parameter variable is named `mileage`. The mileage variable is defined only inside of `convert_miles_to_km()`; if you try to reference `mileage` inside `main()`, you get an error from the compiler telling you that `mileage` is an unknown identifier.

Functions are an important part of C++ programming. In addition to enabling you to create functions, C++ provides several libraries of prewritten functions to perform many useful operations. By using C++'s prewritten functions, you save yourself the trouble and time needed to write the code. Because the library routines are pretested, your program is assembled quickly and with few errors. You learn more about using library functions and defining and using your own functions in Chapter 6, "Functions and Macros."

Summary

This chapter introduced you to the Visual C++ program development system and the basic components of a C++ program. In subsequent chapters, you explore each of these topics in-depth. You also learn how to use the enhanced features of C++ to write object-oriented programs. In this chapter, you learned the following:

- In Microsoft Windows and the Visual Workbench, you use standard pull-down menus and dialog boxes, and you use the editor to type, save, and get C++ source files.

■ Most C++ programs have one or more `#include` directives at the beginning of the source program. These `#include` directives give the compiler additional information to create your program. Your program typically uses `#include` to gain access to functions defined in library files.

■ Each program must include a function named `main()` (except for Microsoft Windows applications, which must include a function named `WinMain()`). Most programs have many functions in addition to `main()`.

■ In C++, you use the `cin` stream and the >> extraction operator to obtain input from the keyboard.

■ To display output to the screen, you use the `cout` stream and the << insertion operator.

■ C++ supports the use of many types of variables, including the `int` and `float` types that you learned about in this chapter. You use variables to store information during the execution of your program.

■ The `if` statement is one of C++'s selector statements. You use `if` to conditionally execute one or more statements in your program.

■ A block of statements can be grouped together by surrounding the statements with { and }.

■ When you want to have a section of code execute repeatedly, you use a loop statement, such as the `for` loop.

■ Because of the design of the underlying 80386, 80486, or Pentium microprocessor, you must choose an appropriate memory model when you compile a program in Visual C++. Visual C++ supports six memory models: Tiny, Small, Compact, Medium, Large, and Huge. You learn more about these memory models in Chapter 7, "Projects."

■ Visual C++ provides several options to enable you to quickly compile, link, and execute your C++ programs.

Review Questions

1. What is the Visual Workbench? What command do you use to compile, link, and run your program? What command do you use to save your program to disk? What command do you use to load an existing program from disk?

2. What is QuickWin?

3. In a dialog box, what keystroke do you use to move from one control to another?

4. How do you select or deselect a radio button or check box item?

5. What are some of the keystrokes you use to move around inside the editor and to make changes to your program source code?

6. C++ source code files must always end in a specific file name extension. What is that file name extension?

7. You have learned two ways to write comments in your C++ program statements. What are the two methods? What is the default color the Visual Workbench uses to display comments?

8. What is the name of the function that each program must contain?

9. What C++ data type do you use for integer variables? For floating-point variables?

10. What are the shorthand notations for incrementing and decrementing an integer variable?

11. Which stream identifier do you use for input from the keyboard? What is the operator symbol that you should use to extract input from the stream to a variable?

12. Which stream identifier do you use for output to the display? Write a typical output statement to output a text string, the value of a variable, and two blank lines.

13. Identify one or more good reasons for using symbolic constants in your programs.

14. What expression operators are used to indicate addition, subtraction, multiplication, and division?

15. What six operators are used to test for equality and relative differences between values?

16. What is the name of the >> operator?

17. What is the name of the << operator?

18. What is the syntax of a `for` loop?

19. What is the syntax of the `if` statement?

20. C++ programs can be written as one large `main()` function; however, they seldom are. What is one reason to split a large program into many smaller functions?

21. When do you need to use the semicolon character in your C++ programs?

Exercises

1. Practice adding more source comments to the sample programs presented in this chapter. Experiment with both the `//` and the `/* */` comment characters. See if you can include comments within comments.

2. Modify the FORLOOP1.CPP program to count downward and display the result on the screen.

3. Add an `if` statement to ANTENNA.CPP to avoid executing the calculations when `frequency` is equal to 0.0.

4. Write a program to input two numbers from the user, add them, and display the result. Store the two numbers in separate variables and assign the result of their addition to a third variable.

Chapter 2

C++ Data Types and Expressions

In Chapter 1, "The Fundamentals of C++ Programming," you learned about the integer and floating-point data types. Visual C++ has several more data types for representing other types of data, as well as several techniques for representing more elaborate data. An example is an address record containing a name, an address, and a ZIP code. It is important to understand the various types of data that you can work with in C++ programs. After all, working with data is what computer programming is all about.

In this chapter, you learn the basic Visual C++ data types, plus more arithmetic operators and other operators that you can use in expressions. In the next chapter, you learn about more advanced data types, such as arrays, structures, and unions, and you are introduced to the concept of an object.

C++ has several basic data types, plus many rules and guidelines for how to define these identifiers. Some variable identifiers are accessible to your entire program, whereas others are accessible only within a function. As you begin to learn C++ data types, you may be a bit overwhelmed with the details. As you read this chapter and the next, you can make your task easier by focusing your attention initially on the following topics:

- Variable naming.

- The `int` integer type for storing integer numbers and the `const int` type for creating symbolic constants.

- The `char` character type for storing characters.

- The `float` type for storing floating-point numbers.

- The C++ expression operators for performing arithmetic. Concentrate on the simple operators, such as addition, subtraction, division, and multiplication; and the equality and relational tests, such as == (equal to) or < (less than).

- The array, especially one-dimensional arrays and character arrays used for text strings.

- Simple structures.

Don't try to learn all the details about each of the data types right away. Get comfortable with the basic data types and master the more complicated data types only as you become more experienced. Use this chapter and the next as references when you need to understand the other C++ data types and capabilities.

Understanding the topics just outlined will enable you to write sophisticated programs. After you have mastered the core set of data types and techniques, you can advance to other topics such as unions, objects, and enumerated types. The object type, introduced in Chapter 3, "C++ Advanced Data Types," is at the core of object-oriented programming. You learn much more about objects in Chapter 8, "Classes."

Identifier Names

Variables, as you learned in Chapter 1, hold data values for your program to process, and a constant symbol holds a value that is not changed during your program's execution. A variable or constant is designated with an *identifier name*, such as Count, number_of_dogs, index, or the single letter i. Each identifier must begin with an alphabetic letter or the underscore character (_) and may then consist of any combination of upper- or lowercase letters, digits, and underscores. In Visual C++, the identifiers can be up to 247 characters in length.

Following are several examples of valid identifiers in C++:

i	I	Index
index	Total	Total_Amount
Acceleration	Antenna_Height	Room116
Control_Value	Valve_Open_Flag	Valve_1_Set

C++ is a *case-sensitive* language. Thus, C++ recognizes ALPHA, alpha, and Alpha as distinct identifiers. Because C++ is sensitive to the case of identifiers (unlike other programming languages such as Pascal or BASIC), you should choose your variable names in a consistent manner to avoid hard-to-find names. In my experience, I have seen professionally written code that included two variables named Index and index in the same function. Both variables may coexist in the same program or same function even though their use may lead to confusion. I don't know why the program's author defined two variable names like this, but I can assure you that it made reading his source code difficult. I have a hunch that the use of these variables also
made finding program errors more difficult and time-consuming than was necessary.

To avoid problems with the case-sensitivity of C++, many programmers write variable identifiers in lowercase, constants in uppercase, and functions in mixed case. Using this approach, you can avoid problems that may occur when you intentionally or unintentionally mix the case with various identifiers. Other programmers prefer to use other naming conventions for their identifiers. In this book, variables are written both in all lowercase and in mixed case.

The Basic Data Types

In addition to the int and float types that you used in Chapter 1, Visual C++ has additional data types, primarily as variations of the basic int and float types. The additional types provide different value ranges and enable you to optimize the memory and calculation efficiency of your program. Remember that the int type can accommodate numbers from –32,768 to +32,767. A variation on this data type, known as unsigned int, alters the allowable range to accommodate numbers from 0 to +65,535. Another variation defines values only in the range of 0 to 255.

Why would you want to use these different data types? The answer is that you can customize the size and speed of calculation to the type of problem you are solving. For instance, the integer types require less memory than the floating-point types, and the microprocessor can perform integer arithmetic faster than it can perform floating-point arithmetic. As a general rule, the smaller the range of allowed values, the less memory the data type requires, and the faster the computer processes the data.

Note

Keep in mind that the range of some data types is machine-dependent. For example, an int data type in Visual C++, on an IBM PC-compatible computer running Microsoft Windows, represents values in the range of –32,768 to +32,767. However, if you used VAX C on a DEC VAX 8200 running VAX-VMS, an int represents values in the range of –2,147,483,648 to +2,147,483,647. And an int type in Visual C++ for NT, on an IBM PC-compatible computer running Windows NT, would represent the same value as an int on the VAX.

Conversely, standards guarantee the same numerical ranges for other data types, such as long int and short int, no matter what machine, compiler, or operating system you use to compile and execute the program.

Integers

You use integer variables for counting, for control variables in for loops, for indexing into arrays (you learn about arrays in the section "Arrays" in Chapter 3, "C++ Advanced Data Types"), and for a variety of other purposes. Integers are ideally suited for these purposes because their range of values matches these types of problems, and because the microprocessor is optimized for maximum performance when you use integer variables. Table 2.1 summarizes the three basic integer types. All these types are stored internally in 2 bytes (or 16 bits) of memory.

Table 2.1 The Three Integer Data Types

C++ Type	Range of Values	Suggested Use
int	–32,768 to +32,767	Integer arithmetic, for loops, or counting
unsigned int	0 to 65,535	Counting, for loops, or indexing
short int	–32,768 to +32,767	Integer arithmetic, for loops, or counting

To define a signed integer variable, use the int type, as in

```
int part_number, num_items;
```

This line declares the part_number and num_items variables to be of type int. You can assign values to these variables:

```
part_number = 1135;
num_items = 55;
```

In C++, you can also initialize the value of a variable at the point where the variables are defined. You do this by adding the values to be assigned immediately after the declaration, as in the following line:

```
int part_number = 1135, num_items = 55;
```

You type negative values by prefacing the integer constant with a hyphen or minus sign:

```
int water_level = -5;
```

An `unsigned int` is a special integer that represents only positive values. The `unsigned int` can represent values from 0 to 65,535 and is especially well suited for counting items or for use as a control variable in a `for` loop. Use an `unsigned int` data type when you need a positive number greater than that provided by the signed `int`. In Visual C++, the `short int` type is equivalent to the `int` type.

For general application programming, you write integer constants in *decimal* or *base 10 notation*—for example, `100`, `999`, or `1500`. To write an unsigned constant, you may want to append the letter `U` (or `u`). Adding `U` causes the compiler to ensure that the constant is treated as an unsigned integer rather than as a signed integer value. For example, to write 40,000 as an unsigned integer, write `40000U`.

If you use C++ to develop operating system software and other software that interacts with the computer's hardware, C++ enables you to write integer constants in *octal* (base 8) or *hexadecimal* (base 16). An octal constant is any number that begins with a `0` and contains digits in the range of 1 to 7. For example, `0377` is an octal number. A hexadecimal constant begins with `0x` and is followed by the digits 0 to 9 or the letters A to F (or a to f). For example, `0xFF16` is a hexadecimal constant. If you are new to C++ (or C) programming, it is not terribly important at this point that you know how to use octal and hexadecimal constants.

Long Integers

When the range of the basic integer types is not great enough for your needs, consider using the `long` integer type. The `long` integer can represent extremely large values, and the computer processes this type more efficiently than it does the floating-point types. Table 2.2 shows the two `long` integer data types. Both types require 4 bytes of memory (or 32 bits) for storage.

Caution

The range of integer values—at –32,768 to +32,737 or 0 to 65,535—seems fairly large. However, when you multiply integer values together, exceeding the limits of the integer type is surprisingly easy. For example, if you multiply 3,000 by 40, you'd expect to get 120,000; however, 120,000 exceeds the valid range for integers. When the computer tries this multiplication, it overflows its internal registers but does not generate an error. Instead, it produces the result of –11,072. Because integer *overflow* during multiplication is a reasonably common problem in programs, you need to keep a sharp eye out for potential trouble spots in your programs.

Table 2.2 The Long Integer Data Types

C++ Type	Range of Values
long	–2,147,483,648 to +2,147,483,647
unsigned long	0 to +4,294,967,295

Use the type name long or unsigned long to define long integer variables. Note this example:

```
long millimeter_measure;
unsigned long spacecraft_distance;
```

As with the integer types, you can write long constants in decimal, octal, or hexadecimal. When you write large constants, you may want to ensure that the compiler treats your constant value as a true long and not as an integer. To force the compiler to treat your constant as a long, append the letter L (or l) to your constant, as in this example:

```
long big_numbers = 40000L;
```

Characters

C++ processes character data (such as text) by using the char data type. Along with the array structure, you can use the char data type to store *character strings* (or groups of characters). You can use the char data type also for performing certain types of arithmetic. You define a character variable by writing

```
char one_character;
```

This line defines one_character to be a char variable that holds a single character. To write character constants, place the character within single quotation marks, as in

```
one_character = 'A';
```

Internally, characters are stored as numbers. The letter *A*, for instance, is stored internally as the number 65. The letter *B* is 66, the letter *C* is 67, and so on. This internal numbering scheme is standardized among PCs and is known as the American Standard Code for Information Interchange (ASCII). ASCII codes define the meaning of each number from 0 to 127. Therefore, the basic char type represents values in the range of –128 to +127.

IBM-compatible computers, however, provide more characters than can be represented in the standard ASCII definition. For this reason, IBM-compatible computers extend the ASCII definitions to use character codes from 128 to 255. This extension provides for a maximum of 256 characters (0 through 255). The English alphabet has just 26 uppercase and 26 lowercase letters, plus 10 digits and assorted punctuation symbols such as parentheses, commas, and periods. The extra character codes represent letters that appear in international alphabets (such as ì, Ä, and û) and represent graphical line-drawing characters.

Because the char type stores values in the range of –128 to +127, C++ provides the unsigned char type to represent values from 0 to 255. You must use the unsigned char type if your application uses the international ASCII character codes.

You may wonder how to enter the single quotation mark as a character if a character constant is written between single quotation marks. The answer is to use *escape sequence characters* (sometimes referred to as *escape codes*). Using an escape sequence, you can substitute other characters for the character that you cannot type. C++ defines the set of standard escape sequences shown in table 2.3.

Table 2.3 Escape Sequences Available in Visual C++		
Sequence	**ASCII Value**	**Use**
\a	7	Rings the "bell" on the PC
\b	8	Equivalent to the Backspace key
\f	12	Performs a formfeed (page eject) on a printer
\n	10	C++ "newline" or linefeed character
\r	13	Carriage return character
\t	9	Tab character

(continues)

Table 2.3 Continued		
Sequence	ASCII Value	Use
\v	11	Vertical tab (seldom used)
\\	92	Backslash
\'	39	Single quotation mark
\"	34	Double quotation mark
\0	0	Null character
\0nnn		Where nnn equals up to three octal digits
\Xnn		Where nn equals up to two uppercase hexadecimal digits
\xnn		Where nn equals up to two lowercase hexadecimal digits

To use an escape sequence, substitute the sequence shown in table 2.3 within the single quotation marks. For example, you enter a single quotation mark as a character by typing the following:

```
char single_quote = '\'';
```

Note that each escape sequence begins with the backslash character. Hence, to enter a single backslash, you must use an escape sequence. Many of the escape sequences shown in table 2.3 are used extensively in the C programming language; other than \', \", \0, and \\, however, these sequences are not used nearly as much in C++ as in C.

Using *char* Types for Arithmetic

Because characters are stored internally as numbers, you can perform arithmetic operations on char data. For example, you can convert a lowercase letter *a* to an uppercase *A* by subtracting 32 from the ASCII code (see the ASCII chart in Appendix A for the entire set of ASCII and extended ASCII codes available on IBM-compatible computers). To perform the conversion, subtract 32 from the char data type:

```
char single_char = 'a';
  .
  .
  .
single_char = single_char - 32;
```

This converts *a* (ASCII code 97) to *A* (ASCII code 65). In a similar manner, adding 32 converts the character from uppercase to lowercase:

```
single_char = single_char + 32;
```

Many C++ programmers use `char` and `unsigned char` variables to perform arithmetic on small integer values in the range of –128 to +127 or 0 to 255, respectively. Because the `char` types require just 1 byte of storage, they use little memory, and the microprocessor can manipulate them at maximum speed.

In addition, the `char` types are proper subsets of the integer types, so you can assign a `char` type to an integer. Here is an example:

```
int sum = 0;
char value;
 .
 .
 .
cin >> value;
sum = sum + value;
```

Floating-Point Types

The floating-point data types represent fractional numbers that contain a decimal point (such as 3.14159) or very large numbers (such as $1.7 * 10^{15}$). Use the floating-point types when you must work with decimal fractions or when you need scientific notation to represent large or small magnitude numbers. The primary disadvantage of the floating-point type is that floating-point calculations are more time-consuming than integer calculations, especially on the older 8088, 80286, and 80386 microprocessors. These microprocessors were designed to perform only integer arithmetic in hardware; floating-point calculations had to be performed using software subroutines. For these microprocessors, you could purchase a separate math coprocessor that would substantially increase the speed of floating-point operations. Today, most 80486-based computers have the floating-point processor built into the 80486 chip.

Visual C++ supports three floating-point formats, which are described in table 2.4. The `float` type requires 4 bytes of memory, `double` requires 8 bytes, and `long double` requires 10 bytes. The more digits of accuracy, the greater the amount of memory required to store the value. Similarly, more digits of accuracy require more processing time.

Table 2.4 Visual C++ Floating-Point Data Types		
C++ Type	**Range of Values**	**Accuracy**
float	3.4×10^{-38} to 3.4×10^{38}	7 digits
double	1.7×10^{-308} to 1.7×10^{308}	15 digits
long double	3.4×10^{-4932} to 1.1×10^{4932}	19 digits

Floating-Point Constants. You can write floating-point constants in several ways. If your value is a whole number, you can write the number with or without a decimal point, as in these examples:

    15

    15.0

If the floating-point value has a fractional part, you write that after the decimal point, as in this example:

    3.14159

To write a negative value, preface the number with a hyphen (or minus sign):

    -3.14159

To write numbers in exponential notation, you must follow the decimal part of the number with the letter E (or e) and then the exponent part, as in these examples:

    4.5E+5

    -3.2E-2

    7.12E6

Comparison of Data Sizes. You have seen in the descriptions of the char, int, and floating-point data types that each type requires a different amount of memory storage than the other types. Figure 2.1 summarizes the differences in storage requirements for each data type. When you write your own program, always strive to choose the smallest data type that can accommodate the range of values your application needs. Because the microprocessor can process the smaller values more quickly, using them boosts your program's overall speed.

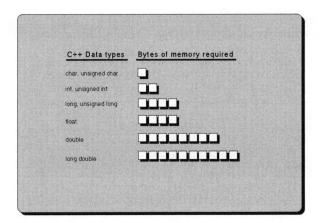

Fig. 2.1
A comparison
of the memory
storage require-
ments for each
data type.

Duration of Variables

Depending on where and how C++ variables are defined, variables can be used throughout the entire program or only within a function, or they may exist temporarily within a block within a function. How long a variable is active is often referred to as a variable's *scope*.

Here are the basic types of C++ variables:

- Local variables

- Global variables

- Dynamic variables

- Object fields

Local variables are defined inside functions. Local variables come into existence only when the function is executed. When the function is completed, the memory space used by the local variables is recycled. Another name for local variables is *automatic* variables (or *auto* variables) because they are automatically created on entry to a function and automatically disposed of when the function exits. Listing 2.1 is a program that uses a local variable.

Listing 2.1 Using a Local Variable

```
1   // TEMPTBL.CPP
2   // Demonstrates the use of local variables by
3   // calculating a Celsius-to-Fahrenheit temperature
4   // conversion table.
5   #include <iostream.h>
6
7   void display_table()
8   {
9     // Variable temperature is local to
10    // this function. It is undefined outside of
11    // display_table().
12    int temperature;
13    for (temperature=0; temperature <= 100; temperature++ )
14      cout << temperature << " degs C. = "
15           << (temperature * 9/5) + 32 << " degs. F. "
16           << endl;
17  }
18
19  void main(void) {
20
21    cout << "Displays a table to convert Celsius temperatures "
22         << " to Fahrenheit."
23         << endl << endl;
24
25    display_table();
26
27    cout << "Press Enter to continue." << endl;
28    cin.get();
29
30  } // end main
```

Listing 2.1 displays a conversion table to be used in converting degrees Celsius to degrees Fahrenheit. The table is displayed by calling the display_table() function (see line 25). This function defines a local variable named temperature (see line 12) for use as the control value in the for loop (lines 13 to 16). The temperature variable is defined only within display_table(). Any attempt to use temperature in the main() function, for example, results in a compiler error. The temperature variable is local to the display_table() function.

If a local variable must retain its value between function calls, you can mark the local variable as *static*. A static local variable remains local to the function that defines it; however, instead of being created and disposed of automatically, memory space is allocated permanently so that the static variable retains its value across function calls. Listing 2.2 is a program that uses a static variable.

Listing 2.2 A Program That Uses a Static Variable

```
1   // STATIC1.CPP
2   // Demonstrates the use of a static local variable by
3   // calculating a sum of entered values. The running
4   // total is kept in a static local variable, demonstrating
5   // that the value of the static variable is held across
6   // function calls.
7   #include <iostream.h>
8
9   void current_sum()
10  {
11      static int sum = 0;       // sum's value will be retained
12                                // across calls to current_sum().
13      int data_value;           // Holds the current input value.
14
15      cout << "Enter a data value? ";
16      cin >> data_value;
17      sum = sum + data_value;
18      cout << "Current sum=" << sum << endl;
19  } // current_sum
20
21  void main(void) {
22      int how_many;             // The number of data values to
23                                // process.
24      int number;               // for loop control variable.
25
26      cout << "Calculates a sum of data values."
27          << endl << endl;
28
29      cout << "How many numbers to sum? ";
30      cin >> how_many;
31
32      for (number=1; number<= how_many; number++)
33        current_sum();
34
35      cout << "Press Enter to continue." << endl;
36      cin.ignore(1);  // Ignore leftover Enter key.
37      cin.get();
38
39  } // main
```

The program in listing 2.2 calls the current_sum() function (see lines 9 through 19) to input and process a data value. Line 17 adds the input value (from the variable data_value) to the static local variable sum. Each time that current_sum() is executed, the next data_value is added to the current value of sum. The value of sum is retained across function calls, unlike normal local variables, because sum is declared using the static keyword before its definition (see line 11). Note that sum is initialized to zero as part of its definition. In the case of a static variable, this initialization is performed once and is not repeated on subsequent calls to current_sum().

Global variables are defined outside functions. These variables can be used by any function in the source file, and they retain their value across calls to different functions.

The memory allocated to a global variable remains allocated throughout the program's execution, taking up valuable memory space whether or not it is used. For this reason, you should avoid using too many global variables within a program. Another common problem that occurs when you use global variables is that one function may set a global variable to a specific value. Then you may forget and let another function make changes to the same variable. These unexpected changes can produce difficult-to-locate program errors. You might be better off using a static local variable in place of a global variable if this design is appropriate for your application.

Listing 2.3 is a program that defines the global variable sum. sum is defined in line 10, outside the scope of any function. Therefore, sum is available to all functions within the program file.

Listing 2.3 A Program That Uses a Globally Defined Variable

```
1   // GLOBAL.CPP
2   // Demonstrates the use of a global variable. Here,
3   // the global variable is used to retain a running sum
4   // (just like STATIC1.CPP). However, the global variable
5   // can be accessed by more than one function. The sum
6   // is calculated in the current_sum() function
7   // by the separate function print_sum().
8   #include <iostream.h>
9
10  int sum = 0;        // sum's value stored here. sum is defined
11                      // outside any function, so sum becomes
12                      // a global variable, accessible to all
13                      // functions in this source file.
14
15  void current_sum()
16  {
17    int data_value;        // Holds the current input value.
18
19    cout << "Enter a data value? ";
20    cin >> data_value;
21    sum = sum + data_value;
22  } // end current_sum
23
24  void print_sum()
25  {
26    cout << "Current sum= " << sum << endl;
27  }
28
```

```
29   void main(void) {
30     int how_many;            // The number of data values to
31                              // process.
32     int number;              // for loop control variable.
33
34     cout << "Calculates a sum of data values."
35         << endl << endl;
36
37     cout << "How many numbers to sum? ";
38     cin >> how_many;
39
40     for (number=1; number<= how_many; number++) {
41       current_sum();
42       print_sum();
43     } // end for
44
45     cout << "Press Enter to continue." << endl;
46     cin.ignore(1);  // Ignore leftover Enter key.
47     cin.get();
48
49   } // end main
```

In listing 2.3, the variable sum is defined as a global variable. Any variable that is defined outside a function becomes a global variable and is accessible to all functions within the source file. Line 21, inside the current_sum() function, adds the data value that is input to sum. A separate function, print_sum() (lines 24 to 27), displays the value of sum. Note that both functions can access sum because sum is a global variable. The main() function can also access sum directly, although the function does not do so in this sample program.

Dynamic variables have qualities that are in some ways similar to both local and global variables. Like a local variable, a dynamic variable is created and disposed of during program execution. The difference between a dynamic variable and a local variable is that the dynamic variable is created at your request (rather than automatically, like local variables) and is disposed of when you no longer need it. As with a global variable, you can create dynamic variable allocations that are accessible to multiple functions. Dynamic variables are discussed in Chapter 5, "Pointers."

Objects are aggregate data types that can hold multiple variables and functions together. Objects are introduced in the section "Introduction to Objects" in Chapter 3, "C++ Advanced Data Types," and are discussed more thoroughly in Chapter 8, "Classes."

Defining Symbolic Constants

Whereas variables hold values that may change during program execution, constants hold values that do not change—hence, the name *constants*. You learned about constants in the section "Symbolic Constants" in Chapter 1. Constants can be used to represent the following:

- The maximum size of a valid input number

- Conversion factors such as the multiplier to use when converting kilometers to miles, or degrees Fahrenheit to Celsius

- The size of a list of data values

- Mathematical constants such as *pi* (3.14159...)

In each of these examples, the value of the constant does not change during the program's execution.

You can always write constants directly into your source code. Suppose that the maximum input value for your program is 500. Values greater than 500 should cause an error message to display. You could write the following section of code to handle this input:

```
cout << "Enter data value? ";
cin >> data_value;
if (data_value > 500) {
  cout << "Data values must be less than 500." << endl;
  .
  .
  .
};
```

Later, if you decide to change the maximum value to a new maximum such as 1000, you must locate and change each occurrence of 500 within your program.

Using *const*

A simpler approach is to create a symbolic constant that is set equal to 500:

```
const int MAXIMUM = 500;
```

Later, if the maximum value changes, you just need to change this definition statement. The new code section looks like the following:

```
const int MAXIMUM = 500;
  .
  .
  .
```

```
    cout << "Enter data value? ";
    cin >> data_value;
    if (data_value > MAXIMUM) {
      cout << "Data values must be less than " << MAXIMUM << endl;
        .
        .
        .
    };
```

Note that MAXIMUM is shown here in uppercase letters. Many programmers write constants in uppercase to distinguish them from variables. You can write symbolic constant names in lowercase or mixed case if you want.

A second advantage to using symbolic constants is that symbolic constant names can be more meaningful than constants like 500 or 99. Therefore, when you create constants, be sure to invent useful names. Don't use cryptic notations like the following:

```
    const int M = 500;
```

Two weeks later, you may not remember that M is your shorthand for *maximum*.

You can write all data types as constants. Here are more examples:

```
    const float PI = 3.14159;
    const char LAST_LETTER = 'Z';
    const long EARTH_RADIUS = 6370000; \\ in meters
```

Using *#define*

C++ was originally developed as a superset of the C programming language. Therefore, you often see continued use of C language features that have been largely replaced with newer C++ features. One such feature is the #define directive used for creating symbolic constants. In C, as well as in C++, the #define directive enables you to create user-defined macros (a topic that you don't need to know about right now). As a consequence of how macros are created, you can also use #define to create symbolic constants.

The #define directive equates a symbol with text so that the statement

```
    #define PI 3.14159
```

sets the symbol PI equal to the characters 3.14159. Wherever PI is referenced in the source code, the compiler substitutes 3.14159.

You should recognize the following distinctive features of the #define directive:

■ When you write the #define directive, note that there is no = between the symbol name and the text that follows.

■ A symbol created with #define is a text substitution, not a reference to a variable. When you write

```
diameter = PI * 2;
```

the compiler translates your source code into

```
diameter = 3.14159 * 2;
```

before compiling the statement into machine code.

■ The #define statement, when used for symbolic constants, should not have a semicolon at the end of the line because the symbol is equal to all of the remaining characters on the line. If you write

```
#define PI 3.14159;
```

PI is equivalent to 3.14159;. If you then reference PI in an arithmetic expression, the compiler incorrectly substitutes PI as well as the trailing semicolon. For example, the expression

```
diameter = PI * 2;
```

incorrectly becomes

```
diameter = 3.14159; * 2;
```

■ const and #define are similar, but they are not equivalent. The most important distinction is that const creates a typed symbol. When you write

```
const float PI = 3.14159;
```

the compiler knows that PI is a floating-point number. The #define directive creates only a text substitution that the compiler makes blindly. The compiler makes the substitution regardless of whether it is correct to do so.

■ You can declare a const symbol local to a function. You can also use #define within a function; however, the definition it creates remains in effect for the rest of the source file. Therefore, if you write

```
#define FACTOR 7.5
```

in the f1() function, you cannot redefine FACTOR in the f2() function. FACTOR, once defined, becomes a global text substitution.

■ If the program doesn't need a previously defined symbol, you can undefine it by using the #undef directive. To remove FACTOR's definition, for example, write

```
#undef FACTOR
```

Listing 2.4 is a sample program that uses `#define` instead of a `const` variable. As shown in this program, `#define` is located outside any functions (see line 5). Because the symbol created by `#define` is globally defined, most symbols created with `#define` are created at the beginning of source files. In this program, the compiler replaces each occurrence of the symbol `KILOMETERS_PER_MILE` with `1.609344`.

Listing 2.4 Using *#define* to Create a Symbolic Constant

```
 1   // DEFINE1.CPP
 2   // This is the METRIC2.CPP source code, modified to
 3   // use #define in place of a const symbol.
 4   #include <iostream.h>
 5   #define KILOMETERS_PER_MILE 1.609344
 6
 7   void main(void) {
 8     float miles;
 9
10     cout << "English-to-metric conversion calculator."
11         << endl << endl;
12
13     // Display prompt for frequency.
14     cout << "Enter number of miles:  ";
15
16     // Read keyboard input.
17     cin >> miles;
18
19     // Display the calculated result.
20     cout << endl << miles << " converts to "
21         << miles*KILOMETERS_PER_MILE
22         << " kilometers." << endl << endl;
23
24     cout << "Or, " <<  (miles*KILOMETERS_PER_MILE)/1000
25         << " meters." << endl << endl;
26
27     cout << "Press Enter to continue." << endl;
28     cin.ignore(1); // Ignore leftover Enter key.
29     cin.get();
30
31   } // main
```

Although C++ offers the improved `const` variable modifier, many C++ programmers began their programming experience by using the C language and `#define`. Hence, you will see `#define` used in many places in existing programs (written by experienced programmers) where const might be better suited. Because #define is used widely, you should become familiar with its use for defining constants; however, you should use const in your own programs.

Expressions and C++ Operators

Visual C++ programs consist of data, program statements, and expressions. An *expression* is typically a mathematical equation, such as 3 + 5. In this expression, the + (plus symbol) is the addition operator, and the numbers 3 and 5 are called *operands*. When you use the + between numbers (or variables), it is called a *binary operator* because the addition operator adds two numbers. Another type of C++ operator is the *unary operator*, which operates on a single value. If the variable x holds the value 3, for example, -x is the value –3. The - (minus symbol) is the unary minus operator. In Chapter 1, you learned to use the ++ increment operator to add 1 to a variable, such as count++. The increment operator is also a unary operator.

Visual C++ supports a powerful suite of unary and binary operators and other types of operators for the creation of arithmetic and other kinds of expressions. Most of these operators are described in this chapter, although a few are not introduced until later in the book.

Because C++ has so many operators (especially when compared to a programming language like Pascal), you may feel overwhelmed trying to remember what each operator means. You should start by learning the arithmetic and relational operators plus the basic assignment operator (=). As you gain experience, you should then explore and learn the additional operators. The C language (the predecessor to C++) became popular in part because its rich repertoire of operators enables programmers to write complex statements concisely. Consequently, as you review C++ code written by others, you'll see frequent examples of C++'s rich operator syntax in use. Ultimately, you need to be familiar with most C++ operators so that you can read other programmers' source code and can optimize your programs to achieve peak performance.

Arithmetic Operators

You use the arithmetic operators shown in table 2.5 to perform basic arithmetic. Note that + and - have two meanings: when used between two operands, the symbols refer to addition and subtraction, respectively;

when + and - are used in front of a single operand, the operators refer to unary plus and unary minus, respectively. When you see 5 - 2, the - symbol refers to subtraction; when you see -5, the - symbol is a unary minus, meaning *minus 5*.

Table 2.5 The C++ Arithmetic Operators		
Symbol	**Use**	**Description**
+	*a* + *b*	Addition
-	*a* - *b*	Subtraction
*	*a* * *b*	Multiplication
/	*a* / *b*	Division
%	*a* % *b* is the remainder of *a* / *b*	Remainder, or modulus
-	-*a*	Unary minus
+	+*a*	Unary plus (seldom used)
++	++*a* and *a*++	Preincrement and postincrement operators
- -	- -a and a - -	Predecrement and postdecrement operators

Arithmetic operators in C++ follow the algebraic rules of hierarchy that you learned in high school (you do remember them, don't you?). These rules specify the precedence of arithmetic operations when multiple operators appear in an expression. Consider the following expression:

    3 + 5 * 2

Does this expression have the value 16—(8 * 2)? Or 13—(3 + 10)? According to the hierarchy rules, multiplication is performed before addition. Therefore, C++ computes the correct answer as if the expression were written with parentheses:

    3 + (5 * 2)

In C++, expressions within parentheses are evaluated first. Then unary operations are performed, followed by multiplication, division, the remainder operation, and then the addition and subtraction operations. (For a complete list of operator precedence, refer to table 2.13 later in this chapter.)

When operators in an expression have equal precedence, such as

```
3 + 5 - 18 + 20 + 75 - 5
```

the order of evaluation is not guaranteed to be the order implied by the expression. The C++ compiler may rearrange the statement if the compiler determines that doing so can improve the efficiency of the calculation. The compiler rearranges only where it can guarantee that the result is unaffected by the reordering, and where an evaluation precedence does not override possible reordering (such as the requirement to perform multiplication before addition).

The ++ and -- operators are unique in that they may appear either in front of or behind an operand. However, there is a subtle difference in the operator's function depending on whether it appears in front or behind. Consider the following code section:

```
int i = 10;
int j;
.
.
.
j = i++;
```

What value does the variable j contain after the assignment statement? At first glance, you might think that j contains 11. However, when ++ appears after the operand (here, the variable i), the original value of the variable is used in the expression before the ++ operator is applied. The effect is that j is assigned the value i, and then i is incremented to 11. This interpretation of the ++ operator can produce subtle problems that are not easy to spot. If you want to ensure that i is incremented before being used in an expression, use the prefix form of ++, as in

```
++i
```

When you use the division operator on integer values, the division operation ignores (or throws away) the remainder of the division result. For example, if you have

```
int x=5;
```

and then use

```
x / 2
```

in an expression, the computed result is 2, and the fractional portion of the result is discarded. If you want to obtain the remainder of a division operation, you should use the remainder operator %, as in

```
x % 2
```

This expression produces the result of 1 because 5 / 2 is 2 with a remainder of 1 (or stated another way, 2 * 2 + 1 equals 5).

Assignment Operators

C++ contains several *assignment operators*, with the most important being the equal symbol (=). You use = to assign the value of an expression to a variable. Where a is a variable, for example, you assign the result of an expression to a by writing

```
a = b + 10;
```

If b has the value 20, a is assigned the value 20 + 10, or 30. In this example, a is referred to as the *left-hand side* of the expression, or *LHS*. The part of the expression to the right of the assignment operator is referred to as the *right-hand side* of the expression, or *RHS*. A constant value cannot be the LHS of an *assignment* expression. That is, you cannot write the assignment

```
5 = b + 10;
```

without the compiler generating an error. This restriction applies only to assignment expressions.

Earlier in the chapter, you learned that C++'s operator syntax enables you to write concise code. One example of this conciseness is to use the assignment operator to initialize several variables within a single statement:

```
int a, b, c;
a = b = c = 5; // Note that the constant 5 appears at the end.
```

This example works because the assignment statement itself has a value. In the example, c = 5 has the value 5, which in turn is assigned to b. The assignment statement (b = c = 5) also has the value 5 and is assigned to a.

Another example of this conciseness is where the assignment operator is sometimes used in a conditional or loop statement. Suppose that you need to set a equal to b, and if b is 0, then execute a specific statement. You could write

```
a = b;
if ( b == 0 ) { ... }
```

or you could write

```
if ( ( a=b ) == 0) { ... }
```

The latter statement combines the assignment and conditional test into a single expression. Personally, I find that code is easier to understand if it does only one function at a time, as in the first example. Historically, the concise format enabled the compiler to generate a more efficient set of machine instructions. Modern compilers (such as Microsoft's Visual C++ compiler) perform internal optimization of your program, resulting in the same code, regardless of which of the preceding statements you use.

Other problems may occur as a result of writing excessively concise expressions. Avoid writing expressions that modify and use a variable within a single expression. Doing so can create ambiguous expressions, such as the following:

```
value = 10;
  .
  .
  .
total = (value = 5) + value++;   // Don't do this.
```

When the compiler evaluates this statement, should value++ be 11 or 6?

Besides the = assignment operator, C++ provides five additional assignment operators that you use chiefly for writing concise code. All six assignment operators appear in table 2.6.

Table 2.6 The C++ Assignment Operators

Symbol	Use	Description
=	a = b	Assigns value of b to a
*=	a *= b	Multiplies a * b and assigns the result to a
/=	a /= b	Divides a by b and assigns the result to a
%=	a %= b	Sets a to the remainder of a / b
+=	a += b	Adds b to a and assigns the result to a
-=	a -= b	Subtracts b from a and assigns the result to a

These assignment operators act like shorthand notation for frequently used expressions. Suppose that you want to multiply the variable i by 15. Using the = operator, you can write

```
i = i * 15;
```

C++ provides a shorthand assignment operator (*=) to perform the equivalent assignment. Using *=, you write

```
i *= 15;
```

This statement means "multiply the value of i by 15," which is actually more clear than trying to translate i = i * 15 into English. That translation works out as "multiply the value of i by 15 and store the result back into i."

The shorthand notation can appear also within conditional statements:

```
if ( i*=15 ) == 150 ) { ... }
```

As a new C++ programmer, you may find it difficult to remember all these operators. Remember that each operator begins with the arithmetic operation (*, /, %, +, or -) followed by = and a single operand. Keep in mind that you don't have to use these operators; you can always perform an equivalent function by using the assignment statement and an arithmetic expression if you like. Remember, however, that C++ programmers tend to exercise the language to its limits. You will encounter these operators when you review source code elsewhere in this book, read programming magazines, and review source code written by other C++ programmers.

Relational Operators

When you write a conditional expression, such as that used in an if selection statement, your expression is testing a condition. You use the relational operators to test for equality, inequality, and relative difference. Table 2.7 shows the C++ relational operators.

Table 2.7 The C++ Relational Operators		
Symbol	**Use**	**Description**
==	a == b	Has the value 1 if a is equal to b; has the value 0 if a is not equal to b
!=	a != b	Has the value 1 if a is not equal to b; has the value 0 if a is equal to b

(continues)

Symbol	Use	Description
Table 2.7 Continued		
<	a < b	Has the value 1 if a is less than b; has the value 0 if a is equal to or greater than b
>	a > b	Has the value 1 if a is greater than b; has the value 0 if a is equal to or less than b
<=	a <= b	Has the value 1 if a is less than or equal to b; has the value 0 if a is greater than b
>=	a >= b	Has the value 1 if a is greater than or equal to b; has the value 0 if a is less than b

Although the relational operators are typically used in an if or while loop statement (described in Chapter 4, "Selection and Loop Statements"), they may also be used in expressions. When used in an expression, the relational operator produces a 0 or 1 result value depending on the condition being tested. 0 is returned for a False condition and 1 is returned for a True condition. For instance, if in C++, you write

```
c = 3 < 5;
```

the variable c is set to 1. Because 3 is less than 5, the < operation returns a value of 1. If, instead, you write

```
c = 5 < 3;
```

c is set to 0.

A common use of a relational operator in an expression is to set a *flag variable*. A flag variable is any variable that holds two values, such as 1 or 0, on or off, or True or False. Programmers often set a flag variable by using a relational operator. If the flag variable is set to 1, the flag is said to be *set* or *True*; if the flag is set to 0, the flag is said to be *cleared* or *False*.

Suppose that you have a program which is processing a set of input data. The program can process a maximum of MAX_LINES (a constant defined somewhere in your program). When the maximum number of lines has been processed, you want to set a flag so that other elements of your program are made aware of the maximum allowable lines condition. To do this, you might write

```
int all_done;
    .
    .
    .
all_done = (line_count >= MAX_LINES);
```

As long as the maximum number of lines has not been reached, `all_done` has the value 0. When `line_count` exceeds the maximum line limitation, however, `all_done` is set to 1 or True. You can use the flag variable in `while` loops or `if` statements to control the execution of the program. Note this example:

```
if (all_done)
    { ... }
else
    { ... }
```

Caution

When you write a conditional expression, it's easy to inadvertently confuse the assignment operator (=) with the equality operator (==). When you mean to write a conditional expression like

```
if ( a == b ) {...}
```

you can easily mistype the line as

```
if ( a = b ) {...}
```

The latter case is a valid conditional statement and compiles without error. However, the effect of this statement is to set a equal to b, and if a is nonzero, to execute the statement that follows. Where you expected a simple relational comparison, you have clobbered the value of a, resulting in potential problems later in the program. This error is common in C++ (and C) programming. As a matter of fact, it's so common that Visual C++ issues the message `warning C4706: assignment within conditional expression` when it sees an assignment during a conditional test. Receiving this message will require you to set certain options within the Visual Workbench, which you learn about in Chapter 12, "Debugging Visual C++ Programs."

You can avoid this type of error provided you are testing against a constant value, as in `if ( a == 0 )`. Remember that constant values cannot appear as the LHS of an assignment expression, but they can appear on the left-hand side of a relational expression. You could rewrite the expression as `if ( 0 == a )`, and if you accidentally typed the assignment operator (=) rather than the equality operator (==), the compiler would report this code as an error instead of as a possible warning.

You can explicitly set a flag variable by assigning the value 1 or 0 to the flag. To make your program easier to read, you can use symbolic constants for the values 0 and 1. For instance, you can create two constants named FALSE and TRUE by writing

```
const int FALSE = 0;
const int TRUE = 1;
```

or

```
#define FALSE 0
#define TRUE 1
```

You can also use a special C++ type called an *enumerated type* to create a symbolic name for flag values. See the section "Enumerated Types and Constants" later in this chapter.

Logical Operators

When you test conditional expressions, some conditions are more complex than a simple

```
if (a == b) {...}
```

Consider the situation in which you need to test whether a is equal to b, and c is equal to d, and e is equal to f. To construct a conditional statement to test these three separate conditions, you must use the logical AND operator (&&). Here is an example:

```
if ( (a==b) && (c==d) && (e==f) ) { ... }
```

In another situation, you might want to perform an operation if any of the equality expressions test True. To test for this condition, use the logical OR operator (¦¦):

```
if ( (a==b) ¦¦ (c==d) ¦¦ (e==f) ) { ... }
```

In some situations, you need to test for an opposite condition. Earlier in this chapter, you learned about flag variables. Suppose that you have a flag variable named all_done and you need to check whether all_done is not True. One way to make this test is to write

```
if ( !all_done) {...}
```

in which the exclamation point symbol (!) is pronounced *not*. You read the preceding if statement as "if not all_done then...."

Bit Manipulation Operators

One of the reasons that C (and C++) became popular on personal computers is that the language offers many low-level bit manipulation operators. For early software to run fast on the original, slow IBM PC and on clone computers, programmers resorted to extremely low-level programming tricks to squeeze every microsecond of performance out of the machines. C was the only language then available for PC computers (other than the more primitive and, for most people, much more difficult to use assembly language) that could provide access to low-level features such as bit manipulation.

Today's high-level applications no longer need to fiddle with the machine's bits to the extent that was once required. However, most professional-level applications still use bit manipulation operators for a variety of reasons. One reason, of course, is historical: it's the way programmers have been doing things for a long time. A second reason is that much low-level software is now written in C and C++ (such as compilers and operating systems), and these complex programs require low-level access to the system's hardware registers. Another reason is that programs sometimes use individual bits of data as flags. This is especially true of programs written for Microsoft Windows.

To understand the bit manipulation operators, you must first understand a little bit (sorry for that!) about how data is stored on the computer. The basic unsigned integer data type, storing numbers in the range of 0 to 65,535, occupies 16 bits of memory. On the PC-class computer, 8 bits make up 1 byte. Figure 2.2 illustrates the layout of a 16-bit integer. Integers on the PC have their least significant bit on the right and their most significant bit on the left. That's why the bit positions are numbered from right to left. That is also the way you write a decimal number. The number 1,234 has a 1 in the most significant—or thousands—place, and a 4 in the least significant—or ones—place.

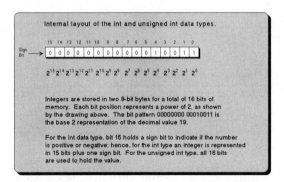

Fig. 2.2
The layout,
in bits, of an
integer variable.

In a decimal number, the value is determined by the digit in the tens column, the digit in the hundreds column, the digit in the thousands column, and so on. You know that the number 1,234 is determined by the following equation:

$$1{,}234 = 1 \times 1000 + 2 \times 100 + 3 \times 10 + 4$$

A number is stored in base 2 (as compared to base 10) by changing the multiplier to a power of 2 instead of a power of 10. In base 2, each bit position contains 0 or 1 (compared to the digits 0 to 9 in base 10). In base 2, the multipliers are 1, 2, 4, 8, 16, 32, 64, 128, 256, 512, 1024, and so on, up to the maximum number of bits. Now take a look at how the value 19 is represented as the 8-bit binary number 00010011:

$$19 = 1 \times 16 + 0 \times 8 + 0 \times 4 + 1 \times 2 + 1 \times 1$$

The bit positions containing a 0 evaluate to 0, so the final result is determined from $16 + 2 + 1$, or 19.

You can test and set the individual bits by using the bit manipulation operators. You can also shift the bits to the left and to the right. In the next section, the shift operators are introduced first because they are the easiest to understand.

Using << and >> to Shift Left and Right. To shift or slide bits to the left, use the << shift operator followed by a single operand indicating the number of bit positions to shift. For example, to shift the value 19, represented by 00010011, over to the left by 1 bit position, you should write

```
int num = 19;
num = num << 1;
```

After this shift operation, the value of num contains the following:

```
00100110
```

You can see that this value is the same bit pattern shifted 1 bit position to the left. Note that a 0 bit is inserted at the right. Excess bits shifted off the left are discarded. If you substitute a different value for the shift amount, the bit pattern is shifted by a different number of bits. The shift amount may be a constant, a variable, or an expression.

To shift bits to the right, use the >> shift operator. Any bits shifted beyond the rightmost bit are discarded, and 0 bits are inserted on the left.

> **Note**
>
> The left and right shift operators are identical to the insertion and extraction opera-
> tors used for stream input/output in C++. The compiler can distinguish your use of
> the insertion and extraction operators from the shift operators by examining the
> context in which the << and >> symbols appear. As a result, the compiler generates
> the correct machine code depending on where and how you have used the operator
> symbols.

Testing Individual Bits. To test or set individual bits requires an understanding of the Boolean arithmetic AND, OR, and exclusive OR operators.
These operators combine 2 bits and produce a result. If you have 2 bits, and
bit1 contains a 1 and *bit2* contains a 1, then *bit1* AND *bit2* equals 1. If either
bit is 0, *bit1* AND *bit2* equals 0. To understand the interpretation of the AND
operation, refer to table 2.8. In C++, you perform Boolean arithmetic on bits
using the & (pronounced *and*) bit-wise Boolean operator, the ¦ (pronounced
or) Boolean operator, and the ^ (exclusive OR) operator.

Table 2.8 Values Produced by the & Operator		
Bit1 &	**Bit2 =**	**Result**
0	0	0
0	1	0
1	0	0
1	1	1

From table 2.8, you can see that if either bit contains 0, the result of *bit1* &
bit2 is always 0 (or False). Only when both bits contain 1 is the result of *bit1* &
bit2 a 1 (or True). Because of this property of the & operator, you can detect
whether an individual bit is set. Consider the bit pattern 00001010. To detect
whether the second bit from the right is set, you can use the & operator to test
the bit pattern with the value 00000010 and then check the result:

```
00001010 & 00000010 = 00000010
```

If the result equals the test pattern, the selected bit is set. When you use bit
testing, one variable can contain an entire series of flags.

For the general case of a single bit test, you can test bit n of a variable x integer by performing the conditional test

```
if ((x & p) == p) { ... }
```

in which p is 2 to the nth power.

To test whether bit number 4 is set, use the following:

```
if ((x & 16) == 16) { ... }
```

Table 2.9 shows powers of 2 up to 32,768.

Table 2.9 Decimal Equivalents for Testing Individual Bits	
Bit Position	**Decimal Equivalent**
0	1
1	2
2	4
3	8
4	16
5	32
6	64
7	128
8	256
9	512
10	1024
11	2048
12	4096
13	8192
14	16384
15	32768

If you want, you can test multiple bits in a single & operation. For example, to test whether the lower 4 bits are all set, you can write

```
if ((x & 15) == 15) { ... }
```

15 is the sum of 1 + 2 + 4 + 8, thereby testing all 4 bits simultaneously.

Setting Bits. You can use the ¦ (pronounced *or*) Boolean operator to set bits within a value. Table 2.10 shows the effect of the ¦ operator between two bits. If either bit is a 1, the result of the ¦ operation is a 1. Only when both bits are 0 does the ¦ operation result in a 0. Use the ¦ to set a bit by ORing the original value with the bit you want to set. To set the first bit in the pattern 00100110, for example, you OR this value with a 1:

```
001000110 ¦ 00000001 = 001000111
```

To set the fifth bit from the right, you write

```
001000110 ¦ 00010000 = 001010110
```

For the general case, you can set bit n of a variable x integer by performing the expression

```
x = x ¦ p;
```

in which p is 2 to the nth power.

If you want, you can set multiple bits in a single ¦ operation. To set the lower 4 bits to 1, for example, write

```
x = x ¦ 15;
```

If a bit is already set before the ¦ operator is used, the bit remains set and is unchanged.

Table 2.10 The Effect of the ¦ Operator		
Bit1 ¦	**Bit2 =**	**Result**
0	0	0
0	1	1
1	0	1
1	1	1

The Exclusive OR Operator. Another common Boolean operation is the exclusive OR, represented in C++ with the ^ symbol. The exclusive OR operation is shown in table 2.11.

Table 2.11 The Effect of the ^ Operator		
Bit1 ^	**Bit2 =**	**Result**
0	0	0
0	1	1
1	0	1
1	1	0

Whereas exclusive OR is similar to the OR operation, note that in the last row of table 2.11, 1 exclusive ORed with 1 equals 0. This means that exclusive OR results in a 1 only when one operand is a 0 and the other is a 1. This property results in a unique consequence:

```
(x ^ p) ^ p is equal to x
```

To understand this principle, watch how the bit pattern 1010 is exclusive ORed with 0110:

```
1010 ^ 0110 = 1100
```

Examine table 2.11 to verify that this result is correct. Next, exclusive-OR the result again with the pattern 0110:

$$1100$$

$$\char`\^\ \ 0110$$

$$=\ 1010$$

To perform several common functions in C++ programs, you can use the capability to exclusive-OR a value twice and get back what you started. You can use this property of the exclusive OR to quickly encrypt or code a set of data values to ensure data security. For example, given a group of data values you must keep hidden, you can exclusive-OR the values with an arbitrary value, producing what appears to a casual observer to be gibberish. To decode your encrypted data, just exclusive-OR the data with your original value, and all your data comes back. You explore this technique in the CHAR-XOR.CPP sample program in the section "Arrays" in Chapter 3, "C++ Advanced Data Types."

Another use for exclusive OR is in graphics programs. When the graphics routines draw a line across the screen, you can use the exclusive OR property both to draw and then to quickly erase a line. Because the graphics screen is effectively a screen full of bit values, you draw a line by setting appropriate bits on the screen. Instead of explicitly setting each bit to represent the line, you can set each bit with the exclusive OR operator. When you set each bit using the exclusive OR, you can erase the line, strangely enough, by drawing the line again! Because each bit already drawn is exclusive-ORed with a new line, bits are cleared, effectively erasing the line.

Additional Assignment Operators

As with the arithmetic operators, shorthand assignment operators are also available for the bit manipulation operators. These operators are shown in table 2.12.

Table 2.12 Additional Assignment Operators		
Symbol	**Use**	**Description**
<<=	a <<= b	Shifts a left by b bits and assigns the result to a
>>=	a >>= b	Shifts a right by b bits and assigns the result to a
&=	a &= b	Assigns a the value a & b
^=	a ^= b	Sets a to a ^ b
¦=	a ¦= b	Sets a to a ¦ b

The Conditional Expression Operator. The C++ conditional expression operator provides a shorthand substitute for the common if statement. Consider how you might calculate the maximum of two values, represented by a and b, using the if statement:

```
if (a > b)
     max = a;
else
     max = b;
```

Using the conditional operator, you write this test as an expression:

```
max = (a > b) ? a : b;
```

The conditional expression operator is a *ternary operator* because it has three operands (unlike a binary operator, which has two operands, or a unary operator, which has one operand). In the general case, you write the conditional expression as follows:

```
expression1 ? expression2 : expression3;
```

The conditional expression operator evaluates *expression1*. If *expression1* is nonzero, the result of the overall expression is *expression2*; if *expression1* is zero, the result is *expression3*. *expression2* and *expression3* are evaluated only if they are selected (thereby saving execution time).

As you can see, the conditional expression operator provides a shorthand substitute for certain kinds of if statements. You can also use the ?: operator within more complex expressions. For example, suppose that the calculated maximum is to be used within a calculation. Rather than assign the maximum to the variable max, you can use the conditional expression's result directly. Here is an example:

```
array_size = 100 * ( (num_values < max_allowed) ?
                      num_values : max_allowed );
```

If num_values is less than max_allowed, the array_size is calculated as 100 * num_values. If num_values exceeds max_allowed, array_size is calculated as 100 * max_allowed.

The Comma Operator. The comma operator enables you to evaluate multiple expressions in a single statement. The rightmost expression determines the overall result. In the generic case, you use the comma operator as follows:

```
expression1, expression2, expression3, ... , expressionn
```

Each expression is evaluated starting from the left and proceeding to the right. The result of the overall expression is determined by the value of *expressionn*. Note an example:

```
int i,j, result;
result = j = 10, i = j; i++;
```

The value of this expression is 11. First, j is assigned the value 10; then i is assigned the value of j. Finally, i is incremented to 11.

The comma operator is seldom used in C++ programming; however, you sometimes see it used to initialize multiple variables in a single statement. For example, to initialize five variables to different values, you can write

```
a = 1, b = 2, c = 3, d = 4, e = 0;
```

There is no speed or efficiency benefit to writing values this way; in this form, the comma operator is strictly a notational convenience. Another example is the use of two variables to simultaneously control execution of a for loop. This method is illustrated in Chapter 4, "Selection and Loop Statements."

Operator Precedence

You learned earlier that some operators take precedence over others. For instance, multiplication is always performed before addition. Use table 2.13 to determine which operations are performed before others. Note that the table contains some operators that you have not yet learned. Don't be alarmed; these operators are described in other portions of this book.

Table 2.13 Operator Precedence in C++	
Highest	() [] -> :: .
precedence	! - + - ++ -- & * (*typecast*) sizeof
	new delete .* ->* * / % + - << >>
	< <= > >=
	== !=
	&
	^
	|
	&&
	||
Lowest	?:
precedence	= *= /= %= += -= &= ^= |= <<= >>=

As you can see in table 2.13, expressions within parentheses are always performed before other arithmetic operations. This means that if you write

    2 * (2 + 3)

the compiler evaluates this expression as 2 * (5) because it performs the arithmetic that is enclosed within parentheses first. You can see also from the table that multiplication, division, and the remainder operations (*, /, and %) are performed before addition and subtraction (+ and -). This means that the expression

    2 + 3 * 2

is evaluated as if it has an imaginary set of parentheses around the (3 * 2) expression. Thus, the compiler performs the arithmetic as 2 + (3 * 2) or 2 + (6).

Converting One Type to Another

As you have seen, variables are each assigned a data type, such as char, int, long, float, double, or another type. Constants also have a type, which is implied by how the constant is written:

Constant	Type
'a'	char
1575	int
98.6	float

When you write arithmetic expressions in C++, you must be sensitive to the types of operands with which you are working. Some operations can be performed only between similar data types. Consider what happens if you write the following:

```
int num;
num = 35.7;
```

Because num is an integer, the compiler converts 35.7 to the integer 35 before assigning 35 to the variable num. Internally, a float constant is represented in a format that bears no relation to that used by the int type. So the compiler performs the conversion for you.

In certain instances, such as when you call functions and especially when you use C++ pointers (see Chapter 5, "Pointers"), you must explicitly tell the compiler how to make the conversion. C++ provides a *typecast* operator for this purpose. You use the typecast operator by enclosing the desired type in parentheses. In the assignment

```
num = 35.7;
```

you could make the conversion to int explicit by writing

```
num = (int) 35.7;
```

In the general case, the typecast operator is used as

```
(typecast) expression
```

in which *typecast* is the desired type and *expression* is an appropriate expression. Be forewarned that some typecasts simply do not make any sense, but the compiler lets you make the typecast anyway and does not issue a warning or error message. For instance, the following section of code compiles without error but doesn't produce the results you want:

```
float frequency = 1296.70;
char c;
c = frequency;
```

Because a `char` type supports values in the range of –128 to +127, when you execute this code, c is given the character equivalent of ASCII 16.

> **Note**
>
> The Microsoft Visual C++ compiler will issue the message `warning C4051: type conversion; possible loss of data` if you do not provide an explicit typecast to such assignments.

Another place for a typecast is the calling of a function whose parameter types are different from the values you want to pass to the function. (You learn more about defining and using functions in Chapter 6, "Functions and Macros.") To see how a function parameter may need typecasting, consider the `exp()` function defined in the Visual C++ runtime library. The function named `exp()` calculates the exponential function e^x, in which x is determined by the double parameter to `exp()`. Usually, you are expected to call `exp()` with an expression of type `double`, as in this example:

```
double x = 2.2345;
cout << exp( x );
```

If you want to use `exp()` with an `int` type parameter, typecast the `int` to a double by using the `(double)` typecast operator:

```
int x = 2;
cout << exp( (double) x );
```

Enumerated Types and Constants

You learned about symbolic constants in the section "Defining Symbolic Constants" earlier in this chapter. C++ has another kind of constant, the enumeration constant or enumerated type. An *enumerated type* is a group of constants for which the compiler automatically generates values. You define the enumerated type by using the `enum` keyword, an optional identifier, and then a list of symbolic constants. For example, you can enumerate constants for the seven days of the week by writing

```
enum { MON, TUE, WED, THU, FRI, SAT, SUN };
```

The symbols inside the { and } braces are called *enumeration constants*. The compiler automatically assigns the value 0 to MON, 1 to TUE, 2 to WED, and so on, up through SUN. If you want to specify a different starting point, such as 1 for MON, you can assign the starting value in the list of enumerated constants:

```
enum { MON=1, TUE, WED, THU, FRI, SAT, SUN };
```

Each value after the first initialized value is numbered sequentially (TUE becomes 2, WED becomes 3, and so on). If you want, you can set new values anywhere inside the enumerated list:

```
enum { MON=1, TUE, WED, THU, FRI, SAT=100, SUN };
```

Here, TUE equals 2, WED equals 3, THU equals 4, FRI equals 5, SAT equals 100, and SUN equals 101.

Each identifier used in an enumeration statement must be unique; once the identifier is defined, it cannot be defined again as a variable, symbolic constant, or enumerated constant. You can, however, use duplicate values within the enumerated constant, as shown in the following example:

```
enum { MON=1, TUE, WED, THU, FRI, SAT=1, SUN };
```

Because the enumerated constant declaration is evaluated from left to right, you can even use the already defined constant symbols in your initializations:

```
enum { MON=1, TUE, WED, THU, FRI, SAT = MON, SUN };
```

You can use the symbols defined for the enumerated type (such as TUE) as regular integer constants. The enumerated constants defined with an enumerated type can be used like any other constant symbol. Enumerated constants are automatically treated as type int. Note this example:

```
enum { MON, TUE, WED, THU, FRI, SAT, SUN };
int today;
   .
   .
   .
today = MON;
   .
   .
   .
today = MON + 2;
```

To create enumerated character constants, use the same format for the enum
statement but specify character constants for the symbol values:

```
enum { MenuOpen = 'O', MenuClose = 'C',
       MenuNew = 'N', MenuExit = 'X' };
```

Using *enum* to Create an Enumerated Type

You can use the enum declaration also to create an enumerated type symbol
that you can use for declaring variables. By specifying an enumeration type
name, you create a new data type (like int or char). You must write the type
name immediately after the enum keyword:

```
enum week_days { MON, TUE, WED, THU, FRI, SAT, SUN };
```

The symbol week_days is now an enumerated type that you can use to declare
variables to hold only the values MON, TUE, WED, THU, FRI, SAT, and SUN. You use
the enumerated type in a declaration such as the following:

```
week_days today;
```

This line declares today to be of the type week_days, having values from MON to
SUN. You can therefore write statements such as

```
today = SUN;
```

but you cannot write a statement such as

```
today = 1;
```

without the compiler issuing this error message: error C2446: '=' : no
conversion from 'const int ' to 'enum ::week_days '.

When you declare a variable as an enumerated type, the C++ compiler provides *type-checking* to ensure that only valid values are assigned to the variable. Type-checking helps you prevent programming errors by catching
invalid assignments like the following:

```
today = 10;
```

The type-checking feature of the C++ compiler is an important part of C++.
You should use type-checking whenever possible, because it can help you
spot programming errors during the compilation phase of your program's
development.

You can use enum to declare variables directly. To define the enumerated type
and to declare one or more variables, add the variables after the enumerated

list. For example, the following statement declares today and work_day to be variables holding values from MON to SUN:

```
enum { MON, TUE, WED, THU, FRI, SAT, SUN } today, work_day;
```

Using Enumerated Types for Flag Variables

Earlier in this chapter, a flag variable was referred to as being a variable that is used to indicate whether a condition is True or False. Typically, the flag variable is set to 1 when a condition is True, and to 0 when a condition is False. As you've learned, a variable that has just two values, 0 or 1, is a Boolean value. In computer programming, these values are often described as being False (for 0) and True (for 1). Previously, you saw how to define constants for FALSE and TRUE. You may also use an enumerated constant to declare FALSE and TRUE, using the following definition:

```
enum boolean (FALSE, TRUE);
```

You can then declare your flag variables as type boolean:

```
boolean valve_open_flag;
boolean end_of_file = FALSE;
```

The C++ compiler checks to make sure that your boolean variables hold only TRUE or FALSE and issues you a warning if you attempt to assign some other value to a boolean variable.

Listing 2.5 uses a boolean enumerated type to declare a flag variable named time_to_quit. The do-while keywords represent a special type of loop. As long as the condition specified at the while statement (see line 19) is TRUE, the loop executes repeatedly. Hence, if you press N in response to the prompt in line 14, the value of time_to_quit stays at its initial value of FALSE. The expression !time_to_quit (read this as "not time_to_quit") computes the opposite of the current value of time_to_quit: when time_to_quit is FALSE, then !time_to_quit is TRUE; and when time_to_quit is TRUE, then !time_to_quit is FALSE. As a result, the while loop continues to execute until time_to_quit is set to TRUE. This usage of a Boolean flag variable is common in C++ programs.

Listing 2.5 A Program That Uses a Boolean Enumerated Type for a Flag Variable

```
1   // ENUM.CPP
2   // Demonstrates use of enumerated type to create
3   // a boolean variable type.
4   #include <iostream.h>
```

```
 5
 6  void main(void) {
 7    enum boolean {FALSE, TRUE};
 8    boolean time_to_quit = FALSE;
 9    char keystroke;
10
11    // Repeatedly prompt for a keystroke until user
12    // types Q to quit the program.
13    do {
14      cout << endl << "Enter Q to quit or N to continue:  ";
15      cin >> keystroke;
16      cin.ignore(1);
17      if ((keystroke == 'Q') || (keystroke == 'q'))
18        time_to_quit = TRUE;
19    } while (!time_to_quit);
20
21  } // main
```

Summary

This chapter presented the basic types of data that you can work with in a C++ program. You used expressions to perform operations on data, such as adding or multiplying values together. In this chapter, you learned the following:

- C++ identifier names must begin with an alphabetic character, followed by any number of alphabetic or numeric characters, or the underscore (_) character.

- The basic C++ data types are integer (int), long integer (long), character (char), and floating-point (float, double, and long double). Each of the integer types has an unsigned counterpart for storing positive values. The double type has an expanded long double that increases the number of decimal places slightly and significantly expands the size of the exponent.

- The character data type uses just 1 byte of memory; the integer type uses 2 bytes; the long integer uses 4 bytes; and the floating-point values use 4, 8, or 10 bytes of storage.

- Data types that require less memory usually take less time for the computer to process. Therefore, for optimal efficiency in your programs, it is important that you select a data type appropriate to your program's needs. Microprocessors perform the fastest arithmetic on integers. Floating-point operations are the slowest, although using an optional math coprocessor significantly improves the performance of programs that rely on many floating-point calculations.

■ C++ contains a wealth of arithmetic operators. Here are the most important:

+   Addition

-     Subtraction

*   Multiplication

/   Division

%   Remainder

++   Increment operator

--   Decrement operator

■ You use relational operators to compare two values to one another. The relational operators are these:

==   Tests whether two values are equal

!=   Tests whether two values are not equal

<   Tests whether one value is less than another

<=   Tests whether one value is less than or equal to another

>   Tests whether one value is greater than another

>=   Tests whether one value is greater than or equal to another

■ The basic assignment operator is the single equal sign (=), which you use to assign the result of an expression to a variable. C++ includes many shorthand assignment operators to enable you to write concise statements.

■ You typically use the logical operators in if conditional statements when you must test whether more than one condition is True. These operators include the ¦¦ (logical OR) and the && (logical AND).

■ The bit manipulation operators—¦ (OR), & (AND), and ^ (exclusive OR)—enable you to set and test the state of individual bits inside a variable. These operators are typically used by software that must work very closely with the hardware, such as operating systems and compilers.

■ Operator precedence governs the order in which the pieces of an expression are evaluated. As you learned long ago, you should perform multiplication and division before addition and subtraction. Those old rules still apply when writing C++ expressions. Because C++ has many more operators than the arithmetic problems you solved when you were young, C++ has correspondingly more complex operator precedence rules. Table 2.13 shows which operators have higher precedence than others.

■ You use type conversions or typecasts (sometimes just called *casts*) to convert one type to another. The compiler automatically performs many type conversions as a convenience to you, the programmer. For instance, if you assign an integer to a `float` variable, the compiler automatically converts the integer value to a `float` type. You may also choose to explicitly request a type conversion by prefacing the variable or expression with `(type)`, in which *type* is a valid data type.

■ Using enumeration constants is an easy way to create a sequentially numbered set of constant identifiers.

In Chapter 3, "C++ Advanced Data Types," you learn how to use groups of related data elements, such as a group of `int` variables or a group of `char` variables. Chapter 3 also shows how to store character strings, which are groups of characters, rather than the individual characters that can be stored in the basic `char` type.

Review Questions

1. Which of the following identifiers are invalid:

   ```
   ALPHA       Summer      winter
   11-Holes    Holes_11    #potatoes
   ```

2. You need to store some data in the range of 0 to 100,000. Which of the following data types would work for this range of values, and which would be the best for this purpose?

   ```
   unsigned int long    unsigned long
   float                double
   ```

3. You need to store data in the range of −30 to +50. What is an appropriate data type to use for this range?

4. You've just been hired to maintain reflectorized lane markers on a 1,000-mile stretch of interstate highway. You need to track the number of lane markers that have been installed (about every six feet apart along each lane stripe). What is a good data type to store the count of lane markers, and why?

5. Are any of the following variable names equivalent?

   ```
   Number_of_gears
   number_of_gears
   Number_of_households_in_Los_Angeles_with_kids
   Number_of_households_in_Los_Angeles_without_kids
   ```

6. Compute the value of the following expression. Be sure to take into consideration the C++ operator precedence rules.

   ```
   2 * 5 * 7 + 35 - 10 * (3 + 2 * (4 + 4 * ( 3 + 8 )))
   ```

7. What are escape sequences?

8. What is the difference between a char and an unsigned char?

9. Your warehouse stocks thousands of toy parts that customers (usually stores or chains of stores) can order. A typical order consists of 20 to 100 different part types, with a typical customer ordering 2,000 to 5,000 parts of each type. What is the most efficient data type to use in calculating the total number of parts that each customer has ordered?

10. Describe the difference between a local variable and a global variable.

11. Describe the three separate types of symbolic constants that you can create and use in C++ programs.

12. Provide at least two reasons why your programs should use symbolic constants.

13. In the following code section, what is the value of height after the last statement has executed?

   ```
   int building_size = 10;
   int height;
   .
   .
   .
   height = building_size++;
   ```

14. What do LHS and RHS mean? Can you use constants on the LHS of a relational expression? Can you use constants on the RHS of assignment expressions?

15. Which operators should you use when you have an `if` conditional statement that must test for four separate conditions being True before deciding which course of action to take?

16. Write a typecast to convert a `float` type variable that contains a small number (in the range of 0 to 100) to a `char` type.

17. Write out an `enum` type to create symbols for each of the 12 months of the year.

Exercises

1. Write a program to input two numbers and then perform various calculations with those numbers. Experiment to see what happens when you multiply integer values together, producing a multiplication overflow. Modify your program to work with `int`, `unsigned int`, `long`, and `float` types. Print out the results of your calculations by using the `cout` stream. To input two numbers, use a statement like the following:

```
cin >> number1 >> number2;
```

When you type a pair of numbers in response to this prompt, type both numbers on the same line, separated by a blank, as in the following:

```
100 200
```

2. Write a program that has two functions. Inside both functions, define and use a local variable named `index`. Observe how the two variables, although they have the same name, are independent of one another because they are local to the function in which they are defined. You can test this by assigning values to the variables, performing calculations, and displaying their values.

3. Write a program to convert dollars to yen. Use a conversion factor of 125 yen per dollar. Prompt and input a dollar amount and then display the corresponding dollar amount, converted to yen. You may also want to display the dollar converted to the British pound (use about $1.50 per pound), the dollar converted to the Canadian dollar (use about $0.80 per Canadian dollar), and the dollar converted to the German mark (use about 1.5 marks per dollar). You may want to look in the business pages of your local newspaper for more recent currency exchange rates. Use a `const` symbolic constant to control the conversion rates.

Chapter 3

C++ Advanced Data Types

In Chapter 2, "C++ Data Types and Expressions," you learned about the basic character, integer, and floating-point values. You learned also how to define and use symbolic constants by using `const`, `#define`, and the `enum` type. Chapter 3 continues the discussion of C++ data types, looking especially at the array type (and its use for character strings), the structure, and the union. The chapter also provides an introduction to the important concept of objects.

In this chapter, you first learn about arrays. An *array* stores many elements of the same type, such as 10 integers, 30 floating-point values, or 15 characters. The array is important for many reasons. One important use for arrays is to store text strings. As you have seen, C++ provides only a simple `char` type for holding a single character. By using the array type, you can create a variable that holds a group of characters.

This chapter also examines the idea of structures. A *structure* holds multiple variables, but they may be of different types. The structure is important to the creation of powerful programs such as in-memory databases and other applications that must work with large amounts of data. You can also use the structure as a primitive object type in C++.

Some additional topics are covered, including bit fields and unions. Some of these topics are considered advanced; you can safely ignore these sections for now and return to them for later reference when needed.

The C++ Aggregate Data Types

In addition to the simple data types used to represent individual characters, integers, and floating-point numbers, C++ has special types for organizing collections of data values. These special types are known as the *aggregate data types*. The word *aggregate* is derived from the Latin *aggregatus* and means roughly *the object formed by the collection of items into a larger body*. If you have ever seen a rock that was formed by lots of little rocks seemingly glued together, you know what an aggregate rock looks like and why the term *aggregate* is appropriate for the C++ data types that hold many values simultaneously.

In the following sections, you learn about the three aggregate data types: the array, the structure, and the union. The array holds a group of items that are all of the same type. You could, for example, use an array to store the high-temperature measurements of each day of the year.

The structure holds values of different types. A classic example is a mailing list that must hold a name, street address, city, state, and ZIP code. If you are familiar with databases, you will notice the similarities between a structure in C++ and a record in a database.

The union is an advanced type that enables you to access the same piece of data in different ways. If your programming background includes the Pascal programming language, you should know that the C++ union is similar to the Pascal case variant record.

Arrays

As noted, an array stores many items of the same type. The type of items stored in the array may be any C++ type, including user-defined structures that you read about later in this chapter. Typically, you use the array to store such types as the `char`, `int`, and `float` types. The following sections show you how to declare, initialize, and use an array of values.

Declaring an Array
You declare an array similarly to other data types, except that you must tell the compiler how large the array must be. To tell the compiler the array size,

you follow the type with the array size in brackets. To create an array of 10 integer variables, for example, you write

```
int numbers[10];
```

This declaration causes the compiler to set aside sufficient memory space to hold 10 integer values. In Visual C++, integers occupy 2 bytes, so an array of 10 integers occupies 20 bytes of memory. Figure 3.1 shows the layout of this 10-element array. Each element of the array can have its own value.

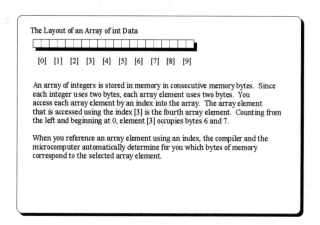

The Layout of an Array of int Data

[0] [1] [2] [3] [4] [5] [6] [7] [8] [9]

An array of integers is stored in memory in consecutive memory bytes. Since each integer uses two bytes, each array element uses two bytes. You access each array element by an index into the array. The array element that is accessed using the index [3] is the fourth array element. Counting from the left and beginning at 0, element [3] occupies bytes 6 and 7.

When you reference an array element using an index, the compiler and the microcomputer automatically determine for you which bytes of memory correspond to the selected array element.

Fig. 3.1
How an array is stored in memory.

You access each element of the array by using an index into the array. For example, the line

```
cout << numbers[3] << endl;
```

displays the value of element 4 in the array. Arrays always begin at element 0 (this may be confusing if you have used other programming languages which assume that arrays begin at index position 1). In C++, the array begins with element 0 so that the numbers array contains the following individual elements:

```
numbers[0]    numbers[1]    numbers[2]
numbers[3]    numbers[4]    numbers[5]
numbers[6]    numbers[7]    numbers[8]
numbers[9]
```

Because the elements are numbered from 0 to 9, no element is indexed as numbers[10]. C++ does not check that your array subscripts are within the defined range of the array. You can inadvertently access array elements that don't exist (such as numbers[10] or numbers[11]), which can cause your program to fail depending on the context in which you make this mistake.

Array Subscripts

The index into an array is often called an *array subscript*. This term comes from mathematics, in which a subscript is used to denote a particular element. Using subscript notation, you write array elements as the following:

$$numbers_0 \qquad numbers_1 \qquad numbers_2$$

In this form, you read each of these elements as *numbers-sub-zero*, *numbers-sub-one*, and *numbers-sub-two*. C++ does not use subscript notation; however, the terminology of array subscripting is used often enough in the world of programming that you should know that when you hear *subscript*, you can substitute the word *index*.

Initializing an Array

You assign values to individual array elements just as you assign values to variables. To assign values to each element of numbers, you write

```
numbers[0] = 10;
numbers[1] = 20;
numbers[2] = 35;
numbers[3] = 40;
numbers[4] = 60;
numbers[5] = 73;
numbers[6] = 15;
numbers[7] = 25;
numbers[8] = 90;
numbers[9] = 65;
```

The index selects which element of the array is to hold the result of the expression. The first statement sets numbers[0] to the value 10; this assignment affects none of the other array elements.

Another way to assign values to an array is to initialize the array in the declaration statement. Just as you can assign an initial value to a variable, you can assign a set of values to an entire array. To do this, place the initial array values in braces and place a comma between the initial values:

```
int numbers[6] = { 10, 20, 35, 40, 60, 73, 15, 25, 90, 65};
```

If you want, you can substitute symbolic constants for numeric values so that the preceding statement becomes

```
const int JAN = 10, FEB = 20, MAR = 35, APR = 40,
    MAY = 60, JUN = 73, JUL = 15, AUG = 25,
    SEP = 90, OCT = 65;
  .
  .
  .
int numbers[10] = { JAN, FEB, MAR, APR, MAY, JUN,
                JUL, AUG, SEP, OCT};
```

You can also assign values by using a `for` loop. To set all the values to 0, for example, use the following statement:

```
for ( index=0; index <=9; index++ ) numbers[index] = 0;
```

Because the value of `index` varies from 0 to 9, each of the elements in the `numbers[]` array is set to `0`.

Character Arrays and Text Strings

A text string is a set of characters, such as `"ABCDEF"`. C++ supports text strings by using an array of `char` to hold a character sequence. Figure 3.2 shows how the letters `"ABCDEF"` are represented in an array of `char`.

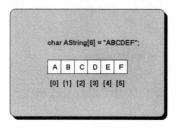

Fig. 3.2
Storing character data in a `char` array.

To define a `char` array to hold `"ABCDEF"`, write

```
char AString[7];
```

Define `AString` to be 6 characters in length, because that size is sufficient to hold the 6 characters. To hold a variable-length string, however, you need a way to mark the string's end. The easiest way to mark the end of the string is to place a special end-of-string character as the last character in the string. C++ uses a *null character* (or `\0`)—which has an ASCII value of 0—as the terminating character of the string.

The easiest way to initialize a `char` array is to make the initialization part of the declaration:

```
char AString[7] = "ABCDEF";
```

The compiler automatically inserts a null character at the end of the string so that the byte sequence shown in figure 3.3 is stored.

If you change the declaration to read

```
char AString[7] = "ABC";
```

the null character is placed immediately after the letter `C`. The internal representation of `AString` then looks like that shown in figure 3.4.

Fig. 3.3
Storing `"ABCDEF"`
as a null-
terminated
string.

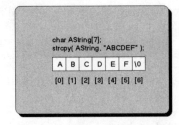

Fig. 3.4
The null
character is
placed immedi-
ately after the
last character of
the string.

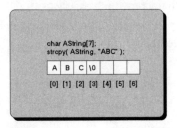

Alternatively, if you want to assign values to individual characters within the character array `AString`, write

```
AString[0] = 'A';
AString[1] = 'B';
AString[2] = 'C';
AString[3] = '\0'; // That's "slash zero", not "slash oh".
```

You may be tempted to write

```
AString = "ABC";
```

but C++ does not allow you to assign a string to an array in this manner (even though you can write a similar-looking assignment as part of a `char` array's declaration). To copy a string constant or to copy a string variable to another string variable, you must use the `strcpy()` function described in the next paragraph.

C++ provides a large set of library routines that you can use to find the current length of a string, change characters within a string, extract characters from a string, and perform many other useful functions. These library functions are described in the section "Using String Functions" in Chapter 6, "Functions and Macros." One string function that you use often is the library function named `strcpy()` (pronounced *string copy*). You use `strcpy()` to copy one string into another, and you use it also as another way to initialize a `char` array. To use `strcpy()`, you must place `#include <string.h>` at the beginning of your program file. The `#include` statement causes the compiler to access a special file named STRING.H, which gives the compiler information about the `strcpy()` function.

To use `strcpy()` to initialize a `char` array, declare the `char` array of the appropriate size and write a statement like the following:

```
strcpy( BString, "This string will be copied." );
```

`strcpy()` sets `BString` equal to `"This string will be copied."`; `strcpy()` also adds a null character to the end of the string.

In Chapter 2, you learned about several escape sequences you can use to represent certain characters inside a text string. Because a text string is always surrounded by double quotation mark characters, the only way to insert a double quotation mark within a text string is to use the escape sequence `\"`. For example, to set the variable `BString` to a quoted string, such as

```
"Jump! Jump!" he yelled.
```

you must use the `\"` sequence to embed quotation marks within the string. Therefore, you must write your string assignment as

```
strcpy( BString, "\"Jump! Jump!\" he yelled." );
```

When the compiler processes the `strcpy()` function, it translates each occurrence of `\"` into a `"` character.

Using an Array

Listing 3.1 illustrates the use of an array in a simple application to track the number of students in grade levels 1 through 6. The sample program, ARRAY.CPP, uses an array variable `num_students[]` to hold the number of students in each grade.

Listing 3.1 Using an Integer Array

```
1   // ARRAY.CPP
2   // Demonstrates the use and manipulation of an array.
3   // In this sample program, an array is used to hold
4   // the number of students in grades 1 through 6.
5   #include <iostream.h>
6
7   void main(void) {
8     const int MAX_GRADES = 6;
9     int num_students[MAX_GRADES];
10    int grade_level;
11
12    cout << "Demonstrates use of an integer array" << endl
13        << endl;
```

(continues)

Listing 3.1 Continued

```
14
15    for (grade_level = 0; grade_level < MAX_GRADES;
16         grade_level++) {
17          cout << "How many students are in grade #"
18               << grade_level+1 << ":   ";
19          cin >> num_students[grade_level];
20        }; // for
21
22    cout << endl
23         << "The number of students in each grade is:"
24         << endl;
25    for (grade_level = 0; grade_level < MAX_GRADES;
26         grade_level++) {
27          cout << "Grade level #" << grade_level+1
28               << " has " << num_students[grade_level]
29               << " students." << endl;
30        }; // for
31
32    cout << endl << "Press Enter to continue." << endl;
33    cin.ignore(1); // Delete leftover Enter key from
34    cin.get();     // previous cin statement.
35
36  } // main
```

ARRAY.CPP uses the variable named grade_level to increment through each of the grades. Note that in line 15, the for loop increments grade_level from 0 up to one less than the MAX_GRADES constant, or 5. When the program runs, it prompts with the following line:

```
How many students are in grade # 1:
```

You can see in line 18 that cout displays grade_level+1 rather than grade_level. The reason for this addition operation is that the data values are stored in elements 0 through 5, but the prompt displays grade levels 1 through 6. Line 19 inputs the number of students and stores the result in num_students[] at the element indexed by grade_level. After you enter each value, the code in lines 25 through 30 displays the values you entered.

An Example That Uses a *char* Array

Listing 3.2 presents CHAR-XOR.CPP, a sample program that uses a char array. CHAR-XOR inputs a string and then demonstrates the use of the exclusive OR operator (the ^ symbol) to encrypt the text string temporarily into an unreadable format. (You can use the technique shown in this program whenever you need a simple method of securing data from prying eyes.) A detailed explanation of how the program works is provided after the listing.

Listing 3.2 Encrypting a *char* Array with the Exclusive OR Operator

```
1   // CHAR-XOR.CPP
2   // Demonstrates the use and manipulation of a character array.
3   // This program inputs a string, and exclusive ORs the
4   // input string with a byte value. The result is then
5   // displayed. On exclusive ORing the previously
6   // exclusive ORed string, the original string is restored.
7   // This use of the exclusive OR operator provides a quick
8   // and easy method of encrypting a character string so
9   // that others cannot read it.
10  #include <iostream.h>
11  #include <string.h>
12
13  void main(void) {
14    const char BYTEVALUE = 255;
15    int i;
16    char input_string[80];
17
18    cout << endl
19        << "Demonstrates use of exclusive OR on "
20        << "a character string" << endl << endl;
21
22    cout << "Enter an input string: ";
23    cin.getline(input_string, sizeof(input_string));
24
25    cout << "You entered:  " << input_string << endl;
26
27    // Apply exclusive OR to each character in string.
28    for (i=0; i<strlen(input_string); i++ )
29      input_string[i] = input_string[i] ^ BYTEVALUE;
30
31    cout << "After conversion, the string is: "
32        << endl << input_string << endl << endl;
33
34    // Applying exclusive OR to each character in string
35    // a second time causes the original string to reappear.
36    for (i=0; i<strlen(input_string); i++ )
37      input_string[i] = input_string[i] ^ BYTEVALUE;
38
39    cout << "The restored string is: "
40        << input_string << endl << endl;
41
42    cout << "Press Enter to continue." << endl;
43    cin.get();
44
45  } // main
```

CHAR-XOR.CPP inputs a text string from the keyboard (lines 22 and 23) and stores the text in the char array named input_string. The program processes the input by using the exclusive OR operator (lines 27 through 29), displays the result (lines 31 and 32), and then restores the result (lines 34 through 37).

This program introduces you to two new features of C++. In line 23, you see `cin.getline()`. This special `cin` method is for inputting text strings. You've already seen how `cin` is normally used with the extraction operator >> to read data from the keyboard into a variable. When you use >>, C++ scans the input text that you type until it finds the first blank character. The text to the left of the blank is assigned to the first input variable in the `cin` extraction statement. When you want to input a text string that contains blank characters, the extraction operator stops reading the input when it reaches the first blank character. Obviously, when you want to read text input, the extraction operator is insufficient because you are unable to read an entire sentence containing blank characters.

The solution is to use the `getline()` method. `getline()` has three parameters, but you need to use only the first two parameters shown in line 23. The first parameter to `getline()` is the name of the `char` array in which the input should be stored. The second parameter is the size of the `char` array that will hold the input. `getline()` uses the size to ensure that it does not accept more input than there is room to store.

The second new feature is the `strlen()` function (pronounced *string length*). `strlen()` returns the length, in characters, of the `char` array parameter. You see `strlen()` in use in lines 28 and 36, where `strlen()` computes the length of the `input_string` variable. The `strlen()` function is declared in the included STRING.H header file.

The `input_string` variable is specially processed by using the exclusive OR (^) operator that you learned about in Chapter 2. The ^ operator sets bits within a data element in a most interesting way: when you apply the ^ operator twice in a row, you get back what you started with. For example, if you compute 65 ^ 255, you get 190. If you then compute 190 ^ 255, you get back 65. CHAR-XOR.CPP uses this capability to encrypt or scramble the input string by applying the exclusive OR operator to every character in the string (lines 28 and 29). This produces a piece of data that is no longer recognizable as text, keeping your information private. When you apply the exclusive OR operator a second time (lines 36 and 37), the encrypted text is unscrambled back to its original value.

Multidimensional Arrays

Arrays that have a single index are called one-dimensional arrays. It's entirely possible for an array to have two or more indexes. Such an array is known as a *multidimensional array*. Multidimensional arrays are not used very frequently (certainly not nearly as much as one-dimensional arrays), but they have their place in C++ programming. In this section, you learn how to declare and use a variety of two-dimensional arrays. Although this section contains no example, in C++ you can create arrays with as many dimensions as your application requires, whether that is three, four, or more dimensions.

You declare a multidimensional array by appending additional array dimensions to the array declaration. Suppose that you have a tic-tac-toe board with three squares across and three squares down. To keep track of the current setting of each position on the board, you can create a two-dimensional array of char. Within the array, you can store a '.' to indicate that the space is not selected, or 'X' or 'O' to indicate that the space is selected. The declaration for a tic-tac-toe board looks like the following:

```
char tic_tac_toe[3][3];
```

This declaration defines a square, two-dimensional array having three elements in both directions. Figure 3.5 illustrates what this multidimensional array looks like in memory. The first index selects the row, and the second index selects the column. tic_tac_toe[0][0] refers to the board square in the upper-left corner, whereas tic_tac_toe[2][1] refers to the board square in the middle of the bottom or lowest row.

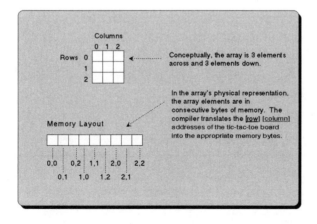

Fig. 3.5
A tic-tac-toe board represented as a 3-by-3 array of integers.

Listing 3.3 shows the simple program that you use to set the squares on the tic-tac-toe board.

Listing 3.3 A Demonstration of a Multidimensional Array

```
1    // TICTACTO.CPP
2    // Shows how a two-dimensional array can be used
3    // to keep track of spaces on a tic-tac-toe board.
4    // This is a very simple program; it assumes
5    // that two players are sitting by the keyboard.
6    // (Since nobody's looking, you can pretend to be
7    // both players, okay?) Each player takes turns
8    // selecting board squares; player 1 marks spaces
9    // with an X, and player 2 marks spaces with an O.
10   // The program really is simple: It prompts
11   // 4 times for each of you to make a move and then quits.
12   #include <iostream.h>
13   #include <string.h>
14
15   // This array holds the content of the
16   // tic-tac-toe board.
17   char tic_tac_toe[3][3];
18
19   void show_board() {
20   // Displays the current state of the
21   // tic-tac-toe board on the screen.
22     int row, col;
23
24     cout << endl;
25     for( row=0; row<3; row++) {
26       for( col=0; col<3; col++)
27         cout << tic_tac_toe[row][col];
28       cout << endl;
29     } // for
30   } // show_board
31
32   void main(void) {
33     int row, col;
34     int iterations;
35
36     cout << "Demonstrates use of a two-dimensional array"
37          << endl
38          << "for use as a tic-tac-toe board." << endl << endl;
39
40     // Initialize the board to all dots '.'.
41     // Simultaneously display the coordinate
42     // positions.
43     for( row=0; row<3; row++) {
44       for( col=0; col<3; col++) {
45         tic_tac_toe[row][col] = '.';
46         cout << "(" << row << ", " << col << ")  ";
47       }
48       cout << endl;
49     }
50
51     // This is a simple program! For all 9
52     // board spaces, ask Player #1 and Player #2
53     // which space they want to select.
54     for ( iterations = 1; iterations <= 4; iterations ++) {
```

```
55      show_board();
56
57      // Note: The prompt is split across two lines solely
58      // so that the line fits on the printed page in the
59      // book.
60      cout << "Player #1:  Select a row and column "
61          << "number (e.g. 0 2)? ";
62      cin >> row >> col;
63      cin.ignore(1);  // Skip over trailing Enter key.
64      // Allow selection of only blank entries. You forfeit
65      // your turn if you select an already selected space.
66      if (tic_tac_toe[row][col]=='.')
67        tic_tac_toe[row][col] = 'X';
68
69      show_board();
70
71      cout << "Player #2:  Select a row and column number? ";
72      cin >> row >> col;
73      cin.ignore(1);  // Skip over trailing Enter key.
74      if (tic_tac_toe[row][col]=='.')
75        tic_tac_toe[row][col] = 'O';
76   } // for
77
78   // Display the final result.
79   show_board();
80
81   cout << endl << "Press Enter to continue." << endl;
82   cin.get();
83   } // main
```

The tic_tac_toe array is declared as a global, two-dimensional array in line 17. tic_tac_toe is defined as a global variable so that it can be accessed from inside the show_board() function (lines 19 through 30) and the main() function. Lines 43 through 49 initialize the tic_tac_toe array so that it contains all dot ('.') characters. Line 46 also displays a map showing the coordinates used to select each position on the board.

The loop beginning in line 54 causes the enclosed statements (lines 55 through 76) to be executed several times. Inside the loop, the program prompts Player 1 to select a row and column (typed as two digits separated by a blank, such as 0 1). If the space is not already taken (as determined by the if test in line 66), the space is marked with an x. Player 2 is then given a chance to select a space. The process repeats until all the spaces are taken. (This simple program is intended to demonstrate creation and use of a two-dimensional array. You may want to change the program logic so that instead of a fixed number of iterations through the loop, the program checks to see whether any more blank spaces are available. If there are no more blank spaces, the program can quit right away.)

Another popular use of multidimensional arrays is to create an array of strings. As you know, a character string is represented in C++ using an array of char. If you want to have an array of strings (an array in which each element is itself a string), you must create an array of an array of char. That becomes a two-dimensional array. Listing 3.4 illustrates how you do this by creating an array of month names.

Listing 3.4 Using a Two-Dimensional Array to Store an Array of Character Strings

```
1   // MULTI1.CPP
2   // Demonstrates a multidimensional array.
3   #include <iostream.h>
4   #include <string.h>
5
6   void main(void) {
7     char month_names[12][10];
8     int i, j;
9
10    strcpy( month_names[0], "January" );
11    strcpy( month_names[1], "February" );
12    strcpy( month_names[2], "March" );
13    strcpy( month_names[3], "April" );
14    strcpy( month_names[4], "May" );
15    strcpy( month_names[5], "June" );
16    strcpy( month_names[6], "July" );
17    strcpy( month_names[7], "August" );
18    strcpy( month_names[8], "September" );
19    strcpy( month_names[9], "October" );
20    strcpy( month_names[10], "November" );
21    strcpy( month_names[11], "December" );
22
23    // Output the content of month_names, character
24    // by character.
25    for( i=0; i<12; i++) {
26      for( j=0; j<strlen(month_names[i]); j++ )
27        cout << month_names[i][j];
28      cout << endl;
29    } // for
30
31    cout << endl;
32    // Output month_names as 12 separate strings.
33    for( i=0; i<12; i++)
34      cout << month_names[i] << endl;
35
36    cout << "Press Enter to continue." << endl;
37    cin.get();
38
39  }
```

Line 7 declares month_names to be a two-dimensional array of 12 elements, each up to 10 characters long. Lines 10 through 21 assign strings to each of the array strings. You can see in lines 25 through 29 that by indexing both subscripts of the array, you can output the array in a byte-by-byte manner. Alternatively, you can access each month_names element as an individual string type. Line 34 accesses each element to output the content of each month_names element.

The MULTI1.CPP program may seem somewhat peculiar to you; after defining a two-dimensional array, lines 10 through 21 and line 34 each reference month_names as if the array had only one dimension. What is going on? The answer is that the compiler is smarter than you think, and many details are being handled behind the scenes. To understand this process, look at figure 3.6. This illustration shows how the month names are stored in an area of memory 12 rows high by 10 columns across. When you reference only the first dimension—for example, month_names[2]—the compiler is smart enough to figure out that you mean the third row. The compiler treats this reference as if you had placed an invisible [0] next to month_names, giving you month_names[2][0]. By doing so, the compiler has no trouble locating the third row (at index 2).

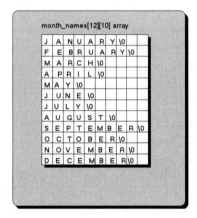

Fig. 3.6
How the
month_names
array is stored in
memory.

When you use a multidimensional array, especially for arrays of strings, it is convenient to initialize the array at the point of declaration. Lines 7 through 10 of listing 3.5 show how to perform this initialization. Put the initializer in braces, as you have seen before, and specify each element of the array.

Listing 3.5 Initializing an Array of Strings

```
1  // MULTI2.CPP
2  // Shows a way to initialize an array of strings.
3  #include <iostream.h>
4  #include <string.h>
5
6  void main(void) {
7    char month_names[12][10] =
8    { "January", "February", "March", "April", "May",
9      "June", "July", "August", "September", "October",
10      "November", "December" };
11   int i, j;
12
13   // Output month_names as 12 separate strings.
14   for( i=0; i<12; i++)
15     cout << month_names[i] << endl;
16
17   cout << "Press Enter to continue." << endl;
18   cin.get();
19 }
```

Structures

A structure is a special C++ data type used to hold groups of related data. Within the structure, you can hold different types of data (unlike the array, which holds a set of the same type of data). Consider, for instance, a program that tracks books. This program must keep track of the book's title, author's name, publisher, and year the book was published. You can store this information in separate, independent variables:

```
char title[60];
char author[40];
char publisher[30];
int year;
```

But what if you have more than one book to track? You could create separate variables for each book, such as book1_title, book2_title, and so on. Clearly, this approach quickly becomes cumbersome and leads to much confusion. A better way is to combine all the related information into a convenient package, called a *structure*. Here is an example of how the preceding information looks when collected together in a C++ structure (struct):

```
struct book_info
{
  char title[60];
  char author[40];
  char publisher[30];
  int year;
};
```

This definition creates a structure type that you can use as a template for creating variables that hold information about books. Each variable defined within the structure is a *member* of the structure (other languages use the term *field* in place of *member*).

The symbol `book_info` is a structure tag. You use the `book_info` tag like an `int` or `float` type to declare variables. The declaration

```
book_info book1, book2, book3;
```

creates three variables named `book1`, `book2`, and `book3`. When you define structure variables, you can preface the definition with the `struct` keyword, followed by the structure tag and the names of the variables (the use of the `struct` keyword is required in C but is optional in C++). Each of the created variables has space for `title`, `author`, `publisher`, and `year`. Figure 3.7 shows how space is allocated in memory for this structure. Note that each member is allocated one after the other.

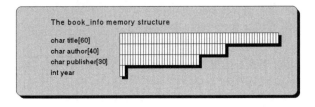

Fig. 3.7
How memory is allocated for the `book_info` structure.

To access the members within a particular variable, use the member-of operator (.):

```
strcpy( book1.title, "Object-Oriented Programming with Visual C++ 1.5"
);
strcpy( book1.author, "Jack Tackett, Jr." );
strcpy( book1.publisher, "Que" );
book1.year = 1994;
```

As you can see, you can use the member variables of a structure like all other C++ variables. The structure serves to collect related information about each book title into a single entity.

When you declare the structure and define the structure tag name, you can also define your variables simultaneously. Simply add the variables after the definition:

```
struct book_info
{
  char title[60];
```

```
        char author[40];
        char publisher[30];
        int year;
} book1, book2, book3;
```

This example defines the book_info tag and the three structure variables book1, book2, and book3. If you want to declare additional structure variables later, you can do so by referencing the book_info tag, as in the line

```
struct book_info book4, book5, book6;
```

or

```
book_info book4, book5, book6;
```

Using Structures in an Assignment

Because a structure is an entity, similar to an int or char, you can assign one structure to another. Say, for example, that you would like to make book4, book5, and book6 have the same values as book1. Therefore, you need only assign book1 to each of the other structures:

```
book4 = book1;
book5 = book1;
book6 = book1;
```

Alternatively, you can write this assignment in shorthand:

```
book4 = book5 = book6 = book1;
```

Initializing a Structure Declaration

You can initialize a structure within the code section of your program, or you can initialize the structure as part of the declaration. With the latter method, you specify the initial values, in braces, after the declaration. To see how to do this, look at the following example:

```
struct book_info
{
  char title[60];
  char author[40];
  char publisher[30];
  int year;
} book1 = { "Object-Oriented Programming with Visual C++ 1.5",
            "Jack Tackett, Jr.", "Que", 1994 };
```

Note that in the initializer list you can specify different types of values corresponding to the different types of members within the structure. You can see this in the three strings, followed by the integer 1994, corresponding to the year member. Be sure to place your initializers in the correct order; otherwise, your structure members may have different values than you expected.

Arrays of Structures

You create an array of structures just as you create an array of other types. For instance, to create an array named books, you write

```
book_info books[100];
```

This line allocates a 100-element array named books. To access the members of each structure element, use array notation. To initialize the first element of books, for instance, your code must reference the members of books[0], as in the following lines:

```
strcpy( books[0].title, "Object-Oriented Programming with Visual C++ 1.5" );
strcpy( books[0].author, "Jack Tackett, Jr." );
strcpy( books[0].publisher, "Que" );
books[0].year = 1994;
```

You access the other elements by replacing the 0 index with the index number of the desired array element. Listing 3.6 shows a complete program that enables you to enter a number of titles into an array of structures. When you run the program, it displays the following menu:

```
Enter:  1) Add book, 2) List books, 3) Quit ?
```

To add a new title, select 1 from the menu. The program prompts for title, author, publisher, and date of publication. To see a list of titles already entered, select 2. When you are finished using the program, select option 3.

You may also initialize an array of structures at the point of declaration by enclosing the initializer list in { and } braces. Note this example:

```
book_info books[2] = {
"Object-Oriented Programming with Visual C++ 1.5", "Jack Tackett, Jr.", "Que", 1994,
"DOS Programmer's Reference", "Terry Dettman", "Que", 1991,
"Principles of Digital Audio", "Ken Pohlmann", "Sams", 1992
};
```

Listing 3.6 Using an Array of Structures

```
1   // STRUCT1.CPP
2   // Demonstrates an array of structures.
3   // This sample program creates an array of structures
4   // to keep track of book titles, authors, and publishers.
5   #include <iostream.h>
6
7   void main(void) {
8      // Here is the structure definition that describes
9      // how the data is collected together into a
```

(continues)

Listing 3.6 Continued

```
10    // structure.
11    struct book_info
12    {
13      char title[60];
14      char author[40];
15      char publisher[30];
16      int year;
17    };
18
19    // MAX_BOOKS is set to 101 to create an array from
20    // [0] to [100] (which is 101 elements). Element [0]
21    // is not used in this program.
22    const int MAX_BOOKS = 101;
23
24    // books[] is an array of book_info structures.
25    struct book_info books[MAX_BOOKS];
26
27    int num_books = 0;    // Counts the number of books.
28    int index;            // Used as for loop index.
29    int command;          // Stores an entered command.
30    char extraline[40];   // Pauses for Enter key to continue.
31
32
33    cout << "Simple database of book titles." << endl
34        << endl;
35
36    do {
37      cout << "Enter:  1) Add book, 2) List books, 3) Quit ?  ";
38      cin >> command;  // Reads the integer digits.
39      cin.ignore(1);   // Reads the Enter key.
40
41      if ( command == 1 )
42      {
43        num_books++;
44        cout << "Enter new title:  ";
45        cin.getline( books[num_books].title,
46                     sizeof( books[num_books].title ) );
47        cout << "Enter new author name:  ";
48        cin.getline( books[num_books].author,
49                     sizeof( books[num_books].author ) );
50        cout << "Enter new publisher name:  ";
51        cin.getline( books[num_books].publisher,
52                     sizeof( books[num_books].publisher ) );
53        cout << "Enter the year the book was published:  ";
54        cin >> books[num_books].year;
55        cout << endl;
56      } // if
57      else if ( command == 2 )
58      {
59        for (index = 1; index <= num_books; index++) {
60          cout << "Book #" << index << " is:" << endl;
61          cout << "Title:   " << books[index].title << endl;
62          cout << "Author:  " << books[index].author << endl;
63          cout << books[index].publisher
64              << ", " << books[index].year << endl;
```

```
65          } // for
66        } // else if
67        else if ( command != 3 ) {
68          cout << "Please type 1, 2, or 3." << endl
69              << "Press Enter to continue." << endl;
70          // Reset the input stream.
71          cin.clear();
72          // And prompt for the Enter key.
73          cin.getline( extraline, sizeof( extraline ));
74        }; // else if
75    } while (command != 3);
76
77  } // main
```

Calculating the Amount of Memory Used

Arrays of structures can quickly consume a great deal of memory. Because each book_info structure occupies 132 bytes of memory, 100 book_info structures require 13,200 bytes. As you can see, you must keep memory limitations in mind when creating your programs. Indeed, a programming maxim says, "All programs grow to fill the maximum amount of available memory." Somehow, regardless of the amount of memory you have available, it never seems to be enough.

One way to determine the size of any data element in your C++ program is with the sizeof() compiler directive. You use sizeof() like a function. sizeof() takes a single parameter—the data item whose size you want to determine—and calculates the number of bytes of memory needed for that item. You can experiment with sizeof() by writing

```
    cout << "Memory size in bytes =" << sizeof( variablename )
        << endl;
```

in which you can replace variablename with the name of any variable, array, structure, or other C++ data type or object.

Lines 11 through 17 of listing 3.6 describe the structure of the book_info data record. Line 25 allocates the array of structures named books. Note that in this sample program, the constant MAX_BOOKS is set to 101, providing an array that extends from books[0] to books[100]. The variable num_books counts the number of titles that have been entered into the array. num_books begins at zero and increments by 1 for each new book added to the array. For the sake of simplicity, num_books is used directly as an index into books[]. When the first title is added, num_books is incremented by 1, and the first book is stored at books[1]. This results in books[0] being unused, which keeps the program simpler.

Line 36, together with line 75, introduces another type of looping statement known as the do-while loop. Everything inside the loop, from line 37 to line 74, is repeated as long as the condition specified in line 75 remains True. In this program, as long as the Quit command (option 3) is not entered, the program continues to loop around and around inside this section of code. After option 3 is selected from the menu, the loop terminates, and execution continues with the statements after line 75. You learn more about do-while in Chapter 4, "Selection and Loop Statements."

The guts of this sample program are located inside the do-while loop, in lines 37 through 74. Line 37 displays the menu of options, and line 38 reads the selected command into the variable command. When you use cin to obtain keyboard input, the >> extractor reads the numeric digits only until reaching a blank or the end of the line. This means that when you type **1** and press the Enter key, the extractor reads only the single digit 1 and leaves the Enter key (↵) character for the next input statement. This means that the next input statement sees the ↵ keystroke already pending and thinks that you decided to type a blank line, resulting in incorrect operation of your program. As you can see in line 45, the next input statement reads the book title. Seeing the ↵ that is still unprocessed by the program, cin.getline() reads and accepts the ↵ keystroke and assumes that you've entered a blank title. The solution to this problem is to add line 39:

```
cin.ignore(1);      // Reads the Enter key.
```

This special function of cin reads and disregards the single keystroke ↵ character. Now, line 45 calls cin.getline() and correctly waits for you to type a book title.

Lines 42 through 56 are processed only when you elect to add a new title. These lines prompt you to enter a title, author name, publisher name, and the year of publication. Line 43 increments num_books. num_books is then used as an index into the books[] array (in lines 45, 48, 51, and 54).

Lines 58 through 66 are processed when you want to display a list of the titles already entered. This section of code uses a for loop to display each entry in the books[] array, ranging from 1 up to the value of num_books.

Finally, lines 67 through 74 handle the situation in which you or your program's user enters an incorrect or invalid menu selection. Line 68 instructs the user as to the valid inputs for the menu prompt and waits for the user to press the ↵ key before proceeding. Line 71 is another new feature that clears any error conditions that may have occurred in the input. Consider what happens if the user selects A instead of 1, 2, or 3. The extraction in line 38 fails because A cannot be converted to the integer type of the command variable, which sets an error condition on the cin input stream. No further input can be processed until the error condition is cleared by calling cin.clear() in line 71. After clearing the error condition, line 73 waits for the user to press the ↵ key before redisplaying the menu prompt line.

Structures within Structures

You have just seen how you can combine aggregate types, such as an array of structures. You have seen also a structure containing an array (the strings inside the book_info structure are character arrays). A structure, interestingly enough, may also contain one or more structures within itself.

Consider a structure designed to hold financial transaction information. This structure must hold an account number, an amount of money, the transaction type (such as deposit or withdrawal), and the date and time the transaction is posted. For convenient access to the month, day, and year fields, plus access to the hours and minutes components of the transaction time, you can write both of these members themselves as structures. Thus, you produce a struct definition, like the following:

```
struct transaction_record {
  long account_number;
  float amount;
  type_of_transaction transaction_type;
  struct {
    int month, day, year;
    } date;
  struct {
    int hours, minutes;
    } time;
} A_transaction;
```

Note carefully how the date and time members are defined using struct. You access the members of date or time using the member-of operator (.), as in these lines:

```
A_transaction.date.month = 11;
A_transaction.date.day = 10;
A_transaction.date.year = 1993;
```

If you want, nested structures themselves can have nested structures. Each time that a struct is located deeper and deeper inside an existing struct, you must use the member-of operator (.) to access each member, one after the other, until reaching the desired member. Listing 3.7 demonstrates access to all the members of the transaction_record structure.

To initialize the structure members at declaration, you must enclose the substructure values in braces also. Here is an example:

```
struct transaction_record transaction =
  { 19983, 100.0, DEPOSIT, {10,11,1993}, {10,30} };
```

Listing 3.7 Nesting Structures inside Structures

```
1   // STRUCT2.CPP
2   // Shows how to define a structure inside another
3   // structure and how to access the members of
4   // such a structure.
5   #include <iostream.h>
6
7   enum type_of_transaction {DEPOSIT, CREDIT};
8
9   struct transaction_record {
10    long account_number;
11    float amount;
12    type_of_transaction transaction_type;
13    struct {
14      int month, day, year;
15      } date;
16    struct {
17      int hours, minutes;
18      } time;
19  };
20
21  void main(void) {
22    struct transaction_record transaction;
23    transaction.amount = 100.00;
24    transaction.transaction_type = DEPOSIT;
25    transaction.date.month = 12;
26    transaction.date.day = 1;
27    transaction.date.year = 1993;
28    transaction.time.hours = 9;
29    transaction.time.minutes = 10;
30  } // main
```

Bit Fields

You can use a structure to define a bit field, which is a way of laying out actual bit usage within an area of memory. Bit fields are especially useful for machine-level interface routines that must access hardware registers. Using bit fields, you can match a C++ struct definition to the exact layout of a hardware register.

Note

Be advised that bit fields are an advanced topic. Feel free to skip this section, especially if you are new to either C or the C++ programming language. The use of bit fields is not essential to the applications you are likely to write. Bit fields are used primarily in low-level system software and also in some applications for efficient storage of bit flags and small values.

A bit field enables you to create variable names for individual bits or groups of bits. To understand how to set up a bit field, consider an application that must talk to the computer's serial port interface. The serial port is the connection that your PC uses to talk to modems and sometimes other devices, including mice and printers. Inside the PC, a special routine is provided that programs can use to initialize certain serial port parameters. To use this routine, your program must set individual bits within a byte value. These bit settings are used to control serial port options such as 7- or 8-bit bytes, 1 or 2 stop bits, parity selection, and bit transmission rate. You don't need to understand all these terms, however, to understand how bit fields operate.

To set the individual bits within the serial port control byte (actually, the PC's basic input/output system, or BIOS, control routine), you can set up a bit field structure, as in this example:

```
struct serial_port_bitfield {
  unsigned int size : 2;
  unsigned int stop_bits : 1;
  unsigned int parity : 2;
  unsigned int bit_rate : 3;
} serial_init;
```

Note that you declare each variable within the bit field structure like a normal variable except for adding the colon (:) character and a number. The number specifies how many bits to allocate to the indicated variable. In this example, 2 bits are allocated to the size variable, 1 bit to the stop_bits variable, 2 to parity, and 3 to bit_rate. The layout of this structure is shown in figure 3.8.

As you can see, the bits are allocated beginning from the rightmost bit and move toward the left. You can assign values to the serial_init structure using the regular member-of operator (.), as in these lines:

```
serial_init.size = 3;
serial_init.stop_bits = 0;
serial_init.parity = 2;
serial_init.bit_rate = 7;
```

Fig. 3.8
The layout of
the serial port
interface bit
field.

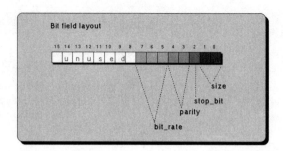

You must be certain that the bit fields are large enough to hold the values you assign. If you use signed integers (the int type), the leftmost bit within the bit field is treated as a sign bit. If you write

```
int size : 2;
```

the leftmost bit of size becomes a sign bit. If you then assign size the value 3, as in

```
serial_info.size = 3;
```

the 2 bits of size are both set, but the leftmost bit is treated as a sign bit. Consequently, size actually has the value of –1.

The Use of *typedef*

A typedef declaration enables you to create a new type name for an existing type name. For example, you can create a unique type name for all declarations that require a year value for a date. To do this, use typedef in the following way:

```
typedef int YearType;
```

Now YearType is synonymous with int. You can use YearType in place of int wherever you want to declare an integer variable for storing a date. Instead of writing

```
int date1, date2, date3;
```

you can use YearType in place of the int type:

```
YearType date1, date2, date3;
```

The major purpose of using typedef to create a new type identifier name is to improve the readability of your program. When you look at the declaration, it is clear that date1, date2, and date3 are intended to store YearType values, not necessarily arbitrary integers. This use of `YearType` helps make your program easier to read.

There are other uses of `typedef`, especially in connection with structures and pointers. You learn about these uses in Chapter 5, "Pointers."

Unions

The union aggregate type uses a definition that looks much like a `struct` definition, but produces a very different result. The `union` type is an advanced C++ feature.

> **Note**
>
> You may want to skip this section at this time and refer back to this chapter when your programming experience increases.

To understand the union, first look at the definition of a typical `union` type:

```
union misc_data {
  char command;
  int  help_topic;
  float miles_traveled;
  char key_pressed;
};
```

As you can see, the union looks just like a `struct` except that the keyword `struct` is replaced with `union`. The difference is in how the data within the union is laid out in memory. Remember that in a structure, the data items in the structure are laid out one after the other within memory. In the union, however, the data items are laid out so that they overlap one another. The effect is that the items are arranged in memory as shown in figure 3.9.

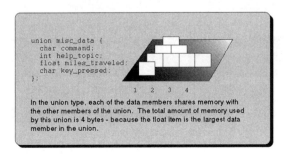

Fig. 3.9

The `misc_data` union includes four overlapping members.

The total size of the union is the size of the largest individual element within the union. In the preceding `misc_data` example, the size of `misc_data` is four bytes because the `float` variable `miles_traveled` is the largest item within the union. (If `misc_data` were a structure, the size of `misc_data` would be the size of the individual elements added together.)

One reason to use a union is to save memory. In many programs, you must have several variables, but they don't need to be used at the same time. Consider the situation in which you need to have several character strings for input. You can create several character string arrays, such as the following:

```
char command_line[80];
char error_message[80];
char help_text[80];
```

Together, these three variables occupy 240 bytes of memory. However, if your program does not need to use all three variables simultaneously (and it should not try to do so), why not let them share the same memory space by using a union? When combined into the following `union` type, these variables occupy a total of just 80 bytes:

```
union some_strings {
  char command_line[80];
  char error_message[80];
  char help_text[80];
} strs;
```

You refer to the members of the union by using the member-of operator (.), as in the line

```
cin.getline( strs.command_line, sizeof( strs.command_line ) );
```

or

```
strcpy( strs.error_message, "Press 1, 2, or 3." );
```

You can demonstrate to yourself that the three strings occupy the same memory by executing the program shown in listing 3.8.

Listing 3.8 A Program Demonstrating That Union Variables Share Their Memory

```
1   // UNION.CPP
2   // Demonstrates that variables within a union
3   // really do occupy the same space!
4   #include <iostream.h>
5   #include <string.h>
6
```

```
 7  void main(void) {
 8    union some_strings {
 9      char command_line[80];
10      char error_message[80];
11      char help_text[80];
12    } strs;
13
14    strcpy( strs.error_message, "Press 1, 2, or 3." );
15
16    cout << strs.error_message << endl
17         << strs.command_line << endl
18         << strs.help_text << endl;
19
20    cout << "Press Enter to continue." << endl;
21    cin.get();
22
23  } // main
```

Another use for unions is to refer to a piece of data in more than one way. For example, if you create the union

```
union some_data {
  char a_short[2];
  unsigned int a_number;
} conversion;
```

you can easily convert two-byte character sequences into an integer equivalent. For example, the section of code

```
conversion.a_short[0] = 'A';
conversion.a_short[1] = 'B';
cout << conversion.a_number << endl;
```

produces the following output:

```
16961
```

You might use this type of conversion if you want to encode your data bytes into numbers, or if your application is reading data from a disk file (see Chapter 11, "C++ Input and Output"). In the case of reading data from a disk file, your program may normally expect character data, but occasionally it must switch to reading a binary integer value stored in two bytes. If you use the union, your program can read the data as characters but switch to an integer format when needed.

Introduction to Objects

In this chapter, you've learned how to use the aggregate types, such as the array and the structure, to store related kinds of data. As you learn to write more complex programs, you learn also how to break your program into pieces called *functions*. Each C++ program is typically made up of data elements and functions (see Chapter 6, "Functions and Macros"). In most programs, the functions perform some type of operation on the data. In the simple book-tracking program that used an array of structures, for example, you could split the operation to add a new title to the array into its own function, perhaps called `AddTitle()`. You might place the operation that lists or displays the books into a function named `DisplayTitles()`.

A large program may consist of many pieces of data and many functions. It is up to you to remember which function operates on which piece of data. Sometimes programmers make mistakes. (Programmers really are human, although some pride themselves on being a little ambiguous about their membership in the human race!) One common mistake is when several functions each change a data value, and each function assumes that it alone has complete control over the piece of data. The result, of course, is that the program fails to operate as expected.

One solution to this dilemma of multiple functions operating on data is to combine the data and functions into a single entity called an *object*. The result is that only authorized functions (those that are part of the object) can make changes to the data. Furthermore, by looking at the definition for the object, you can tell at a glance exactly which functions are allowed direct access to the data. By encapsulating data and functions, you improve the functions' information-hiding capabilities. By keeping internal information hidden, you help to eliminate the temptation to make inappropriate changes to an object's internal information. Information hiding gives the object total control over its own data.

Another purpose for object-oriented programming lies in the power of a feature called *inheritance*. Inheritance enables you to create new objects by telling the compiler that you want a new object to be like some existing object, but with a few twists or modifications. Through inheritance, you can build an application from many existing components in an easier and more flexible manner than that provided by a mere library of functions. These concepts are explained and illustrated in later chapters of this book, especially Chapter 8, "Classes," Chapter 9, "The Power of Inheritance," and Chapter 10, "Virtual Functions and Polymorphism."

To understand how to put object orientation into operation, consider a simple structure to hold a time value. This structure is called `time_record`; it holds two values, `hours` and `minutes`:

```
struct time_record {
  int hours;
  int minutes;
};
```

To declare a structure variable named `current_time` to hold a `time_record`, write

```
struct time_record current_time;
```

You can now write a program to track time values, using the `current_time` structure. Then you can set the value of `current_time` directly by writing

```
current_time.hours = 2;
current_time.minutes = 45;
```

To display `current_time`, write the following:

```
cout << current_time.hours << ":" << current_time.minutes;
```

Now suppose that at some later date you decide that your application must store time internally as the number of minutes since midnight. In this form, 2:45 becomes 165 minutes. To make this modification, you must go through your entire program, find each use of `current_time`, and change your code to reflect this new requirement. That could take a lot of time!

After a moment's thought, you realize that a better implementation of the timekeeper is to set the current time by using a function. So you write a function such as the following:

```
void set_time ( int new_hours, new_minutes )
{
  current_time.hours = new_hours;
  current_time.minutes = new_minutes;
};
```

If you decide to store the time internally as minutes only, you can make a simple change to your `set_time()` function, saving a great deal of searching and editing. The change might look like this:

```
void set_time ( int new_hours, new_minutes )
{
  current_time.hours = 0;
  current_time.minutes = new_hours*60 + new_minutes;
};
```

You can add a show_time() function to display the current hours and minutes settings. A complete program to do this is presented in listing 3.9.

Listing 3.9 Managing a Time-Information Record

```
1   // TIMEOBJ1.CPP
2   // Demonstrates a non-object-oriented
3   // implementation of a time record.
4   #include <iostream.h>
5
6   struct time_record {
7       int hours;
8       int minutes;
9     };
10
11  struct time_record current_time;
12
13  void set_time ( int new_hours, int new_minutes )
14  {
15    current_time.hours = new_hours;
16    current_time.minutes = new_minutes;
17  } // set_time
18
19  void show_time (void)
20  {
21    cout << current_time.hours << ":"
22         << current_time.minutes << endl;
23  } // show_time
24
25  void main(void)
26  {
27    cout << "Demonstration of a simple object."
28         << endl << endl;
29
30    set_time ( 2, 45 );
31    show_time();
32
33    cout << "Press Enter to continue." << endl;
34    cin.get();
35
36  } // main
```

As you can see from the features of the TIMEOBJ1.CPP program, the set_time() and show_time() functions are tightly coupled to the definition of current_time. Indeed, why not combine the definition of the record with the definition of the function? That is the essence of an object. You can combine both data and functions into a structure definition:

```
struct time_record {
  int hours;
  int minutes;
  void set_time ( int new_hours, int new_minutes );
  void show_time (void);
};
```

Using this `struct` definition, you can create a `current_time` object:

```
struct time_record current_time;
```

So far, everything you see is just a minor extension of the structure concept. However, the `time_record` structure definition defines only what the parameters to `set_time()` and `show_time()` look like. The actual implementation requires the use of the `::` *scope resolution operator*. You can see this operator in use in listing 3.10.

Listing 3.10 Demonstrating an Object-Oriented Implementation of a Simple Time-Information Structure

```
 1   // TIMEOBJ2.CPP
 2   // Demonstrates an object-oriented
 3   // implementation of a time record.
 4   #include <iostream.h>
 5
 6   struct time_record {
 7     int hours;
 8     int minutes;
 9     void set_time ( int new_hours, int new_minutes );
10     void show_time (void);
11   };
12
13   void time_record::set_time ( int new_hours, int new_minutes )
14   {
15     hours = new_hours;
16     minutes = new_minutes;
17   } // set_time
18
19   void time_record::show_time (void)
20   {
21     cout << hours << ":"
22          << minutes << endl;
23   } // show_time
24
25   void main(void)
26   {
27     struct time_record current_time;
28
29     cout << "Demonstration of a simple object."
30          << endl << endl;
31
32     current_time.set_time ( 2, 45 );
33     current_time.show_time();
34
35     cout << "Press Enter to continue." << endl;
36     cin.get();
37
38   } // main
```

In TIMEOBJ2.CPP, the time_record structure is modified to include the declaration of the set_time() and show_time() functions. You can see the new definition in lines 6 through 11. The actual implementation of set_time() and show_time() is placed elsewhere in the program. You can see the implementation of set_time() in lines 13 through 17 and the implementation of show_time() in lines 19 through 23. Note the use of the :: scope resolution operator. Here, you use the :: operator to show that set_time() and show_time() are actually components of the time_record structure. Although their code is located outside the time_record struct definition, they are properly part of the time_record structure. The use of the :: operator tells the compiler that these two functions are associated with time_record.

Because set_time() is now a part of time_record, set_time() has direct access to the hours and minutes variables. Compare this direct access to that used in lines 15 and 16 of TIMEOBJ1.CPP (listing 3.9). In TIMEOBJ1, set_time() directly referenced the current_time variable. But what if your program needs two time records? You would need two set_time() functions, or you would have to pass the current_time structure as a parameter to set_time(). In addition, you can see that show_time() (lines 19 through 23) also has direct use of the structure variables. The direct access to the structure variables provided by object orientation has an important benefit that becomes apparent in the next sample program, TIMEOBJ3.CPP.

The declaration of current_time in line 27 of main() looks just like any other declaration of a struct variable. The main difference is that set_time() and show_time() are each member functions of current_time. You already know that hours and minutes are member variables of the structure. You access member *variables* using the member-of operator (.), and you access member *functions* using the same operator (see lines 32 and 33). When you write

```
current_time.set_time( 2, 45);
```

the compiler knows that you are calling the set_time() member function of the current_time structure. In effect, you tell the current_time object to set its time values.

When set_time() is called, an invisible piece of information is passed along by the compiler, so that when set_time() assigns new values to hours and minutes, set_time() knows that hours and minutes mean the variables owned by the current_time structure.

This object-oriented implementation of the time_record makes possible a neat trick: you can now have multiple time records that share the same set_time() and show_time() routines. Listing 3.11 illustrates this trick by declaring three time_record structures—current_time, last_time, and next_time. In object-oriented parlance, three instances of the time_record object type now exist.

Listing 3.11 Creating Multiple *time_record* Objects

```
1   // TIMEOBJ3.CPP
2   // Demonstrates the creation of
3   // multiple time_record objects.
4   #include <iostream.h>
5
6   struct time_record {
7       int hours;
8       int minutes;
9       void set_time ( int new_hours, int new_minutes );
10      void show_time (void);
11      };
12
13  void time_record::set_time ( int new_hours, int new_minutes )
14  {
15    hours = new_hours;
16    minutes = new_minutes;
17  } // set_time
18
19  void time_record::show_time (void)
20  {
21    cout << hours << ":"
22         << minutes << endl;
23  } // show_time
24
25  void main(void)
26  {
27    struct time_record current_time, last_time, next_time;
28
29    cout << "Demonstration of a simple object."
30         << endl << endl;
31
32    current_time.set_time ( 2, 45 );
33    current_time.show_time();
34
35    last_time.set_time( 10, 30 );
36    last_time.show_time();
37
38    next_time.set_time( 4, 15 );
39    next_time.show_time();
40
41    cout << "Press Enter to continue." << endl;
42    cin.get();
43
44  } // main
```

Line 27 declares three `time_record` objects: `current_time`, `last_time`, and `first_time`. Each of these objects has its own private copy of `hours` and `minutes`, yet shares the common member functions `set_time()` and `show_time()`. Lines 32 through 39 initialize each of the objects and display their time settings.

The TIMEOBJ3.CPP program merely touches on the power of object programming. You've seen how the generic `time_record` object can support multiple time variables and how you can use object orientation to hide the underlying details of your program. Using the object design, you can easily change how the time information is stored. The use of objects makes your program cleaner, easier to read, and more flexible than a program that does not use objects.

In addition to the `struct` definition, C++ supports another type known as the *class*. The class definition is central to the full capabilities of C++'s object-oriented programming tools. You learn about the class type starting in Chapter 8, "Classes." This introduction to objects is here because it's important to begin thinking of your own programming problems in terms of objects. You use this form of the `struct` type in the next several chapters, where appropriate, to help you begin seeing your own programming challenges more objectively.

Summary

In this chapter, you learned the aggregate types of C++. The aggregate types hold collections of data, such as arrays of integers or structures that contain different kinds of data. After reading this chapter, you should have a good understanding of the basic array types and the use of a `struct` type variable.

The following topics were covered in this chapter:

- You define an array much like any other simple variable, except that you specify a number of array elements in brackets after the name of the variable. An example of an integer array declaration looks like the following:

  ```
  int monthly_totals[12];
  ```

- Arrays of `char` hold text strings. In C++, you terminate most of these strings by placing the null character `\0` as the last byte in the string.

- You can use the `strlen()` function to obtain the current length of a string stored in an array of `char` (but only when the string is terminated with a null character). Use `strcpy()` to copy one string to another.

- C++ supports multidimensional arrays. Such arrays are defined as having more than one index, like the following:

  ```
  int monthly_totals[12][4];
  ```

  You may think of a multidimensional array as being an array of arrays.

- You define a structure using the `struct` keyword, a tag name, and then a set of variables within braces. An example of a structure type is the following:

  ```
  struct employee_data {
    char name[30];
    long employee_number;
    char phone_num[32];
  };
  ```

- You declare a structure type variable by prefacing the declaration with the `struct` keyword and then the structure tag name. To create a variable that is laid out as specified for the `employee_data` type, write

  ```
  struct employee_data employee_record;
  ```

- To determine the size, in bytes, of any C++ data type, use the `sizeof()` directive.

- Bit fields are an advanced feature of the `struct` type, used to create bit-sized variables within a structure. Bit fields are often used in software that must work directly with the operating system or the hardware.

- Use `typedef` to create a synonym for other type identifiers. For example, the line

  ```
  typedef int Str_Length;
  ```

  makes `Str_Length` a synonym for `int`. You can use `Str_Length` in declarations to clarify your intended purpose of variables:

  ```
  Str_Length name_size, title_size;
  ```

- By using a `union` type, you can cause your variables to coexist in the same memory space. By allocating variables so that they share memory, you can reduce the total memory requirements of your programs.

■ You learned about some additional features of the `cin` input stream, including `cin.getline()` and `cin.clear()`.

C++ is best known for its object-oriented programming capabilities. This chapter has just scratched the surface of object technology. However, the introduction here is sufficient for you to begin viewing your own programming problems in terms of objects. The main thrust of C++'s object technology is presented in Chapters 8 through 10.

Review Questions

1. Why are arrays, structures, and unions known as aggregate data types?

2. Are the index values `0`, `15`, `25`, and `30` valid indexes into an array declared as `int values[30]`?

3. In the array `int numbers[6]`, does a reference to `numbers[2]` refer to the second element of the array or the third element of the array?

4. You have a program that uses the array `char alphabet[26]`. Write two kinds of statements to initialize `alphabet` so that it contains all 26 letters of the English alphabet.

5. What is the null character? Must every string have a null character?

6. For null-terminated strings, can you think of a way to find the length of the string without using the `strlen()` function?

7. Write a text string that contains double quotation mark characters within the string.

8. Why should you use `cin.getline()` in place of the `>>` extraction operator when reading strings from the keyboard?

9. Write a multidimensional array for an array of strings that holds the names of each day of the week.

10. Write a structure definition to hold the following items: a person's name, telephone number, age (in years), height (in inches), and weight. Give the structure a tag name and use the tag to declare two variables named `me` and `you`.

11. If you have an array of 100 structures of the type declared in question 10, approximately how many bytes of memory does this structure require?

12. Write a short program that uses `sizeof()` to calculate the actual size of the array of 100 structures, using the `struct` type you created in question 10.

13. How do you assign values to members of a structure?

14. When you use `cin` and `>>` to read a single character or number from the keyboard, why must you follow the input statement with `cin.ignore()`?

15. Write out a bit field `struct` definition that creates eight variables, each two bits wide.

16. A `union` definition looks like a `struct` definition. What is the main difference between a `union` and a `struct`?

17. An object combines what two aspects of a program into a single entity?

18. When you define a function inside a structure, what special operator do you use to link the function's implementation to the definition inside the `struct`?

Exercises

1. Practice using character arrays, `cin.getline()`, `strcpy()`, and `strlen()`. Write a program to input a string from the keyboard, and then display the string, character by character, to the screen. Your routine should use a `for` loop to iterate from the first character to the last character in the string. You can detect the end of the string by using `strlen()`, or you can search for the null character `\0` at the end of the string.

2. Create a program to track a group of employees. Create a structure to hold each employee name, employee number, and the year the employee started work. Model the program similarly to the book-title record-keeping program you used in this chapter.

3. Create a program to store and update a structure containing a date in the form of three variables: `month`, `day`, and `year`. Create the program so that it has two functions: `set_date()` and `show_date()`.

4. Modify the program created in exercise 2 to encapsulate the date member variables and functions into a single structure. Use this program to create several instances of the date structure, such as `todays_date`, `birth_date`, and `vacation_date`.

Chapter 4

Selection and Loop Statements

Chapter 1, "The Fundamentals of C++ Programming," introduced some of the C++ statements. C++, fortunately, has relatively few programming statements compared to many other programming languages. You've already learned about the basic if statement for conditionally executing sections of your program. In this chapter, you study additional examples of the if statement and learn about the switch statement. You use the switch statement to select one alternative from many possible outcomes; it is better suited than if for certain types of decision problems.

In this chapter, you also learn more about the basic for loop as well as the while and do-while loop constructions. You finish this chapter by looking at the goto statement, a C++ language feature that is not used much but does have its place in the programming art.

After reading this chapter, you should be familiar with and be able to use each of the following C++ keywords:

if	for loops
if-else	while loops
if-else if	do-while loops
switch	goto and statement labels
break and continue	

Decision and Selection Statements

In Chapter 1, you learned to use the `if` statement to control execution of portions of your program selectively. In Chapter 2, "C++ Data Types and Expressions," you saw several program examples that use the `if` statement. The following sections explore in greater detail the use of the `if` statement and introduce the `switch` statement.

The *if* Statement

The basic `if` statement lets your program make decisions about which parts of the program should be executed next. The `if` statement consists of a test expression followed by a statement or a group of statements. In response to a prompt, for example, your program must determine whether the user pressed Y for yes or N for no. Your program can use the `if` statement to select a course of action based on the input, as in the following example:

```
if (input == 'N')
    cout << "About to exit program." << endl << endl;
```

Only when the input keystroke is equal to N does the program display the warning message that you are about to exit the program.

The general format for the `if` statement is

```
if (test-expression)
    statement;
```

The `if` statement checks the value of *test-expression*. If *test-expression* is nonzero (or True), *statement* is executed. If *test-expression* is zero (or False), *statement* is not executed, and the program skips ahead to the next program statement in sequence. To clarify, you might think of the formal definition of an `if` statement as

```
if (test-expression is true)
    then execute this statement;
```

The *test-expression* can be any expression that results in an integer. Usually, the *test-expression* uses a relational operator (such as ==, <, or >) to compare values to one another. The relational operator produces a value of 1 when the relation tests as True, or 0 if the relation tests as False. For instance, if the variable named `delta` has the value of 10 and you write

```
if (delta == 10) ...;
```

the expression `delta == 10` evaluates to a value of 1 or True, and the *statement* part of the `if` is executed. If, instead, you write

```
if (delta == 5) ...;
```

then the expression evaluates to 0 or False.

In some cases, you can use an integer value directly, without performing a relational comparison. If you have a program that counts down from 10, for instance, you can test whether the counter has a value of zero by using the counter variable as the `test-expression`. Note this example:

```
int counter;
.
.
.
if (counter) ...;
```

Here, if `counter` is nonzero, the `statement` part of the `if` is executed. When `counter` reaches zero, the `statement` part is not executed. If your program is decrementing a counter, you can combine the decrement operation and the conditional test into a single operation, as in

```
if (--counter) ...;
```

In this form, the value of `counter` is decremented, and then the test is performed. Remember that when the decrement operator appears before an operand, the operand is decremented before using its value in the expression. As long as `counter` is still greater than zero, the `statement` part of the `if` is executed.

Sometimes you must selectively execute a group of statements. You can do this by placing braces around the group of statements to be executed. Following is an example of an `if` statement that selectively performs two operations:

```
if (input_value > maximum_value)
{
  maximum_value = input_value;
  cout << "New maximum value is " << input_value << endl;
}
```

When you group statements by using the left and right braces (`{ }`), the group of statements is called a *compound statement* or a *block*. You don't need to place a semicolon after the right brace of a block. However, no harm is done if you use the semicolon; the compiler merely ignores the unneeded semicolon.

Any statement can appear inside a block, including more `if` statements, as in this example:

```
if (frequency >= frequency_max)
{
        frequency = frequency_max;
        frequency_delta = -frequency_delta;
```

```
            if (turn_around_hold)
                  delay(turn_around_hold);
    }
```

The statement that follows the if statement may itself be another if statement, as in this example:

```
if (frequency <= frequency_max)
  if (frequency >= lower_frequency)
    frequency_delta = 0.1 * frequency_delta;
```

The two if statements are equivalent to a single if statement that uses the logical && operator, as in the following example:

```
if ( (frequency <= frequency_max)
         && (frequency >= lower_frequency) )
       frequency_delta = 0.1 * frequency_delta;
```

In both examples, if the first test fails, the second test is not executed at all. This "short circuit" evaluation can lead to some hard-to-track-down programming bugs when assignment is combined with evaluation, as in

```
if ((frequency <= frequency max) &&
     (frequency = lower_frequency))
        frequency _delta = 0.1 * frequency delta;
```

In the preceding example, if the statement (frequency <= frequency_max) tests out to 0 or False, the second test that also does an assignment is never executed, and frequency is not equated to lower_frequency.

The *if-else* Statement

In some situations, your program must decide between two outcomes. To make such a decision, you should use the if-else form of the if statement. The formal syntax of the if-else statement is

```
if (expression)
  statement1;
else
  statement2;
```

If *expression* is True, *statement1* is executed; if *expression* is False, *statement2* is executed. The following is an example of an if-else statement:

```
if (error_code)
  cout << "Error # " << error_code << endl;
else
  cout << "Operation completed successfully." << endl;
```

If error_code is not zero, an error message is displayed. If error_code is zero, the else part of the statement is executed, displaying a success message to the user.

When you use an `if-else` statement as the statement part of another `if` statement, to which `if` does the `else` belong? Consider the following:

```
if (expression1)
    if (expression2)
        statement1;
    else
        statement2;
```

Does the `else` part belong to the first or second `if`? The answer is that the `else` keyword always matches the closest `if`. Therefore, *expression2* decides which statement, *statement1* or *statement2*, is executed.

The *if-else if* Statement

Additionally, when you need to test for a whole series of conditions, you can string many `if` statements together by using the `if-else if` form of the `if` statement. Here is the format for this statement:

```
if (expression1)
    statement1;
else if (expression2)
    statement2;
else if (expression3)
    statement3;
else
    statement4;
```

You can add as many `else if` statements as your application requires. The following is an example of the `if-else if` in operation:

```
// Calculate # of decimal places to show.
int ndigits;
if(fabs(dy) < 10/nDivs)
        ndigits = 2;
else if(fabs(dy) < 100/nDivs)
        ndigits = 1;
else
        ndigits = 0;
```

The *switch* Statement

Now you've learned how you can write a long series of `if-else if` statements to test for many possible conditions. You can see that a long list of `if-else if` statements can become confusing and difficult to follow. A better solution is to use the easier `switch` statement. The C++ `switch` statement chooses one statement from among many possible outcomes.

The C++ `switch` statement, together with the `case` keyword, compares a value to many possible values (or *cases*) and executes the statement or statements whose `case` equals the `switch` value. In most instances, using the `switch` statement is more efficient than using a list of `if-else if` statements.

The general form of the `switch` statement is

```
switch (test-expression)
{
  case constant-value1: series of statements; break;
  case constant-value2: series of statements; break;
  case constant-value3: series of statements; break;
  .
  .
  .
  default: series of statements; break;
}
```

The value of *test-expression* must evaluate to an integer value (which includes values of type `char`). The integer value is then compared to each of the constant values in the `case` statements. When a match is found, the statement or block that follows the colon (`:`) is then executed. If *test-expression* does not match any of the cases, program control flows to the statement or block after the `default` keyword.

To understand how to use the `switch` statement, consider a program that displays a menu of selections. Depending on which selection is chosen, the program performs only certain operations. Listing 4.1 shows a program set up to use a `switch` statement to process user input. Note in listing 4.1 that you can list several constants for each case.

Listing 4.1 Using a *switch* Statement to Select from Many Possible Outcomes

```
1   // SWITCH1.CPP
2   // Demonstrates use of the switch statement to select
3   // a course of action based on user input.
4   #include <iostream.h>
5
6   void main(void) {
7     char keystroke;
8
9     cout << "Editing Program 1.0" << endl << endl
10         << "Choose an option from the following menu:" << endl;
11
12    cout << "  L - Load file" << endl
13        << "  S - Save file" << endl
14        << "  E - Edit mode" << endl
15        << "  P - Print file" << endl
16        << "  X - Exit program" << endl;
17    cin.get(keystroke);
18    cin.ignore(1); // Ignore trailing Enter key.
19    switch (keystroke)
20    {
21      case 'L': case 'l':
22        cout << "You selected Load file." << endl;
23        break;
```

```
24      case 'S': case 's':
25        cout << "You selected Save file."  << endl;
26        break;
27      case 'E': case 'e':
28        cout << "You selected Edit file." << endl;
29        break;
30      case 'P': case 'p':
31        cout << "You selected Print file." << endl;
32        break;
33      case 'X': case 'x':
34        cout << "You selected Exit program." << endl;
35        break;
36      default:
37        cout << "I do not recognize what you typed." << endl;
38    } // switch
39
40    cout << "Press Enter to continue.";
41    cin.get();
42  } // main
```

Line 19 sets up switch to use the value of keystroke as the selection value. The value of keystroke is then compared to each of the constants specified in the case statements in lines 21, 24, 27, 30, and 33. If a match is found, the statements following the matching case are executed. The break statement tells the computer that, after processing the statements for this case, it should break execution and resume processing at the first statement following the switch's right brace (}). You learn about break in the next section.

If no match is found, control falls through to the default case specified in lines 36 and 37. The default keyword is optional; you don't have to specify a default case. However, you should use a default condition when processing user input that is prone to mistyped keystrokes and errors. In instances where the switch value is guaranteed to be one of the case values, you can omit the default selection.

Multiple Cases

Notice that listing 4.1 uses two cases for each match so that the user can enter either uppercase or lowercase letters. Multiple cases are often used to provide a series of match conditions to trigger a certain response, as in

```
case '1':
case '2':
case '3':
case '4':
  cout <<"digit in range 1 - 4";
  break;
```

This example outputs its message if the input matches any number from 1 through 4.

The *break* Statement

You use the break statement to break out of the current flow of execution and resume after the end of the switch statement. Listing 4.1 in the preceding section shows how you use break at the end of each of the cases. If you don't insert break at the appropriate points, the program flows to the next group of statements after the next case. In other words, if you write your case statement like the following, your output will not be what you might expect:

```
case 'L': case 'l':
  cout << "You selected Load file." << endl;
case 'S': case 's':
  cout << "You selected Save file."  << endl;
case 'E': case 'e':
  cout << "You selected Edit file." << endl;
case 'P': case 'p':
  cout << "You selected Print file." << endl;
case 'X': case 'x':
  cout << "You selected Exit program." << endl;
```

If you press L, the first case is matched, but instead of seeing

```
You selected Load file.
```

on your display, you see instead

```
You selected Load file.
You selected Save file.
You selected Edit file.
You selected Print file.
You selected Exit program.
```

This erroneous output occurs if you omit the break statement after each case. Program control flows from one case into the next and does not stop until reaching the last case. This mistake is easy to make, so keep in mind the necessity of placing a break after each statement or block inside the switch statement.

Looping Statements

When a section of code must be executed many times, you should use one of the C++ looping statements. The looping statements cause a statement or block of statements to execute repeatedly until some stopping condition is met. You saw many examples of the for loop in the first three chapters. The following sections provide additional details on the use of the for loop and present the while and do-while loops.

The *for* loop

You use the for loop to repeat a section of code a specific number of times. The for loop, as you've already seen, uses a loop control variable to control the number of iterations through the loop. The general form of the for loop is

```
for ( initial-condition; ending-condition; increment )
   statement or block to repeatedly execute;
```

For example, to execute a single statement exactly 10 times, you write

```
for ( counter = 1; counter <= 10; counter++ )
   cout << counter << endl;
```

This example initializes counter to 1, checks that counter is still less than or equal to 10, and then executes the single statement to output the value of counter. Then counter is incremented and compared to 10. If counter is still less than or equal to 10, the loop repeats until the ending condition is satisfied.

To execute a block of statements 10 times, enclose the group of statements within braces ({ }):

```
for ( counter=1; counter <= 10; counter++ )
{
   cout << "The value of counter is " << counter << endl;
   cout << "counter * 10 = " << (counter * 10) << endl;
}
```

Figure 4.1 shows the steps going on in a for loop by translating it into its pseudocode equivalent. Before the for loop executes, the counter=1 assignment is made before any other statements within the loop are executed. Indeed, when the compiler translates the for loop into machine instructions, it places the initialization code outside the for loop altogether.

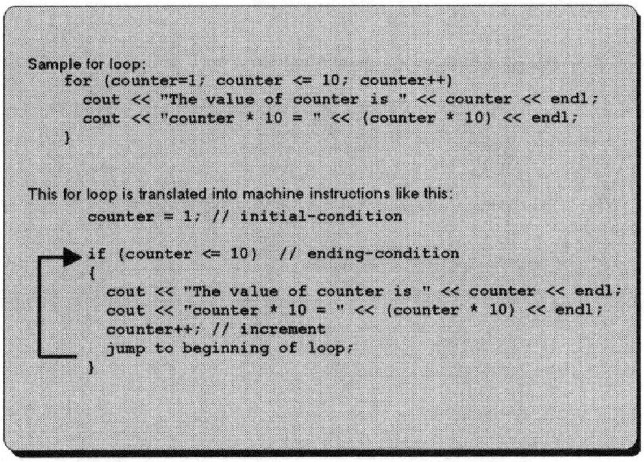

```
Sample for loop:
   for (counter=1; counter <= 10; counter++)
      cout << "The value of counter is " << counter << endl;
      cout << "counter * 10 = " << (counter * 10) << endl;
   }

This for loop is translated into machine instructions like this:
   counter = 1; // initial-condition

   if (counter <= 10)  // ending-condition
   {
      cout << "The value of counter is " << counter << endl;
      cout << "counter * 10 = " << (counter * 10) << endl;
      counter++; // increment
      jump to beginning of loop;
   }
```

Fig. 4.1
When the compiler translates the for loop, this sequence of instructions results.

Next, the `for` loop checks whether the `ending-condition` is True. If it is False, the program jumps around the body of the loop and does not execute any of the enclosed statements. If the `ending-condition` is True, the loop executes one iteration. Then the control variable is incremented, and the program jumps back to the `ending-condition` test and repeats the cycle.

A `for` loop can also decrement its control variable, producing a `for` loop that counts down rather than up. Be sure to set the initial condition to a value larger than the `ending-condition`, as shown in the following example, which counts down from 10 to 1:

```
for ( counter=10; counter >= 1; counter-- )
{
    cout << "The value of counter is " << counter << endl;
    cout << "counter * 10 = " << (counter * 10) << endl;
}
```

After the loop finishes executing, what is the value of the `counter` variable? In Visual C++, when the loop terminates, `counter` is left with the value of 0. Although you can use the value of the control variable outside the loop, doing so is usually considered bad programming practice because the value may not always be what you expect. Depending on the specific compiler you use (such as some compilers other than Visual C++) and depending on the compiler options you have selected, the value could be different. For this reason, you should not rely on the value of the loop control variable outside the scope of the `for` loop. If you must have access to the last value, save the value to a temporary variable, as in the following lines:

```
for ( counter=1; counter <= 10; counter++ )
{
    cout << "The value of counter is " << counter << endl;
    cout << "counter * 10 = " << (counter * 10) << endl;
    saved_value = counter;
}
// Okay to use saved_value here.
```

Defining the Control Variable within the *for* Loop. You can use a special feature of C++ to define the control loop variable within the `for` loop. Such a declaration looks like this:

```
for ( int counter=1; counter <= 10; counter++ )
{
    cout << "The value of counter is " << counter << endl;
    cout << "counter * 10 = " << (counter * 10) << endl;
}
```

By placing the `int` data type in front of `counter`, you declare and initialize `counter` as part of the `for` loop. The declaration of `counter` remains in effect for the rest of the function in which this `for` loop appears.

Note

The definition of the C++ language is evolving; the treatment of variables defined within a `for` loop might change in future editions of C++. In future versions of C++, `counter` may become a variable that is local to the `for` loop, and any attempt to use `counter` outside the `for` loop will result in an error message stating that `counter` is undeclared. By making the `for` loop variable local, the problems associated with using a control variable outside the loop are eliminated.

Using the *char* Type as a Loop Control Variable. Because the `char` data type is a subset of the `int` data type, you can use `char` variables as control values. For example, to display the alphabet, you can write the following:

```
for (char alpha='A'; alpha <= 'Z'; alpha++ )
    cout << alpha;
cout << endl;
```

Using Complicated Expressions for the Increment. The increment expression of a `for` loop need not be simple addition or subtraction. You can use any expression that makes sense for the problem you are solving. To print the values 1, 2, 4, 8, 16, 32, and 64, use `i*=2` for the increment. This expression results in the following `for` loop:

```
for (i=1; i<100; i*=2)
    cout << i << " ";
```

Leaving Out Parts of the *for* Loop. Each part of the `for` loop—the *initial-condition*, the *ending-condition*, and the *increment*—is optional. You can omit the control sections if that is appropriate for your program. For example, the following `for` loop increments the control loop variable independently from the looping mechanism:

```
for (int i=0; i < 10;) i++;
```

If you do omit a portion of the loop control section, you must still include the semicolon (;), as in this example:

```
int i=0;
for ( ; i<10; i++) ...
```

Two Examples of Using a *for* Loop. Two examples that use the for loop are shown in listings 4.2 and 4.3. The program in listing 4.2 uses the for loop to iterate an expansion of the Maclaurin series (a topic you may have learned in a calculus course) to calculate the value of e^x. The program in listing 4.3 demonstrates how you can place more than one control variable inside a for loop.

Listing 4.2 Using a *for* Loop to Calculate a Mathematical Function

```
1   // FORLOOP2.CPP
2   // Uses a for loop to calculate the value of
3   // e to x'th power using the Maclaurin series:
4   //
5   //   x              2    3
6   // e = 1 + x + x  + x  + ...
7   //             --   --
8   //             2!   3!
9   //
10
11  #include <iostream.h>
12
13  void main(void) {
14    int n;                 // for loop control variable.
15    float e_to_x;          // Accumulates the value of e.
16    float x = 1;           // Set x=1 for calculating e.
17    float x_to_nth;        // Tracks x to the nth power.
18    float factor = 2;      // Used to compute the factorial.
19    float factorial = 2;   // Equals factor!
20
21    // Let e_to_x accumulate the result. Initialize e_to_x
22    // to the first two terms of the Maclaurin series.
23    e_to_x = 1 + x;
24
25    //                          n
26    // Let x_to_nth accumulate x  value.
27    x_to_nth = x * x; // Initialize to x squared.
28
29    // Expand the Maclaurin series out 9 terms.
30    for (n=1; n<10; n++ )
31    {
32      // Add the next factor.
33      e_to_x = e_to_x + x_to_nth / factorial;
34
35      //            n
36      // Calculate x  by simple multiplication.
37      x_to_nth = x_to_nth * x;
38
39      // Calculate factorial divisor by simple
40      // multiplication.
41      factor = factor + 1;
42      factorial = factorial * factor;
43    }
44
```

```
45    cout << "e to the " << x << "th power is=" << e_to_x << endl;
46
47    cout << "Press Enter to continue.";
48    cin.get();
49 } // main
```

The Maclaurin series calculates the value of e^x by using an infinite power series. Note the following equation:

$$e^x = \sum \frac{x^n}{n!} = 1 + x + \frac{x^2}{2!} + \frac{x^3}{3!} + \dots \text{ for all } x$$

As you can see from this equation, the calculation of e^x is an iterative calculation, where the value of n ranges from 0 to infinity. This formula is implemented in C++ by using a `for` loop and several variables to simplify the calculation of x^n and $n!$. Within the `for` loop (lines 30 through 43), each term in the series expansion is added to the variable e_to_x so that e_to_x accumulates the sum of all the terms. This series converges rapidly, so it is not necessary to iterate a large number of terms of the series. Hence, the stopping condition is set to `n < 10`. Each time through the loop, the variables x_to_nth, factor, and factorial are used to calculate x^n and $n!$.

Listing 4.3 Using the Comma Operator to Include More Than One Control Variable in a *for* Loop

```
 1  // FORLOOP3.CPP
 2  // Demonstrates use of the comma operator to
 3  // provide two control variables inside a for loop.
 4  // This program takes string alpha1 and copies the
 5  // string to alpha2 so that the characters in alpha2
 6  // are reversed from those in alpha1. In other words,
 7  // if alpha1 = "ABCDEFGHIJKLMNOPQRSTUVWXYZ", then after
 8  // this program runs, alpha2 = "ZYXWVUTSRQPONMLKJIHGFEDCBA".
 9
10  #include <iostream.h>
11  #include <string.h>
12
13  void main(void) {
14    int n,m;                 // for loop control variables.
15    char alpha1[27] = "ABCDEFGHIJKLMNOPQRSTUVWXYZ";
16    char alpha2[27];
17
18    // Note the use of two control variables. m indexes
19    // alpha1 from the end of the string back down to 0
20    // while n indexes alpha2 from 0 up to the string length.
21    for (n=0, m=strlen(alpha1)-1; n < strlen(alpha1); n++, m--)
22      alpha2[n] = alpha1[m];
23    // Set the last byte of alpha2 to a null terminator.
24    alpha2[strlen(alpha1)] = '\0';
25
```

(continues)

Listing 4.3 Continued

```
26    // Display the result.
27    cout << "Alpha1=" << alpha1 << endl
28         << "Alpha2=" << alpha2 << endl;
29    cout << "Press Enter to continue.";
30    cin.get();
31  } // main
```

Normally, you use just one control variable inside a for loop. But sometimes it is convenient to use more than one control variable. By using the comma operator (see the section "The Comma Operator" in Chapter 2, "C++ Data Types and Expressions"), you can place two or more expressions in any part of the for loop control expressions. The for loop in lines 21 and 22 uses two control variables, n and m, to copy alpha1 and simultaneously reverse the order of the characters into alpha2. Variable n counts up from 0 while m counts down from the length of the string. Line 22 assigns alpha1[m] to alpha2[n].

As the loop begins execution, n = 0 and m = 25. An assignment is made from alpha1[25] to alpha2[0]. This sets alpha2[0] to the letter Z. n is incremented to 1, and m is decremented to 24. Then alpha2[1] is set to alpha1[24], or Y. This process continues until n reaches the length of alpha1 and the loop terminates. Line 24 sets the last byte of alpha2 to the null character so that alpha2 is properly terminated with a zero byte.

The use of the comma operator is fairly rare in C++ programming. Principally, you use it when you need to use two control variables in a for loop, as in listing 4.3. Remember that the comma operator causes the expressions to be evaluated from left to right. If you use the comma operator within the *ending-condition* part of the for loop, the overall expression value is the value of the rightmost expression. In other words, if you add the test for m == 5 into the *ending-condition*, as in

```
for (n=0, m=strlen(alpha1)-1; m == 5, n < strlen(alpha1); n++, m--)
```

the *ending-condition* is still determined by the value of n < strlen(alpha1), not whether m == 5. This is true because the value of the overall expression

```
m == 5, n < strlen(alpha1)
```

is the value of the rightmost expression, or n < strlen(alpha1).

The *break* Statement as a Loop Exit

Earlier in the chapter, you learned how to use the break statement to break out of a switch statement. You can also use break to make an immediate exit from a for loop. When you use break in this manner, the loop terminates immediately, and the program resumes executing at the first statement after the end of the for loop. The program in listing 4.4 would normally display the numbers 0 to 99 on the computer's monitor. However, because of the conditional statement in line 12, the for loop is terminated as soon as n reaches 50.

You can use the break statement in any of the C++ looping statements, including the while and do-while loops.

Listing 4.4 Using the *break* Statement within a *for* Loop

```
1   // BREAK1.CPP
2   // Uses the break to terminate a for loop
3   // prematurely.
4   #include <iostream.h>
5
6   void main(void) {
7     int n;
8
9     for (n = 0; n < 100; n++ )
10    {
11      cout << n << " ";
12      if (n == 50) break;
13    }
14
15    cout << "Press Enter to continue.";
16    cin.get();
17  } // main
```

The break statement suspends execution of the current loop only. This means that if you have a for loop inside another for loop, a break inside the inner loop terminates only the inner loop. Run the program in listing 4.5 to see how this approach works.

Listing 4.5 Using *break* inside a Nested *for* Loop

```
1   // BREAK2.CPP
2   // Demonstrates that the break only breaks out of
3   // the current for loop. When for loops are nested
4   // within one another, a break in the innermost loop
5   // only breaks out of the innermost loop.
6   #include <iostream.h>
7
8   void main(void) {
9     int n;
10
11    for (m = 0; m < 5; m++ )
```

(continues)

Listing 4.5 Continued

```
12      for (n = 0; n < 100; n++ )
13      {
14        cout << n;
15        if (n == 50) break;
16      }
17
18      cout << "Press Enter to continue.";
19      cin.get();
20    } // main
```

The *continue* Statement

The continue statement is similar to break, except that continue does not jump outside the loop; it merely jumps to the end of the loop. This way, a continue statement is used to begin the next iteration of the loop immediately. You can use continue with the for, while, and do-while loops. Listing 4.6 shows how you might use the continue statement in a program.

Listing 4.6 Using the *continue* Statement

```
 1   // CONTINUE.CPP
 2   #include <iostream.h>
 3   #include <string.h>
 4
 5   void main(void) {
 6     int index;
 7     char alpha[27] = "abcdefghijklmnopqrstuvwxyz";
 8
 9     cout << "Before conversion:  " << alpha << endl;
10
11     for (index = 0; index < strlen(alpha); index++ )
12       {
13         if (alpha[index] < 'a') continue; // To next iteration.
14         // If we reach here, alpha[index] must be a
15         // lowercase letter. Convert it to uppercase.
16         alpha[index] -= 32;
17         // Internally, characters are stored as ASCII values
18         // (see Appendix A). The lowercase letters are
19         // exactly 32 higher than their uppercase counterparts.
20         // By subtracting 32, a lowercase value is converted
21         // to uppercase.
22       }
23
24     cout << "After conversion:  " << alpha << endl;
25
26     cout << "Press Enter to continue.";
27     cin.get();
28   } // main
```

The *while* Loop

Use the `for` loop when you must repeatedly execute a section of code a specific number of times. In other situations, however, you may need to execute a code section over and over until a condition changes. The `while` loop executes a statement or block as long as its controlling expression is True. The general form for the `while` loop is

```
while (expression)
  statement or block;
```

If *expression* is nonzero, the *statement* or *block* of statements is executed. When *expression* becomes zero, the `while` loop terminates, and the program resumes processing at the first statement beyond the loop.

The following is an example of a `while` loop that repeats a single C++ statement:

```
int i=1;
while (i < 10)
  cout << i++ << endl;
```

Because the ++ increment operator is used within the `cout` insertion, there is no need, in this example, to increment `i` in a separate statement.

Here is an example of a `while` loop that repeats the execution of a block of C++ statements:

```
char keystroke = '1';
int i = 0;
while ( keystroke == '1' )
{
  cout << i++ << endl;
  cout << "Press 1 to continue or 2 to stop.";
  cin.get(keystroke);
  cin.ignore(1);
}
```

The `while` statement is well suited for many tasks. One such task is processing input from the keyboard, as shown in the preceding example. In many applications, you may want the program to prompt the user repeatedly until the user enters a value to terminate the program. Listing 4.7 shows a program that sums an arbitrary sequence of numbers entered at the keyboard. The `while` statement is used to repeatedly prompt, input, and process the entered value until a terminating value is typed.

Listing 4.7 Using the *while* Loop to Process User Input

```
1   // WHILE.CPP
2   // Demonstrates use of the while loop.
3   #include <iostream.h>
4
5   void main(void) {
6     float input_value = 1;
7     float sum = 0;
8
9     cout << "Accepts any number of values as input ";
10    cout << "and sums the values." << endl << endl;
11    cout << "Enter 0.0 to quit program." << endl << endl;
12    while (input_value != 0.0)
13    {
14      cout << "Enter value (0.0 to quit):  ";
15      cin >> input_value;
16      cin.ignore(1); // Ignore trailing Enter key.
17      sum += input_value;
18      cout << "Total so far:  " << sum << endl;
19    } // end while
20
21    cout << "The sum of all values entered is:  " << sum
22        << endl << endl;
23
24    cout << "Press Enter to continue.";
25    cin.get();
26  } // main
```

The while statement in line 12 executes the block of statements in lines 13 to 19 as long as input_value is not equal to zero. For the loop to operate the very first time, you must initialize input_value to a nonzero value, as in line 6.

Lines 14 through 16 prompt and input the next value to add to the accumulating sum variable. You must enter a value of 0 to terminate the loop; otherwise, the program continues to prompt for a new value to add to sum.

Another common use for the while statement is to process data from a disk file. This use is similar to that of the keyboard input program in listing 4.7 except that the input values are read from a disk file. In this form, the while statement terminates file reading when the end of file is reached. You learn how to use disk files in Chapter 11, "C++ Input and Output."

An important consideration when writing a while loop (or its cousin, the do-while) is to identify the proper values to place in the loop's controlling expression. In some instances, you use a simple relational test, as in line 12 of listing 4.7. In many other applications, you can use the while to test the value of flag variables. For example, if `error_occurred` and `end_of_file` are flag variables having values of 0 or 1, you might write the following:

```
while ( !error_occurred || !end_of_file ) { ... }
```

As long as no errors occur and the end-of-file flag is not set, the loop continues to execute. If a problem arises, you can add code inside the loop to set the `error_occurred` flag. Or you can use the `break` statement to escape out of the loop.

When you use the `while` loop, sooner or later you will encounter a frequent programming problem: the *infinite loop*. An infinite loop is one that never terminates. Failure to terminate is caused when the condition that is tested never becomes False, so the `while` loop repeatedly executes its statement block forever. If you want to see an infinite loop, you can type the following short section of code:

```
while (1) cout << "You'll never stop me!" << endl;
```

Be forewarned that you must use the Exit command (Ctrl+C) from the QuickWin **F**ile menu to suspend your program. In some situations, you may have to reboot your computer.

The *do-while* Loop

The `do-while` loop is just like the `while` statement except that you place the stopping condition test at the end of the loop. The format for a `do-while` statement is

```
do
   statement or block;
while (expression);
```

You can use `do-while` with a single statement or with a group of statements. In the latter case, you should enclose the group of statements with a leading left brace ({) and a trailing right brace (}).

Because you place the conditional test at the end of the loop, the statement or block is always executed at least once. For the type of problem shown in listing 4.7's summation program, the `do-while` statement is a better choice than the `while` statement. By replacing the `while` statement with `do-while`, you no longer have to initialize `input_value` to a known value before entering the loop. The first input statement assigns a value to `input_value`. Listing 4.8 shows the `do-while` loop.

Listing 4.8 Using the *do-while* Loop

```
1  // DOWHILE1.CPP
2  // Demonstrates use of the do-while loop.
3  #include <iostream.h>
4
5  void main(void) {
6    float input_value;
7    float sum = 0;
8
9    cout << "Accepts any number of values as input ";
10   cout << "and sums the values." << endl << endl;
11   cout << "Enter 0.0 to quit program." << endl << endl;
12   do
13   {
14     cout << "Enter value (0.0 to quit):  ";
15     cin >> input_value;
16     cin.ignore(1); // Ignore trailing Enter key.
17     sum += input_value;
18     cout << "Total so far:  " << sum << endl;
19   } while (input_value != 0.0);
20
21   cout << "The sum of all values entered is:  " << sum
22       << endl << endl;
23
24   cout << "Press Enter to continue.";
25   cin.get();
26 } // main
```

Optimizing Loops

Because loops contain code that is executed repeatedly, programs tend to spend much of their time within the confines of the looping statements. Any improvements you make to the program statements inside a loop, even small ones, are magnified by the number of times that the loop gets executed. Therefore, if you want to optimize the performance of your program, you should pay particular attention to the code you place inside loops.

The key to making a loop run faster is to reduce the amount of code that must be executed. First identify calculations that do not change inside the loop; then move these calculations outside and assign them to a temporary variable for use inside the loop. For example, the for loop shown in the following code section performs a time-consuming trigonometric calculation during each execution through the loop:

```
for( item = 1; item <= MaxValues; item++ )
{
  X = 1.1 * Radius[item] * cos ( AngleInRadians );
  Y = - 1.1 * Radius[item] * sin ( AngleInRadians )*(Xasp/Yasp);
```

```
    EndX = X * 1.4;
    EndY = Y * 1.4;
    line (X, Y, EndX, EndY );
};
```

`cos()` and `sin()` are standard C++ library routines used to calculate the cosine and sine, respectively, of their parameter. `line()` is a library function that draws a line on the screen. By rewriting this code fragment, you can move the time-consuming calculation outside the loop and store it in a temporary variable. In many instances, the compiler's optimization features catch this type of duplicate code and create a temporary variable for you automatically, as in the following lines:

```
TempMultX = 1.1 * cos (AngleInRadians);
TempMultY = 1.1 * sin(AngleInRadians) * (Xasp/Yasp);
for( item = 1; item <= MaxValues; item ++ )
{
  X = TempMultX * Radius[Radius];
  Y = - TempMultY * Radius[Radius]
  EndX = X * 1.4;
  EndY = Y * 1.4;
  line (X, Y, EndX, EndY );
};
```

You should also identify duplicate calculations appearing inside loops. Avoid repeated calculations of values that you can place in a temporary location. Consider the following statement, which calls a function named `copy()`:

```
if  ((EndPos-StartPos+1) < MaxAllowed)
    copy( S, StartPos, EndPos-StartPos + 1 );
```

By rewriting this statement, you can eliminate the duplicate calculation of `EndPos-StartPos+1`:

```
amount = EndPos - StartPos + 1;
if  (amount < MaxAllowed)
    Copy( S, StartPos, amount );
```

In the conditional expression of the `while` and `do-while` loop, keep the number of items in the conditional expression to a minimum. If each iteration of the loop requires a time-consuming or complicated calculation to be evaluated as the test condition, overall execution of the loop will be slowed.

Using *goto* and Statement Labels

In this chapter, you've learned about using the `break` statement to escape out of a loop, and you've seen how to use a flag variable to control execution of a `while` or `do-while` loop. Each of these methods is well suited for terminating a simple loop. However, if your program must escape out of a deeply nested loop structure, you can use the `goto` statement to execute an immediate jump to a statement label location outside the loop.

> **Note**
>
> Most modern programming books explicitly forbid you from using the `goto` statement. The reason dates back to the early history of programming, when computer languages did not have `while` and `do-while` statements. To make a program repeat itself, you had to explicitly use a `goto` statement to cause the program to jump back to the beginning of a code section. Those early languages also lacked `if-else` statements; instead they used something akin to `if (expression) goto label` and then placed the conditionally executed statement after the label. Such frequent use of the `goto` statement produced what became known as "spaghetti code" for its likeness to a bowl of spaghetti. You never can find the start and end of a piece of spaghetti, can you?
>
> Because of the problems caused by spaghetti code, new programming structures, such as `if-else` and the looping statements, were created so that you no longer needed to use the `goto` statement. And because using the `goto` resulted in terribly complicated programs that were difficult to make run correctly, using the `goto` has since been strongly discouraged. However, in a few instances, using `goto` makes sense and causes little harm. These instances are described in this section.

A statement label is an identifier you place at the beginning of a line and is followed by a single colon (`:`). You use the `goto` keyword to redirect the program's execution to a label. Figure 4.2 shows how the `goto` statement redirects the flow of the program.

Fig. 4.2
How the `goto` statement redirects the flow of a program.

```
      ┌── goto handle_error;
      │   ...
      └─▶ handle_error:
              cout << "An error has occurred." << endl;
```

You can use any sequence of characters for a label, if the identifier you choose meets the same identifier requirements used by variables. This means that statement labels must begin with an alphabetic character or the underscore, followed by alphabetic, numeric, or underscore characters.

One place to use a `goto` statement is where your program must jump out of a series of nested loops. Consider a situation in which you have a series of nested loops, such as the following:

```
while (!end_of_file) {
  // Read input from file into month_summary.
  .
  .
  .
  index = 0;
  while (index <= strlen(month_summary)) {
    if ( month_summary[index] == '*' )
      goto abort_processing;
  } // while
} // while
.
.
.
abort_processing:
```

In this example, you use the goto statement to jump outside the scope of both loops to handle a special situation. You can use the goto to jump to any location within the current function. You cannot use a goto to jump to statements inside other functions, however.

Another place that it sometimes makes sense to use a goto is where you want to optimize certain while test expressions. Many programmers avoid using goto statements by setting a flag inside a while loop and then testing the flag in the while's expression. This is a perfectly reasonable way to create an exit from a loop; indeed, this approach is recommended. In some cases, however, the number of flags that must be checked in the while's expression can become exorbitant. For example, you can eliminate the goto statement in the preceding code segment by setting a flag variable. Use time_to_abort as the flag and set it to False (or 0) before entering the loop:

```
int time_to_abort = 0;
while (!end_of_file && !time_to_abort) {
  // Read input from file into month_summary.
  .
  .
  .
  index = 0;
  while (index <= strlen(month_summary) && !time_to_abort) {
    if ( month_summary[index] == '*' )
      time_to_abort = 1;
    else
    {
      // Process input.
      .
      .
      .
    } // if - else
  } // while
} // while
```

As you can see, you've eliminated the use of goto. However, two separate while loops must now test the value of time_to_abort. If this were a time-critical routine, you might not want to have those two extra tests performed each time through the loop. And if your routine had to test many flags (not just one or two), tracking down where each flag is set can be just as difficult and confusing as a plate of spaghetti code. Therefore, in a very few situations such as this, you may choose to use the goto statement to jump ahead to a single location inside the function. You should definitely avoid using goto to jump backward in your code, and you should try to restrict the goto's destination to a single location, such as error-processing code at the end of a function. By using if-else, the C++ looping statements, and flag variables, you should have little need for the goto statement in your programs.

Indiscriminate use of goto statements can result in programs that are hard to debug and difficult to understand. When you scan through a program that is laced with goto statements and statement labels, you'll find it very hard to follow the path the program follows during execution. When control jumps from place to place and sometimes back again, understanding what the program was meant to do becomes extraordinarily difficult. Therefore, as a general rule, you should avoid using the goto statement wherever you can use an alternative control structure, such as if-else or a while loop. By using the while (or do-while), you have no need to use a goto to repeat a section of code. And by using if-else, you rarely need to interrupt the flow of a program by jumping to other locations.

Summary

In this chapter, you learned the C++ selection statements (if and switch) and the three kinds of looping statements (for, while, and do-while). You also saw the few situations in which using a goto statement is useful to your programs.

Following is a summary of each of the statements introduced in this chapter:

■ The if statement executes selectively one or more statements in your program. The general form of the if statement is

```
if (expression)
    statement;
```

in which *statement* is executed only when *expression* is not equal to zero.

■ `if-else` selects between two courses of action. The general form of the
`if-else` statement is

```
if (expression)
  statement1;
else
  statement2;
```

statement1 is executed if *expression* is not equal to zero; *statement2* is
executed if *expression* is equal to zero.

■ `if-else if` selects from several courses of action. The format for the
`if-else if` statement is

```
if (expression1)
  statement1;
else if (expression2)
  statement2;
else if (expression3)
  statement3;
else statement4;
```

The `if-else if` is identical to the `if-else` statement except that additional test conditions are added at each `else if`.

■ The `switch` statement is used to select one course of action from many
possible options. The `switch` statement has the following format:

```
switch (test-expression)
{
  case constant-value1: statement or series-of-statements; break;
  case constant-value2: statement or series-of-statements; break;
  case constant-value3: statement or series-of-statements; break;
    .
    .
    .
  default: statement or series-of-statements;
}
```

■ The `for` loop provides an easy way to have your program repeatedly
execute a statement or group of statements a specified number of times.
The format of the `for` loop is

```
for (initial-condition; ending-condition; increment)
  statement or block;
```

■ The `while` loop repeatedly executes a section of code an unspecified
number of times. The loop repeats as long as a test expression evaluates
to True (or nonzero). The `while` statement has the following form:

```
while (test-expression is true)
    statement or block;
```

- Use do-while when the loop must execute at least once. The do-while does not test its controlling expression until the end of the loop, so it always runs through the loop code at least one time. The general form of the do-while statement is

```
do
    statement or block;
while (test-expression is true);
```

- You should use the goto statement sparingly. Using goto too much leads to "spaghetti code" that is difficult to debug and extremely difficult to modify.

Review Questions

1. Your program must decide between two courses of action. What is the best selection statement to make this decision?

2. As the result of an if statement, your program must execute a block of code. How do you specify that a group of statements, rather than an individual statement, should be executed?

3. Do you need to use a relational operator in every conditional expression used in if statements?

4. What value does the if statement consider to be a False condition?

5. What values are considered to be True conditions?

6. Can you specify another if statement as the *statement* part of an if or if-else statement?

7. Your program must decide on one course of action among many possible outcomes. What is the best selection statement to use for this type of problem?

8. When you use the switch statement, you can specify a large number of cases for selection. When C++ statements are executed for each case, what is the last statement that you should place before the next case keyword?

9. Your program must repeat a section of code exactly 100 times. What is the best loop statement to use for this purpose?

10. Your program must prompt for an input value, process the input, and decide whether another input value should be entered. This process must be repeated until the user enters a value to stop executing the program. What is the best loop statement to use for this purpose and why?

11. What are some simple steps that you can take to ensure that your loops run as fast as possible?

12. Name one or two reasons to use the goto statement. Identify reasons that the goto statement is neither needed nor used much in C++.

Exercises

1. Your program displays a menu containing five options: New test, Load test, Run test, Print test report, and Quit. The user selects a menu item by entering the first character of a command. Write a series of if-else if statements to process this input. Then write a switch statement to process the same commands.

2. Write a simple program to print out the values in a character string, character by character. Then modify the program to print the string in the reverse order.

3. Write a program to produce the arithmetic mean of a set of input values. In addition to tracking the sum of the values entered, you must count the total number of values that were typed. To compute the mean, divide the sum by the total number of values.

4. Modify the program in exercise 3 to calculate the standard deviation of the data. To perform this calculation, use the following formula:

$$s = \sqrt{\frac{n(\Sigma x^2) - (\Sigma x)^2}{n(n-1)}}$$

You can translate this statistical formula into C++ by writing a formula such as

```
s = sqrt( (n * sum_x_sqrd - mean*mean ) / (n * (n - 1) ));
```

in which

    s = calculated standard deviation

    n = total number of values entered

    sum_x_sqrd = sum of each individual value squared (in other words, square each value before adding to the sum)

    mean = calculated mean or average value

    `sqrt()` is a library function. To use this function, you must place `#include <math.h>` at the beginning of your program.

5. Write a program to calculate prime numbers from 3 to 500. Your program should print the list of prime values as

    3 5 7 11 13 17 23 ...

A simple way to calculate prime numbers is to set up a loop running from 3 to 500. Then test whether each number is prime by dividing the candidate number by every lower valued number but itself. For example, if the candidate number is 12, begin dividing by 3, then 4, and then 5. If there is no remainder (use the `%` remainder operator), the number is prime, and you don't need to make any additional division tests. Perform the division test inside a `while` loop. As soon as you determine that the number cannot be prime (because division produces no remainder), set a flag or use `break` to exit the `while` loop, and proceed to the next candidate number.

6. After writing the prime number program in exercise 5, modify the program, as described here, to improve its performance.

You know that all even numbers are divisible by 2. Therefore, in the loop from 3 to 500, test only odd values such as 3, 5, 7, 9, 11, 13, 15, and so on.

For the divisor test, you must test divisors only up to the square root of the candidate number. In other words, if you are testing the value 65, you need only test divisors of 3, 5, and 7.

Chapter 5

Pointers

Every time you declare a C++ variable, the compiler sets aside an area of memory to store the content of the variable. When you declare an int variable, for example, the compiler allocates two bytes of memory. The space for the variable is placed at a specific location in memory known as the variable's *memory address*. When you reference the value of the variable, the Visual C++ compiler automatically accesses the memory address where the integer is stored. You can also gain access to this memory address by using C++ *pointers*. A pointer is a variable that contains a memory address. By using pointers, your program can perform many tasks that are not possible using the standard data types.

The pointer is a type that is distinct from the int, char, float, and other types you learned about in Chapter 2, "C++ Data Types and Expressions." In this chapter, you learn about the following:

- Memory addresses

- The declaration and initialization of pointer variables

- The use of pointers

- Dynamic memory allocation

- The creation of complex data structures

- The differences among near, far, and huge pointers

Many new C++ programmers find that pointers are a confusing subject. Indeed, many intermediate and advanced programmers get confused with pointer operations. But pointers are essential to the creation of advanced programs that work with complex organizations of data. You also find pointers at work when you begin to use object-oriented class libraries to speed up your application development. To exploit fully C++'s object-oriented programming capabilities, you must understand pointers.

Understanding the Pointer

Every variable that you declare in C++ has an address associated with it. You can find out what the address is by using the C++ address-of operator (&). Normally, you use this operator with a pointer variable and assign the address to a pointer. The following code section declares a pointer variable p and assigns to it the address of the character variable named alpha:

```
char * p;
char alpha = 'A';
p = &alpha;
```

The first line, char * p;, declares p to be a pointer to a char. The * symbol tells the compiler that p is not a char but is instead a pointer to a char, as figure 5.1 illustrates. p's value is the memory address of alpha (or 100, as shown in fig. 5.1). You can access the value at the address to which p points by using * as a dereferencing or indirection operator. Therefore, while p stores an address, *p is the value located at the address.

> **Note**
>
> The & operator is also the bitwise AND operator. The * operator is also the multiplication operator. The compiler determines which operator to use, depending on the context in which it appears.

Fig. 5.1
p's value is the address of alpha; *p is the value stored at alpha.

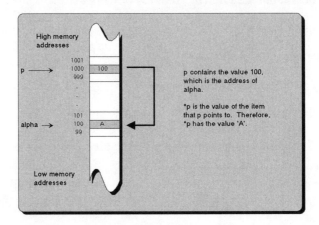

Study this concept carefully. p is a variable whose value is the memory address of another variable (or other location in memory). *p uses the address as a pointer to that memory location and returns the value stored at that location.

Using a Pointer

Pointers have many uses in C++ programming, including the following:

- Implementing complex data structures whose data elements are linked to other data elements

- Allocating space for variables dynamically (while the program is running, rather than at compile time)

- Assisting in passing parameters to functions

- Substituting for array indexes to speed up the processing of data in arrays

This chapter discusses each of these topics (except for passing parameters by using pointers, which is described in Chapter 6, "Functions and Macros").

Using the *NULL* Pointer

Normally, a properly initialized pointer points to some location in memory. However, an uninitialized pointer, like any variable, has a random value until the pointer is initialized. Using an uninitialized pointer can result in your program failing to execute, hang your computer, or even result in loss of data. For this reason, you must use caution when working with pointer variables to ensure that the pointers you use store valid memory addresses.

You can emphasize that a pointer does not currently have a valid pointer address by assigning the value NULL to the pointer. Note this example:

```
char *p = NULL;
```

Some C++ functions also return the NULL value if they encounter an error. You can add tests for the NULL value by comparing the pointer to NULL, as in

```
if ( p == NULL ) ...
```

or

```
if ( p != NULL) ...
```

Using a Pointer to an Array

To begin exploring the pointer, consider how you can use a pointer in place of an array index. The following redefines the variable `alpha` to be a character string holding the 26 letters of the alphabet:

```
char alpha[27] = "ABCDEFGHIJKLMNOPQRSTUVWXYZ";
```

Again, p is a pointer to a `char`:

```
char * p;
```

You set p to point to the first character element of `alpha` by writing

```
p = &alpha[0];
```

If you write

```
cout << *p << endl;
```

the letter A is displayed because p points to the first element of the string. Try this example using the Visual C++ compiler and verify that this is true.

Note

p points to a `char`. Therefore, you can set p to the address of an individual element of `alpha`, because `alpha` is an array of `char`. For example, you also can write

```
p = &alpha[12];
```

so that p points to the 13th character in `alpha` (the letter M). However, you cannot set p = &alpha. `alpha` is an array whose elements are of type `char`. Therefore, because p is a pointer to type `char`, p may point to elements of `alpha`. p is not a pointer to an array but to the individual character, so if you try to write

```
p = &alpha;
```

the compiler issues an error. (If you doubt this, try it.)

Performing Arithmetic on a Pointer

Even though p is a pointer, you can perform addition and subtraction on pointers. An addition operation effectively moves the pointer so that it points to a new address. For example, if p currently points to the letter A in string `alpha`, if you write

```
p = p + 1;
```

p now points to the letter B in string alpha. You can use this technique to scan each element of the string alpha without using an index variable. Here is an example:

```
p = &alpha[0];
for (i = 0; i < strlen(alpha); i++ )
{
  cout << *p << endl;
  p = p + 1;
};
```

This example uses p to point incrementally to each character in the character array alpha. This type of operation is so common that C++ programmers combine the indirection operator (*) with the increment operator, resulting in the following:

```
for (i = 0; i < strlen(alpha); i++ )
  cout << *p++ << endl;
```

In this form, the value that p points to is fetched and written to the output stream, and then p is incremented to point to the next character. In figure 5.2, you can see how p is incremented at each character position to point to the next character in sequence.

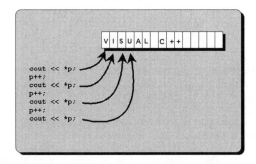

Fig. 5.2
*p++ is used to access incrementally each character in the string.

A Shortcut

You can shorten this example to scan across a string by taking advantage of the null terminator at the end of the string. Use the while statement to loop through each character until reaching the null or zero byte at the end of the string. This eliminates the need for the for loop and its control variable. The result is this section of code:

```
while (*p) cout << *p++ << endl;
```

As long as *p has a nonzero character value, the while loop executes, the character is printed, and p is incremented to point to the next character. On reaching the zero byte at the end of the string, *p has the value of '\0', or zero. The zero value causes the while loop to terminate. There is not much you can do to make this while loop more efficient.

Listing 5.1 shows a program that uses a pointer to scan across a character string and convert any lowercase characters to uppercase characters. The conversion of the entire string occurs in lines 19 and 22.

Listing 5.1 A Program That Uses a Pointer in the Conversion of Lowercase Characters to Uppercase

```
1   // PTR-LC.CPP
2   // Uses a pointer to index a character array and
3   // convert lowercase characters in the character
4   // array to uppercase.
5   #include <iostream.h>
6
7   void main(void)
8   {
9     char *p;
10    char TextString[80];
11
12    cout << "Enter string to convert:   ";
13    cin.getline( TextString, sizeof(TextString) );
14
15    // Set p to point at first character of the string.
16    p = &TextString[0];
17
18    // Loop until *p points to a zero byte.
19    while (*p)
20        // Use the conditional statement to subtract 32
21        // from lowercase letters 'a' to 'z'.
22        if ((*p >= 'a') && (*p <= 'z')) *p++ = *p-32; else p++;
23        // Because the = assignment operator has the lowest
24        // precedence, the assignment to *p is performed last.
25        // For this reason, it's okay to place *p++ to the left
26        // of the assignment. This causes p to be incremented
27        // after evaluating the expression to the right of =,
28        // and after assigning the new value to *p.
29
30    cout << "The converted string is:" << endl;
31    cout << TextString << endl;
32
33    cout << "Press Enter to continue.";
34    cin.get();
35  } // main
```

Line 16 initializes p to point to the first character in the string. Line 19 is the start of the while loop, which executes until encountering the zero byte at the end of the string. In line 22, an if() statement determines whether the character falls between `'a'` to `'z'`. If the character is a lowercase character, the assignment

```
*p++ = *p - 32;
```

is executed. Subtracting 32 from a lowercase ASCII code converts the lower-case letter to uppercase.

p is incremented as part of the assignment so that p points to the next charac-ter in the string. You may find this confusing because it looks like p is incremented before evaluating the assignment statement. Fortunately, this is not the case. The C++ compiler evaluates the expression to the right of the assignment operator = first. Therefore, where *p is used to the right of the = operator, *p points to the current character. Only after computing the result of the conditional expression does the compiler look to the left of the = assignment operator. In the case where the character is already an uppercase letter, p is incremented to point to the next character; no conversion is necessary.

Using a Pointer to Speed Up Array Access

Using a pointer in place of an array index can result in more efficient code for two reasons:

- The code you write is shorter. For example, if you use a `while` loop and a pointer to scan through a null-terminated string, as the preceding section demonstrated, the variable i is eliminated entirely, and fewer operations are performed to access the string character by character.

- You eliminate the internal calculations that the computer must perform to convert an array index into a memory position. Therefore, using a pointer is faster than using an array index.

In C++, providing access to arrays through a pointer makes perfect sense, especially because of its efficiency. You can use the pointer type for all types of arrays, including arrays of `int`, `float`, and other types you learn about later in this chapter. Whenever your program must sequentially access the ele-ments of an array, your program is more efficient if it uses a pointer instead of indexing by using the brackets (`[]`) as in the example `MyArray[count]`. Therefore, where it makes sense in your programs, use pointers for maximum efficiency.

Pointer Arithmetic

When you perform arithmetic on the pointer, the amount you add to (or subtract from) a pointer adjusts the address stored in the pointer. The amount of adjustment is determined by what the pointer points to. When the pointer is used to index the char type, the statement

```
p = p + 1;
```

increments p by 1 byte to point to the next character. However, if p points to a type that is not 1 byte, such as the integer

```
int *p;
```

then the statement

```
p = p + 1;
```

increments p by 2 bytes, not 1, because integers are 2 bytes in size. When you perform arithmetic on a pointer, the pointer is adjusted to point to the next element of the given type. To clarify this point, consider the following section of code:

```
float *fp;
float Revenue[12];
 .

 .

 .
fp = &Revenue[0];
cout << *fp++ << endl;
```

After execution of

```
*fp++;
```

fp points to Revenue[1], whose address is 4 bytes away, because floats are 4 bytes in size.

The only type of arithmetic that you can perform on a pointer is addition or subtraction. You can use either the + or - binary arithmetic operator, or the ++ increment or -- decrement unary operator. You cannot, however, add a pointer to a pointer.

Setting One Pointer Equal to Another

You can also assign one pointer to another, although you must use caution when doing so, for reasons explained in the next section, "Dynamic Memory Allocation." Consider the following code:

```
float *fp1;
float *fp2;
float Revenue[12];
```

```
        .
        .
        .
    fp1 = &Revenue[0];
    fp2 = fp1;
    cout << *fp2++ << endl;
```

This code sets fp1 to point to the first element of the Revenue array. fp2 is then set equal to fp1. This means that the address stored in fp1 is copied to fp2. Both pointers now point to the same location, which in this example is Revenue[0]. When you dereference *fp2, you obtain the same value as when you dereference *fp1. (Remember that to dereference a pointer means to trace the address stored in the pointer to reach the item that is stored at that address.)

Note that after executing the output statement, fp2 points to the second element of the Revenue array, and fp1 still points to the first element (see fig. 5.3). Using a pointer assignment to save the location of a pointer is a particularly good use of the pointer assignment statement.

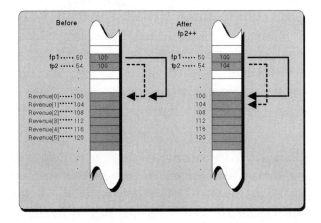

Fig. 5.3
After fp2 is incremented, fp1 and fp2 no longer point to the same element of the Revenue array.

Dynamic Memory Allocation

The variables you have declared in your programs had their memory space set aside by the compiler (in the case of global variables) or in a special memory area called the *stack* (in the case of local variables). For global and local variables, you had to tell the compiler exactly how many variables to allocate. But you can easily imagine problems in which you do not know how much memory to allocate before the program executes.

Consider a program to evaluate student test scores. This program stores each of the student scores in an array. The size of the array must be large enough to accommodate the largest class of students. If the class size increases, you must be able to modify and recompile the program. For this type of problem, you can create a more versatile program by using pointers and *dynamic memory allocation*.

A dynamically allocated variable's space is created during the program's execution (unlike a global variable's space, which is set aside at compile time). Dynamic memory allocation gives you direct control of your program's memory requirements. The program can create or destroy the dynamic allocation at any time during program execution. You can determine the amount of memory needed at the time the allocation is made. Depending on the memory model in use, you can also create variables larger than 64K.

As your program runs, areas of memory are set aside for the program to use. Compiled program code is placed in memory segments called *code segments*. The program's data, such as global variables, is placed in an area called the *data segment*. Local variables and program control information (needed to keep track of function calls) are placed in an area called the *stack*. The memory that remains is called *heap memory* (as if all the remaining memory were thrown into a big heap). When the program requests memory for a dynamic variable, the desired memory space is allocated from the heap.

The Heap

As your program runs, its memory layout might look like that shown in figure 5.4. The exact layout differs somewhat depending on the memory model the program uses. For large data models, the heap refers to the area of memory existing beyond the program's stack and running up to the top of available memory. The heap is essentially all the memory remaining after the program is loaded. When you request a dynamic memory allocation, the Visual C++ memory management system, which operates transparently behind the scenes, carves out a chunk of memory from the heap and returns a pointer to the memory block.

The *new* Operator

To request an allocation of memory from the heap, use the C++ new operator. new has the form

```
pointer = new typename (optional-initializer);
```

where *typename* is a C++ data type or `typedef` name, and *optional-initializer*
is an optional initial value for the allocation. The following example uses `new`
to allocate space for an integer quantity:

```
int *pInt;
.
.
.
pInt = new int;
```

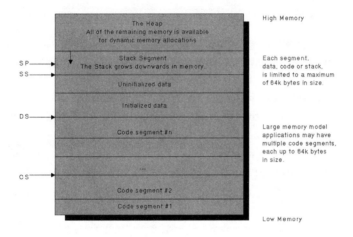

Fig. 5.4
The memory
layout of a large
model program.

This call to `new` allocates space for an `int` (two bytes) and stores the address of
the allocation in `pInt`. `pInt` now points to the location in the heap where
memory is set aside. Figure 5.5 shows how `pInt` points to the allocation in the
heap.

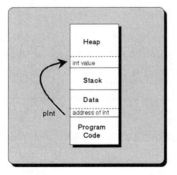

Fig. 5.5
After using `new`
to allocate an
integer variable,
`pInt` points to
the location in
the heap where
space has been
allocated for the
integer.

You use the allocation the same way you would access any other variable
through a pointer. To assign the value 750 to the allocated variable, write

```
*pInt = 750;
```

This places the value 750 in the allocated area in the heap. You can use this variable in statements and arithmetic expressions like this:

```
cin   *pInt;
sum = sum + *pInt;
```

The *delete* Operator

When you no longer need the allocation, you can discard the memory space by using the C++ delete operator, as in the following example:

```
delete pInt;
```

You must always delete a dynamic allocation when the allocation is no longer used. If you forget to discard the memory used by the allocation, the memory remains locked up and unavailable for other purposes in your program. If your pointer is declared local to a function and you forget to deallocate the memory block, you lose your ability to discard the allocation when you exit the function. This occurs because a local pointer variable is discarded when the function terminates. Without access to the pointer variable, you cannot discard the now unneeded memory allocation. Over time, the program may slowly eat its way through the heap memory and then suddenly die of memory starvation. Always make certain that you properly discard your memory allocations when you no longer need them.

To avoid accidentally writing data to the old memory address, you should also set pInt equal to NULL after deleting the memory to which it was pointing.

Examples That Use *new* and *delete*

You can use the new operator with any data type, including char, int, float, arrays, structures, and typedef identifiers. Using new is particularly convenient for arrays. Consider a character string formed by an array of char. By using new, you can create a pointer to a variable length array so that you can adjust the amount of memory needed for the text string during the program's execution.

First consider the allocation of a simple 80-byte character string. Create a pointer to a char, like this:

```
char *p;
```

To allocate the character string, write

```
p = new char[80];
```

The C++ memory management system reserves 80 bytes of memory for the char array, and the address of the allocation is stored in p. Listing 5.2 is a complete program that implements this dynamic allocation.

Listing 5.2 An Example of a Dynamically Allocated Array of *char*

```
1   // CHAR80.CPP
2   // Demonstrates dynamic allocation of a character string.
3   #include <iostream.h>
4   #include <string.h>
5
6   void main(void)
7   {
8     char *p;
9
10    p = new char[80];
11
12    strcpy( p, "I am a character string allocated using"
                  " the new operator." );
13
14    cout << p << endl;
15
16    delete p;
17
18    cout << "Press Enter to continue.";
19    cin.get();
20  } // main
```

In line 12, a string constant is copied to the allocated string. When a string constant does not fit on a single line, you can break the constant into multiple lines, as shown in line 12. The compiler stitches the individual string constants together into a single long string. Note that the first parameter to strcpy() is p and not *p. strcpy() copies its rightmost parameter to the address specified on the left. The value of p is the address that strcpy() needs for the copy destination; *p is the value stored at that address. Similarly, line 14 displays the string to which p points. If you wrote *p in line 14, the cout insertion operator would think you meant a single char because *p's value is a single character. To enable the insertion operator to display the entire string, you must use the address of the string.

A neat feature of new is that you do not have to use a constant for the allocation size. By using a variable, you can adjust the size of the array's dimension as the program is running. Listing 5.3 shows how to allocate a variable amount of memory, depending on the string size needed.

Listing 5.3 A Program in Which the Size of the String Array Is a Variable

```
1   // CHAR80A.CPP
2   // Demonstrates dynamic allocation of a character string
3   // using a variable-sized array.
4   #include <iostream.h>
5   #include <string.h>
6
7   void main(void)
8   {
9     int string_size;
10    char *p;
11
12    cout << "How many characters to allocate? ";
13    cin  string_size;
14    cin.ignore(1);
15
16    p = new char[string_size];
17
18    strcpy( p, "I am a character string allocated using "
                  "the new operator." );
19
20    cout << p << endl;
21
22    delete p;
23
24    cout << "Press Enter to continue.";
25    cin.get();
26  } // main
```

The size parameter of the array does not specify the number of bytes to allocate, although it certainly looks as if it does in these examples using the char data type. The size parameter actually specifies the number of elements in the array. Therefore, if you allocate an array of the float type, as in

```
float *fp;
  .
  .
  .
fp = new float[50];
```

you allocate a 50-element floating-point array that occupies 200 bytes of memory (remember that each individual float element occupies 4 bytes).

Using *new* for Multidimensional Arrays

To allocate a multidimensional array, you indicate each array dimension just as you would normally declare a multidimensional array. For example, to allocate a pointer to an array of month names that is [12] by [10], write

```
p = new char[12][10];
```

When you use new to allocate a multidimensional array, only the leftmost size may be a variable. Each of the other dimensions must be a constant value.

Running Out of Memory

If there is insufficient heap storage for your dynamic memory allocation request, the new operator returns NULL. To write a completely safe program, you should test the value returned by new to ensure that it is not NULL. NULL is a constant that C++ defines for you. You must reference #include <iostream.h>, <stdlib.h>, or other standard C++ header files to obtain the definition of NULL.

Initializing a Dynamic Allocation

Another benefit of new is that new can also initialize your allocation to a value that you specify. For example, you can initialize an allocated int type by writing

```
p = new int(999);
```

The value in parentheses is the initializer. This allocation request is equivalent to initializing *p, as in

```
*p = 999;
```

Unfortunately, initialization is not available for array types.

Problems with Pointers

You must use care when using pointer variables. Some of the most common C++ program defects are due to erroneous use of pointers. When you declare a pointer variable as

```
int *p;
```

the address stored in the pointer, like any variable, is undefined until you initialize the variable. The compiler, however, does not prohibit you from using the pointer before initialization, and this can cause your program to fail. Such a pointer is known as a *dangling pointer* because the location it points to could be anywhere in memory. If you assign a value, as in

```
*p = 0;
```

you may have just written a 0 value over a critical value in memory. Worse, you may not encounter this erroneous zero value until much later in your program, which makes tracking down the actual problem much more difficult.

Another problem is caused by continuing to use a pointer after its allocation has been deleted. Consider what happens when you execute a `delete` operation:

```
delete p;
```

The memory allocation to which p pointed is discarded and no longer available. However, the address of the now invalid memory location is still stored in the pointer p. In many instances, you can continue to use this pointer to the discarded memory because the memory manager has not yet decided to reassign the memory block. The data becomes invalid only after the memory manager finally decides to reassign the memory block for another use. Consequently, your program erroneously can continue to use a pointer that is no longer valid.

Warning

As mentioned earlier, you can assign one pointer to another, as in the following example:

```
int *p1, *p2;
  .
  .
  .
p1 = new int;
p2 = p1;
```

Now both p2 and p1 point to the same location in the heap, which is also called aliasing. When you execute

```
delete p1;
```

both pointers become invalid. If you now use p2 (forgetting that p1 and thus p2 are now both deleted), you can damage memory. If you are not paying close attention, your use of two pointers to the same spot can quickly result in a program error. For this reason, using multiple pointers to the same location is discouraged except where absolutely necessary.

Using Pointers with Arrays

You have already seen how to create and use a pointer to an array of char. In this section, you learn how to create and use a pointer to an array of integers and how to access individual array elements by using the pointer.

You can choose from three different methods to access elements of an array by using a pointer. Suppose that you have an integer array declared as

```
int AnArray[10];
```

and that pArray is declared as a pointer to an int, like this:

```
int *pArray = AnArray[0];
```

You can access elements of AnArray by using conventional array notation, such as AnArray[1] or AnArray[2].

Method 1: Using Only the Pointer. You can also gain access to the array elements by using the pointer variable pArray. You already know one method of using the pArray pointer to gain access to the elements of AnArray: you use pArray to point to each element in the array, as in

```
for (i=0; i<10; i++)
  cout << *pArray++ << endl;
```

pArray begins by pointing at AnArray[0]. After the first iteration of this loop, pArray is set to point to AnArray[1], then AnArray[2], and so on, for each iteration. Using this technique, you can sequentially access each element of the array. This is the fastest and most efficient method available to access each element of an array. The only drawback is that you cannot access individual elements in random order.

Method 2: Using the Pointer and an Offset. To access individual array elements, you must add a constant value to the pointer and then dereference the result. Remember that the pointer variable is just the address of the array in memory. By adding an offset to the pointer's address, you create a new pointer value to reach any element in the array. For example, to set the third element of the array (starting from index 0) to the value 99, you write

```
*(pArray + 2) = 99;
```

The compiler knows that pArray points to an int type. Therefore, when you add 2 to pArray, the compiler knows that you mean the third int after where pArray is pointing. This concept is undoubtedly confusing, so consider how the compiler internally works with arrays and pointers.

Figure 5.6 shows the layout of AnArray, stored at address 1000 in memory. The pointer pArray is also stored somewhere in memory and is set to point to &AnArray[0], or 1000. When you write a conventional array index, such as AnArray[2], the compiler computes the location of the indexed element by adding two times the sizeof(int) to the location of AnArray[0] (or, using C++ notation, &AnArray[0]). Therefore, &AnArray[2] is 1000 + 2*2 or 1004. When you write *(pArray + 2), the compiler uses the address in pArray, or 1000, and adds 2*2 to produce 1004. The calculation for the array element at *index* is equivalent to

```
&AnArray[0] + index * sizeof(int)
```

The pointer form is equivalent to

```
pArray + index * sizeof(int)
```

In effect, the internal computation to reach a specific array element is the same, whether you use an array index or an offset from a pointer. Therefore, you can use a pointer and an index (or offset) to reference an element of any array type by writing

```
*(pointer + index)
```

Fig. 5.6
The relationship between array elements and a pointer to an array.

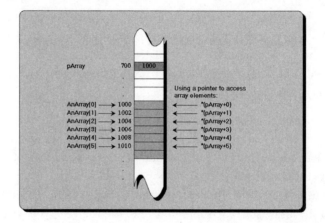

Method 3: Using the Pointer as an Array. You have just seen that the compiler computes the address of an element of AnArray[] by evaluating

```
address = &AnArray[0] + index * sizeof(int)
```

You have also seen that when you have a pointer set equal to the first element of the array, such as

```
pArray = &AnArray[0];
```

the computation to access an array element is identical:

```
address = pArray + index * sizeof(int)
```

Because pArray has the same address as AnArray[0], the compiler lets you use pArray in place of AnArray in an indexing operation. In this form, you use the arrays as

```
pArray[index]
```

and this is equivalent to writing

```
AnArray[index]
```

This means that when pArray is a pointer to an array, you use an index by appending the indexing expression in brackets after the pointer value. The next listing, listing 5.4, shows an example of this technique.

Summary of the Three Methods. This section described the three primary methods for using pointers to access array elements:

- Use the pointer directly, as in *p, and increment p to point to each array element in sequence.

- Add the index value to the pointer, as in *(p+index), to reach the array element at the indexth position.

- Use the pointer as an array and write p[index].

A Sample Program That Uses a Pointer to an Array

Now that you know the three methods of using pointers to access array elements, you can put theory into practice. Listing 5.4 shows a program that dynamically allocates an array of integers. The program then uses each of the three techniques to display the values stored in the array.

Listing 5.4 Using a Pointer to Create an Array of Integers Dynamically

```
1   // NEW-INT.CPP
2   // Dynamically allocates an array of int.
3   // Demonstrates ways to use the pointer variable
4   // to access elements of the array.
5   #include <iostream.h>
6
7   void main(void)
8   {
9     int array_size;   // Size of array.
10    int *pArray;      // Pointer to allocated array.
11    int *p;           // Used for access.
12    int i;            // for loop control variable.
13
14    cout << "Demonstrate use of pointers to access arrays."
15         << endl << endl;
16
17    cout << "How many array elements to allocate? ";
18    cin  array_size;
19    cin.ignore(1);
20
```

(continues)

Listing 5.4 Continued

```
21   // ================================================
22   // Allocate an array of array_size elements.
23   pArray = new int[array_size];
24
25   // Demonstrate the use of arrays by adding an offset
26   // to the pointer. Set each element of pArray to i.
27   for (i=0; i < array_size; i++)
28     *(pArray + i) = i;
29
30   // Display the elements on-screen.
31   for (i=0; i < array_size; i++)
32     cout << *(pArray + i) << endl;
33
34   // ================================================
35   // Demonstrate using a pointer as an array.
36   cout << "Reference as an array, using the pointer."
37       << endl;
38   for (i=0; i < array_size; i++)
39     cout << pArray[i] << endl;
40
41   // ================================================
42   // Demonstrate using a pointer, without indexing.
43   cout << endl
44       << "Demonstrate array access without indexing."
45       << endl;
46   // Let p point to start of the array.
47   p = pArray;
48   for (i=0; i < array_size; i++ )
49     // And use p directly to scan through the array
50     // elements.
51     cout << *p++ << endl;
52
53   delete pArray;
54
55   cout << "Press Enter to continue.";
56   cin.get();
57 } // main
```

Line 23 uses the new operator to allocate memory space for the array. The address of the array (corresponding to element 0) is placed in the pointer, pArray. You can alter the declared array size while the program is running by setting different values for array_size. When you run this sample program, you should use a small array size such as 5 or 10. This makes it easier to understand the program's behavior.

Lines 27 through 32 use the *pointer + index* method of accessing array elements. These lines set the elements of the array so that element 1 is 0, element 2 is 1, element 3 is 2, and so on. Lines 38 through 39 demonstrate the pointer-as-array method, using a bracketed index value to access the array elements. Last, lines 47 through 51 use a pointer to scan sequentially across the array. Note in line 47 that the second pointer variable, p, is initialized to pArray before the for loop begins in line 48. If pArray were incremented, you could not delete the memory allocation, as is done in line 53.

An Array of Pointers

A pointer variable is like the other data types. This means that you can declare an array of pointers or place a pointer inside a structure (the latter case is described in the next section, "Pointers and Structures").

In Chapter 3, "C++ Advanced Data Types," you learned about multidimensional character arrays used as strings, and you saw the example of an array of character strings used to store the names of the months. This array is declared as

```
char month_names[12][10];
```

and allocates the 12-by-10-byte block of memory (for a total of 120 bytes) shown in figure 5.7. Notice that for those months with short names, such as May and June, a large amount of the array space is wasted.

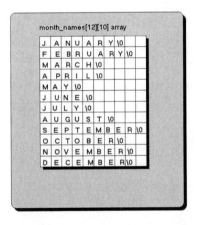

Fig. 5.7
How month_names is laid out in memory.

One way to fix the problem of unused memory is to change the declaration to use an array of pointers:

```
char *month_names[12];
```

This changes the declaration of month_names to an array having 12 elements, where each element is a pointer to a character string that is allocated dynamically using the new operator.

For each month, use new to allocate only the minimum space needed for each string, as in

```
month_names[0] = new char[8]; // "January"
strcpy( month_names[0], "January" );
month_names[1] = new char[9]; // "February"
strcpy( month_names[1], "February" );
month_names[2] = new char[6]; // "March"
strcpy( month_names[0], "March" );
month_names[3] = new char[6]; // "April"
strcpy( month_names[3], "April" );
month_names[4] = new char[4]; // "May"
strcpy( month_names[4], "May" );
```

This produces the memory layout shown in figure 5.8, in which each element of month_names[] points to the memory location at which the corresponding month string is stored. This type of array is called a *ragged array* because of the varying lengths of the array elements. For many applications, an array of pointers, particularly pointers to strings, can make better use of memory than a multidimensional array.

Fig. 5.8
An array of pointers to character strings.

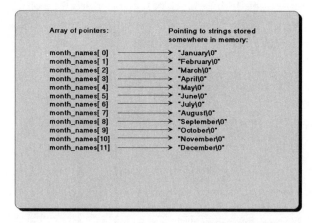

Initializing an Array of Pointers to Strings

Initializing the array of pointers, as shown in the preceding code fragment, is tedious and creates a great deal of machine code. In C++, you don't have to go through so much work just to initialize an array of pointers to strings. Instead, you can use an initializer list as part of the declaration:

```
char *month_names[12] = {"January", "February", "March",
                         "April", "May", "June", "July",
                         "August", "September", "October",
                         "November", "December"};
```

The compiler stores the character strings in a data memory area and automatically sets each of the pointers in the month_names[] array to point to the corresponding strings.

Listing 5.5 shows how you can create an array of pointers to arbitrary strings and then access the strings or individual characters within the strings.

Listing 5.5 Using an Array of Pointers to Character Strings

```
1   // ARRAY-P.CPP
2   // Allocates an array of pointers to character strings.
3   #include <iostream.h>
4   #include <string.h>
5
6   void main(void)
7   {
8     const int MAX_STRINGS = 5;   // Maximum number of strings.
9     char *strings[MAX_STRINGS];  // An array of pointers.
10    int i;                       // Used for for loop control.
11    char input_line[80];         // Temporary holder for input.
12
13    cout << "Demonstrates use of an array of pointers."
14        << endl << endl;
15
16    cout << "At each prompt, enter a character string:"
17        << endl;
18
19    // Prompt and accept input for each string.
20    for (i=0; i < MAX_STRINGS; i++ )
21    {
22      cout << "Enter text for string #" << i << ": ";
23      cin.getline( input_line, sizeof(input_line) );
24      // Allocate just enough memory to store the input string.
25      // Note the use of +1 on the strlen() to accommodate the
26      // null byte at the end of the string.
27      strings[i] = new char[strlen(input_line)+1];
28      // Copy the input string to the location stored in
29      // the pointer array. strings[i] points to the
30      // allocated memory block.
31      strcpy( strings[i], input_line );
32    } // for
33    cout << endl;
34
35    cout << "You entered the following strings:" << endl;
36    for (i=0; i< MAX_STRINGS; i++)
37      cout << "String #" << i << " " << strings[i] << endl;
38
39    /* Demonstrate access to individual elements of the
40       strings. This section of code displays the first
41       character string (strings[0]), character by character.
42       To access the individual characters of the first string,
43       realize that strings[0] points to the start of a
44       character array. Accessing the individual elements of
45       the character array requires the use of an index.
46       Remember that, in general, you can access an array element
47       via a pointer by using
48           *(pointer+index)
49       In this code section, pointer is replaced by strings[0],
```

(continues)

Listing 5.5 Continued

```
50        which is the address of the first character string. You
51        use index to access the individual characters in that string.
52   */
53   for (i=0; i < strlen(strings[0]); i++)
54     // Access the i'th character of the string pointed
55     // to by strings[0].
56     cout << *(strings[0]+i) << " ";
57   cout << endl;
58
59   // Delete each of the memory blocks pointed to by
60   // the array elements.
61   for (i=0; i < MAX_STRINGS; i++)
62     delete strings[i];
63
64   cout << "Press Enter to continue.";
65   cin.get();
66 } // main
```

The ARRAY-P.CPP program declares a small array of pointers to strings by using the following declaration:

```
char *strings[MAX_STRINGS];
```

You can set the constant MAX_STRINGS, in line 8, to a larger value. Next, the program prompts you to enter a text string (lines 22 through 23). In line 27, the new operator allocates just enough memory to hold the character string you typed. Note the use of strlen(input_line)+1: the +1 is needed to ensure that you allocate space for the trailing zero byte used to mark the end of a null-terminated string. Line 31 uses strcpy() to copy the contents of input_line to the memory location that has just been stored in strings[i].

Lines 35 through 37 output each of the strings to the display. Next, the program demonstrates access to each of the individual elements within a particular string, as shown in lines 53 through 56. Carefully read the comments in lines 39 through 52; these comments explain how the individual characters are accessed.

Lines 59 through 62 use delete to destroy each memory allocation. Because each array element contains a pointer, you must use a for loop to iterate through the entire array and delete each character string.

An example of where you might use an array of pointers is in a simple text-editing program that keeps all the edited text in an array of character strings. Before learning about pointers, you probably thought a text editor stored the text lines in a multidimensional array of char. Such a definition might look like the following:

```
const int MAX_LINES = 500;
char text_lines[MAX_LINES][80];
```

With this definition, storing 500 lines requires 500 × 80 or 40,000 bytes of memory. Because most text lines are less than 80 characters long, using a multidimensional array wastes large amounts of memory. A much better solution is to use an array of pointers and allocate the minimum memory needed for each line. Your declaration then changes to

```
char *text_lines[MAX_LINES];
```

Then use new to allocate only the needed memory for each line stored in the ragged array.

Pointers and Structures

Putting a pointer into a struct definition opens up a whole new world of possibilities in C++ programming. By placing a pointer into a structure, your application can create complex data structures. A data structure represents an organization for storing data. The array is an example of a data structure that stores its elements sequentially in memory, one after the other. But many structures in the real world do not fit into the limited data models provided directly by C++.

Consider the corporate organizational structure shown in figure 5.9. This is called a tree structure, and in this case, a binary tree, because each node of the tree has two branches. This type of structure is best implemented in C++ using pointers.

As you may remember from a previous chapter (see the section "Structures" in Chapter 3, "C++ Advanced Data Types"), a structure is a storage element that contains a group of related data elements. If some of the data elements are pointers to other structures, complex relationships can be defined and maintained. The binary tree in figure 5.9 can be represented by a structure that contains two pointers to as many as two subordinates.

Placing a Pointer into a *struct* Definition

You can place a pointer into a struct definition as you would place any other type of variable. Note this example:

```
struct company_official {
  char title[20];a
  char *name;
} Manager;
```

Fig. 5.9
A tree data
structure used to
represent the
members of a
corporate
organization.

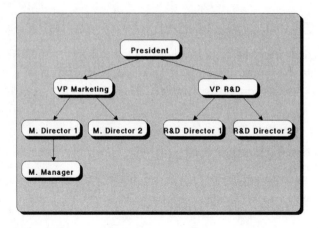

To allocate space for the name member and initialize the string, you write

```
Manager.name = new char[30];
strcpy( President.name, "George Smithson, Jr." );
```

Because `Manager.name` contains the address of the null-terminated character
string, to display the `name` field, you write

```
cout << Manager.name << endl;
```

Access to the individual characters within the `name` member is the same as
with any other pointer to a string. The following code references the `name`
field, character by character, so that it can display a blank between the letters
in the name:

```
for (int i=0; i<strlen(Manager.name); i++)
  cout << *(Manager.name+i) << " ";
cout << endl;
```

Using Self-Referential Structures

To implement the organizational structure suggested earlier in this section,
you must use a special type of structure called a *self-referential structure*, which
is a fancy way of saying that the structure definition contains a pointer to
another instance of the same type of structure. Because this is a complicated
concept, two sample programs that use pointers in this manner are presented.

Look at a possible structure definition that can be used as a building block to
construct the organizational structure shown in figure 5.9. Each entry in the
chart consists of a job title and two pointers, where each pointer points to a
possible subordinate (or is set to NULL to indicate that there is no subordinate). This suggests the following `struct` definition:

Yes, This Is Hard!

Using pointers in C++ is certainly one of the most confusing aspects of the C++ programming language. Almost all newcomers to C++ (and many experienced programmers) find the concept of a pointer difficult to fathom. Do not be discouraged. You can master these concepts, but you must work through this section slowly. Try to draw pictures of the data structures used in the examples and sample programs. Draw lines to link the structures together, like the pointers do in memory. Again, be patient and try not to be discouraged. This is a difficult topic to master.

```
struct company_official {
  char title[20];
  company_official *sub_1; // subordinate #1
  company_official *sub_2; // subordinate #2
}
```

The last two items are self-referential pointers to the structure in which they are defined. What in the world does this mean?

Self-referential pointers don't really point to this particular structure. Instead, they point to memory allocations that look like this structure definition. In this way, you can string together several instances of the company_official record. Figure 5.10 shows the result. Each memory allocation is a copy of the company_official structure. This means that each memory allocation looks like the company_official structure. Within each allocation, pointers link one structure to two other memory allocations.

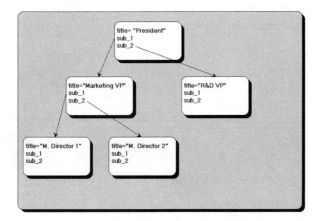

Fig. 5.10
The use of self-referential pointers to link similar records.

To see how this structure may be laid out in C++ code, begin by creating a pointer to the company_official struct type. To do this, declare the variable

President to be a pointer to a `company_official` structure:

```
company_official *President;
```

President is now a pointer to a structure containing the `title` and subordinate information. To create an instance of this structure in memory, you must use the `new` operator:

```
President = new company_official;
```

To initialize the `title` member of the structure, you might write

```
strcpy( *(President).title, "President" );
```

The peculiar expression `*(President).title` dereferences the `President` pointer to reach the structure containing the `title` member. Specifically, `*(President)` reaches the object to which `President` is pointing. Because that memory object is a structure, you can then append `.title` to access the `.title` member of the structure.

Using a pointer to reach a structure member is so common that C++ has a special operator, `->`, to assist in this indirection. You can use the `->` operator to provide an easier alternative to the `*(...)` operation. Here is an example:

```
strcpy( President->title, "President" );
```

`*(President).title` and `President->title` are exactly equivalent in meaning. In the latter case, the `->` operator tells C++ that `President` points to a structure; the name of any structure member can then be placed after the `->` operator. C++ programmers prefer to use the `->` operator because it produces a cleaner and easier-to-read dereference.

Listing 5.6 helps you understand how to use pointers to create abstract data structures. The program constructs a part of the company organization chart shown in figure 5.9.

Listing 5.6 A C++ Implementation of the Corporate Organizational Chart

```
1   // COMPANY.CPP
2   // Partial implementation of the organizational
3   // structure described in Chapter 5.
4   #include <iostream.h>
5   #include <string.h>
6
7     struct company_official{
8       char title[20];
```

```
 9      company_official *sub_1;
10      company_official *sub_2;
11    };
12
13  // Recursive function to display structure.
14  void display_org( company_official *position ) {
15    // Display title at current position.
16    cout << position->title << endl;
17    // Call us again to display any subordinates on
18    // left half.
19    if (position->sub_1 != NULL)
20      display_org( position->sub_1 );
21    // Call us again to display any subordinates on
22    // right half.
23    if (position->sub_2 != NULL)
24      display_org( position->sub_2 );
25  } // display_org
26
27
28  void main(void) {
29    company_official *President;
30    company_official *position;
31
32    President = new company_official;
33    strcpy( (*President).title, "President" );
34    strcpy( President->title, "President"  );
35
36    President->sub_1 = new company_official;
37    strcpy( President->sub_1->title, "Marketing VP" );
38
39    President->sub_2 = new company_official;
40    strcpy( President->sub_2->title, "R&D VP" );
41
42    // Let position point to Marketing VP.
43    position = President->sub_1;
44    position->sub_1 = new company_official;
45    strcpy( position->sub_1->title, "Marketing Director 1" );
46    position->sub_1->sub_1 = NULL;
47    position->sub_1->sub_2 = NULL;
48
49    position->sub_2 = new company_official;
50    strcpy( position->sub_2->title, "Marketing Director 2" );
51    position->sub_2->sub_1 = NULL;
52    position->sub_2->sub_2 = NULL;
53
54    // Let position point to R&D VP.
55    position = President->sub_2;
56    position->sub_1 = new company_official;
57    strcpy( position->sub_1->title, "R&D Director 1" );
58    position->sub_1->sub_1 = NULL;
59    position->sub_1->sub_2 = NULL;
60
61
62    position->sub_2 = new company_official;
63    strcpy( position->sub_2->title, "R&D Director 2" );
64    position->sub_2->sub_1 = NULL;
```

(continues)

Listing 5.6 Continued

```
65      position->sub_2->sub_2 = NULL;
66
67      display_org( President );
68  } // main
```

Lines 7 through 11 define the structure used to represent each position in the company. The structure contains a field to hold the title and two pointers to point at subordinates. The program starts by allocating the first employee, the President (see line 32). This employee's title is set, in line 33, to President. Next, the President hires two subordinates, a Marketing VP and an R&D VP. These are incorporated (pun intended) into the data structure by allocating new company_official structures. Line 37 allocates and initializes the Marketing VP position; line 40 allocates and initializes the R&D VP position.

Lines 36 and 39 both add an extra level of indirection. After executing line 65, the data structure is implemented as shown in figure 5.11.

Fig. 5.11
The data structure implemented by COMPANY.CPP.

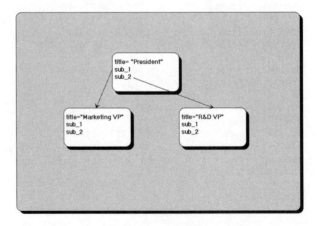

Each arrow in the drawing is equivalent to the -> indirection operator in the C++ code. Therefore, the first indirection reaches the sub_1 member of the President position; the second indirection through sub_1 reaches the subordinate structure, which also contains a title field.

Line 43 uses a temporary pointer variable to simplify the construction of the subordinate offices. By setting position equal to the first subordinate, you do not have to use as many indirect pointer operations. In effect, position points directly to the Marketing VP's structure, as shown in figure 5.12.

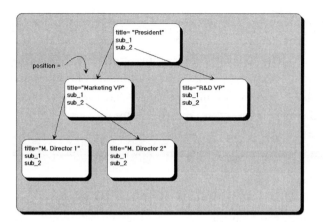

Follow through the C++ code carefully and manually draw the structure on a piece of paper. This exercise helps you understand the actions being done. When you finish, your drawing shows the first few positions of the organization structure represented in figure 5.9.

Last, in line 67 the program calls a function named display_org(), which displays the position titles of all who have been added to the company. The implementation of display_org() is in lines 13 through 25.

When display_org is called, its single local parameter variable, position, points to the President. Line 16 outputs the title, President, stored at this location. If the sub_1 pointer is not NULL, the function calls itself to display the subordinate's position. (A function that calls itself is known as a *recursive function*.) Each time a function is called recursively, it gets a new copy of its parameter and local variables. On the second invocation of display_org(), a new copy of the position variable points at Marketing VP. Line 16 outputs the title Marketing VP. And again, because the Marketing VP has a subordinate, display_org() is called for a third time.

On the third entry to display_org(), line 16 displays Marketing Director 1. At this point, this Marketing Director has no subordinate, so display_org() completes and returns to its caller.

After the third invocation of display_org(), the program returns to inside the previous or second invocation, where position still points to Marketing VP. Having displayed the sub_1 positions, display_org() now calls itself to display the sub_2 positions. The display_org() function continues in this manner, traversing down, up, and across the data structure.

A recursive function is a complex concept to master. Again, take your time and don't worry too much if you do not yet understand all this material. If you have made it this far, you probably now appreciate the warning given at the beginning of this section regarding the difficulty of mastering this material. You probably are also beginning to appreciate the power that the use of pointers and data structures can unleash in your programs. To help understand this difficult material, the next section provides a second sample program, which constructs a data structure known as the *linked list*.

Implementing a Linked List

A linked list uses pointers to connect structures together in memory. You can build *singly linked lists* by using a single pointer, enabling traversal of the list in one direction only. Or the list can use two pointers: one to point in the forward direction and one to point in the reverse direction. A list with two pointers is called a *doubly linked list*. Figure 5.13 shows both a singly linked list and a doubly linked list.

Fig. 5.13

The structure of singly and doubly linked lists.

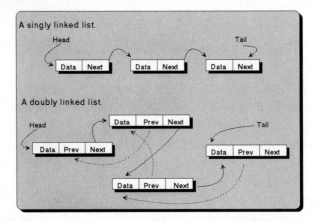

The major components of a linked list are the following:

- A *data record* that contains the information stored in the list, such as name, address, and phone number fields. This data record also stores a pointer to the next record in sequence, and optionally a pointer to the previous record in the sequence.

- A *head pointer*, pointing to the first element of the list.

- A *tail pointer*, pointing to the last element of the list.

Before any elements are added to the list, the head and tail pointers are both set to NULL. As items are added to the list, the head pointer is set to the first element in the list, and the tail pointer is continually updated to point to the last record in the list. By using the tail pointer to keep track of the last item in the list, the program that manages the list knows where new elements should be attached to the list structure. Listing 5.7 is a program that implements the insertion and display of a doubly linked list. This sample program enables you to enter an unlimited number of names that are then stored in the list. (The actual limit is determined solely by how much memory you have in the program's heap storage area.)

Listing 5.7 The Implementation of a Linked List Data Structure

```
1   // LISTTYPE.CPP
2   // Demonstrates the use of pointers in structures by
3   // implementing a doubly linked list of records.
4   #include <iostream.h>
5
6   void main(void) {
7
8     // Define the structure and its data
9     // members. You can add more members than
10    // the mere name field that is shown here.
11    struct list_type
12    {
13      char name[20];
14      // The following point to the next entry in
15      // the list and the previous entry in the
16      // list, respectively.
17      list_type *next;
18      list_type *prev;
19    };
20
21    // head points to the front of the list.
22    list_type *head = NULL;
23    // tail points to the end of the list.
24    list_type *tail = NULL;
25    // next_entry points to the entry you are adding.
26    list_type *next_entry;
27
28    // Used to process keyboard command input.
29    char command_ch;
30
31    do {
32      cout << "Select A)dd, L)ist or Q)uit? ";
33      cin.get(command_ch);
34      cin.ignore(1);
35
36      switch(command_ch) {
37        // Add a new entry to the list.
```

(continues)

Listing 5.7 Continued

```
38          case 'a': case 'A': {
39              // Allocate next entry in list.
40              if (head == NULL) { // If list is now empty...
41                  next_entry = tail = head = new list_type;
42                  next_entry->next = NULL;
43                  next_entry->prev = NULL;
44              } // if
45              else { // List is not empty.
46                  next_entry = new list_type;
47                  // Set previous pointer to point at what
48                  // was the last entry.
49                  next_entry->prev = tail;
50                  // Set the previous entry's next pointer to
51                  // point at the new entry.
52                  tail->next = next_entry;
53                  // And set tail to point at the new entry.
54                  tail = next_entry;
55                  // And the last entry does not point
56                  // anywhere, so set it to NULL.
57                  next_entry->next = NULL;
58              } // else
59              cout << "Enter name:  ";
60              cin.getline( next_entry->name,
61                           sizeof( next_entry->name ) );
62              break;
63          } // case
64          // Display the contents of the list.
65          case 'l': case 'L': {
66              list_type *an_entry; // Temporary pointer to entries.
67              char direction_ch;
68              cout << "Display in F)orward or R)everse direction? ";
69              cin.get(direction_ch);
70              cin.ignore(1);
71              switch (direction_ch) {
72                case 'f': case 'F': {
73                  an_entry = head;
74                  while (an_entry != NULL) {
75                      cout << an_entry->name << endl;
76                  an_entry = an_entry->next;
77                  } // while
78                  break;
79                } // case
80                case 'r': case 'R': {
81                  an_entry = tail;
82                  while (an_entry != NULL) {
83                      cout << an_entry->name << endl;
84                      an_entry = an_entry->prev;
85                  } // while
86                } // case
87                default: break;
88              } // switch
89
90              break;
```

```
 91              } // case
 92          // Quit running the program.
 93          case 'q': case 'Q': {
 94              // Delete all the entries and free up
 95              // their memory allocations. This code
 96              // starts at the end of the list and removes
 97              // each entry, one by one, until reaching
 98              // the beginning of the list (where
 99              // next_entry->prev = NULL).
100              while (tail != NULL) {
101                  next_entry = tail->prev;
102                  delete tail;
103                  tail = next_entry;
104              } // while
105              break;
106          } // case
107          default:
108              break;
109      } // switch
110  } while ((command_ch != 'q') && (command_ch != 'Q'));
111
112      cout << "Press Enter to continue.";
113      cin.get();
114
115  } // main
```

Before examining the program in detail, look at the sample program output shown in figure 5.14.

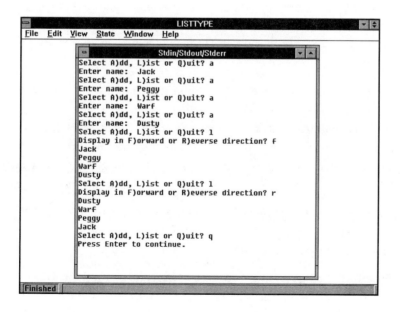

Fig. 5.14
Output generated by the LISTTYPE.CPP program.

In this sample output, four names are added to the list structure. Then the L (for List) command is given, and the names are displayed in the order you entered them. If you select the R)everse option, the names are displayed from the last to the first.

The definition of the list structure appears in lines 13 through 19. A single field, name, is available for storing a person's name. You can easily modify this program to add street address, city, state, and ZIP code members. The next pointer links to the next list entry, in the forward direction, or is set to NULL if there are no additional items in the list. The prev pointer, which links back to the previous entry in the list, is needed so that the list can be traversed in the backward direction.

To understand the program's operation, begin by looking at the code in lines 38 through 63, which handles the addition of a name. The addition of a new element is split into two cases, depending on whether the list is empty or already contains entries. For the empty list, the head and tail pointers are both set to point to the first entry (see line 41), and the next and prev pointers of the list record are both set to NULL.

If the list is not empty, a new list element is allocated and its address is stored temporarily in the next_entry pointer variable. Next, a complicated series of pointer adjustments are made. Because the next_entry is attached after the tail of the list, next_entry->prev is set equal to the current tail. The original last element, pointed to by tail, has its next member adjusted to point at the new last entry, next_entry (see line 52). Finally, the tail pointer is set to point at next_entry. The prompt and input statements in lines 59 through 61 handle the name input.

Displaying the content of the list is a simple matter of tracing the pointers that link the elements together. In lines 73 through 77, a temporary pointer, an_entry, is set to the head pointer that points to the start of the list. As long as an_entry is not a NULL pointer, the while loop in lines 74 through 77 repeats. Line 75 displays the name member stored at the current list element, and line 76 sets an_entry to point to the next element in the list.

Displaying the list in reverse order is identical to displaying the list in the forward direction except that tail is used as the starting point and the prev member is used to trace the list in the backward direction.

Chapter 14, "The MFC General-Purpose Classes and Collection Classes," shows you how to use object libraries that provide the linked list functionality. By using the libraries, you can gain access to frequently used data structure code, saving yourself the time and trouble of writing and debugging the routines.

Near, Far, and Huge Pointers

Visual C++ has three flavors of pointers known as *near*, *far*, and *huge*. For most of the programs you write, you can ignore these different pointer types and use whatever the compiler assumes is appropriate for the compiler options you have selected. But to use Visual C++ to its maximum capabilities, you must understand the differences between these pointer types, especially the near and far pointer.

To understand the need for the different pointer types, you must learn a bit about the design of the 80x86 family of microprocessors. When Intel Corporation designed the first members of this microprocessor group, the 8088 and the 8086, it wanted the new microprocessor to have some compatibility (albeit very limited) with an earlier microprocessor called the 8080. The 8080 worked only with up to 64K of memory (65,536 bytes), which is quite small by today's standards. From the standpoint of memory, that meant that all code and data combined had to fit in a 64K address space.

When Intel designed the 8088 and 8086, the original 64K limitation of the 8080 (as well as some other features) was incorporated into the new processors. But the 8088 and 8086 introduced a distinctly new twist: program addressing was still limited to a 64K per memory segment, but the computer could use multiple 64K memory segments to support up to a total of 1M of memory.

To meet this need, the 8088/86 introduced segment registers to point to the start of memory segments. Within each segment, a 16-bit address is used to reach any part of the 64K address space. The same concept applies to the 80286, 80386, and 80486 processors, which are upward-compatible with the original 8086.

To use the full memory capacity of the CPU, the Visual C++ compiler translates your program so that internally, the program uses the CPU's special segment registers. You can write your programs to operate within the 64K limitation of each memory segment, or, by using the segment registers, you can write your programs to access the full range of memory.

Programs that operate wholly within a 64K segment can use near addressing. Such programs use a 16-bit-sized memory address to reach any byte within a 64K segment. (A 16-bit unsigned integer holds values from 0 to 65,535, so you can see how a 16-bit address works with up to 64K of memory.)

To address more than 64K of memory, you must use a far address that has two components: the *segment address* and the *16-bit offset address*. The segment address selects the start of a memory segment that is up to 64K. The offset chooses a specific byte within that 64K segment. In effect, the segment and offset addresses are combined to form a single address.

At this point in your programming experience, you need to know that there are two kinds of addresses, near and far. A *near memory reference* is a 16-bit address used entirely within a segment. A *far memory reference* is made to a separate segment and requires two 16-bit addresses to specify both a segment and an offset. The segment and offset values are combined, as shown in figure 5.15, to produce a 20-bit address. You learn more about memory addresses in the section "Memory Addressing" in Chapter 7, "Projects."

Fig. 5.15
A memory address computation that uses the far pointer.

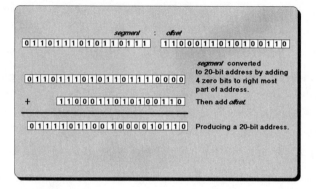

A near memory reference requires half as many address bytes as a far memory reference, so using near memory references produces smaller programs. Fewer instruction bytes also means faster execution.

The compiler generates machine instructions that use either near or far addressing, depending on the memory model you are using or whether you explicitly tell the compiler to use near or far addressing. By default, when you use the tiny, small, or compact memory models, all your pointers are near pointers. The maximum possible memory that you can address in these models is 64K. In the medium, large, and huge models, the default pointer is the far pointer. In these models, your program can address up to 1M of memory.

A huge pointer is a special kind of far pointer used only when your program needs to access a data item that exceeds 64K. Whenever a single piece of data exceeds 64K, that data must spread across more than one memory segment. The huge pointer handles data that extends across segment boundaries.

32-bit Addressing

The 80386, 80486, and Pentium microprocessors can access memory by using a true 32-bit address in place of the segment and offset pair now in use. Using this flat memory addressing requires new compilers, and new operating systems such as Windows NT, or special software known as *DOS protected mode interfaces*. You cannot use the 32-bit addressing capability of the newer microprocessors with Visual C++ 1.5 Professional Edition and Visual C++ 1.0 Standard Edition. However, 32-bit processing is becoming widely available and Microsoft has introduced a 32-bit version of Visual C++ for Windows NT, its 32-bit operating system. Soon you will no longer have to be concerned with the use of near and far pointers, because all pointers become true 32-bit pointers. The 32-bit mode of operation still supports a segmented memory architecture, but you are able to use 32-bit near pointers. For now, though, to use the full capabilities of the existing Visual C++ and Windows operating system, you must be familiar with the concept of near and far pointers.

To understand why you cannot use a far pointer, consider what happens when you perform arithmetic on a far pointer (remember that you can perform addition and subtraction on all pointer types). Whenever you add a value to a far pointer, your addition affects only the offset value of the pointer. If you add 1 to a far pointer, the offset value increments by 1. If the addition causes the offset to exceed 16-bits (as in 65,535 + 1), an arithmetic overflow occurs. Because a 16-bit address holds only addresses in the range of 0 to 65,535, the offset becomes reset to zero.

The huge pointer uses special routines to process the increment or decrement operations on far pointers so that both the segment and offset addresses are adjusted properly. Using these special routines results in slower pointer arithmetic, so you should use a huge pointer only if your application must manage chunks of data much larger than 64K (for example, a large array of strings).

When you select the huge memory model, the compiler still uses far pointers by default. To declare a huge pointer, you insert the huge keyword between the data type and variable name, like this:

```
int huge *p;
```

Summary

This chapter introduced the power of C++ pointers. You learned how to perform basic pointer operations. You learned also how to apply pointers to improve your use of character strings and to implement complex data structures.

Pointers add great flexibility to the creation of dynamic and complex data structures in C++ programs. Mastering C++ pointers is a difficult topic—many C++ programmers, even experienced programmers, can get lost trying to trace structures linked together by the magic of pointers. In many respects, this chapter is only an introduction to the application of pointers in C++ programming.

In this chapter, you learned the following:

- A pointer variable holds the address of another location in memory.

- To declare a pointer, you place an asterisk between the data type and the variable name, as in `int *p;`.

- To obtain the value stored at the address used by the pointer, you use the indirection or dereference operator (`*`). The value of `p` is a memory address, and the value `*p` is the quantity stored at that memory address.

- To obtain the address of an existing variable, use the address-of operator (`&`).

- Use the `NULL` constant to initialize a pointer to point to nothing. Using an uninitialized pointer, which contains a random memory location, can harm your program and operating system.

- By setting a pointer to the address of the first element in an array, you can use the pointer to access each element sequentially in that array.

- You can also use a pointer to access array elements, by using the form `*(pointer + index)` or `pointer[index]`.

- The heap is the free memory remaining after your program is loaded into memory and ready for operation. The Visual C++ memory management system, built into Visual C++, coordinates use of the heap.

- You use the `new` operator to allocate blocks of memory from the heap. `new` returns a pointer to the allocated block.

- Each allocation that you make should eventually be discarded when it is no longer used. Use the `delete` operator to eliminate unused memory blocks.

■ By using a pointer to a char together with new, you can dynamically allocate space for character strings so that your string variables exactly fit the size of the desired text strings.

■ By combining pointers and struct definitions, you can create complex data structures that link disparate structures together.

■ To access an element of a structure when the structure is accessed by a pointer, you can use the -> operator. For example, when p is a pointer to a structure containing name and address members, you can use -> to access the members, like this:

```
p->name // Reference name member of structure pointed to by p.
p->address // Reference address member of structure pointed to by p.
```

■ Visual C++ provides three kinds of pointers: near, far, and huge. For the purposes of the applications you are most likely to write at this point in your C++ experience, you can let the compiler automatically decide which type of pointer to use.

Review Questions

1. To obtain the address of an array element, which operator should you use?

2. Your program must copy string1 to string2, where both variables are declared as arrays of char. Which of the following is the most efficient way to perform the copy and why?

A. for(int i=0; i <=strlen(i); i++)

string2[i] = string1[i];

B. char *p1 = string1[0]; char *p2 = string2[0];

while (*p1) *p2++ = *p1++;

3. Your program has a pointer, pS, which points to a structure that has a member named mpg. What are the two equivalent ways of using pS to reach the member mpg?

4. What problem can occur when you set two pointers to point to the same dynamically allocated variable?

5. What is a self-referential data structure?

6. What is a recursive function?

7. Visual C++ has three types of pointers. What are their names?

8. pWeekly is a pointer variable that was initialized to point at the first element of an array named Weekly_Total[]. Which of the following is a valid method of accessing the elements of the array?

   A. pWeekly[index]

   B. *(pWeekly + index)

   C. Weekly_Total[index]

   D. All of the above

Exercises

1. This chapter described a corporate organizational structure and showed a way to use pointers to implement this structure. You can also implement a structure similar to this by using arrays and array indexes in place of pointers. If you define an array as

```
struct {
  char title[20];
  int sub_1;
  int sub_2;
} org[100];
```

you use elements of this array to store each of the company positions. Set org[0] to President, org[1] to Marketing VP, org[2] to R&D VP; then set org[0].sub_1 to 1 and org[0].sub_2 to 2. In this way, the indexes link the corporate structure. Implement the corporate structure by using an array.

2. Modify the LISTTYPE.CPP program to add fields to the struct definition. Modify the input and display routines to display these values.

3. Add to LISTTYPE.CPP a feature that deletes a specific record from the list. To perform a delete operation, you must snip the pointer links to the deleted record. This means that you must trace the deleted record's previous link to the previous entry in the list, and then set that entry's next pointer to skip over the deleted entry. You will need to do the same for the entry that follows the deleted record. Be sure to use `delete` to discard the deleted record properly.

4. Use pointers to implement a singly linked list structure similar to the doubly linked structure in LISTTYPE.CPP. For the data stored in each list node, use a pointer to store a dynamically allocated string. Your program should input a set of values to store in each node, and then display the entire list that was entered.

Chapter 6

Functions and Macros

You already know that every C++ program has at least one `main()` function (or a `WinMain()` function if the program is intended for use with Microsoft Windows). Most C++ programs consist of many functions rather than one giant `main()` function. By separating code into functions, you can reuse it in your program and in other programs. After you write and test your function, you can use it over and over again. To reuse a function within your program, you need only to call the function.

If you group functions into libraries or as member functions in class libraries, other programs can reuse the functions, thereby saving development time. And because libraries presumably hold tested routines, you increase the reliability of the entire program.

In this chapter, you learn about the following:

- Using the functions provided with Visual C++ and using the C++ standard libraries

- Declaring and implementing your own functions

- Passing parameter variables to functions

- Making your function return a result value

- Using macros, which resemble functions but are not really functions at all

Using Library Functions

The Visual C++ package includes hundreds of prewritten functions you can use in your programs. The Visual C++ package does include a library reference book, so you can also use the on-line help messages for documentation. This section introduces a number of the library features and shows you how to use some of the standard functions in your programs.

Table 6.1 lists the categories of routines available in the standard library. For example, the math routines contain functions to compute sin( ), cos( ), tan( ), and other mathematical operations. The time and date routines provide functions to obtain the current clock setting and system date on your PC. Visual C++ includes a very capable set of graphics functions you can use to display graphics on-screen. The graphics routines are described in Chapter 13, "Graphics Programming with QuickWin."

Table 6.1 Types of Routines Available in the C++ Standard Library	
Classification routines	Memory routines
Conversion routines	Miscellaneous routines
Diagnostic routines	Process control routines
Directory control routines	Standard routines
Graphics routines	String and memory routines
Inline routines	Text window display routines
Input/output routines	Time and date routines
Interface routines	Variable argument list routines
Math routines	

Many of the functions, such as the input and output routines and the memory routines, are not used much in C++ programming. Instead, they have been replaced by C++'s streams (such as cin and cout) and by the new and delete operators. The older routines are still present in the library so that the Visual C++ compiler can be used to write programs in the older C language.

You can obtain information on any of the available library routines in three different ways:

■ To see a list of all functions organized by category, choose **H**elp and then choose **C**/C++ Language from the **H**elp menu. The Windows help program, WinHelp, displays the Language Help topic as shown in figure 6.1. Use the mouse to click the box next to Run-Time Routines, which displays the help topics shown in figure 6.2. You can click any category to see a list of the functions available in that category. Then, by clicking on any function name, you can learn more about the function. Figure 6.3 shows the functions available in the Time category.

■ You can use WinHelp's Search button, as described in Chapter 1, "The Fundamentals of C++ Programming," to see information on a specific library function whose name you already know.

■ You can see information on a specific library function while you are editing a source file. You simply place the cursor on the function name and press the F1 function key. The appropriate WinHelp dialog box is displayed, provided that help is available, or a message appears indicating that there is no help for the indicated function name.

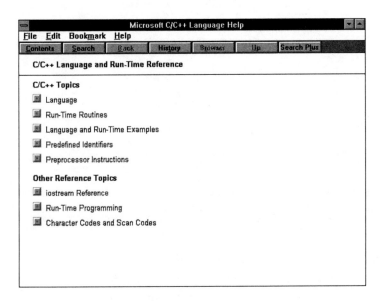

Fig. 6.1
The Language Help topic displayed in the WinHelp dialog box.

Fig. 6.2
Some of the
function
categories
available from
the Run-Time
Routines help
topic.

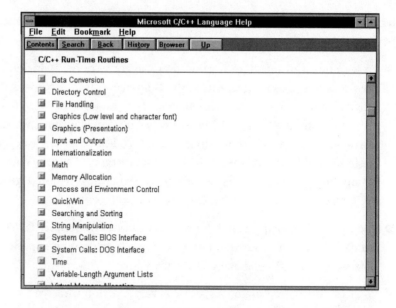

Fig. 6.3
The functions
available in the
Time category.

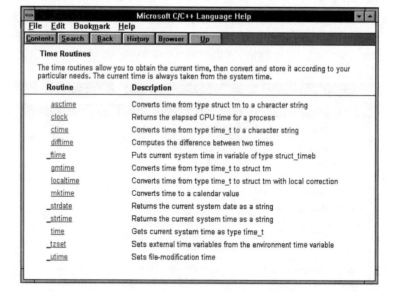

Using a Specific Library Function

To find a routine that serves your program's needs, use one of the on-line
help search techniques discussed in the preceding section. For example, if
your program needs to obtain the current time, this information is available
through the time() function. If you search through the help messages for
time routines and click this selection, the search dialog box displays

information on several time-related functions. One of these functions is
time(), declared as the following:

```
time_t time(time_t *timer);
```

Near the top of the help dialog box is the notation #include <time.h>, as
shown in figure 6.4. This means that the declaration for the time() function
is contained in the file TIME.H and that you must reference this file by adding the #include compiler directive to your program. The .H file name extension is short for *header*, and .H files are known as *header files*.

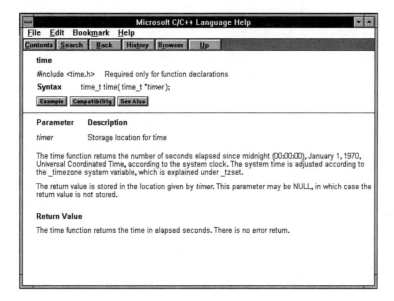

Fig. 6.4
The help
information
available for the
time() function.

Note that the time information is returned as a time_t type, which can be
stored in the passed parameter. This variable holds the number of seconds
that have elapsed since January 1, 1980. This value is not very useful for displaying a date. You can, however, use it as a parameter to another library
function called ctime(), which can display the date represented by the time_t
value. You can use the methods described in the preceding section to get
more information on the ctime() function.

With this information, writing a small program to extract and display the
current system date is simple. Listing 6.1 shows the result. Note the use of the
#include <time.h> directive. The TIME.H file informs the compiler about the
time() and ctime() functions.

Listing 6.1 Using the Library Routines *time( )* and *ctime( )*

```
 1  // GETTIME.CPP
 2  // Demonstrates using the library routine time() and ctime().
 3  #include <iostream.h>
 4  #include <time.h>
 5
 6  void main(void)
 7  {
 8    time_t ATime;
 9
10    time( &ATime ); // You could also use ATime = time(NULL);
11
12    cout << "Current time = "
13         << ctime( ATime )
14         << endl;
15
16    cout << "Press Enter to continue.";
17    cin.get();
18
19  } // main
```

Line 10 calls the library routine `time()` and passes to the function the address of the `time_t` variable `ATime`. When used in this context, the `&` operator is called the *address-of operator*. You saw examples of this operator used to compute the address of variables in Chapter 5, "Pointers." You learn more about using the `&` address-of operator in the section "Pass-by-Reference Parameters" later in this chapter.

Next, you pass the value of `ATime` to the `ctime()` library routine, which returns a character string containing the date and time represented by `ATime`.

Using String Functions

When you write programs that process text, you often use a set of functions known as *string functions*. You have already learned about the `strlen()` function, which determines the length of a character string, and the `strcpy()` function, which copies one string to another. Table 6.2 provides definitions of several frequently used string functions. The Visual C++ library includes even more string functions than are shown in the table. To use any of the string functions, you must place the following in your program file:

```
#include <string.h>
```

All the string functions have a parameter variable declared that is similar to

```
char *s1
```

This means that the function expects a pointer to a string. When you use the function, you can use a pointer to a string or you can specify the name of a char array variable. When you pass an array to a function, C++ automatically passes the address of the char array. As you learned in Chapter 5, "Pointers," the address of a variable is equivalent to a pointer to the variable. The sections that follow show an example that demonstrates the use of some string functions.

Problems with Linking and Libraries

If Visual C++ encounters problems when linking your program and the required libraries, the cause of the problems may be that Visual C++ cannot find one or more of the libraries. First check the Directories dialog box (choose **O**ptions and then **D**irectories). The **L**ibrary directories combo box shows the correct subdirectory name containing the Visual C++ libraries. The default directory is \MSVC\LIB. If your libraries are in a different location, edit this field in the dialog box.

Another possibility is that, when you installed Visual C++, you chose not to install all the required library models. For example, if you installed only the Small memory model library, you may not be able to access the correct functions when compiling a Large memory model program. Be sure that you select the correct memory model. Do this by choosing the **P**roject command from the **O**ptions menu, which displays the Project Options dialog box. Click the **C**ompiler button to display the C/C++ Compiler Options dialog box, and then click the Memory Model list item. You can select **T**iny, **S**mall, **M**edium, **C**ompact, **L**arge, or **H**uge, depending on the libraries you have installed and the requirements of your application. You learn more about this procedure in Chapter 7, "Projects." You can also run the Visual C++ installation program again to install any additional libraries you need.

Table 6.2 Some Popular String Functions

Function	Function Header
strlen()	`size_t strlen(const char *s);` Returns the length of string s.
strcpy()	`char *strcpy(char *dest, const char *src);` Copies the src string to the dest string.

strcmp()	`int strcmp(const char *s1, const char *s2);`
	Compares string s1 to s2 and returns the following:
	  0 if s1 = s2
	  <0 if s1 < s2
	  >0 if s2 > s2

(continues)

Table 6.2 Continued	
Function	**Function Header**
strcmpi( )	int strcmpi(const char *s1, const char *s2); Same as strcmp( ) but treats the characters as if they are all the same case.
strcat( )	char *strcat(char *dest, const char *src); Appends string src to the end of dest.
strnset( )	char *strnset(char *s, int ch, size_t n); Uses strnset( ) on an existing string to set n bytes of the string to character ch. See also the section "Using memset( )" later in this chapter.
strstr( )	char *strstr(const char *s1, const char *s2); Searches for string s2 in s1 and returns a pointer to the characters where s2 is found.

You have seen examples of the strlen( ) and strcpy( ) functions earlier in this book. Most of the time, you will ignore the return value from strcpy( ); but if you do choose to use the return value, strcpy( ) returns a pointer to the dest string. Many other string functions also return a pointer to the dest string, but most programmers ignore the return value.

Using *strcat( )*. strcat( ) appends one string to the end of another string. For example, if s1 has the value of ABC and s2 has the value of XYZ, the function call

```
strcat( s1, s2 );
```

sets s1 to ABCXYZ. Listing 6.2 shows an example that calls the strcat( ) function.

Listing 6.2 Using the *strcat()* Function

```
1   // STRCAT.CPP
2   // Demonstrates the use of the strcat() function to
3   // append or "concatenate" one string to the end
4   // of the other.
5   #include <iostream.h>
6   #include <string.h>
7
8   void main(void)
9   {
10     char s1[80], s2[80];
11     cout << "Enter string #1: ";
12     cin.getline(s1, sizeof(s1));
13     cout << "Enter string #2: ";
```

```
14    cin.getline(s2, sizeof(s2));
15
16    strcat(s1,s2);
17
18    cout << "String 1 + String 2 = "
19         << endl
20         << s1 << endl;
21
22    cout << "Press Enter to continue.";
23    cin.get();
24
25  } // main
```

Using *strcmp( )*. When you want to determine whether one string is equal to another, or greater than or less than another, you should use the strcmp( ) function. strcmp( ) compares its first parameter to its second parameter and returns 0 if the two strings are identical, a value less than zero if string 1 is less than string 2, or a value greater than zero if string 1 is greater than string 2. "Less than" and "greater than" refer to the *alphabetical ordering* (also known as *lexicographical ordering*) of the strings. For example, *Alpha* is less than *Beta*.

A peculiarity of how characters are represented internally on the computer is that uppercase letters are considered "less than" lowercase letters. The letter *A* is less than the letter *a*; the capital letter *Z* is less than the letter *a*! For this reason, when performing a string comparison, you may sometimes want to have the case of the letters ignored (that is, treat both strings as if they were all uppercase or lowercase). The Visual C++ library provides a second function, named stricmp( ), that is identical to strcmp( ) except that stricmp( ) ignores the case of the letters when making comparisons. This means that when you use stricmp( ), the strings "abcdef" and "ABCDEF" are considered to be equivalent.

Listing 6.3 demonstrates how to use the strcmp( ) function in a program. If you want, you can change strcmp( ) to stricmp( ).

Listing 6.3 A Demonstration of the *strcmp( )* Function

```
1  // STRCMP.CPP
2  // Demonstrates the use of the strcmp() function to
3  // compare one string to another string.
4  #include <iostream.h>
5  #include <string.h>
```

(continues)

Listing 6.3 Continued

```
6
7  void main(void)
8  {
9    int result;
10   char s1[80], s2[80];
11
12   cout << "Enter string #1: ";
13   cin.getline(s1, sizeof(s1));
14   cout << "Enter string #2: ";
15   cin.getline(s2, sizeof(s2));
16
17   result = strcmp(s1,s2);
18   if (result < 0 )
19     cout << s1 << " is less than " << s2 << endl;
20   else
21   if (result == 0)
22     cout << s1 << " is equal to " << s2 << endl;
23   else
24     cout << s1 << " is greater than " << s2 << endl;
25
26   cout << "Press Enter to continue.";
27   cin.get();
28
29 } // main
```

Using *strstr( )*. When you need to locate the position of a word of text, such as a word within a sentence, you can use the strstr( ) function. The strstr( ) function has two parameters, s1 and s2, which are both pointers to strings. (You can also use a char array, because the address of a char array is equivalent to a pointer address.) The second string parameter, s2, specifies the string to search for within the larger string, which is specified by s1. If s2's string is found within the larger s1 string, strstr( ) returns a pointer to the starting position of the string that matches the value of s2, relative to the s2 string's position within the s1 string.

For example, if s1 has the value "Programming in C++ is fun" and s2 has the value "C++", the function call

```
ps = strstr( s1, s2 );
```

sets ps (a char * pointer) to point to the first byte of "C++" inside s1. If no match is found, strstr( ) returns NULL. Listing 6.4 demonstrates the use of the strstr( ) function.

Listing 6.4 Using the *strstr( )* Function

```
 1  // STRSTR.CPP
 2  // Demonstrates the use of strstr() to search for one
 3  // string within another string.
 4  #include <iostream.h>
 5  #include <string.h>
 6
 7  void main(void)
 8  {
 9     // Initializes s1 to point to the string constant shown.
10     char *s1 =
11       "The quick brown fox jumped over the lazy brown dog.";
12     // s2 is the string to find in s1.
13     char *s2 = "fox";
14     // ps points to the location where s2 is found.
15     char *ps;
16
17     // strstr() returns a pointer to the location in
18     // s1 where s2 is found.
19     ps = strstr( s1, s2 );
20     cout << "s2 begins here: " << ps << endl;
21
22     cout << "Press Enter to continue.";
23     cin.get();
24
25  } // main
```

Using *memset( ).* If you want to initialize a string to a specific character sequence, such as all blanks or asterisks, use memset( ). It is not one of the string
functions but is instead part of a collection of routines used for directly accessing memory. However, you can use memset( ) quite easily, as shown in
listing 6.5.

To use memset( ), you must include the file MEM.H by placing the following
statement near the beginning of your program file:

```
#include <mem.h>
```

memset( ) has three parameters:

```
memset( void *s, int c, size_t n);
```

The first parameter is a void *s, which roughly means that s can be a pointer
to any type. c is the character to which the area of memory should be initialized, and n is the size of the area (or number of characters) to initialize. The
following example sets the first 10 characters of the string str to asterisks:

```
char str[50];
memset( str, '*', 10 );
```

Be very careful when using memset() because it does not know anything about the declared size of a char array. If, in the preceding example, you used 100 for the third parameter, memset() would merrily write asterisks through memory continuing past the end of str. As you can imagine, writing bytes over unintended memory locations is dangerous and can cause your program to fail.

Listing 6.5 Using *memset( )* to Initialize a String

```
1   // MEMSET.CPP
2   // How to initialize a string to a specific character
3   // by using the memset() function.
4   #include <iostream.h>
5   #include <mem.h>
6
7   void main(void)
8   {
9     char s1[40];
10
11    // memset() copies the character parameter to
12    // string s1. You must specify the number of
13    // characters to set - if you specify too many,
14    // memset() will initialize memory bytes beyond
15    // the end of the string, possibly causing your
16    // program to fail. So be careful!
17    memset( s1, '*', sizeof(s1) );
18    // Adding a null byte. The null byte is not
19    // required in this example because cout
20    // will display only up to the size of s1;
21    // however, if you need to add a null byte
22    // after initializing a string, here is how
23    // to do so:
24    s1[sizeof(s1)] = '\0';
25    cout << "s1 = " << s1 << endl;
26
27    cout << "Press Enter to continue.";
28    cin.get();
29
30  } // main
```

Defining Your Own Functions

Using functions enables you to break your large programs into many smaller functions, making programming tasks easier to manage and easier to understand. By placing code and data into functions, you hide the underlying implementation details from the rest of the program. When the details of a working function are hidden, you can concentrate on the requirements of your program. Furthermore, by placing program features into functions, you increase the opportunities to reuse your functions in other programs later. You will quickly find that functions are an essential feature of C++.

To write your own function, write a function header (or declaration) followed by the C++ statements that are a part of the function. The function header may also include optional parameter variables. Parameter variables are used to pass information to or from the function. Here is an example of a simple function that sums the values in a global array named Data:

```
float sum( int array_size )
{
  int index;
  float total = 0.0;
  for (index=0; index < array_size; index++)
    total += Data[index];
  return total;
} // sum
```

The function sum( ) encapsulates the code needed to sum the values in the Data array. The function header consists of a return type (float), the function name (sum), and a single parameter (array_size). The return type tells the compiler that sum( ) is a function which returns a value to the caller. The array_size variable is a parameter that tells the function how many elements of the Data array are to be summed. Before looking at the implementation details, look at how this function might be called from within a C++ program. The following code section shows an example of a call to sum( ):

```
float Data[100];// global Data array

void main(void)
{
  int num_elements;

  cout << "How many values? ";
  cin >> num_elements: // Check to see if < 100, or you may
                       // have problems.

.
. // Code to input values to Data goes here.
.
  cout << sum( num_elements ) << endl;

} // main
```

When the last cout output statement calls sum( ), the value num_elements is passed to the function sum( ) and becomes sum's local parameter array_size. Therefore, if num_elements has the value of 35, then when the cout statement calls sum( ), the value 35 is assigned to the local parameter array_size.

Inside the sum() function, the array_size, index, and total variables are all local to the function. A *local variable* is created automatically on entry to the function, stored on the stack, and discarded on exiting from the function. These variables exist only when sum() is called. Next, a for loop adds up the values in the Data array. Finally, the return statement passes the computed total back to the caller. In effect, return sets sum() equal to total, and this value is then used to produce output at the caller's cout statement.

In summary, every function has a function header declaration that includes a function result type, the function name, and an optional set of parameter variables. Within the function's body, you can define additional variables that are local to the function. You use a return statement to pass a value back to the caller.

Function Result Types

Every function that you write has a result type. This type should be one of the simple C++ types (such as int, char, or float), a pointer to any C++ type, or a struct type. If your function does not return a result, you can use the void type.

Here are some sample function declarations that return different types of results:

```
int compute_mpg(int gallons, int miles_travelled);
char upcase(char ch);
float StdDev(void);
char * position(char *s);
void DisplayResults(int n);
struct PersonInfo FetchRecord(int record_number);
```

In C++, the use of the struct keyword is optional for functions that return a structure type. You can use the structure tag alone, as in the following function declaration:

```
PersonInfo FetchRecord(int record_number);
```

Be Careful with the *return* Statement

A common programming error is to forget to include the return statement, or to place the return statement within a section of code that does not get executed, as in

```
if (Total >= 0.0)
   return Total;
```

If Total is less than zero, no return statement is executed. Visual C++ flags this omission as a compiler error and generates the error message error C2202: '<function name>' : not all control paths return a value.

Using the *void* Return Type. Many functions that you write will not return a result, because you can use a function as a subroutine to perform a complete task. A function that does not return a result is sometimes called a *procedure*. To tell the compiler that a function does not return a result, use the void return type, as in this example:

```
void DisplayResults( float Total, int array_size)
```

When a function does not return a specific value, the use of the return statement is optional. You can place the return statement at the end of your functions, or you can use the return statement to exit conditionally from a function from any point within the function. For example, depending on a particular condition, you might decide to exit immediately from a function rather than continue processing. Here is an example:

```
if (std_deviation < 1.0) return;
```

If you omit a return type for a function, as in

```
DisplayResults( float Total, int array_size)
```

the C++ compiler assumes that the return type is int, making this declaration identical to the following:

```
int DisplayResults( float Total, int array_size)
```

Always specify your function result types; this clarifies your intent and helps eliminate any confusion that might arise when reading through the source code.

Function Parameters

A function's use of parameters can take several forms. For example, a function may use *pass-by-value* and *pass-by-reference* parameters, or may have no parameters at all. This section examines the mechanism that Visual C++ uses to pass parameters to functions, as well as how to optimize parameter passing depending on the data type in use.

Using *void* in Place of Parameters. If your function has no need for parameters, you should specify the void type without any parameter variables. You have seen this technique used in the sample programs of this book to declare the main( ) function:

```
void main( void )
```

This declaration states that main( ) has no parameters and does not return a result.

Defining Parameter Variables. You define parameter variables as you would other local variables, except that you place the parameter variable definitions within parentheses immediately following the function name. A function can have any number of parameters, depending on the function's requirements. For example, to define a function that takes three floating-point parameters, you would write

```
float ImpRatio(float SecLoadImp,
               float PrimaryTurns,
               float Secondary Turns)
```

When you call `ImpRatio()`, you must pass three parameters to this function. At the calling point, each parameter may be a constant, a variable, or an expression, as in the following example:

```
Impedance = ImpRatio( LoadImpedance, 80, turns*2);
```

Using Pass-by-Value Parameters. In the function examples you have seen so far, the parameters have been passed by value. *Pass-by-value* means that when Visual C++ compiles the function and the code that calls the function, the function receives a copy of the parameter values. If you change the value of a local parameter variable, the change is confined to the function and has no effect outside the function. The program in listing 6.6 makes clear the local nature of a pass-by-value variable.

Listing 6.6 A Demonstration of Pass-By-Value

```
1   // PASSBYVA.CPP
2   // Demonstrates that pass-by-value parameters
3   // can be changed inside a function without
4   // changing the caller's parameter variable.
5   #include <iostream.h>
6
7   void DemoLocal(int value)
8   {
9     cout << "Inside DemoLocal, value=" << value << endl;
10    value = 99;
11    cout << "Inside DemoLocal, value=" << value << endl;
12  } // DemoLocal
13
14  void main(void)
15  {
16    int n = 10;
17    cout << "Before calling DemoLocal, n=" << n << endl;
18    DemoLocal( n );
19    cout << "After calling DemoLocal, n=" << n << endl;
20    cout << "Press Enter to continue.";
21    cin.get();
22  } // main
```

Line 10 shows that the parameter variable value is assigned the value 99; however, the program's output shows that this assignment has no effect outside the function:

```
Before calling DemoLocal, n=10
Inside DemoLocal, value=10
Inside DemoLocal, value=99
After calling DemoLocal, n=10
```

As the output shows, the value of variable n remains unchanged despite the assignment of 99 to the parameter variable value. The parameter variable is private to the DemoLocal() function. If you want your function to alter the parameter variable and to have this change appear also in the original parameter variable used by the caller, you must use pass-by-reference or pointer methods for the function parameters.

Using Pass-by-Reference Parameters. When your function must alter the value of the parameter value and have that altered value percolate up to the caller, you must use the pass-by-reference method of passing parameters. In this method, the compiler does not create a copy of the caller's parameter values. Instead, the compiler passes the memory address of the parameter value to the function. Inside the function, when the local parameter variable is referenced, the code is really accessing the caller's original parameter value.

To understand how this works, look at a program example. To declare a parameter variable as pass-by-reference, you must preface the variable name with the & reference symbol. The reference, when used in the function header's parameter declaration, tells the compiler to use the pass-by-reference method for handling the parameters. Listing 6.7 uses the & reference symbol.

Listing 6.7 A Program That Uses a Pass-by-Reference Parameter

```
1   // PASSBYRE.CPP
2   // Demonstrates the use of pass-by-reference parameters.
3   // Shows that a parameter reference variable can be used
4   // to change the value of the caller's parameter variable.
5   #include <iostream.h>
6
7   void DemoLocal(int &value)
8   {
9     cout << "Inside DemoLocal, value=" << value << endl;
10    value = 99;
11    cout << "Inside DemoLocal, value=" << value << endl;
12  } // DemoLocal
13
14  void main(void)
15  {
```

(continued)

Listing 6.7 Continued

```
16    int n = 10;
17    cout << "Before calling DemoLocal, n=" << n << endl;
18    DemoLocal( n );
19    cout << "After calling DemoLocal, n=" << n << endl;
20    cout << "Press Enter to continue.";
21    cin.get( );
22  } // main
```

This sample program produces the following output:

```
Before calling DemoLocal, n=10
Inside DemoLocal, value=10
Inside DemoLocal, value=99
Before calling DemoLocal, n=99
```

The output shows that the assignment statement inside the DemoLocal( ) function changed the value of n.

One limitation of the pass-by-reference method is that you can pass only variables to the function. You cannot use constants or expressions at the point where the caller invokes the function. In other words, the following call to DemoLocal( ) is invalid because the caller is not using a variable:

```
DemoLocal( 20 + n );
```

Establishing Default Parameter Values. A wonderful feature of C++ functions is that you can establish default values for the parameters. When default values are declared, you can optionally omit values for the default parameters. The only restriction is that you must include all variables from the left up to the first omitted parameter. This restriction is clarified shortly.

Listing 6.8 demonstrates the use of a function that has default parameter values.

Listing 6.8 A Program That Shows How to Assign Default Values to Parameter Variables

```
1   // DEFAULT.CPP
2   // Demonstrates the use of default parameter values.
3
4   #include <iostream.h>
5   void f(int a=10, int b=20, int c=30)
6   {
7     cout << "a=" << a << endl
8          << "b=" << b << endl
9          << "c=" << c << endl;
10  } // f
```

```
11
12   void main(void)
13   {
14       f();
15       f(1);
16       f(1,5);
17       f(1,2,3);
18       cout << "Press Enter to continue.";
19       cin.get();
20   } // main
```

Line 5 shows that the function parameters have been assigned default values, just as you would initialize variables as part of a simple variable declaration. When you call function f(), you can optionally omit all the parameters, because they have default values. Line 14 is a call to f() that omits the parameters and accepts the default values. You can also choose to assign new values to some or all of the parameters, as shown in lines 15 through 17. In line 15, where only one parameter is specified, the value of 1 is assigned to the first parameter variable, and a, b, and c each receive their respective defaults. Line 16 assigns a the value of 1, b the value of 5, and c the default value of 30. Line 17 assigns new values for each of three parameter variables.

You can omit parameters only to the right of the last parameter used. In other words, you can omit parameters as

```
f();
f(a);
f(a,b);
f(a,b,c);
```

but you cannot write

```
f(,,c);
```

The compiler flags this as an error. Therefore, you can omit values only to the right of parameters that you are specifying.

Parameter Type-Checking. The C++ compiler uses the data types that you specify for function parameters in several ways. The compiler uses a data type to ensure that, when your program calls a function, you use the proper type for the function parameter. For example, if you have a function defined as

```
f(char ch);
```

and you try to call this function with a string rather than a character, as in

```
f("Just kidding!");
```

Visual C++ issues an error message. This type-checking helps you spot programming errors before they can cause erratic program operation.

C++ also provides a feature known as overloaded functions (see the section "Function Overloading" later in this chapter). By using overloaded functions, you can define several functions that have the same name, if their parameter types differ from one another. Note this example:

```
f(char ch);
f(int a);
f(float x);
```

Using the overloaded function feature of C++, the compiler processes the following function calls so that each call refers to the appropriate function:

```
f('!');
f(75);
f(3.14159);
```

By examining the type of the parameters, the compiler matches your call to the desired function. The capability of the compiler to support overloaded functions relies on the declared data types for each parameter variable.

Understanding Parameter Passing. Although you don't have to understand how parameter passing works internally, you may find the subject interesting. And understanding what's going on "under the hood" can help you optimize your programs. This section looks at both pass-by-value and pass-by-reference parameter passing in more detail.

How Pass-by-Value Works. When your program invokes a function, each of the parameter values is placed on the stack. Consider the function f(), used in listing 6.8:

```
void f(int a, int b, int c)
{
  cout << "a=" << a << endl
       << "b=" << b << endl
       << "c=" << c << endl;
} // f
```

To call function f(), you write a statement like this:

```
f(1,2,3);
```

The compiler translates this statement into a sequence of machine instructions that resembles the following:

```
push 3
push 2
push 1
call f
add sp, 6
```

The first three instructions place the desired parameter values on the stack. The stack grows downward on the 80x86 family of microprocessors, which produces a stack like that shown in figure 6.5.

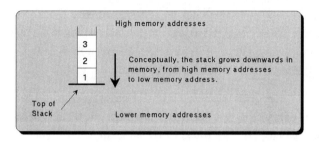

Fig. 6.5
The stack produced by passing the values 3, 2, and 1 using pass-by-value parameter passing.

When the call instruction is executed, the current location of the program is also stored on the stack. The current location is called the *instruction pointer* and is kept in a special microprocessor register named IP. Figure 6.6 shows what the stack looks like when the value of the IP register is pushed on the stack.

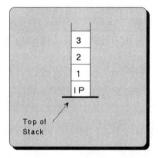

Fig. 6.6
How the stack appears when the value of the IP register is pushed on the stack.

Inside the function f(), when the compiler sees a reference to the parameter variable named a, the compiler knows that a is stored in the stack. Therefore, the compiler produces compiled code that references the memory address of a. The values placed on the stack are copies of the original parameters. Any change you make to these local variables is discarded when the function exits. When the function encounters the return statement (or the assumed return, if the C++ source code does not include a return statement), the microprocessor looks at the top of the stack to determine the location where the function was called. Because the IP register is stored at the stack top, the computer uses this address to return execution to the next statement after where function f( ) was called. Then the computer executes the last machine instruction in the previously shown series of machine instructions:

```
add sp, 6
```

This instruction adds 6 to the stack pointer. Because each of the three parameters is 2 bytes, adding 6 to the stack pointer repositions the stack pointer to the position just before the location where the parameter values were pushed on the stack. This effectively discards the parameter values.

How Pass-by-Reference Works. Pass-by-reference operates analogously to pass-by-value except that the address of the variable, rather than the value of the variable, is placed on the stack. Consider again the function f( ), which is now modified to use pass-by-reference for its parameters:

```
void f(int &a, int &b, int &c)
{
  cout << "a=" << a << endl
       << "b=" << b << endl
       << "c=" << c << endl;
} // f
```

For each reference parameter in the function's parameter list, you must use a variable, instead of a constant, for each of the parameter values. In the following code, the addresses of x, y, and z are passed to the function f( ):

```
int x=1;
int y=2;
int z=3;
f( x, y, z );
```

Because the parameters to f( ) are reference parameters, the compiler will not allow you to write

```
f( 1, 2, 3 );
```

because the compiler cannot generate an address for a simple constant.

For the call f(x, y, z), the compiler produces code that resembles the following:

```
push segment:offset address-of-z
push segment:offset address-of-y
push segment:offset address-of-x
call f
add sp, 12
```

This produces the stack arrangement shown in figure 6.7.

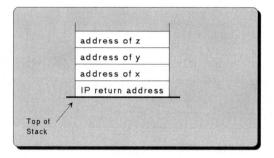

Fig. 6.7
The stack arrangement produced by pass-by-reference parameter passing.

Inside the function f( ), the compiler now knows that the value stored on the stack is not the value of the local parameter variable a, but is instead the memory address of the variable passed by the caller. Notice that a reference parameter and a pointer are equivalent. In the example

```
cout << "a=" << a << endl
```

the compiler treats this reference to a as if a were a pointer variable, and you had written *a to dereference the pointer, like this:

```
cout << "a=" << *a << endl
```

When the function exits, 12 is added to the stack pointer (this value varies depending on the memory model in use). In this example, because a 4-byte *segment:offset* address is used to track each of the three variables, 12 bytes must be removed from the stack to discard the memory addresses.

Using Pointers for Parameter Variables. You can also use pointers to implement pass-by-reference parameters. Indeed, pointers were the only way that C programmers could implement pass-by-reference parameters. In the previous section, you saw how a reference parameter is similar to a pointer variable. In this section, you learn how to use pointers to implement pass-by-reference.

Using pointers for parameter variables requires great attention to detail. You must be sure to use the pointer's address rather than the value to which it points; in some cases, you must use the address-of operator, & (which is distinguished from the & reference operator by the context in which it is used) to obtain the proper address. Consider the case of implementing the f( ) function (shown in the preceding section) so that it uses pointers for the function parameters:

```
void f(int *a, int *b, int *c)
{
  cout << "a=" << *a << endl
       << "b=" << *b << endl
       << "c=" << *c << endl;
} // f
```

In this form, `f()` expects to receive three pointers: a, b, and c. Within the function, each pointer is dereferenced as `*a`, `*b`, or `*c` to obtain the value to which the respective pointer points.

In the preceding sample code, how would you pass the variables x, y, and z to the function `f()`? Use the & address-of operator and write

```
f( &x, &y, &z );
```

When you place & in front of a variable, you obtain the variable's address rather than its value. You saw this notation used when you were introduced to pointers in Chapter 5, "Pointers." Using the address-of operator results in a sequence of machine instructions identical to that used for pass-by-reference:

```
push segment:offset address-of-z
push segment:offset address-of-y
push segment:offset address-of-x
call f
add sp, 12
```

The major distinction between using the address-of operator and using reference parameters is that when you use the address-of operator, you must manually specify the & address-of operator at each location where you call the function `f()`. If your program has numerous functions, you must keep track of which parameters require that you insert the & address-of operator. If you fail to specify the & address-of operator, the compiler will not issue an error. On even a modest-sized program, you can easily lose track of which function calls require parameters to be prefaced by &. The lack of an & address-of operator can result in a dangling pointer, which can produce incorrect results or a crashed program. For this reason, you should use the reference operator form of pass-by-reference in place of pointers.

In some cases, to pass a pointer as a parameter makes perfect sense. Consider a program that uses a pointer to index through all elements of an array. When the program finds a particular value, it calls a function to modify the array entry. The following section of code uses a pointer variable p to efficiently scan through an array of data values in sequential order:

```
int *p;
p = &Data[0];  // Data[] is an array of integers.
while (*p != 0) {
  if (*p < 0) compute_value (p);
  p++;
}
```

When the program finds a data value that is less than zero, the program passes the address of the data element, which is contained in the variable p, to a function named compute_value(). Inside the compute_value() function, the pointer is used to directly access the following array:

```
void compute_value(int *ptr) {
  int new_value;
  .
  . // Perform some computation using *ptr.
  .
  *ptr = new_value;  // Place modified value into the array.
};
```

Remember that ptr holds the address of the array element pointed to by p. Therefore, the assignment

```
*ptr = new_value;
```

places a new value in the original Data array. Using a pointer as a parameter in such a program results in efficient operation of your program and makes perfect sense.

Reference Parameters Are Preferred to Pointer Parameters

Whenever possible, use the & reference operator to pass parameters; it produces an easier-to-read program than pointers. Since the birth of the C language, pointers have been the only way to pass parameters by reference. Not until the recent invention of C++ has the language supported true "pass by reference." Consequently, many C programmers have grown accustomed to using pointers as part of parameter passing. But using pointers for parameter passing was simply a way of working around C's lack of a pass-by-reference mechanism. Many programming errors are caused by incorrect use of pointers for parameter passing, even when coded by expert programmers. You should use the & reference operator because it is more convenient, is easier to use, and results in cleaner source code that is easier to maintain. However, there are uses for pointers as a parameter—just make sure to use reference parameters when it makes sense to use them, and to restrict the use of pointers when it is more appropriate to use pointers.

Using Arrays as Parameters. Use the parameter mechanism to pass array types to functions. C++ always uses the pass-by-reference mechanism to pass entire arrays; when you call a function and use an array as the parameter, internally, C++ automatically treats the function call as if you had placed the & address-of operator in front of the array name. You must therefore be careful never to modify arrays in a called function; doing so also modifies the array in the calling function.

Consider the C++ program in listing 6.9, which implements a Length( ) function to calculate the length of a null-terminated string. In line 8, the parameter variable str is declared as a character array of unknown size. Because no size is specified, C++ lets you call Length( ), which uses character arrays of varying sizes.

Listing 6.9 A Program That Uses an Array as a Parameter

```
 1  // LENGTH1.CPP
 2  // Defines the function Length() to calculate the
 3  // length of a zero-byte terminated string. This
 4  // program demonstrates passing an array as a
 5  // pass-by-value parameter to a function.
 6  #include <iostream.h>
 7
 8  int Length(char str[])
 9  {
10    int count=0;
11    while (str[count++] != '\0');
12    return count;
13  } // Length
14
15  void main(void)
16  {
17    cout << Length("C++ is better than C.") << endl;
18
19    cout << "Press Enter to continue.";
20    cin.get();
21  } // main
```

On calling Length( ) in line 17, the code passes the address of the string constant to the Length( ) function. The body of Length( ) scans through the str[] array by using a simple while loop to count the non-null characters. The while loop terminates when it encounters the null byte at the end of the string.

Using the Reference Operator for Array Types. Another way to write the
Length( ) function is to use the C++ & reference operator. When you use this
operator, your code clearly shows that you are using pass-by-reference for the
array types. Listing 6.10 uses the & reference operator for the Length( ) parameter variable.

**Listing 6.10 A Program That Uses Pass-By-Reference to Pass an
Array Parameter to a Function**

```
 1  // LENGTH2.CPP
 2  // Defines the function Length() to calculate the
 3  // length of a zero-byte terminated string. This
 4  // program demonstrates passing an array as a
 5  // pass-by-reference parameter to a function that
 6  // is more efficient than pass-by-value.
 7  #include <iostream.h>
 8
 9  typedef char string80[80];
10
11  int Length(string80 &str)
12  {
13    int count=0;
14    while (str[count++] != '\0');
15    return count;
16  } // end Length
17
18  void main(void)
19  {
20    string80 s = "C++ is better than C.";
21
22    cout << Length( s ) << endl;
23
24    cout << "Press Enter to continue.";
25    cin.get();
26  } // main
```

In the pass-by-reference version of the program, a typedef is used to create
the string80 type (see line 9). Line 11 then uses the string80 type in the parameter definition. Note the use of the & reference operator. (You must use a
typedef here, because the compiler does not accept char &str[ ]—this is interpreted as an array of references, which is not what you want.)

Within the body of Length( ), when you access str[ ], the compiler translates
this access into a reference to the original variable that was passed to the
Length( ) function (which, in this example, is the s variable defined in line
20). Because Length( ) uses a pass-by-reference parameter, the amount of stack
space required by the parameter variable is only that needed for a memory
address.

Using Pointers to Pass a String. For historical reasons (harking back to the C language), many C++ programmers use a pointer to pass an array to a function. This process is so common that you should make certain you are familiar with the technique. Consider a function to extract numerous characters from one character string and copy them to another. Such a function must have a source string, a destination string, and a parameter indicating the number of characters to copy, as in listing 6.11.

Listing 6.11 A Program That Uses Pointers to Pass Arrays to Functions

```
1   // EXTRACT.CPP
2   // Demonstrates the common use of pointers when
3   // passing arrays to functions.
4   #include <iostream.h>
5
6   // The extract function copies num_chars characters
7   // from the source string to the dest string.
8   int extract(char *dest, char *source, int num_chars)
9   {
10    int count;
11    for(count=1; count <= num_chars; count++)
12      *dest++ = *source++;
13    *dest = '\0';
14    return count;  // return the number of chars processed.
15  } // end extract
16
17  void main(void)
18  {
19    char s1[40] = "C++ is better than C.";
20    char s2[40];
21
22    extract( &s2[0], &s1[0], 3 );
23
24    cout << s2 << endl;
25
26    cout << "Press Enter to continue.";
27    cin.get();
28  } // main
```

Take a look at the extract() function in lines 8 through 15. Note that in the parameter declarations no arrays are defined—only pointers to type char. In line 12, the pointers are used to access the destination and source strings, respectively. Note in line 22 the use of the & address-of operator to obtain the address of the destination and source strings—this is very important. By varying the array index on the source string, you can extract a subset of the source string beginning from a character position other than the first. For example, if you write

```
extract( &s1[0], &s2[4], 2 );
```

you extract the word is from the source string.

Using Structures as Parameters. You can use either the pass-by-value or pass-by-reference technique to pass structures to functions, just as you can pass arrays to functions. As with all pass-by-value parameters, if the structure is large, the time needed to copy a struct parameter to the stack may be prohibitive. In such cases, seriously consider using pass-by-reference instead.

Listing 6.12 shows a program that passes a structure to a function by using the pass-by-value method. To change the program to pass-by-reference, you need only place the & reference operator between CPersonInfo and Data in the DisplayInfo() function header.

Listing 6.12 A Program That Passes a Structure by Value

```
 1   // STRUCT3.CPP
 2   // Demonstrates using a structure as a
 3   // pass-by-value parameter to a function.
 4   #include <iostream.h>
 5
 6   // Define the CPersonInfo structure type.
 7   struct CPersonInfo {
 8     char name [20];
 9     char street[25];
10     char city[30];
11     char state[3];
12     char zip[9];
13   };
14
15   void DisplayInfo( CPersonInfo Data )
16   {
17     cout << Data.name << endl
18          << Data.street << endl
19          << Data.city << " " << Data.state
20          << " " << Data.zip << endl;
21   } // DisplayInfo
22
23   void main(void)
24   {
25     // Declare DataRecord as a CPersonInfo structure.
26     CPersonInfo DataRecord = { "Paul Barrett",
27                                "37 King Street",
28       } // main;
```

(continues)

Listing 6. 12 Continued

```
29
30    DisplayInfo ( DataRecord );
31
32    cout << "Press Enter to continue.";
33    cin.get( );
34
35  } // main
```

Passing an Array of Structures. Passing an array of structures is a bit more complicated, because you must use a typedef if you want to use the pass-by-reference method. Listing 6.13 shows one way to pass an array of structures. Note in line 15 the use of typedef to define CDataBase as a synonym for an array of 100 CPersonInfo structures. The CDataBase type is then used as the parameter to DisplayInfo( ) (lines 17 through 27). Inside DisplayInfo( ), the members of the CDataBase array are referenced through the Data[] array parameter (see lines 22 through 25).

Listing 6.13 A Program That Passes an Array of Structures to a Function

```
1   // STRUCT4.CPP
2   // Demonstrates passing an array of structures,
3   // by reference, as a parameter to a function.
4   #include <iostream.h>
5
6   // Define the CPersonInfo structure type.
7   struct CPersonInfo {
8     char name [20];
9     char street[25];
10    char city[30];
11    char state[3];
12    char zip[9];
13  };
14
15  typedef CPersonInfo CDataBase[100];
16
17  void DisplayInfo( CDataBase &Data, int num_records )
18  {
19    int index;
20    for (index=0; index < num_records; index++)
21    {
22      cout << Data[index].name << endl
23           << Data[index].street << endl
24           << Data[index].city << " " << Data[index].state
25           << "  " << Data[index].zip << endl;
26    }
27  } / /  DisplayInfo
28
29  void main(void)
```

```
30  {
31      // Declare DataRecord as a CPersonInfo structure.
32      CDataBase DataRecords = { "Jack Tackett, Jr.",
33                                "4606 Millbrook Rd",
34                                "Cary", "NC", "27604",
35                                "Peggy Tackett",
36                                "4606 Millbrook Rd",
37                                "Cary", "NC", "27604",,
38                                        };
39
40      DisplayInfo ( DataRecords, 2 );
41
42      cout << "Press Enter to continue.";
43      cin.get();
44
45  } // main
```

Line 15 declares DataRecords to be an array of 100 CPersonInfo structures
(using the CDataBase type name). The first two members of the DataRecords[]
arrays are initialized as part of the declaration. Line 40 calls the
DisplayInfo() function, passing both the array of structures as well as the
number of elements used in the array. To keep the example simple, only the
first two
elements of the array are used.

Using the *const* Parameter Modifier. Your program operates more efficiently when you use pass-by-reference rather than pass-by-value, as you have
seen in two examples. These examples include passing arrays, structures,
and any large data structures to a function. Often, when you use pass-by-
reference, your functions need only to read the values of the parameter
variables; you don't have the need or the intention of making changes to the
parameter variables. To ensure that your variables are not altered in any way,
you can mark your parameters as "read only" by prefacing their declaration
with the keyword const.

Consider again the DisplayInfo() function from listing 6.13. This function
outputs the values from an array of structures. You might assume that a
function with a name like DisplayInfo() would not alter its parameters. To
ensure that the function makes no modifications, you can preface each of
the parameter declarations with the const keyword:

```
void DisplayInfo( const CDataBase &Data, const int num_records )
{
  int index;
  for (index=0; index < num_records; index++)
  {
    cout << Data[index].name << endl
         << Data[index].street << endl
         << Data[index].city << " " << Data[index].state
         << "  " << Data[index].zip << endl;
  }
} // DisplayInfo
```

Inside `DisplayInfo( )`, if you attempt to assign a new value to any of the parameter variables, the compiler issues the following error message:

```
error C2607: 'initializing' : cannot implicitly convert a 'struct
   ::CPersonInfo [100]' to a 'struct ::CPersonInfo __near &[100]'
   that is not const
```

Modify the STRUCT4.CPP program so that it uses `const` parameters. Then attempt to assign a value to `num_records` within the `DisplayInfo( )` function and see what happens.

The use of the `const` keyword in parameter declarations serves two purposes:

- When other programmers reuse your functions in their programs, the use of `const` alerts them that the parameters are read-only.

- In large functions, you can easily make an inadvertent and incorrect assignment to a parameter variable. If you make your parameters `const` where possible, the compiler will prevent you from making an inadvertent assignment.

Using the Ellipsis in Parameters. C++ provides a mechanism to define a variable number of parameters for a function. This mechanism uses an ellipsis ($\ldots$) to denote that additional parameters may be added when the function is called. The following example is such a declaration:

```
int f( int a, int b, ... )
{
   // Function definition goes here.
};
```

This notation should help you recognize the use of a variable number of parameters when viewing other programmers' source code. The actual usage of the variable parameter list is a bit complicated and beyond the scope of this book. Furthermore, variable parameter lists evade the type-checking provided by the C++ compiler, thus increasing the likelihood of programming errors.

Defining Variables within Functions

Many of the sample functions used in this chapter and in earlier chapters declared variables inside the function body. Such variables are said to be local to the function. Local variables cannot be used outside the scope of the function in which they are defined. Most local variables have temporary duration—that is, memory for the local variable exists only while the function is executing. This type of variable is known as an *auto* variable, and such temporary duration is known as *auto duration*.

Auto Variables

By default, any variable that you declare inside a function is said to be an auto variable. *Auto* is short for *automatic*, to indicate that local variables are allocated space automatically on entry to the function and are deallocated on exit. You can optionally preface your local variable definitions with the keyword auto, as in

```
auto int Total;
```

However, you don't have to specify the auto keyword, because auto duration is assigned to local variables by default.

Static Variables

Variables defined outside a function in your source file are *static* variables. The memory for a static variable is allocated throughout the execution of your program. Because static variables remain allocated throughout program execution, they are used to hold values between calls to functions. These variables are said to have *static duration*. You can also declare local variables within functions to be static by prefacing the variable declaration with the keyword static, as in the following example:

```
function TotalResults(float DataValue)
{
  static float Sum;
  .
  .
  .
  Sum = Sum + DataValue;
}
```

Because Sum is a static variable, the memory space allocated for Sum remains untouched after leaving the TotalResults() function. Therefore, you can use Sum to accumulate a sum across calls to TotalResults().

The term *global variable* was used in an earlier chapter to describe the concept of static variables. The term *global*, as used in this book, means that the variable is not a local function variable. Because global variables are defined outside a function, any of the functions within the source file can use them.

Register Variables

Another type of C++ variable is the *register* variable. By prefacing the declaration of a variable with the keyword `register`, you suggest to the compiler that the variable be stored in one of the microprocessor's hardware registers. The `register` keyword is only a suggestion; it is not a mandate to the compiler. The 80x86 family of microprocessors does not have many hardware registers to spare, so the compiler may choose to ignore your suggestion.

Place the `register` keyword before an integer-type variable, like this:

```
register int index;
```

You can use a register variable as a loop control variable. By keeping the loop control variable in a register, you reduce the time that the CPU requires to fetch the value of the variable from memory. Note an example:

```
register int index;
for (index = 0; index<1000; index++) ...
```

Use the `register` keyword sparingly, if at all. Because the compiler automatically tries to optimize your program by placing values in registers, your request to keep a specific variable in a register may disrupt the compiler's capability to optimize register usage.

Defining Functions Separate from the Implementation

Each function must be defined before other functions can call it. The sample programs you have seen so far have met this requirement by declaring each function before the main( ) function. However, you can define function prototypes without an implementation. A function prototype consists of the function name, the function return type, and its parameter list. The implementation of the function's body is omitted. This minimal information provides the compiler with everything it needs to know to process calls to the function. Define the function prototype by terminating the declaration with a semicolon, as in the following:

```
void DisplayInfo( CDataBase &Data, int num_records );
```

Because no function body is present, the compiler knows that this is a function prototype and that the implementation of the function will appear later in the file. Listing 6.14 is a modified version of the STRUCT4.CPP program that appeared in listing 6.13. This listing shows how you might declare a function before its implementation. Note that in the actual implementation you must repeat the function declaration with no changes to the return type or parameters.

Listing 6.14 A Program That Uses a Function Prototype

```
 1   // HEADER.CPP
 2   // Modified version of STRUCT4.CPP used to
 3   // demonstrate the use of function headers.
 4   #include <iostream.h>
 5
 6   // Define the CPersonInfo structure type.
 7   struct CPersonInfo {
 8     char name [20];
 9     char street[25];
10     char city[30];
11     char state[3];
12     char zip[9];
13   };
14
15   typedef CPersonInfo CDataBase[100];
16
17   // The next declaration is a function prototype. This
18   // declaration informs the compiler about the
19   // function DisplayInfo. The semicolon after the
20   // function header tells the compiler that this
21   // line serves as a declaration only; the actual
22   // definition appears later in the file.
23   void DisplayInfo( CDataBase &Data, int num_records );
24
25   void main(void)
26   {
27     // Declare DataRecord as a CPersonInfo structure.
28     CDataBase DataRecords = { "Jack Tackett, Jr.",
29                               "4606 Millbrook Rd",
30                               "Cary", "NC", "27604",
31                               "Peggy Tackett",
32                               "4606 Millbrook Rd",
33                               "Cary", "NC", "27604",,
34                                         };
35     DisplayInfo ( DataRecords, 2 );
36
37     cout << "Press Enter to continue.";
38     cin.get();
39
40
41   } // main
42
```

(continued)

Listing 6.14 Continued

```
43   // And here is the actual implementation of DisplayInfo.
44   //
45   void DisplayInfo( CDataBase &Data, int num_records )
46   {
47     int index;
48     for (index=0; index < num_records; index++)
49     {
50       cout << Data[index].name << endl
51            << Data[index].street << endl
52            << Data[index].city << " " << Data[index].state
53            << "   " << Data[index].zip << endl;
54     }
55   } // DisplayInfo
```

Why Use Function Prototypes?

There are several reasons to use function prototypes in your programs. The sample programs that you have seen so far have all defined their functions before the main( ) function of the program. However, as your programs increase in size, you will eventually have several pages of function source code appearing before the main( ) function. Trying to find the main( ) function and follow the program's logic can be difficult in a large program. For this reason, C and C++ programmers have traditionally placed main( ) as the first function in the source file and then followed with the remaining program functions.

Another reason to use function prototypes is to avoid having to determine which functions must be declared before others. Consider the following program structure:

```
f1(void);
f2(void);
f3(void);

main(void)
{
  f2( );
}

f1(void)
{
  f3( );
}

f2(void)
{
  f1( );
```

```
      }

      f3(void)
      {
          .
          .
          .
      }
```

If you don't use function prototypes, you must structure this program in the following way, so that each function is properly defined before it is called:

```
      f3(void)
      {
          .
          .
          .
      }

      f1(void)
      {
          f3( );
      {

      f2(void)
      {
          f1( );
      }

      main(void)
      {
          f2( );
      }
```

Suppose that your program has 24 functions rather than 4 functions. Without function prototypes, determining the proper declaration order for such a large program becomes quite an ordeal. You will find that your programming task is easier if you declare function prototypes at the top of the source file. Thereafter, you can place your function definitions in any sequence. Figure 6.8 shows the structure that your programs will have when you use this technique.

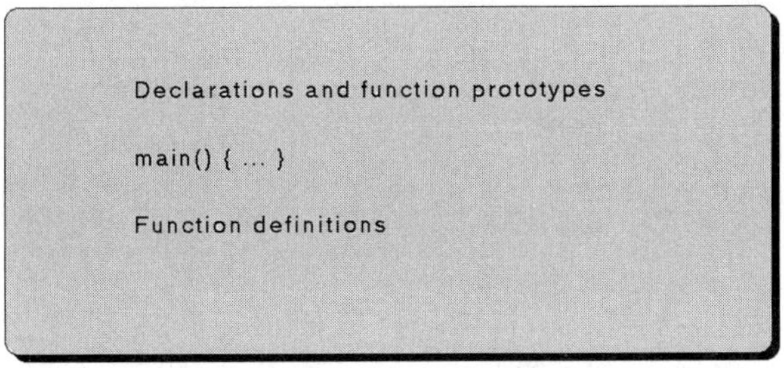

```
      Declarations and function prototypes

      main() { ... }

      Function definitions
```

Fig. 6.8
The overall program structure when function prototypes are used.

In Chapter 7, "Projects," you learn how to place function prototypes into separate .H header files. After you place your definitions in separate files, you can share your code more easily among programs. You learn also how to use this technique to split your programs into several source files for ease in project management.

Putting It All Together into a Sample Program

In this chapter, you have learned much about using functions in C++ programs. To give you a complete feel for using functions in an actual program, look at the object-oriented program in listing 6.15. This program uses function prototypes, pointers, and functions.

Listing 6.15 An Object-Oriented Implementation of List-Manipulation Routines

```
1   // LIST.CPP
2   // This is a modified version of the LISTTYPE.CPP program
3   // from Chapter 5. Here, the program has been restructured
4   // to use functions to add, list, and destroy entries
5   // from the list. Further, the entire program is now
6   // organized in an object-oriented framework.
7   #include <iostream.h>
8   #include <string.h>
9
10  const int FORWARD = 0;
11  const int REVERSE = 1;
12  const int MAXNAMESIZE = 20;
13
14  // Define the list_type object as
15  // a structure containing data fields,
16  // next and previous link pointers,
17  // and the Add_to_Tail() and Display_List()
18  // functions to operate on the list.
19  struct list_element
20  {
21    char name[MAXNAMESIZE];
22    // The following point to the next entry in
23    // the list and the previous entry in the
24    // list, respectively.
25    list_element *next;
26    list_element *prev;
27  };
28
29  struct list_type
30  {
31    list_element *head;  // Points to front of the list.
32    list_element *tail;  // Points to the end of the list.
```

Listing 6.15 Continued

```cpp
33     void Initialize_List(void);  // Initializes head & tail.
34     void Add_to_Tail(char name_to_add[]);
35     void Display_List(int Direction);
36     void Destroy_List(void);
37   };
38
39   //==============================================
40   void main(void) {
41     // Used to process keyboard command input.
42     char command_ch, direction_ch;
43     char TheName[MAXNAMESIZE];
44     list_type TheList;           // The list object.
45
46     TheList.Initialize_List();
47     do {
48       cout << "Select A)dd, L)ist or Q)uit? ";
49       cin.get(command_ch);
50       cin.ignore(1);
51
52       switch(command_ch) {
53         // Add a new entry to the list.
54         case 'a': case 'A': {
55           cout << "Enter name:   ";
56           cin.getline(TheName, sizeof(TheName) );
57           TheList.Add_to_Tail(TheName);
58           break;
59         } // case
60         // Display the contents of the list.
61         case 'l': case 'L': {
62           cout << "List in F)orward or R)everse direction? ";
63           cin.get(direction_ch);
64           cin.ignore(1);
65           switch (direction_ch) {
66             case 'f': case 'F' : {
67               TheList.Display_List(FORWARD);
68               break;
69             } // end case
70             case 'r': case 'R' : {
71               TheList.Display_List(REVERSE);
72               break;
73             } // end case
74             default: break;
75           } // end switch
76           break;
77         } // end case
78         // Quit running the program.
79         case 'q': case 'Q': {
80           TheList.Destroy_List();
81           break;
82         } // end case
83         default:
84           break;
85       } // end switch
```

(continues)

Listing 6.15 Continued

```
86     } while ((command_ch != 'q') && (command_ch != 'Q'));
87
88     cout << "Press Enter to continue.";
89     cin.get();
90   } // end main
91
92   //================================================
93   void list_type::Initialize_List(void)
94   {
95     head = NULL;
96     tail = NULL;
97   }
98
99   //================================================
100  void list_type::Add_to_Tail(char name_to_add[])
101  // Add new data to the tail of the list.
102  {
103    list_element *next_entry;    // Points to next entry in list.
104
105    // Allocate next entry in list.
106    if (head == NULL) { // If list is now empty...
107      next_entry = tail = head = new list_element;
108      next_entry->next = NULL;
109      next_entry->prev = NULL;
110    } // end if
111    else { // List is not empty.
112      next_entry = new list_element;
113      // Set previous pointer to point at what
114      // was the last entry.
115      next_entry->prev = tail;
116      // Set the previous entry's next pointer to
117      // point at the new entry.
118      tail->next = next_entry;
119      // And set tail to point the new entry.
120      tail = next_entry;
121      // And the last entry does not point
122      // anywhere so set it to NULL.
123      next_entry->next = NULL;
124    } // else
125
126    strcpy( next_entry->name, name_to_add );
127  } // Add_to_Tail
128
129  //================================================
130  void list_type::Display_List(int Direction)
131  // Display the content of the list in either
132  // the FORWARD or the REVERSE direction.
133  {
134    list_element *an_entry; // Temporary pointer to entries.
135
136    switch (Direction) {
137      case FORWARD: {
```

Listing 6.15 Continued

```
138        an_entry = head;
139        while (an_entry != NULL) {
140          cout << an_entry->name << endl;
141        an_entry = an_entry->next;
142        } // end while
143        break;
144      } // end case
145      case REVERSE: {
146        an_entry = tail;
147        while (an_entry != NULL) {
148          cout << an_entry->name << endl;
149          an_entry = an_entry->prev;
150        } // end while
151      } // end case
152      default: break;
153    } // end switch
154  } // Display_List
155
156  //=================================================
157  void list_type::Destroy_List(void)
158  // Free up all memory used the list.
159  {
160    list_element *next_entry;
161    // Delete all of the entries and free
162    // up their memory allocations. This code
163    // starts at the end of the list and removes
164    // each entry, one by one, until reaching
165    // the beginning of the list (where
166    // next_entry->prev = NULL).
167    while (tail != NULL) {
168      next_entry = tail->prev;
169      delete tail;
170      tail = next_entry;
171    } // end while
172  } // end Destroy_List
```

LIST.CPP is a significant restructuring of the LISTTYPE.CPP program (listing 5.7) in Chapter 5, "Pointers." In LISTTYPE.CPP, the operation of adding, displaying, and deleting the list elements were all coded inside the main() function. By splitting these tasks into separate functions, you can understand more easily the structure of the program. Furthermore, if you encapsulate the functions and data into a single object, the list code becomes completely reusable, as you will see.

Listing 6.15 reworks listing 5.7's list data structure so that the head and tail pointers (plus the functions for adding, displaying, and destroying the list) are encapsulated into an object description (see lines 29 through 37). The declarations of the Initialize_List(), Add_to_Tail(), Display_List(), and

Destroy_List( ) functions within the list_type structure serve as function prototypes. The actual implementation of these functions is in lines 93 through 97, 100 through 127, 130 through 154, and 157 through 172, respectively. The main( ) function appears at the top of the file in lines 40 through 90.

To understand the program's operation, now look at the code in detail. Line 44 declares TheList as a list_type object that is local to main( ). Because all the code and data needed to support the list is encapsulated in list_type, you can easily modify this program to add more lists. For instance, you can add

```
list_type A_List, B_List, C_List;
```

Because the head and tail pointers are stored within each object, each list is completely independent of the others. Are you beginning to see the value of object orientation in programming? Each of these objects—A_List, B_List, and C_List—becomes a fully functioning, independent list object. The code created to implement the list is now completely reusable within your program or within other programs. This saves you much coding effort later.

Line 46 calls the Initialize_List( ) member function of TheList. This function sets TheList's head and tail pointers to NULL. The rest of the main( ) function handles the user interface to prompt for a command, handle the entry
of new names to add, and exit the program. In line 57, TheList calls the Add_to_Tail( ) member function so that names can be added to TheList. Lines 67 and 71 call the Display_List( ) function to output the current list content, and line 80 calls Destroy_List( ) to delete all the memory allocated to the current list.

Note that in this modified program, the main( ) function now knows nothing about the internal structure of the list. main( ) handles the user interface and calls the list object's member functions to add and display list elements and to destroy the list. The internal structure of the list is so completely encapsulated that its structure is hidden from outside users. This technique of hiding the internal structure of routines is good programming practice. It frees the programmer from worrying about low-level details of library routines or other routines. In Chapter 7, "Projects," you learn how to convert this list code into a precompiled module that other programs can use.

The implementation of the Add_To_Tail( ) and Display_List( ) functions is nearly identical to the similar code used in listing 5.7. Indeed, the code was copied from the original program source and placed into the functions.

Function Overloading

C++ lets you declare several different functions that have the same name. To understand why this is useful, consider a function that returns the square of its input value. You can declare such a function as

```
int square( int x )
{
  return x*x;
}
```

To implement a similar function to process a long or double value, define separate functions by using a different function name for each type, as in

```
long lsquare (long x);
double fsquare (double x);
```

C++, however, lets you declare multiple functions that have the same name. A function name that is reused is known as an *overloaded function*. C++ uses the data types of the parameters to distinguish the functions from one another. Here is an example of square( ) rewritten as an overloaded function:

```
int square(int x);
long square(long x);
double square(double x);
```

In your program, you call the square( ) function as you would any other function:

```
long radius = 40000;
result = square(radius);
```

Visual C++ looks at the type of the parameter variables to determine which of the functions to call. In the preceding example, the call to square( ), Visual C++ calls

```
long square(long x);
```

because the radius parameter variable is a long data type. The next section, "Function Templates," contains an additional example of an overloaded function.

To determine which of the overloaded functions to call, the C++ compiler requires that at least one of the parameter values have a type different from those used by the other functions. Therefore, you could have two overloaded functions declared as

```
int f( int a, int b, int c);
int f( int a, int b, float c);
```

Visual C++ can tell these functions apart because at least one of the parameter values has a different type. However, if you try to write an overloaded function that has similar data types, Visual C++ issues an error. For example, the following definitions would not compile because the compiler cannot distinguish them from one another:

```
int f( int a, int b, int c);
int f( int a, int b, int x);
```

The actual mechanism that Visual C++ uses to select the correct overloaded function involves a sequence of steps and checks on the parameter types. Ideally, Visual C++ finds an overloaded function that exactly matches the parameter types used by the caller. In some cases, though, an exact match cannot be found. For example, if you call the square( ) function with the float type, the compiler sees that square( ) is defined only as the int, long, and double types. However, Visual C++ can easily convert a float parameter to a double, which then causes a match to the overloaded function that uses a double parameter, as in the following:

```
double square(double x);
```

In summary, Visual C++ selects an overloaded function based on the following rules:

- If an exact match between the caller's parameter types and an overloaded function is found, use the overloaded function.

- If an exact match is not available, but if converting a type to a superior type—such as an int parameter to a long, or a float to a double—produces an exact match, use that selected function. (A type is superior to another type if the superior type can handle a larger range of values, such as converting an int to a long or a char to an int.)

- If a match that uses a user-defined cast operator is available, use it. You can define and overload the cast operators (int), (long), and so on. You can also create cast operators for your own class types (classes are defined beginning in Chapter 8, "Classes").

- If an overloaded function is defined with a variable number of parameters (by using the ellipsis, . . .), it may be used as a potential match.

Function Templates

The C++ language defines a mechanism, called a function template, to create a generic function—that is, a single function which can simultaneously support multiple data types for its parameter or parameters. Unfortunately, MSVC Versions 1.0 and 1.5 do not support function templates as defined by the emerging C++ standard. The concept of function templates is, however, very important to the understanding of C++ and object-oriented programming techniques; the next few paragraphs describe how function templates work in the proposed C++ standard.

Microsoft Visual C++ and Templates

Microsoft does not support true C++ templates as described in the *Annotated Reference Manual*, also known as the ARM. The C++ community views this book as the de facto definition of the C++ language, considering that its coauthor is Bjarne Stroustrup, the creator of C++. The ANSI and ISO standards committees used the ARM as their base document for their standard definition of the language, which they are still working to complete. Microsoft has stated that as soon as the standards bodies issue the standard definition of C++, MSVC will support that standard, perhaps even in the next release. Until then, Microsoft provides a tool called TEMPLDEF.EXE, located in the \MSVC\BIN directory, to build template-based objects. Unfortunately, the use of this tool is beyond the scope of this book.

Use a function template when you find yourself writing a sequence of identical overloaded functions. For example, consider a function named abs() that returns the absolute value of its parameter. (The absolute value of a number x is x if x is greater than 0, or $-x$ if x is less than 0.)

To implement abs() so that it can accept int, float, long, and double parameters, you can write the function four separate times and let C++'s overloaded function feature sort out which function to call, depending on the data type. Your set of abs() definitions might look something like this:

```
int abs(int x)
{
  return (x<0) ? -x : x;
}

long abs(long x)
{
  return (x<0) ? -x : x;
}
```

```
float abs(float x)
{
  return (x<0) ? -x : x;
}

double abs(double x)
{
  return (x<0) ? -x : x;
}
```

For this type of problem, however, the C++ standard provides a much better solution called *function templates*. Instead of writing all of those abs() functions, you can write a single function template that looks like this:

```
template <class TYPE>
TYPE abs( TYPE x )
{
  return (x<0) ? -x : x;
};
```

The template keyword indicates to the compiler that a function template is present. The TYPE keyword is a placeholder symbol indicating that the compiler can substitute the appropriate data type. Imagine the preceding template definition and substitute int. That is all you have to do to write a generic abs() function. This function works with any data type, if a unary minus (-) is defined for the data object. (Note that magic word *object*. As you learn in Chapters 8, 9, and 10, you can create your own data objects. A function template works for any object or type, even those that do not yet exist, as long as the object or type has a unary minus operator. You learn how to create such objects later in this book.)

You can declare an overloaded function, like other functions, independent of the function template. For instance, if you separately add a definition for

```
char * abs( char * ) {...}
```

the compiler treats this as an overloaded function.

Function-like Macros

Macros are not functions. However, in many respects, their definition and use is sometimes similar to that of functions. A macro is a defined text substitution that you create by using the #define directive. You have already learned to use #define to create a symbolic constant, as in the following example:

```
#define MAXIMUM 100
```

This equates the symbol MAXIMUM with the text 100. When you use the symbol MAXIMUM within your program, the compiler substitutes the text value of 100 and continues processing as if you had written the characters 100 in your text.

Macros can be used in C++ for more than simple text substitution. You can create and use macros that look very much like functions, complete with parameter values. You create function-like macros by using the #define directive, and they result in a text substitution when invoked. Consider the square() function used to compute the square of a parameter value. This function results in simple multiplication of its parameter variable—x to produce x*x. Because of its simplicity, square() is a reasonable candidate to use as a macro. To implement square() as a macro rather than as a function, use #define to declare the macro:

```
#define square(x) (x*x)
```

This #define directive sets square(x) equivalent to (x*x). At compile time, Visual C++ substitutes the value you use as a parameter to square() for x. If you write

```
float a = 10;
a = square (a);
```

Visual C++ translates this into

```
a = (a*a);
```

and then compiles the statement. Note that the parameter to square(), the variable a, is substituted for x in the text expansion of the macro.

Remember that a function-like macro is not a function; it is a simple text substitution. Therefore, each time you reference the macro in your source, the macro may result in a text expansion and generate more code than it would if you called a traditional function. However, the macro creates inline code that eliminates the overhead caused by making a function call (pushing parameters on the stack, calling a subroutine, accessing the parameter values from with the function, and then popping the parameters when done).

When writing a macro definition, you must use care with the parameters. Consider the following simple macro definition:

```
#define ADD(x,y) x + y
```

When you use this macro in an expression, such as

```
a = ADD(10,20);
```

the macro expands to

```
a = 10 + 20;
```

But consider applying the macro within a more complicated expression:

```
a = c * ADD(10,20);
```

This statement expands to

```
a = c * 10 + 20;
```

and may not produce the result you expected. Remember that under the algebraic rules of hierarchy, the multiplication step is performed before the addition step. This expression is evaluated as if you had written

```
a = (c * 10) + 20;
```

which is probably not the result you intended. You probably wanted this macro to expand within the expression to read

```
a = c * (10 + 20);
```

To achieve the text substitution you want, you must place parentheses around the macro's definition so that the proper expansion takes place. The proper definition for ADD( ) becomes

```
#define ADD(x,y) (x + y )
```

A similar problem occurs when the parameter value is an expression. Suppose that you have a macro defined as

```
#define MULT(x,y) (x*y)
```

and you write

```
a = MULT(3+5,10);
```

This expansion produces the expression

```
a = 3+5*10;
```

which is not the result you want. What you want is

```
a = (3+5) * (10);
```

The solution is to get in the habit of putting parentheses around each argument in a macro definition. The definition of MULT( ) becomes

```
#define MULT(x,y) ((x)*(y))
```

A Common Mistake

A frequent mistake made with the use of #define is to place a semicolon inadvertently at the end of the #define statement. Do not do so; the macro is pure text substitution, not a statement. A semicolon at the end of the macro definition will be inserted into any reference to the macro. If you mistakenly write

```
#define ADD(x,y) (x+y);
```

and then use ADD( ) in the expression

```
a = ADD(10,20) * c;
```

the macro expands incorrectly to

```
a = (10 + 20); *c;
```

Because C++ lets you use an expression as a statement (C++ discards the value of an expression if the expression is not assigned to another variable), the result of the macro substitution is two statements that compile without error. Obviously, though, this text substitution produces erroneous code.

When defining macros, you can use a couple of special macro definition operators: the quoted string operator # and the string concatenation operator ##. The # quoted string operator places quotation marks around the parameter to the macro so that a macro defined as

```
#define printx(x) cout << #x << x
```

can be used to expand the following expression into a suitable output statement:

```
printx(10+10)
```

This becomes

```
cout << "10+10" << 10+10;
```

Note how the macro parameter x, where prefaced with #, is expanded as the quoted string "10+10" rather than the arithmetic expression.

The concatenation operator ## is especially useful when you are using a macro to automatically create a sequence of identifiers. Suppose that your program must have four identifiers named Quarter1, Quarter2, Quarter3, and Quarter4, initialized to 1, 2, 3, and 4, respectively. By creating a macro definition, you can create a shorthand declaration and initialization statement for these identifiers. Using the definition

```
#define ID(x) int Quarter##x = x
```

and the sequence of statements

```
ID(1);
ID(2);
ID(3);
ID(4);
```

Visual C++ expands the macros into

```
int Quarter1 = 1;
int Quarter2 = 2;
int Quarter3 = 3;
int Quarter4 = 4;
```

In the concatenation operation (`Quarter` becoming affixed to the value of x), any extra blanks in the line concatenation are removed so that the value represented by x immediately follows the item with which it is being concatenated. In other words, if you write

```
ID(    1);
```

you will get

```
int Quarter1 =     1;
```

The *#undef* Directive

If you no longer want to use a macro in your program, or if you want to create a new definition for a given macro, you can erase the macro's definition by writing

```
#undef macroname
```

where *macroname* is the name of any macro definition already created in your source file.

Problems with Macros

Although macros are used frequently in C++ programming, they are not needed nearly as much as they were used in C++'s predecessor, the C language. Because so many C++ programmers learned C before learning C++, these programmers continue to use C programming techniques in their C++ coding. In most instances in which a macro might be used, you can use the enhanced features of C++ to eliminate the need for a macro.

For example, you should use `const` symbolic constants in place of `#define` statements so that the compiler can perform type-checking in expressions and parameters to functions. When you define the constant MAXIMIUM as

```
const int MAXIMUM = 100;
```

the compiler now knows that MAXIMUM is of the int type. However, when you use a macro such as

```
#define MAXIMUM 100
```

the compiler cannot perform the same degree of checking that it can perform when the specific type is specified.

Another problem occurs when you use function-like macros. The macro is a blind text substitution. You already read in the text box "A Common Mistake" how the inadvertent placement of a semicolon in a #define statement can result in a flawed text substitution that compiles without error. Consider another example of a problem that can occur when you use a macro. You could define a macro to implement an absolute value function, abs( ), like this:

```
#define abs(x) ((x)<0) ? -(x) : (x) )
```

Whatever type you substitute for x is expanded in the macro, even when x is a struct, union, or array for which it makes no sense to perform the absolute value. What is worse, a macro causes a blanket substitution to occur anywhere in the file. If you later decide to implement an overloaded abs( ) function, such as

```
long abs( struct TagRecord x) {;};
```

you will quickly run into trouble. Your function will never become a function, but instead will translate into this bizarre macro expansion:

```
long ( (struct TagRecord x)<0 ?
     -(struct TagRecord x) : (struct TagRecord x) ) {;};
```

As you might suspect, macro definitions, although wonderfully useful in C, are not needed as much in C++. Instead, you can replace many macros with function templates and overloaded functions that enhance type-checking and resistance to the errors that macros can introduce.

One useful tool that can help locate problems with macros is CPP.EXE. CPP, which is included with your Visual C++ package, runs just the preprocessor to produce a text file that shows all the macros expanded.

Summary

Functions are the base on which C++ programs are built. You use functions to subdivide large problems into smaller tasks. By encapsulating features into functions, you can maintain your program more easily because the program features become isolated pieces that you can test and modify individually. Using functions helps you reduce the size of your program because you can repeatedly call and reuse the code within a function.

In this chapter, you learned the following:

- By using library routines, you can incorporate prewritten code into your programs, shortening the time it takes to write your software. Because commercially produced libraries are extensively tested, using high-quality library routines can help you produce reliable programs.

- You can use the on-line help system to learn about available C++ library functions. When you have found a function that you can use, you must include the function's prototype declaration by using `#include` to read in an appropriate library header file.

- When you define your own functions, you must specify a return type, a function name, and an optional list of parameters. If your function has no return result, use the special `void` type to indicate that the function does not return a value. If your function has no parameters, use the keyword `void` in place of your parameter declarations.

- Functions that return a result should do so by using the `return result;` statement. You can force a function that does not return a result to execute an immediate return by using `return;`.

- Function parameters that are passed by value cause a private, local copy of the parameter value to be created for the function. Any changes that you make to a pass-by-value parameter have no impact on the caller.

- Function parameters that are passed by reference, using the & reference operator, cause the C++ compiler to pass the address of the caller's parameter to the function. Inside the function, the code works directly with the parameter that was passed to the function and may make permanent changes to that parameter.

- You use the `const` modifier when you want your function parameters to have read-only values.

■ You can establish default values for parameters by following the variable declaration with the = symbol and then a constant expression. Parameters that have defaults may be omitted when calling the function; C++ uses the default value when a parameter is unused.

■ Variables may be defined inside functions and are private to the scope of the function. By default, memory space for these variables is created automatically on entry to the function and discarded when the function exits. By using the `static` keyword in front of a local variable definition, you can request C++ to allocate the memory for local variables for the duration of the program.

■ Many programs define functions separately from their implementation. To do so, a program must use a function prototype definition and then a separate function definition later in the program.

■ By using overloaded functions, you can reuse a function name many times, provided that each implementation of the overloaded function has differences in its parameters. The compiler uses the differing parameter types to determine which of the various functions is to be called.

■ Function templates provide a way to automatically create a group of related functions.

■ You can use function-like macros to generate short sections of code automatically.

Review Questions

1. When you use a library function, how do you obtain the function's prototype declaration so that you can use the function in your program?

2. Write a function declaration for a function that has no return result.

3. Write a function that returns a structure type.

4. Write a function declaration that has no parameter variables.

5. Suppose that you must write a function which takes a single int parameter value. Within the function, the parameter value will be set to zero if it is out of range. Should this parameter use pass-by-value or pass-by-reference?

6. Describe two methods of implementing a pass-by-reference parameter in a function.

7. Do you need to use the & address-of operator when passing an array to a function?

8. Suppose that your function has three parameters, each of which is passed by reference. How can you ensure that the function does not modify any variables that are passed to this function?

9. How do you write a function that will let you optionally omit one or more parameters when the function is called?

10. Suppose that your program frequently must compute the value of a variable by using the expression

    $$x*x + 2*x + x$$

    where x may be any variable. Which do you think would be better to handle this calculation—a function or a function-like macro? Why?

11. Describe the term *duration* as it applies to local variables. What is the default duration of a local variable? How do you make a local variable have duration outside the scope of a function?

12. What is a function prototype?

13. Name three reasons to use function prototypes in your programs.

14. What does function overloading enable you to do with functions?

15. How does the compiler distinguish between different implementations of overloaded functions?

16. What method do you use to automatically create a set of functions that work with multiple data types?

17. Is a macro a true function? Explain what you mean by your answer.

Exercises

1. Use the Visual C++ on-line help system to review some functions of the C++ library. Become familiar with looking up functions and translating the information you find into C++ program statements.

2. Write a function that accepts a single character parameter and returns, as the function result, the uppercase equivalent of the char parameter. If the character is lowercase, convert it to uppercase. If the char parameter is already an uppercase letter, return the char without making any changes to it.

3. Modify the function created in exercise 2 so that, instead of returning the converted character as a function result, you use a & reference parameter to pass the character by reference.

4. Develop a function to find the lowest value in an array of integers. Pass the array as a parameter to the function. Let the function's return result be the array index of the lowest value.

5. Modify the STRUCT3.CPP program (listing 6.12) so that it uses a pointer to pass the CPersonInfo structure-type parameter.

6. Develop a function to compute the arithmetic mean of a set of values that are passed to the function as an array. The two parameters to the function should be the array and the number of values in the array. Compute the mean by summing the values in the array and then divide by the number of values. Return the result as the function's value.

7. Write a function named Inverse() that takes a single int parameter and returns, as the function result, the inverse of the parameter (for example, *x* produces -*x*). Then create a sequence of overloaded functions to implement Inverse() for the signed char, long, float, and double types.

8. Write a macro to detect the maximum of two values. *Hint:* Use the ?: ternary conditional operator.

9. Write a function named PrintString() that accepts a single pointer to a char and displays its parameter as a string. Your function will be declared as

```
void PrintString(char * str) {    }
```

Inside PrintString(), display the text string so that each character is separated by a blank. If the input parameter contains ABCDEF, display the result as A B C D E F.

10. Modify the LIST.CPP program (listing 6.15) to include a search function. You will need to add a new command, S)earch, to the `main( )` function, and an appropriate code to prompt for a name to find in the list. Add a function to the `list_type` structure to implement the search command. Use the search function to display a message indicating whether the desired name was found in the list.

11. Modify the LIST.CPP program to add a D)elete command. For this feature, you may want to use the search function developed in exercise 10 to locate a desired name. Then use the list location identified by the search routine and snip out the list element that is to be deleted. Don't forget to use the `delete` operator to destroy the memory allocated to the list element.

Chapter 7

Projects

All the sample programs you have worked with until now have fit within a single source file. As your programs grow, you will find that splitting large programs into multiple source files makes editing and compiling easier. A program split into several files is referred to collectively as a *project*. Visual C++ provides special tools to help you manage projects that contain multiple source files and object modules. This chapter explains how to split your program into multiple files and how to use the Visual Workbench's project manager to manage the compiling and linking of your applications.

Splitting a Program into Multiple Source Files

Separating your program into multiple resource files gives you many important advantages:

- Opening and saving a small source file takes less time than opening and saving a large source file.

- When you use the edit window to edit a smaller file, locating specific functions or other features takes less time.

- Compiling a short file takes less time than compiling a long file.

- By separating your program into multiple files, you can group related functions together. After your functions are working properly, you can compile them into an object (.OBJ) file, and you don't need to compile them again.

■ You can produce separate modules containing commonly used functions. Then you can incorporate the common functions into many different programs merely by sharing the object file.

When you split a program into several files, you rely on the use of header files that you create to tell the compiler about the functions stored in other files. You then use the #include directive to tell the compiler about the header files that describe the code you have placed in other source files.

Each source file (ending in .CPP) is compiled separately, producing a corresponding .OBJ object module. The Visual C++ link step combines the object modules, producing an executable .EXE file. Before looking at the project management features of Visual C++, you first learn about structuring your programs into separate files.

Splitting Up Your Programs Is Easy

There are no definite rules about how to select which functions to place in other files. As a rule of thumb, though, you will find it most convenient to split your programs into files containing common tasks or features. For example, if your program has a set of routines to display a menu of choices, you may want to put that code into a file named MENU.CPP. If your program has special graphics routines, you might place those functions in a file named GRAPHICS.CPP. Each of these files should have a matching header file, such as MENU.H or GRAPHICS.H. The header files declare function prototypes and define constant identifiers, macros, and variables that are available for others to use.

Figure 7.1 shows a program made from four separate source files: MAIN.CPP, SOURCE1.CPP, SOURCE2.CPP, and SOURCE3.CPP. The MAIN.CPP program uses #include to incorporate each of the header files from SOURCE1, SOURCE2, and SOURCE3 so that MAIN.CPP knows which functions the respective source files provide.

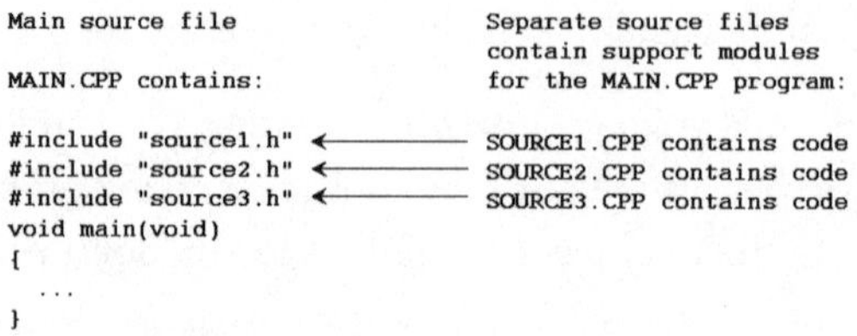

Fig. 7.1
The MAIN.CPP
program uses
the resources of
three other
modules.

```
Main source file                    Separate source files
                                    contain support modules
MAIN.CPP contains:                  for the MAIN.CPP program:

#include "source1.h"  ◄─────────── SOURCE1.CPP contains code
#include "source2.h"  ◄─────────── SOURCE2.CPP contains code
#include "source3.h"  ◄─────────── SOURCE3.CPP contains code
void main(void)
{
    ...
}
```

The LIST.CPP program in listing 6.15 of Chapter 6 is an example of a program that you can split logically into separate files. LIST.CPP uses pointers to implement a list type data structure. As originally written, the entire program fits in a single source file. In the next sections, you see how to split this program into three separate files: a header file named LIST-MOD.H; a source module file named LIST-MOD.CPP; and the main program, LISTDEMO.CPP, which uses the source module.

Many C++ programs that you write are split into many source module files with matching header files and one main program file. Splitting the program into several smaller files makes editing and compiling easier and quicker, saving you valuable time.

Creating Source Modules

A typical source module contains only the code needed to implement the tasks performed by the module. To convert the original LIST.CPP program, you can strip out the main() function and the definitions of the list_type structure that appeared at the beginning of LIST.CPP. The result is the source module shown in listing 7.1. This code is now in a separate file named LIST-MOD.CPP, which is short for *list module*.

Listing 7.1 The LIST-MOD.CPP List Module Source File

```
 1   // LIST-MOD.CPP
 2   // Contains the implementation of the list module code.
 3
 4   #include <iostream.h>
 5   #include <string.h>
 6   #include "list-mod.h"
 7
 8   //=================================================
 9   void list_type::Initialize_List(void)
10   {
11     head = NULL;
12     tail = NULL;
13   }
14
15   //=================================================
16   void list_type::Add_to_Tail(char name_to_add[])
17   // Adds new data to the tail of the list.
18   {
19     list_element *next_entry;   // Points to next entry in list.
20
21     // Allocate next entry in list.
22     if (head == NULL) { // If list is now empty...
23       next_entry = tail = head = new list_element;
24       next_entry->next = NULL;
```

(continues)

Listing 7.1 Continued

```
25      next_entry->prev = NULL;
26    } // if
27    else { // List is not empty.
28      next_entry = new list_element;
29      // Set previous pointer to point at what
30      // was the last entry.
31      next_entry->prev = tail;
32      // Set previous entry's next pointer to
33      // point at the new entry.
34      tail->next = next_entry;
35      // And set tail to point to the new entry.
36      tail = next_entry;
37      // And the last entry does not point
38      // anywhere, so set it to NULL.
39      next_entry->next = NULL;
40    } // else
41
42    strcpy( next_entry->name, name_to_add );
43  } // Add_to_Tail
44
45  //=================================================
46  void list_type::Display_List(int Direction)
47  // Displays the content of the list in either
48  // the FORWARD or the REVERSE direction.
49  {
50    list_element *an_entry; // Temporary pointer to entries.
51
52    switch (Direction) {
53      case FORWARD: {
54        an_entry = head;
55        while (an_entry != NULL) {
56          cout << an_entry->name << endl;
57        an_entry = an_entry->next;
58        } // while
59        break;
60      } // case
61      case REVERSE: {
62        an_entry = tail;
63        while (an_entry != NULL) {
64          cout << an_entry->name << endl;
65          an_entry = an_entry->prev;
66        } // while
67      } // case
68      default: break;
69    } // switch
70  } // Display_List
71
72  //=================================================
73  void list_type::Destroy_List(void)
74  // Frees up all memory used by the list.
75  {
76    list_element *next_entry;
77    // Delete all the entries and free
78    // up their memory allocations. This code
```

```
79    // starts at the end of the list and removes
80    // each entry, one by one, until reaching
81    // the beginning of the list (where
82    // next_entry->prev = NULL).
83    while (tail != NULL) {
84      next_entry = tail->prev;
85      delete tail;
86      tail = next_entry;
87    } // while
88  } // Destroy_List
```

In the next section, you see the header file that makes the code from the LIST-MOD.CPP program available to other programs.

Creating Header Files

When you move source code into separate source files—or *modules*, as they are usually called—you need to create a header file (one that ends with .H) to describe the symbols and functions in the modules. Programs that use the module use the #include directive to read the header file and the list of definitions so that the compiler knows the types of the variables defined in the external module and how to create proper function calls.

Listing 7.2 shows the header file for LIST-MOD.CPP. You can see from the listing that the header file provides the names of functions (in this example, the member functions of the list_type object) and their prototypes. If your source module exports simple functions (as compared to the object member functions in this example), you would place the function prototypes in the header file. Function prototypes consist of the function return type, the function name, and the parameter list, followed by a terminating semicolon. You may want to check the Visual C++ \INCLUDE directory for examples of the header files provided with Visual C++. One file you should take a look at is ALLOC.H in the MSVC\INCLUDE directory. ALLOC.H contains function prototypes for memory allocation routines. (You won't need to use the _Cdecl keyword that you see in ALLOC.H.)

Listing 7.2 The Header File for the LIST-MOD.CPP Source Module

```
1  // LIST-MOD.H
2  // This is the header file containing the definitions
3  // of the symbols that are made available
4  // to this module's users.
5
6  const int FORWARD = 0;
7  const int REVERSE = 1;
8  const int MAXNAMESIZE = 20;
```

(continues)

Listing 7.2 Continued

```
9
10  // Define the list_type object as
11  // a structure containing data fields,
12  // next and previous link pointers,
13  // and the Add_to_Tail() and Display_List()
14  // functions to operate on the list.
15  struct list_element
16  {
17    char name[MAXNAMESIZE];
18    // The following point to the next entry in
19    // the list and the previous entry in the
20    // list, respectively.
21    list_element *next;
22    list_element *prev;
23  };
24
25  struct list_type
26  {
27    list_element *head;  // Points to front of the list.
28    list_element *tail;  // Points to the end of the list.
29    void Initialize_List(void);  // Initializes head and tail.
30    void Add_to_Tail(char name_to_add[]);
31    void Display_List(int Direction);
32    void Destroy_List(void);
33  };
```

Traditionally, header files have a file extension of .H. A few programmers use .HPP to differentiate C++ header files from standard C header files (which use .H), but you are not required to do so. Most programmers use .H for all of their C++ header files.

Creating a Main File

LIST-MOD.CPP and LIST-MOD.H are the files needed to compile the list module. Now it is time to put the list module to work in an application. To do this, you create a main program that uses the list module code. This program, LISTDEMO.CPP, is in listing 7.3.

Listing 7.3 A Program That Uses the List Module

```
1  // LISTDEMO.CPP
2  // Uses the LIST-MOD module. Note the #include
3  // directive to reference the LIST-MOD.H header
4  // file.
5
6  #include <iostream.h>
7  #include "list-mod.h"
8
9  //=================================================
10 void main(void) {
```

```
11    // Used to process keyboard command input.
12    char command_ch, direction_ch;
13    char TheName[MAXNAMESIZE];
14    list_type TheList;           // The list object
15
16    TheList.Initialize_List();
17    do {
18      cout << "Select A)dd, L)ist or Q)uit? ";
19      cin.get(command_ch);
20      cin.ignore(1);
21
22      switch(command_ch) {
23        // Add a new entry to the list.
24        case 'a': case 'A': {
25          cout << "Enter name:   ";
26          cin.getline(TheName, sizeof(TheName) );
27          TheList.Add_to_Tail(TheName);
28          break;
29        } // case
30        // Display the contents of the list.
31        case 'l': case 'L': {
32          cout << "List in F)orward or R)everse direction? ";
33          cin.get(direction_ch);
34          cin.ignore(1);
35          switch (direction_ch) {
36            case 'f': case 'F' : {
37              TheList.Display_List(FORWARD);
38              break;
39            } // case
40            case 'r': case 'R' : {
41              TheList.Display_List(REVERSE);
42              break;
43            } // case
44            default: break;
45          } // switch
46          break;
47        } // case
48        // Quit running the program.
49        case 'q': case 'Q': {
50          TheList.Destroy_List();
51          break;
52        } // case
53        default:
54          break;
55      } // switch
56    } while ((command_ch != 'q') && (command_ch != 'Q'));
57
58    cout << "Press Enter to continue.";
59    cin.get();
60  } // main
```

For a program to use the list module, the program must use the #include directive to bring in the symbol definitions defined in the LIST-MOD.H file. This happens in line 7 of listing 7.3. Note that even though LIST-MOD.CPP required the use of both #include <iostream.h> and #include <string.h>, you do not need to reference the STRING.H file within the main program because none of the string functions are used in LISTDEMO.CPP. Remember that the purpose of header files is to provide the compiler with the information it needs in order to compile the current source file. Functions such as strcpy() are referenced only in LIST-MOD.CPP so that the LIST-MOD.CPP file is the only source file that needs to reference #include <string.h>. By splitting your source files in this way, you reduce the number of lengthy include files included in the other source files, thereby speeding up the overall compilation process.

The example shown here is split so that the main program uses the only source module. However, you can also create source modules that are used only by other source modules. Just be certain that the using source module includes the appropriate .H header files.

Now that your program is split into several files, how do you compile the entire program? You must use the Visual C++ project management tools. You use these tools to select the group of files that makes up a single program (or project). The Visual C++ project manager uses the project list to compile each of the required files automatically to produce a single executable file. The use of the project management tools is the subject of the next section, "Using the Visual Workbench to Create Projects."

The Difference between #*include* <*file*> and #include "*file*"

When you look through C++ sample programs, you notice two kinds of notations for including header files. One has angle brackets around the file name:

```
#include <string.h>
```

The other has the file name in quotation marks:

```
#include "mytypes.h"
```

When the compiler sees angle brackets, it looks for a standard header file (most likely one provided in the Visual C++ package). The compiler looks for standard header files by checking the list of include directories specified in the Directories dialog box. You can see this list by choosing **O**ptions **D**irectories. The second combo box in the dialog box, **I**nclude Directories, lists the directories that Visual C++ checks to locate the standard include files.

When the compiler sees quotation marks around the file name, it first checks the current directory. If the include file is not located in the current directory, the directory search proceeds as if angle brackets were used around the file name. You almost always use quotation marks around the file name when you use #include to access a header file you have created.

Using the Visual Workbench to Create Projects

You use the project manager to create a new project or modify an existing project. You have already used this tool to create the QuickWin programs presented in earlier chapters. In any case, to access an existing project, choose **P**roject from the Visual Workbench menu bar and then choose **O**pen. Visual C++ displays the dialog box shown in figure 7.2.

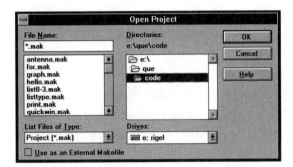

Fig. 7.2
The Open Project dialog box.

To create a new project, choose instead **P**roject **N**ew. Visual C++ displays the familiar dialog box shown in figure 7.3.

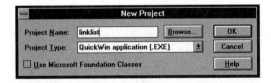

Fig. 7.3
The New Project dialog box.

You enter the name you want to give your new project, as well as the type of executable file you want to create. Visual C++ adds the .MAK file extension to the name you provide. For example, to create a project file for the LISTDEMO.CPP program and its LIST-MOD.CPP source module, enter the name **LISTDEMO** in the dialog box. Then click the down arrow on the drop-down list box and choose QuickWin as the executable type. The **U**se Microsoft Foundation Classes check box indicates that your project uses the MFC class library shipped with MSVC. Chapter 14, "The MFC General-Purpose Classes and Collection Classes," provides more information on this topic, so until then, you can uncheck this box for your projects. When you press the OK button, Visual C++ displays the Edit-<project name> dialog box shown in figure 7.4, enabling you to add files to the new project makefile.

Fig. 7.4
Adding new
source files to
your project
file through
the Edit-
LINKLIST.MAK
dialog box.

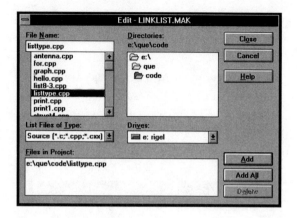

Fig. 7.4
Adding new
source files to
your project
file through
the Edit-
LINKLIST.MAK
dialog box.

Adding Files to the Project

To add files to the project, you just select the name of each file you want
from the File **N**ame combo box, and then click the **A**dd button. You can also
double-click the file to add it automatically to the project. When you have
finished entering the file names you need for your project, click the Cl**o**se
button.

For the LISTDEMO.CPP program, you should add the two files
LISTDEMO.CPP and LIST-MOD.CPP. When you use the project manager to
build your own applications, you normally add only the .CPP source files you
used to build your application. MSVC automatically detects the header files
that your application includes, so you don't need to specify them. In fact,
you cannot specify header files!

For each file that you add to the project, the project manager stores information about where the file is located, the names of the header files referenced
by each source module, and even the compiler options used when compiling
individual sections of the program. This information is contained in the
makefile you specified when you created the project. This is an ASCII file that
you can load into the Workbench's editor and edit by hand, but it is best to
let the Workbench edit the project makefile.

Editing the Files in the Project Makefile. If you want to edit the project,
either to add more files or to delete a file, choose the **E**dit command from the
Project menu. The same dialog box shown in figure 7.4 is displayed. Add
your new files as you did when you first created the project. To remove a file
from the project, click once on the file name in the **F**iles in Project list box
and then click the D**e**lete button. You can also use Alt+E, or you can double-
click the file name to have it deleted from the list.

If you want to change some of the options your project uses, choose **P**roject from the **O**ptions menu. You can alter such options as the type of executable file this project creates or the type of memory model the project uses (memory models are discussed later in this chapter).

Editing the Project Makefile. Figure 7.5 shows the Project Options dialog box. You can use this dialog box to change the type of executable file created. The various buttons enable you to change values used while compiling and linking. This dialog box also allows you to decide whether to build a debug version of your program (the default setting in the Visual Workbench) or a release version.

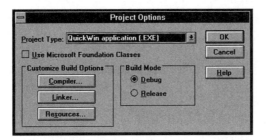

Fig. 7.5
The Project Options dialog box.

Chapter 12, "Debugging Visual C++ Programs," provides information on debugging. Be aware that a debug version of your program is significantly larger and slower than a release version. The reason is that MSVC places extra code in a debug build, which helps out in debugging, and deletes this extra code in the release version.

Debugging

No matter how careful programmers are, eventually they will make mistakes. Sometimes a mistake is easy enough for the compiler or linker to detect and report. Sometimes this is not the case, especially if the error has to do with the logic of the running program. Suppose that in a program built to calculate a payroll figure, the programmer used the wrong value in one of the calculations. The error might show up in a report (or someone's paycheck!), but it might be hard to figure out where in the code the error occurred. In such cases, a programmer must resort to debugging—that is, removing bugs—to fix the problem. This process is shown in Chapter 12, "Debugging Visual C++ Programs." The term *debugging* has been attributed to the late Admiral Grace Hopper who, on removing a moth from a malfunctioning vacuum tube computer, claimed that the computer had been "debugged."

Using the Rebuild All Menu Option

Now that you have split your program into multiple source files and added them to the project makefile, the next step is to compile each of the files and link the resulting .OBJ files into a single .EXE program file. To compile all your program's modules, choose **P**roject **R**ebuild All. Visual C++ compiles each module listed in the project file. If no compilation errors are detected, the resulting .OBJ object modules are linked together to form the .EXE application.

You already may be asking, "But if I edit only one file, do I have to recompile all my source files?" The answer is no. The project manager's **P**roject **B**uild command, described next, automatically selects only the changed files for recompilation, thereby greatly reducing the total time required to compile and link your application.

Using the Build Menu Option

The **P**roject **B**uild command performs a "smart" recompilation of your program. The **B**uild option checks to see which files have changed since the last compilation and recompiles only the files that have changed. **B**uild compares the date and time attached to each file and uses this information to determine which files need recompiling. If the date and time of a .CPP file is more recent (or newer) than the date and time of its matching .OBJ file, Visual C++ recompiles the .CPP file. To "make" your application, choose **P**roject **B**uild. When you develop your applications, you should use the **B**uild command almost exclusively because of the efficiency it brings to the compiling and linking process.

Using the Compile Menu Option

You can use the Com**p**ile option on the **P**roject menu to compile individual source modules. This command is useful when you test whether you have any errors or warnings in the source code of the current module. If you want, you can load and compile each source module individually, and then choose **B**uild or **R**ebuild All to create the executable file. After you have created this file, you can run the program with the **P**roject Execute command.

Using the Toolbar Buttons

If you prefer to use the mouse, each of the menu options mentioned—with the exception of **P**roject Execute <application>—has a corresponding toolbar button, as shown in figure 7.5. The section "The Visual WorkBench Toolbar" in Chapter 1, "The Fundamentals of C++ Programming," described the various components of the Workbench toolbar. The very first button in the toolbar provides a drop-down list of all the files in your project. The fifth button performs the compile-only function. The sixth button performs the **P**roject **B**uild function, and the seventh button performs the **P**roject **R**ebuild All function.

Project
Files   Build

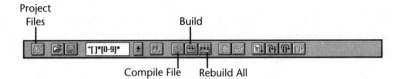

Compile File   Rebuild All

Fig. 7.6
The Project
toolbar buttons.

Dealing with Dependency Problems

Occasionally, when you make an application, the changes you made do not seem to be incorporated in the application. You make the program, run it, and test your changes—but your fixes are not in the program. What's going on? The problem is that, for some reason, your source file (.CPP) is older than the corresponding .OBJ file. This can occur if the clock battery on your computer is exhausted and needs to be replaced. Sometimes errant software can reset the system clock. The result is that, when you edit the file, a new date and time are attached to the file, but that date and time are now older than the date and time of the .OBJ file. **B**uild therefore thinks that the source file has not been changed. If you sense that your changes are not being incorporated in the program, take a look at the date and time associated with the file. If there is a discrepancy, use **R**ebuild All to rebuild all of the application.

Using the DOS Command Line

The project file created by the Visual Workbench is an ASCII file, ending with the .MAK extension. This file is also called a makefile and acts as an input file for the Microsoft tool called NMAKE.EXE. You can compile your project outside the Visual Workbench by exiting to DOS or opening a DOS session under Windows. (You can start a DOS session from within Windows by double-clicking the MS-DOS Prompt icon located in the Main group.) You must then set up some environment variables used by such command-line tools as NMAKE. Microsoft provides a batch file, called MSVCVARS.BAT, to set these variables for you. Execute this batch file and then type the following at the DOS prompt to build your program:

```
NMAKE /f<project-name>.MAK
```

This builds your project just as if you had chosen the **P**roject **B**uild command from within the Visual Workbench. The /f parameter is used to tell NMAKE which file to use as input, because by default it looks for a file named `makefile`.

Conditional Compilation Directives

Sometimes when you use `#include` to bring header files into the compilation, you may encounter situations in which symbols are inadvertently declared more than once. A duplicate declaration causes the compiler to issue an error and the overall compile to fail. This problem can occur when a header file, in turn, uses `#include` to gain access to other header files.

To understand the problem, consider what happens when your program includes the header files for two source modules, and each of these header files must access a common header file named MYTYPES.H:

- MAIN.CPP contains

  ```
  #include "FILES1.H"
  #include "FILES2.H"
  void main() ...
  ```

- FILES1.H contains

  ```
  #include "MYTYPES.H"
  ```

- FILES2.H contains

  ```
  #include "MYTYPES.H"
  ```

The problem is that the identifiers inside MYTYPES.H are effectively included into MAIN.CPP—twice.

At first, you might think to edit the `#include "MYTYPES.H"` statement from the second .H file. This would work for compiling MAIN.CPP, but to compile the FILES2 source module, you must put the `#include` statement back into the file. The solution is to use *conditional compilation directives*. These directives enable you to conditionally compile sections of code, depending on the setting of a flag symbol.

Defining Flag Symbols

You usually create flag symbols with the `#define` directive, which is discussed in the section "Using `#define`" in Chapter 2, "C++ Data Types and Expressions." After creating a macro symbol with `#define`, you can use conditional compilation directives (or statements) to test whether a symbol is defined or to test the value of the symbol.

Using *#ifdef* and *#ifndef*

Visual C++ provides several conditional compilation directives. The simplest
two are the following:

- #ifdef *symbol*

  Evaluates to True if *symbol* is already declared. You can read this directive as "if defined *symbol*, then compile the following statements."

- #ifndef *symbol*

  Evaluates to True if *symbol* is not declared. You can read this directive as
  "if not defined *symbol*, then compile the following statements."

You can use these directives in your source file to conditionally compile sections of code. Here's an example:

```
#define ADDTESTCODE
      .
      .
      .
#ifdef ADDTESTCODE
void TestCondition(int x)
{
  if (x<0) or (x>500)
    cout << "Error:  X is out of range, x=" << x << endl;
}
#endif
      .
      .
      .
void main(void)
{
  int d;
      .
      .
      .
#ifdef ADDTESTCODE
  TestCondition( d );
#endif
      .
      .
      .
} // main
```

When the compiler encounters #ifdef, it checks whether the named symbol
(ADDTESTCODE in this example) was declared previously in a #define statement.
If the symbol was declared, the code between the #ifdef and the #endif is
compiled into the program. However, if the symbol was not defined, the
compiler ignores all the code between the #ifdef and the #endif. You can use
this feature to conditionally include sections of code in your program. As the

preceding example demonstrates, this feature is especially useful for inserting test code in your program. When you are assured that your program is working correctly, you can remove the symbol definition (or use `#undef` *symbol* to undefine the symbol), and the conditionally compiled code will not be included in subsequent compiles. Therefore, using conditional compiles can save you much time and effort if you want to insert test code or change the program's operation from time to time. By using the conditional compilation directives, you can leave your test code in the source for future use in case you later decide to update or change the program.

Using Conditional Compilation to Avoid Duplicate Symbols

You can use `#ifdef` and `#ifndef` to eliminate the problem of duplicate symbols when several header files include one or more common files, as described in the example at the beginning of this section. The solution to the problem is to have the header file define a unique symbol for itself. Later, if that unique symbol is already declared, the header file's content will be ignored. You can put all the conditional compilation directives inside the header file so that the process occurs automatically for any user of the header file. Here is an example for the MYTYPES.H header file:

```
// MYTYPES.H header file
#ifndef _MYTYPES_H
#define _MTTYPES_H
    .
    .
    .
// The rest of the header file goes here
// including all function prototypes and symbols.
    .
    .
    .
#endif
```

The first time the compiler sees MYTYPES.H, the unique symbol `_MYTYPES_H` is unknown, so the compiler proceeds to compile the code between the `#ifndef` and the matching `#endif`. The second time MYTYPES.H is encountered, the compiler processes the `#ifndef _MYTYPES_H` directive and sees that `_MYTYPES_H` has been declared. Therefore, the declarations between `#ifndef` and the matching `#endif` are now ignored, eliminating the potential for duplicate identifier definitions.

The format of the symbol name is entirely up to you. The use of a single underscore, followed by the file name, followed by a single underscore and then the letter H is a standard that many programmers follow; however, you are free to choose your own identifier name in any format you want.

You should use this symbol notation in most header files you create. Before
long, you will have a library of source modules that start by using each other.
If you get in the habit of inserting these conditional compilation directives
now, you can save yourself the trouble of having to fix your header files later
as you begin to share your code.

Using *#if, #elif, #else,* and *#endif*

The #if directive is used to make general conditional tests and is similar to
the C++ if() statement. The format of #if is

```
#if constant-expression
.
. // lines of code
.
#endif
```

If *constant-expression* evaluates to a nonzero value, the enclosed lines of
code are compiled. If *constant-expression* evaluates to zero, the compiler
skips the enclosed lines and resumes compiling at the first statement after
#endif. You can reference any symbols defined in #define statements, and
you can use any of the standard expression operators (such as <, >, ==, &&, ||,
and so on).

You can also extend a simple #if statement to test multiple conditions by
using an if-else type of construct. The following illustrates the full capabilities of the #if conditional directive:

```
#if constant-expression-1
  .
  . // lines of code
  .
#elif constant-expression-2
  .
  . // lines of code
  .
  #endif
#elif constant-expression-n
  .
  . // lines of code
  .
  #endif
#else
  .
  .
  .
#endif
```

Using the #elif directive, you can test for many alternative conditions. Each
code section appearing after the #elif directive must be terminated by its

own #endif directive. You can add an optional #else clause to catch a situation in which none of the conditional tests evaluates to True.

You can place additional #if directives inside the code section after the #if, #elif, or #else directive. However, you must ensure that each conditional statement has a matching #endif statement.

Using the *defined()* Operator

Visual C++ provides a function-like operator, defined(), that you can use in conditional compilation expressions to test whether a macro symbol is defined. For example, to test whether _MYTYPES_H is defined, use

```
#if defined(_MYTYPES_H)
```

To test whether _MYTYPES_H is not defined, use

```
#if !defined(_MYTYPES_H)
```

In these examples, defined() is used identically to #ifdef and #ifndef. Using defined() is advantageous when you want to test whether multiple symbols are defined. Note this example:

```
#if defined(_FILE1_H) && defined(_FILES2_H)
```

Without the use of the defined() operator, you would have to use two #ifdef directives, as in

```
#ifdef _FILES1_H
#ifdef _FILES2_H
  .
  .
  .
#endif
#endif
```

Clearly, when you must check for the definition of multiple symbols, using the defined() operator results in code that is easier to read.

The Scope of Variables

You have learned that, when you define a variable within a function, that variable is local to the function. You can use a local variable only within the function in which the variable is declared. A variable defined within a function is said to have local scope or function scope.

When your program is split across multiple source files, additional scoping rules affect which identifiers are visible within a source file and which identifiers are visible outside the source file. This section explains the different scoping rules.

Function Scope

Variables defined locally to a function have *function scope*. This includes all the variables that you declare at the beginning of the code block after the function's header. In this book, the term *local variable* is used to distinguish variables declared within a function from variables declared outside a function. Local variables are also known as *auto variables* (*auto* is short for *automatic*) to indicate that memory for local variables is set aside automatically on entry to a function and discarded at exit. auto is also a keyword that you can place in front of a local variable to signify that the variable is in use only during the scope of the function. The auto keyword is seldom used, however, because automatic duration is the default for local variables.

Block Scope

A variable confined to a block of code that appears within a function has *block scope*. Variables defined within a block are local to the block and are undefined outside the block. The following code presents an example of block scope:

```
void main(void)
{
  int i;
  for( i=0; i<10; i++ )
  {
    int j;   // Define block scope variable here.
    for( j=0; j<3; j++)
      cout << i << " " << j;
    cout << endl;
  }
  // The compiler issues an error for the
  // following line because j is not defined here,
  // outside the scope of the block.
  cout << i << j << endl;
}
```

The compiler cannot compile the last statement because variable j, defined in the previous code block, is no longer recognized.

File Scope

A variable (or a constant symbol or typedef symbol) that is declared outside any function has *file scope*. Variables having file scope are available for use by all functions in the source file. Normally, you declare variables having file scope (also known as *global variables*) before the first function in the source file.

Function Prototype Scope

Variables defined in a function's parameter list are accessible only during execution of the function and therefore have *function prototype scope*. In most respects, a parameter variable behaves identically to a local variable having function scope.

Accessing Variables and Functions across Source Files

C++ provides two types of variable *linkage*, which means that a variable can be used (linked to) across several functions or from another source file. There are two types of linkage:

- Internal linkage

- External linkage

Internal Linkage

Variables declared inside a function or a block (including function parameter variables) are not visible outside the function. Therefore, these variables have no linkage to the outside world and cannot be accessed by code in other modules of a project.

External Linkage

By default, all variables and functions defined in file scope have external linkage. Such variables and functions are potentially usable by functions contained in other source modules. Variables and functions that have external linkage must have unique names across all source files. In other words, a variable having external linkage must be defined only once (outside of functions) in all the project's source modules.

To understand what this means, consider a sample program that is split into two source modules, MAIN.CPP and MODULE1.CPP. Each defines a variable named Total, as shown in the following code fragments:

```
// MAIN.CPP
int Total;
void main(void)
   .
   .
   .

// MODULE1.CPP
int Total;
```

```
void f(void)
.
.
.


// MODULE1.H
void f(void);
```

In both files, `Total` is defined outside the scope of a function, so `Total` has both file scope and external linkage. Both files compile without error; however, a problem occurs when the object modules are linked together in the link step. The linker sees two definitions of `Total` and issues an error message saying that `Total` is defined twice. Although MODULE1's `Total` declaration does not appear in the header file, `Total` has external linkage. If you want to remove the external linkage from either variable, you should preface either or both of the definitions with the `static` keyword, as in

```
static int Total;
```

The use of the `static` keyword, in this context, is described in the section "Using the `static` Keyword to Restrict Linkage" later in this chapter. The important point for you to understand is that all variables and function names that have external linkage must have a unique name that does not conflict with the names used in any of the other source files making up the project.

Using the *extern* Keyword. Any variable or function that has external linkage can be used in other source modules, if the compiler is given a declaration for the variable or function. Normally, you use header files to declare symbols defined in the other modules. Alternatively, you can use the `extern` keyword to notify the compiler that the declaration on the rest of the line is not defined in the current source file but is located elsewhere. The following example uses `extern`:

```
// MAIN.CPP
int Total;
extern int Sum;
extern void f(void);
void main(void)
.
.
.


// MODULE1.CPP
int Sum;
void f(void)
.
.
.
```

In this example, a header file is not used to access the symbols declared in MODULE1.CPP. Instead, inside MAIN.CPP, the variable Sum and the function f() are both marked as extern, identifying them as being defined externally. Remember that the file scope symbols in MODULE1 all have external linkage. However, the compiler cannot compile MAIN and access those symbols without first seeing a proper declaration for the symbols. All symbols must be declared before they are used in a function. Using the extern keyword enables you to access the external symbols defined in other modules.

Using the *static* Keyword to Restrict Linkage. As you now know, variables defined outside the scope of functions have external linkage. Occasionally, though, you want to keep such variables private to the source file in which they are declared. To make a global variable private to the source file (and thus not usable to other code modules), you can preface the variable declaration with the keyword static. For example, the following variables are declared outside the functions of a source file:

```
static char text_line[80];
static int line_index;
static char Buffer[MAXBUZSIZE];
static char * pBuffer;
```

By prefacing each declaration with the static keyword, the compiler ensures that these external variables are private to the source file. Furthermore, the names themselves are now invisible outside the file, so there is no conflict if another source file reuses these variable names.

You can also place the static keyword in front of a function declaration. By default, all functions that you write have external linkage and are visible to the other program modules. When you place the static keyword in front of the function declaration, however, the compiler makes the function private to the source file. You can then reuse the function name in other source modules in the program.

It is good programming practice to keep variable and function declarations local to the area of the program in which their use is needed. Therefore, where it makes sense in your programs, you should use the static keyword on all file scope (or global) variables and functions that do not have to be used outside the source file in which they are declared.

The following points summarize the use of the static keyword:

■ When you use the static keyword on a function's local variables, the local variables are permanently allocated for the duration of the program. Like all local variables, `static` local variables are private to the function in which they are declared.

- When you use the `static` keyword on a variable that has file scope (declared outside any functions), the variable becomes private to the source file. As with all file scope variables, however, memory is allocated for the duration of the program's execution.

- When you preface a function declaration with the `static` keyword, the function's name becomes private (meaning that it does not have external linkage) to the source file in which the function is declared.

Memory Models

To program the PC, you will find it helpful to know about the structure of the underlying microprocessor (*central processing unit*, or *CPU*) and memory systems. To create the most efficient C++ programs, you must have a basic understanding of how memory is allocated. Your choice of a memory model influences the capacity, speed, and size of your program. Where you place your data storage—in global or local (auto) variables, or in dynamically allocated memory—affects your program's operations and capabilities. This section uncovers some of the mysteries of memory management and the decisions you must make to optimize your use of system memory.

If you are not a nuts-and-bolts person, you may find some of the internal microprocessor description tough to fathom. That's OK—but do read through the material so that you obtain an overview of the internal structure of your microprocessor. This information will help you determine which of the memory model options you should select when compiling your program. A description of the Visual C++ memory model options appears in the section "Choosing a Memory Model" later in this chapter.

MSVC and Windows NT

For this discussion, it is assumed that you are using Visual C++ on an IBM-compatible PC with an 80x86 type of processor. Microsoft also sells a version of Visual C++ for its Windows NT operating system. NT can run on other microprocessors besides the Intel 80x86. If you are running MSVC++ on such a platform, the internal memory map and CPU architecture will be vastly different from those described here.

The 80x86 Memory Structure

For all but small programs, you must decide which memory model the compiler should use when compiling your program. The choice of memory model influences how much code or data you can have in your program, as well as the overall size and speed of your application. To understand how to choose a memory model requires that you first know a little bit about the Intel 80x86 CPU family of microprocessors.

When Intel produced the first members of the 80x86 family, the 8088 and 8086 chips, Intel was building an upgrade (and a big one at that) from the original 8080 microprocessor of the earliest personal computers. The 8080 was an 8-bit processor with a 16-bit addressing capability. From the standpoint of memory, that meant that all code and data combined had to fit within a 64K address space. Therefore, 64K was all the memory there was to work with in those early days.

When the 8088 and 8086 were designed, the original 64K limitation of the 8080 (as well as the 8080's original register-naming convention) was incorporated in the new processors, but with a distinctly new twist: program addressing was still limited to 64K per segment, but the computer could support up to a total of 1M of memory through the use of multiple 64K memory segments. To meet this need, the 8088/86 introduced segment registers to point to the start of memory segments. Within each segment, a 16-bit address is used to reach any part of the 64K address space. The same concept applies to the 80286, 80386, and 80486 processors, which are upward-compatible with the original 8086. An important distinction, from the standpoint of memory, is that the newer processors can address vastly increased memory spaces: up to 4 gigabytes of physical memory.

The 80x86 CPU Registers

The basic 80x86 CPU architecture provides a set of 16-bit registers and addressing of up to 1M of memory. The newer CPUs introduce 32-bit registers and, consequently, can address even greater memory spaces. Table 7.1 shows how the CPU's registers influence the memory-allocation scheme. This table presents the basic CPU registers that are provided in the 8088 and newer processors.

Table 7.1 The Basic Registers Used in the 8088 and Newer Processors

Register	Explanation	Alternative 8-Bit Form
AX	Accumulator register	AH, AL—high and low bytes, respectively, of AX
BX	Base register	BH, BL—high and low bytes, respectively, of BX
CX	Count register	CH, CL—high and low bytes, respectively, of CX
DX	Data register	DH, DL—high and low bytes, respectively, of DX
BP	Base pointer	
SI	Source index	
DI	Destination index	
CS	Code segment	
DS	Data segment	
SS	Stack segment	
ES	Extra segment	
IP	Instruction pointer	
SP	Stack pointer	

In table 7.1, the segment registers—CS, DS, SS, and ES—are most important to the discussion of memory addressing in this chapter. Some of the register names given in the Explanation column are largely irrelevant, particularly those for the AX, BX, CX, and DX registers. The names and use of these registers originated with the A, B, C, and D registers of the 8080 microprocessor. For instance, although the CX register is indeed used as a counter for some instructions, it can also be used for general arithmetic and other functions. Nevertheless, these "explanatory names" have carried over through the years.

Table 7.1 also shows the 8-bit registers—AH, AL, BH, BL, CH, CL, DH, and DL—which address the high and low bytes, respectively, of the AX, BX, CX, and DX registers, enabling easy byte-level operations.

In the 80386 processor, these original 16-bit registers have become subsets of the new processor's 32-bit registers. For example, EAX is the extended AX register, and AX is equivalent to the lower 16 bits of EAX. AH and AL continue to reference the high and low bytes of AX and, therefore, the lowest two bytes of EAX. The 80386 also contains additional 32-bit registers, but this book does not cover them (see an 80386 microprocessor handbook or 80386 assembly language programming guide for details). The 80x87 math coprocessor provides additional registers and instructions not described in this book.

Memory Addressing. The segment registers—CS, SS, DS, and ES—are used to address memory. The index registers, DI and SI, are used with DS and ES to assist with instructions that move or operate large byte blocks. To understand low-level memory addressing, consider the bit representation of registers and addresses.

When you look at the layout of bits within a register, the bits are numbered in ascending order from *right to left*, as shown in figure 7.7.

Fig. 7.7
The layout of bits within a register.

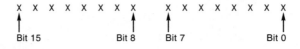

As figure 7.7 shows, the value of decimal 8, stored as a bit pattern, is

    0000 0000 0000 1000

Certain registers—CS, SS, DS, and ES—are called *segment registers* and are used only for memory addressing. The 8086/8088 CPU's segment registers provide 1M addressing—which is a good trick because the 16 bits in each register address only 64K of memory. The secret is in how the segment registers are combined with other values to form a physical memory address. Each of the segment registers points to a 16-byte page. Effectively, the segment registers are equivalent to a 20-bit register whose lower 4 bits are always zero, as shown in figure 7.8.

Fig. 7.8
The layout of bits within a segment register.

Memory addresses are formed by adding the contents of a segment register, shifted 4 bits to the left, to another 16-bit register (such as BX) or a 16-bit offset value, resulting in a 20-bit memory address, as in the following:

```
      xxxx xxxx xxxx xxxx 0000        Segment register value
+          nnnn nnnn nnnn nnnn        Other 16-bit register or constant
      ─────────────────────────
=     aaaa aaaa aaaa aaaa aaaa        Producing a 20-bit address
```

The segment registers are combined in specific ways with other registers and 16-bit constant values to address memory. The CS (code segment) and IP (instruction pointer) registers are added together to point to the next machine instruction to be executed by the CPU. Because the IP register is just 16 bits wide, a single code segment is limited to a maximum of 64K of code. Because these registers are always used together, they are often written as the pair CS:IP.

The SS (stack segment) and SP (stack pointer) registers point to the top of the processor's stack, where temporary values and function call return addresses are recorded. (In the 80x86 family of processors, stacks grow downward in memory, so the stack's top is actually at a lower memory address than the stack's bottom.) Stacks are limited to a total of 64K of memory because of the 16-bit address capability of the SP registers. Just as CS and IP are written as CS:IP, the SS and SP registers are often referenced as SS:SP.

Data stored in the heap area is usually referenced as an offset from the ES (extra segment) register. If you change the value in ES, the entire heap storage area can be accessed. Depending on the specific machine instruction, you can add the DI and SI registers to the DS and ES registers to point to groups of bytes in different memory segments.

Memory segments do not need to be 64K. Indeed, most memory segments, particularly those that contain code, are considerably less than 64K. Each time the program begins to execute machine instructions within a segment, the CS register is set to point to the beginning of the segment, and the IP register is set to an offset within the segment. Control is transferred to other segments when the program executes a far jump or subroutine call to a procedure located in some other segment. Similarly, segments that store data can be less than 64K. You gain access to those data values by setting one of the other segment registers, usually DS or ES, to point to a segment and then use BX, DI, or SI as offsets from the start of the segment.

Near and Far Memory References. Depending on the memory model you are using (see the next section), the compiler can generate machine instructions that use either *near* or *far* addressing. Consider a simple C program containing three functions—main(), func1(), and func2()—all located within a single source module and compiled using the Small memory model. When main() calls func1() or func2(), the CPU sets the CS and IP registers to point to the first instruction in the functions. Because all three functions are located in the same code segment pointed to by CS, only the IP register needs be set to point to the function being called. This means that to call func1(), the call instruction needs only the 16-bit address of func1(), because the value of CS is unchanged. When a function call is made entirely within a segment, only 16-bit addresses are used. This is known as a *near* memory reference.

Now consider what happens when func1() is located in a different source module and the program is compiled using the Large memory model. For main() to call func1(), the CPU is given a new value for both CS and IP. The new CS value is the address of the segment containing func1(). In this form, the program is making a *far* memory reference.

In summary, a near memory reference is a 16-bit address used entirely within a segment. A far memory reference is one that is made to a separate segment and requires two 16-bit addresses to specify both a segment and an offset. As you can see, a near memory reference requires half as many address bytes as a far memory reference. This means that the use of near memory references produces smaller programs. Fewer instruction bytes also mean faster execution.

You can perform limited arithmetic on the address in a far pointer, but it affects only the offset portion of the address. If you add 1 to a far pointer, the offset value is incremented by 1. If the addition causes the offset to exceed 16-bits (as in hex FFFF + 1), the offset wraps around back to zero. Pointers are frequently incremented and decremented using C's postfix and prefix operators (for example, *p++ and *(--p)). The postfix and prefix operators increment and decrement, respectively, the offset portion of a segment and offset pair.

Choosing a Memory Model

Now that you have glimpsed the underlying processor architecture, you can begin to understand how memory models determine the layout of your compiled programs. The memory model determines where and how much code and data can be allocated to your application, as well as how the segment registers will be used to access that code and data.

The simplest memory model is the Tiny model, in which the CS, SS, DS, and ES registers are all set to point to the same area of memory. This limits the total size of your program—including code, data, and stack space—to a maximum of 64K. Within this space, all functions can be reached with a simple 16-bit address. Table 7.2 describes each of the six memory models and indicates their advantages and disadvantages.

Table 7.2 Memory Models Supported in Visual C++	
Model	**Description**
Tiny	In the Tiny model, the CS, SS, DS, and ES registers all point to the same memory address. Maximum program size is limited to a total of 64K. Only near pointers are permitted.
Small	The Small model is often used as a substitute for the Tiny model. Small model programs are divided into two segments: code and data/stack. Each segment is limited to a maximum of 64K, and the DS and SS registers share the same 64K maximum segment. As with the Tiny model, all memory references are made using simple 16-bit near pointers, providing for the smallest and fastest possible memory references.
Compact	The Compact model is designed for small programs that must manipulate much data. There is only one code segment up to 64K; however, multiple data segments permit up to 1M of memory addressing for data.
Medium	The Medium memory model is the mirror image of the Compact model, providing only 64K of data but up to 1M of code space. Because many programs have much code but little data, this memory model is popular.
Large	Large model programs can accommodate up to 1M of both code and data. Far pointers are used for all code and data references. The disadvantage to using the Large model is that far addresses require 4 bytes of memory and are slightly slower to use than are 2-byte near addresses. And although the total data can be up to 1M, the largest single data element can be no larger than 64K.
Huge	The Huge model is essentially the same as the Large model, but without the 64K data element size restriction. Huge model programs can allocate data structures that are larger than 64K, and each code module can have its own data segment up to 64K.

The Tiny, Small, and Compact models are known as *small code memory models* because they all limit the code space to a maximum of 64K. The Medium, Large, and Huge models are referred to as *large code memory models* because they provide multiple code segments with intersegment calls made using segment and offset addressing.

By choosing the correct memory model for your application, you may be able to reduce the size of your program and create faster code, especially if you can use a memory model that uses near pointers for code or data values. The Medium and Compact memory models provide good compromise solutions when your application must have much code or much data.

Memory Model Restrictions. In each memory model, the maximum code size for any module is still 64K. This means that when you compile a source file, the source file must result in no more than 64K of code. This restriction occurs because the IP (instruction pointer) register is a 16-bit register with a 64K addressing limit. Because each source file is compiled into its own code segment, it must necessarily be restricted to a maximum of 64K code bytes. If you exceed the 64K restriction, you must split your code into two or more code modules.

The amount of static data that your program can have depends on the memory model you are using, but is generally 64K or less. Static data includes all variables that have file scope (variables defined outside a function are automatically treated as static), variables declared as static or extern, and all string constants. The following points summarize data memory allocations:

- In the Small and Medium models, the data segment is shared with the stack, limiting the total static data to something less than 64K, depending on the memory required by the stack. Small and Medium model programs can use dynamic memory allocation (using the new and delete operators) to manipulate more than 64K of data memory.

- In the Large and Compact models, the data segment is unshared and permits the maximum 64K of static data.

- The Huge memory model is fundamentally different from the others. The Huge model supports multiple data segments so that each code module can have its own static data segment, each up to 64K.

Memory Model Selection. When you compile your object modules, you must tell the compiler which memory model to use. Generally, all object modules and libraries in a program should use the same memory model, although in some instances, you can mix models. (How you do this is beyond the scope of this book.) To select a memory model in the Visual Workbench, use the Project Options dialog box shown earlier in figure 7.5. Click the **Com**piler button to display the C/C++ Compiler Options dialog box, as shown in figure 7.9. Click the Memory Model entry in the **Ca**tegory list box to display the controls that allow you to change the memory model. Select Tiny, Small, Medium, Compact, Large, or Huge as appropriate for your application.

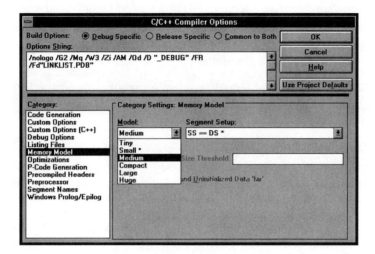

Fig. 7.9
Selecting a memory model with the C/C++ Compiler Options dialog box.

The Future of Memory Models. This may seem like a lot of work in order to choose a memory model for your application—and it is! If you are building simple applications, you can rely on the Visual Workbench's default memory model. If your application behaves strangely or does not compile, the preceding section should help you decide which memory model is more appropriate. You can also take comfort that, in the not-too-distant future, new operating systems will not burden developers with choosing a memory model. These operating systems will present to developers what is called a flat memory space—that is, a large, contiguous address range. You will not have to decide on a memory model because there will be only one!

Summary

This chapter introduced you to the Visual C++ project manager. You must use the project manager when your program is split into several modules. Separating the program into several modules helps you group related functions together. For large programs, using the multiple source modules is essential and helps you speed the edit-compile-link cycle.

In this chapter, you learned the following:

■ You can split a large program into sections in whatever manner makes sense for your application. Usually, you should group related functions and data structures together into one file.

- Each source module usually has a header file, which has the .H extension. The header file contains function prototypes and data declarations.

- A program that uses the functions provided in other modules uses the `#include` directive to read the other module's header files. The header files give the compiler the information it needs to construct calls to the functions defined in the module.

- Source modules can themselves access other source modules. The LIST-MOD.CPP program (listing 7.1) used `#include` to access IOSTREAM.H, STRING.H, and LIST-MOD.H.

- The Visual C++ project manager, contained in the Visual Workbench, helps you manage projects that are built from multiple modules. The project manager optimizes the compilation process by ensuring that only the files which have changed are recompiled.

- You use conditional compilation directives to control which sections within your source files are to be compiled.

- Each C++ variable has an associated scope. The scope of a variable indicates the area of the program in which the variable can be accessed and where it will have a valid value.

- Variables have either internal linkage or external linkage. All functions have external linkage unless prefaced with the `static` keyword. Symbols that have external linkage can be accessed and used from other source files.

- The design of the 80x86 microprocessor family influences how the compiler generates machine code. Because the 80x86 family has a segmented memory architecture, you have six choices for the type of memory model your programs will use: Tiny, Small, Compact, Medium, Large, and Huge. The smaller memory models generate less code and result in slightly faster program execution, but they limit the maximum size of the program's code and data. The larger memory models enable you to create maximum-size programs, but at the potential expense of slightly slower execution and slightly more generated code.

In Chapter 8, "Classes," you begin to learn about the C++ class structure. Using classes is similar to using the `struct` definition to create an encapsulated object, yet classes are more powerful. Ultimately, the class enables you to write program code that is derived from existing code. Using this feature is far more powerful and extensible than using prewritten functions. The concept of the class is introduced in Chapter 8, and important additional features of the class are described in both Chapter 9, "The Power of Inheritance," and Chapter 10, "Virtual Functions and Polymorphism."

Review Questions

1. Why would you want to split a program into multiple source files?

2. What strategy would you use to organize one of your programs into multiple source files?

3. What is a header file?

4. How do you eliminate duplicate definitions of symbols declared in header files?

5. Describe the difference between `#include <file>` and `#include "file"`.

6. How do you create a new project file?

7. During project development, what command do you use to compile and link your application optimally? Which button on the toolbar represents this command?

8. What is a variable's scope?

9. Define file scope, block scope, and function prototype scope.

10. How do you eliminate external linkage from a function?

11. What purpose does the `extern` keyword serve?

12. What are the six memory models supported by Visual C++?

13. Why must you choose an appropriate memory model?

Exercises

1. Modify the LIST-MOD.H header file (listing 7.2) so that it uses conditional compilation to eliminate the potential for duplicate symbols.

2. Create the following separate files:

■ *SOURCE1.CPP.* Contains a function named `f1()` that prints on the display the value of its single parameter. Create also a header file, SOURCE1.H, for this file. Be sure to use conditional compilation to eliminate the potential for duplicate symbols.

■ *SOURCE2.CPP*. Contains a function named f2() that prints on the display the values of its two parameters. Create also the SOURCE2.H header file.

■ *SOURCE.CPP*. Uses #include to access SOURCE1.H and SOURCE2.H. This program can have just a main() function that calls both f1() and f2(). Use the project manager to create a project named SOURCE.MAK, and then add all three source files to the project.

3. Add a function named f3() to SOURCE2.CPP. This function may just print the simple message Inside SOURCE2:f3(). Do not add f3() to the SOURCE2.H header file. Instead, add within SOURCE.CPP a declaration for f3() by using the extern keyword, and then call f3() from inside the main() function. Note that you can use the f3() function even though f3() does not appear in any header file.

4. Now remove the extern f3() declaration from SOURCE.CPP. In its place, write your own f3() function in SOURCE.CPP, but preface the function name with static. Output the message Inside SOURCE:f3() inside this f3() function. Notice that the new version of f3() has internal linkage—your call to f3() goes to the f3() function inside SOURCE.CPP, not to the f3() function inside SOURCE2.CPP.

5. Add a file scope int variable named xyz to both SOURCE1.CPP and SOURCE.CPP. When you build the application, using **B**uild, observe the error message you receive concerning the duplicate identifiers. Make one or both of the identifiers static by prefacing the declaration with the static keyword and then recompile the program. This exercise demonstrates that the static variable is visible only inside the single module and does not have external linkage.

6. Write an application of your choosing. *Suggestion:* Extend the list module code to store a complete name, address, city, and state record for each name entered. Modify the simple one-line menu so that each menu selection is displayed on a separate line. You should place your program in at least three separate source files and use at least two headers. You need to create a project file and add the appropriate source files to the project.

Chapter 8

Classes

In Chapter 3, "C++ Advanced Data Types," you learned how to combine both data and the functions that operate on that data into a single entity called an object. You learned to use the struct declaration to define an object's data and member functions. In this chapter, you are introduced to a new type of object mechanism called the *class*. The class is at the heart of C++ object-oriented programming and provides much more flexibility and power than does the struct definition.

In this chapter, you build on what you have learned about objects created using the struct keyword. You also learn about the following new topics:

- Defining objects using the class declaration

- Creating public and private members of a class

- Using constructor and destructor functions

- Using objects as parameters to functions

- Using friend functions

This discussion of classes and object-oriented programming continues in Chapter 9, "The Power of Inheritance," and Chapter 10, "Virtual Functions and Polymorphism."

Using *struct* to Implement Objects

Before examining true C++ classes in detail, you should review the use of the struct type to declare an object that contains both data and functions. In Chapter 3, "C++ Advanced Data Types," you learned to create a structure object such as the following `CDate_Info` structure, which combines both data and function declarations to produce an object definition:

```
typedef char string80[80];
struct CDateInfo {
    int Month, Day, Year;
    void SetDate( int MonthNum, int DayNum, int YearNum );
    void GetDate( int &MonthNum, int &DayNum, int &YearNum );
    void GetStringDate ( string80 &DateStr );
    void GetMonth ( string80 &MonthName  );
}
```

This declaration defines an object type containing three data members— `Month`, `Day`, and `Year`—plus the member functions `SetDate()`, `GetDate()`, `GetStringDate()`, and `GetMonth()`. You can use this declaration to create an instance of this object type by writing

```
CDateInfo DateInfo;
```

This line creates an object named `DateInfo`. You can reference the data fields of `DateInfo` directly, as in the following:

```
DateInfo.Month = 11;
DateInfo.Day = 28;
DateInfo.Year = 1993;
```

Alternatively, you can use the member function `SetDate()` to set the data members:

```
DateInfo.SetDate(11, 28, 1993);
```

By requiring that users of the `CDateInfo` object type use the defined functions to access the `DateInfo` record, your program practices a form of *information hiding*. The users of your date routines no longer have to know anything about the underlying representation of the `DateInfo` data structure. By using `SetDate()`, users do not have to know or understand the internal format required to store the date. Future changes to the internal data structure of `DateInfo` are now hidden from the users of this simple date module. Information hiding is good programming practice. In a moment, you see how to make these fields *private* so that they cannot be accessed outside the scope of the object.

The object's member functions (sometimes called an object's *methods*) are written as shown in listing 8.1. Notice that the function name in the function body is prefaced by the object name followed by two colons, `::`. The scope resolution operator `::` allows the member function to be implemented separately from the object definition. Within each member function, the code can access the member data fields without using the scope resolution operator. Inside CDateInfo::SetDate, the compiler is able to process

```
Month = MonthNum;
```

because the compiler knows that Month is a member field of the object. Even though the body of the SetDate() function is written outside the class definition, the compiler knows that when you refer to a member variable, you are referring the member defined within the class.

Listing 8.1 Creating an Object Using the C++ *struct* Declaration

```
 1   // OBJECT1A.CPP
 2   // Illustrates the use of the struct declaration
 3   // to define an object-like type named CDateInfo.
 4   #include <iostream.h>
 5   #include <string.h>
 6   #include <stdio.h>
 7
 8   typedef char string80[80];
 9
10   struct CDateInfo {
11     void SetDate( int MonthNum, int DayNum, int YearNum );
12     void GetDate( int &MonthNum, int &DayNum, int &YearNum );
13     void GetStringDate ( string80 &DateStr );
14     void GetMonth ( string80 &MonthName );
15     int Month, Day, Year;
16   };
17
18
19   void CDateInfo::SetDate( int MonthNum, int DayNum, int YearNum )
20   {
21     Month = MonthNum;
22     Day = DayNum;
23     Year = YearNum;
24   };
25
26
27   void CDateInfo::GetDate( int &MonthNum, int &DayNum, int &YearNum )
28   {
29     MonthNum = Month;
30     DayNum = Day;
31     YearNum = Year;
32   };
33
34
35   void CDateInfo::GetStringDate ( string80 &DateStr )
36   {
37     string80 TempStr;
38     sprintf( DateStr, "%d", Month );
39     sprintf( TempStr, "%d", Day );
```

(continues)

Listing 8.1 Continued

```
40    strcat( DateStr, "-" );
41    strcat( DateStr, TempStr );
42    strcat( DateStr, "-" );
43    sprintf( TempStr, "%d", Year );
44    strcat( DateStr, TempStr );
45  };
46
47
48  void CDateInfo::GetMonth( string80 &MonthName )
49  {
50    static char *Months[] =
51      {"January", "February", "March", "April", "May", "June",
52       "July", "August", "September", "October", "November",
53       "December"};
54    strcpy( MonthName, Months[Month-1] );
55  } // GetMonth
56
57
58  void main(void)
59  {
60    CDateInfo DateInfo;
61    string80 DemoStr;
62
63    DateInfo.SetDate ( 2, 18, 1994 );
64    DateInfo.GetStringDate ( DemoStr );
65    cout << "Date, in string format is:  " << DemoStr
66         << endl;
67    DateInfo.GetMonth ( DemoStr );
68    cout << "The month selected is:  " << DemoStr << endl;
69
70    cout << "Press Enter to continue.";
71    cin.get();
72  } // main
```

OBJECT1A.CPP defines an object type named CDateInfo. Line 60 declares DateInfo to be an instance of the CDateInfo class. The program sets the date by calling the SetDate() member function (line 63) and then uses the GetStringDate() member function to obtain a string containing the date in text format.

GetStringDate() is implemented in lines 35 through 45 and uses a function you have not seen before: sprintf(). In the C programming language, you display output to the screen by using a function named printf(), whereas printf() is seldom used in C++ programs. However, its companion function, sprintf(), is especially useful in some C++ applications. sprintf() is a special version of printf() that "prints" to a string rather than to the display. You can see how sprintf() works by looking at line 38:

```
sprintf( DateStr, "%d", Month );
```

Here, `sprintf()` writes to `DateStr` a string representation of the `Month` argument. The `"%d"` parameter is a formatting instruction that tells `sprintf()` to format `Month` (which is an integer) as a decimal number. When `Month` contains the value 12, this statement sets `DateStr` to `"12"`. You can use `sprintf()` to convert all the standard data types into string representations. To read about `sprintf()` and its formatting instructions, use the Visual C++ on-line help. Simply place the cursor on `sprintf` and press F1. To use `sprintf()`, you must use the `#include <stdio.h>` statement.

After `CDateInfo` is defined, you can create multiple instances of a single object type. To create several date objects, for example, write

```
CDateInfo DateInfo;
CDateInfo StartingDate;
CDateInfo EndingDate;
```

Each of these lines is a self-contained, independent object, and each has its own copy of the `Month`, `Day`, and `Year` fields. These separate objects are initialized by calling

```
DateInfo.SetDate ( 8, 29, 91 );
StartingDate.SetDate ( 5, 1, 91 );
EndingDate.SetDate ( 10, 29, 91 );
```

Each of these objects is completely independent of the others. Each object inherits the `SetDate()` function from the `CDateInfo` class. You may think that when you see a set of objects all created from the same class, the compiler duplicates the entire object, including code. Fortunately, that is not the case. Each of the objects—`DateInfo`, `StartingDate`, and `EndingDate`—has private copies of its member data variables `Month`, `Day`, and `Year`; however, the compiler efficiently shares a single copy of the member function code among all the objects.

Introducing the C++ *class* Keyword

In C++, most objects are described using the C++ `class` mechanism. The `struct` form of defining an object is seldom used. You use the `class` keyword to describe the layout of an object, much like you have done using the `struct` keyword. The reasons for using `class` rather than `struct` are many and are explored in this chapter and the next two chapters.

The `class` is similar to the `struct`, at least in its most primitive form. You can define `CDateInfo` as a true class by changing the keyword `struct` (in line 10 of listing 8.1) to `class` and inserting the `public` keyword, as shown in the following class definition:

```
class CDateInfo {
  int Month, Day, Year;
public:
  void SetDate( int MonthNum, int DayNum, int YearNum );
  void GetDate( int &MonthNum, int &DayNum, int &YearNum );
  void GetStringDate ( string80 &DateStr );
  void GetMonth ( string80 &MonthName  );
};
```

The primary differences between the `class` and `struct` mechanisms are the use of the `class` keyword in place of `struct` and the use of the `public` keyword. Structures are public, whereas the members of a class are private and cannot be accessed directly outside the class functions (this restriction enforces information hiding). To make the members of the class visible to the outside world, you must insert the `public` keyword before the items that you want to be publicly accessible to the users of this class definition.

As with the `struct` definition of an object, the class definition is itself not an object but, instead, a template for how you want the object to look. A class definition is sometimes compared to a cookie cutter. Just as you use a cookie cutter to stamp out multiple instances of cookies from cookie dough, you use the class definition to create multiple instances (or objects) that are members of this class type. You use class types to declare objects just as you used the structure type definitions. For example, the line

```
CDateInfo StartingDate, EndingDate;
```

creates two objects, `StartingDate` and `EndingDate`, which are instances of the `CDateInfo` class. To initialize the member fields of the objects, you must use the `SetDate()` member function:

```
StartingDate.SetDate( 11, 28, 1993 );
EndingDate.SetDate( 2, 18, 1994 );
```

The `Month`, `Day`, and `Year` members of `CDateInfo` are private, unlike those declared using `struct`. Because these members are private, you cannot directly access the members by using such code as

```
StartingDate.Month = 11;
```

which forces use of the member functions for data manipulation. The Visual C++ compiler flags this line as an error because `Month` is a private field of the `CDateInfo` class and is not accessible outside the member functions.

C++ also has a `private` keyword so that you can explicitly label some sections of the class as private and some as public. Because class members are private by default, the `private` keyword is not used as often as the `public` keyword. You can see the `private` keyword in use in this example:

```
class CDateInfo {
private:
  int Month, Day, Year;
public:
  void SetDate( int MonthNum, int DayNum, int YearNum );
  void GetDate( int &MonthNum, int &DayNum, int &YearNum );
  void GetStringDate ( string80 &DateStr );
  void GetMonth ( string80 &MonthName  );
};
```

You can place either `public` or `private` at any point in the class definition, and you can have multiple `public` or `private` sections within the class. Because users of your class do not have access to the private members, a good programming practice is to place the public definitions at the beginning of an object declaration and the private definitions at the end. A preferred definition of `CDateInfo`, therefore, is as follows:

```
class CDateInfo {
public:
  void SetDate( int MonthNum, int DayNum, int YearNum );
  void GetDate( int &MonthNum, int &DayNum, int &YearNum );
  void GetStringDate ( string80 &DateStr );
  void GetMonth ( string80 &MonthName  );
private:
  int Month, Day, Year;
};
```

C++ has a third type of data protection called *protected* members. You can read about protected members and their uses in Chapter 9, "The Power of Inheritance."

Out-of-Line and Inline Functions

You can implement the member functions of a class as either *out-of-line* or *inline* functions. Out-of-line functions resemble those shown in listing 8.1, in which the member functions of `CDateInfo` are implemented outside the class definition. The scope resolution operator (::) tells the compiler that each function definition is a member of the `CDateInfo` class. When the compiler sees a function header, as in

```
void CDateInfo::SetDate(int MonthNum, int DayNum, int YearNum);
```

the compiler recognizes that this line is the definition of the SetDate() member function of the CDateInfo class.

You can also define member functions inside the class declaration as shown in the following example. In this example, string80 is a user-defined type declared as

```
typedef char string80[80];
```

Here is the class definition:

```
class CDateInfo {
private:
  int Month, Day, Year;
public:
  void SetDate( int MonthNum, int DayNum, int YearNum )
  {
    Month = MonthNum;
    Day = DayNum;
    Year = YearNum;
  };
  void GetDate( int &MonthNum, int &DayNum, int &YearNum )
  {
    MonthNum = Month;
    DayNum = Day;
    YearNum = Year;
  };
  void GetStringDate( string80 &DateStr );
  void GetMonth( string80 &MonthName  );
};
```

A function defined inside the class declaration becomes an inline function. Inline functions are not called in the traditional sense of calling a function. When your program calls an inline function, the compiler inserts the actual inline function code directly into the compiled machine instructions, instead of issuing a true function call. This process eliminates the overhead of pushing parameters onto the stack, pushing a return address, and then jumping to the function. Because each inline function call results in a duplication of code, however, the use of inline functions is usually reserved for very short functions.

You can also declare out-of-line functions to be compiled as inline functions. To make an out-of-line function an inline function, preface the out-of-line function definition with the inline keyword:

```
inline void CDateInfo::SetDate( int MonthNum, int DayNum, int
YearNum )
{
  Month = MonthNum;
  Day = DayNum;
```

```
    Year = YearNum;
  };
```

In this form, calls to the SetDate() member function are compiled as inline functions, and the assignment statements contained in SetDate() are embedded directly into the output code.

Constructor Functions

A class may have an optional, special function called a *constructor function*. The constructor function is a special-purpose class member function normally used to initialize the data members of the class. A constructor function is called automatically when the object is created. In Chapter 10, "Virtual Functions and Polymorphism," you learn about a special type of class member function known as a *virtual* function; classes that have virtual functions are required to have a constructor function. Most of the classes you define will have virtual functions, so you should get into the habit of creating a constructor method for each of your class definitions.

The constructor function has the same name as the class type. To create a constructor function for the CDateInfo class, insert the following line into the class definition:

```
  CDateInfo(int MonthNum, int DayNum, int YearNum);
```

The constructor function may have parameters, as shown here, or it may have zero parameters. The constructor must not have a return type because C++ provides a special return type for all constructor functions. A typical use of the constructor function is to initialize the members of the class to known values. Later in this chapter, you see how you can put this constructor to use. After adding CDateInfo() to the class definition, the class looks like this:

```
class CDateInfo {
public:
  CDateInfo(int MonthNum, int DayNum, int YearNum);
  void SetDate( int MonthNum, int DayNum, int YearNum );
  void GetDate( int &MonthNum, int &DayNum, int &YearNum );
  void GetStringDate ( string80 &DateStr );
  void GetMonth ( string80 &MonthName  );
private:
  int Month, Day, Year;
};
```

You implement the CDateInfo() constructor as you would any other member function, as shown in this example:

```
CDateInfo::CDateInfo(int MonthNum, int DayNum, int YearNum)
{
  Month = MonthNum;
  Day = DayNum;
  Year = YearNum;
}
```

As you can see, this constructor performs the same operation as the SetDate() member function. In the next section, however, you see how you can use the constructor function to initialize your object declarations.

Using the Constructor Function

You use the constructor function for CDateInfo to initialize the data members of the class. After you have defined the constructor function, you do not call the constructor directly. Instead, after a class has a constructor defined, you use the constructor to initialize the object when the object is declared. To see how this process works, consider the following revised declarations for StartingDate and EndingDate:

```
CDateInfo StartingDate(11, 28, 1993);
CDateInfo EndingDate(2, 18, 1994 );
```

On seeing this declaration, the compiler creates the two variables and calls the constructor function of CDateInfo, passing to the constructor the initialization values shown in the declaration.

You will find that most classes you design have constructor functions. You use the constructors to initialize the data members of the class.

Classes with Multiple Constructors

Each class can have multiple constructor methods through the use of *overloaded functions*—functions with the same name but with different parameter lists. You can use default parameter values, or you can declare a constructor that has no parameters. The following class definition illustrates additional examples of constructor methods:

```
class CDateInfo {
public:
  CDateInfo();
  CDateInfo(int MonthNum, int DayNum, int YearNum);
  CDateInfo( string80 &DateString );
  void SetDate( int MonthNum, int DayNum, int YearNum );
  void GetDate( int &MonthNum, int &DayNum, int &YearNum );
  void GetStringDate ( string80 &DateStr );
  void GetMonth ( string80 &MonthName  );
private:
  int Month, Day, Year;
};
```

Notice that each constructor is named the same as the class. The compiler distinguishes the constructors by looking at the differences in the parameters. If, for example, you declare an object variable CurrentDate, using the declaration

```
CDateInfo CurrentDate;
```

Visual C++ automatically selects the default constructor that has no arguments.

When you declare a constructor that has default parameters, you do not have to supply all the parameter values when you use the constructor. If you omit a value, however, all subsequent parameters in the constructor must have declared default values.

The Copy Constructor

One type of constructor is special: the *copy constructor* function. A copy constructor is a function used to copy one object to another. Consider the following statements:

```
CDateInfo Date_One(11,28,1993);
CDateInfo Date_Two;
Date_Two = Date_One;
```

To implement the assignment of Date_One to Date_Two, you must declare a copy constructor for your class. The copy constructor has a single reference parameter to an instance of the same class and copies the data members from one object to the other object. To implement a copy constructor for CDateInfo, you must declare an additional constructor function that has a CDateInfo parameter, as shown in the following:

```
class CDateInfo {
public:
  CDateInfo(int MonthNum, int DayNum, int YearNum);
  CDateInfo( CDateInfo &Other_Object); // Copy constructor
  void SetDate( int MonthNum, int DayNum, int YearNum );
  void GetDate( int &MonthNum, int &DayNum, int &YearNum );
  void GetStringDate ( string80 &DateStr );
  void GetMonth ( string80 &MonthName  );
private:
  int Month, Day, Year;
};
```

The implementation of the copy constructor copies the data fields from the parameter object to the current object, as in

```
void CDateInfo::CDateInfo( CDateInfo &Other_Object )
{
  Month = Other_Object.Month;
```

```
        Day = Other_Object.Day;
        Year = Other_Object.Year;
    }
```

The compiler calls the copy constructor whenever you assign an object to another object of this class. Therefore, when you write

```
    Date_Two = Date_One;
```

the compiler translates this assignment statement into a function call, passing Date_One as the parameter to the copy constructor. If your objects will never be copied from one to the other, you don't have to create a copy constructor for the class. (See the section "The *this Pointer" later in this chapter for another way of copying the member data from one object to another.)

The Default Constructor Function

If you do not specify any constructor functions for your classes, the C++ compiler automatically creates one for you. The default constructor function initializes the member data fields to zero. If this initialization is sufficient for your needs, you can use the default constructor; however, you may find that for most of the classes you invent, you want to create your own constructor function or functions.

Destructor Functions

As with the constructor method for initializing an object, the destructor method provides for the destruction of an object. A destructor is called automatically when an object is being destroyed. If any of the member functions make dynamic memory allocations, the destructor method is a good place to put the appropriate delete statements. Then when the object is no longer needed, the object's private memory allocation can be cleaned up by calling the destructor. Destructors are most important when you use pointers to objects along with the new operator to allocate object instances dynamically. Using pointers to objects is described in the next section.

Consider, for example, a class that implements a text-editing field. The object's constructor method might use the new operator to allocate a character string for the editing field. When the object is no longer required, the character buffer must be discarded. By placing the delete operator in the destructor function for the class, you ensure that each object created from the class disposes of its memory allocation when the object is destroyed. If you fail to properly discard the text buffer, the buffer continues to occupy a portion of the C++ heap memory for the duration of the program's execution.

In C++, the destructor function has the same name as the class name, except that the name must be preceded by the tilde (~) character. For the `CDateInfo` class, you write the destructor as follows:

```
~CDateInfo();
```

Like the constructor function, the destructor must not have a return type. Unlike the constructor, a destructor function takes no parameters. Because a destructor has no parameters, you cannot create overloaded destructor functions, so each class is limited to having a single destructor function.

You can invoke destructors either by calling them directly or by letting C++ automatically call the destructor for you. Destructors are called automatically in two situations in which an object is destroyed:

- If an object is declared local to a function, the object's destructor is called automatically on exiting the function.

- When an object is declared dynamically using the `new` operator, you normally discard that object using the `delete` operator. When you invoke `delete` on an object instance, `delete` calls the destructor for you.

Consider the case of a class named `CFieldEdit` that is used to implement the text input edit field just described. You use `CFieldEdit` to create, or *instantiate*, an instance of the object, as in

```
CFieldEdit BField(500);
```

To call `BField`'s destructor, explicitly select the function by writing this somewhat peculiar-looking expression:

```
BField.CFieldEdit::~CFieldEdit();
```

This line might be clearer if the compiler enabled you to write

```
BField.~CFieldEdit();
```

but the compiler does not. Instead, you must use the scope resolution operator (`::`) to show the compiler that you are invoking the destructor member function of the `CFieldEdit` class as a member of the `BField` object.

In the next section, you learn how to create and destroy object instances dynamically using `new` and `delete`. When you call `delete` to dispose of an object instance, `delete` automatically calls the object's destructor for you so that you don't have to call it explicitly.

Pointers to Objects

Like all C++ data types, objects can be allocated dynamically using the new operator. To do so requires only that you define a pointer to the class type and then call new. Consider the example described in the preceding section. In that example, a class named CFieldEdit allocates a character string in its constructor function (named Buffer) and deallocates Buffer in its destructor function. The declaration of the CFieldEdit class looks like the following:

```
class CFieldEdit
{
public:
  CFieldEdit ( int FieldSize );
  ~CFieldEdit();

  // Other methods that use the field might go here:
  private:
  char * Buffer;
  int BufferSize;
};
```

To keep things simple, the CFieldEdit class contains just the constructor and destructor functions, plus a pointer to the character string buffer and the size of the buffer. CFieldEdit enables you to specify the size of the desired buffer as a parameter to the constructor.

You declare a pointer to an object instance of the CFieldEdit class by writing

```
CFieldEdit * AField;
```

in which AField points to an object of type CFieldEdit. Keep in mind, however, that for now AField is just like any other uninitialized pointer. Note the similarity to ordinary C++ pointers, such as

```
char * AString;
```

To have AField point to an actual object requires you to use new to allocate an instance of the object. You specify the size of the desired text buffer as a parameter to the constructor:

```
AField = new CFieldEdit(500);
```

Now AField points to an instance of the class CFieldEdit. This particular instance has a buffer of 500 bytes in size. A complete implementation of CFieldEdit is shown in listing 8.2.

Listing 8.2 Using a Destructor to Dispose of a Dynamically Allocated Object Instance

```
 1  // OBJECT2.CPP
 2  // Demonstrates the use and value of a destructor
 3  // method. In this program, the constructor function
 4  // creates a dynamically allocated character string.
 5  // It is essential that the destructor discard this
 6  // character string when the object is no longer needed.
 7  #include <iostream.h>
 8
 9  const int MaxBufferSize = 1023;
10
11  class CFieldEdit
12  {
13  public:
14    CFieldEdit ( int FieldSize );
15    ~CFieldEdit();
16
17    // Other methods that use the field might go here:
18  private:
19    char * Buffer;
20    int BufferSize;
21  };
22
23
24  CFieldEdit::CFieldEdit(int FieldSize )
25  {
26    if (FieldSize > MaxBufferSize)
27      FieldSize = MaxBufferSize;
28
29    Buffer = new char[FieldSize];
30
31    BufferSize = FieldSize;
32
33  };
34
35  // The destructor
36  CFieldEdit::~CFieldEdit()
37  {
38    delete Buffer;
39  };
40
41
42  void main (void)
43  {
44    // Declare AField to have a 500-byte buffer.
45    CFieldEdit * AField;
46
47    AField = new CFieldEdit(500);
48
49    // Using delete to discard a dynamic object instance
50    // automatically invokes the object's destructor.
51    delete AField;
52
53  } // main
```

A Second Example of Using a Pointer

Now look back to the CDateInfo class and see how to create a pointer to an instance of CDateInfo. First declare a pointer variable as a pointer to CDateInfo. Then use new to create and return a pointer to the object. To declare a pointer, write

```
CDateInfo * ADate;
```

This declaration makes ADate a pointer to a CDateInfo object. Then use new to allocate an instance of the CDateInfo object:

```
ADate = new CDateInfo(6, 27, 1992);
```

The new operator allocates memory for the object and calls the constructor method, passing the month, day, and year arguments shown, to initialize the new object.

Because you are using a pointer to an object, reference the member functions of the ADate object instance by using the -> pointer member-of operator:

```
ADate->SetDate( 10, 1, 91 );
ADate->GetDate( AMonth, ADay, AYear );
ADate->GetStringDate ( TheDate );
ADate->GetMonth ( WhichMonth );
```

You can instantiate multiple instances of CDateInfo through multiple pointer variables. To declare four separate object pointers, for example, write

```
CDateInfo *ADate, *BDate, *CDate, *DDate;
```

To instantiate each of these four instances, write

```
ADate = new CDateInfo( 8, 29, 91 );
BDate = new CDateInfo( 1, 1, 92 );
CDate = new CDateInfo( 6, 27, 92 );
DDate = new CDateInfo( 9, 17, 91 );
```

Disposing of Object Pointers

When a dynamically allocated object is no longer required, you must dispose of it with the delete operator. For example

```
delete ADate;
```

disposes of the object pointed to by ADate and frees up the memory that was used. The destructor function for ADate is called automatically.

Arrays of Objects

You can organize objects, such as structures and other C++ types, into arrays. For example, the declaration

```
CDateInfo Dates[12];
```

allocates an array of 12 CDateInfo object instances. You use the array as you do any other array type. To call the SetDate() member function of a specific element of the array, write

```
Dates[1].SetDate( 6, 27, 1994 );
```

You can create a pointer to an array of objects through the use of a pointer and the new operator. To declare a pointer to CDateInfo objects, write

```
CDateInfo * DateInfo;
```

To initialize this pointer to point to an array of CDateInfo objects, write

```
DateInfo = new CDateInfo[12];
```

DateInfo now points to an array of 12 object instances, each of the CDateInfo type.

When you use the delete operator to discard the array pointed to by DateInfo, you should use the following special notation:

```
delete[] DateInfo;
```

The brackets ([ ]) tell the compiler that DateInfo is a pointer to an array. In earlier editions of C++, you were required to use the delete[] operator whenever you deleted a pointer to an array. Now you are required to use delete[] only when the array elements are objects that contain a destructor. Because there is no harm in using the delete[] operator for arrays that do not contain constructors, many C++ programmers use delete[] for all pointers to arrays.

Objects as Function Parameters

You can use objects as parameters to functions. You can pass object parameters by value, or—using the & reference operator—you can pass object parameters by reference. The IncrementDate function, for example, accepts a parameter object of the CDateInfo type and increments the date values to the next date, in sequence, automatically incrementing the month and year as appropriate. To perform this operation requires that the parameter be passed by reference, as shown here:

```
void CDateInfo::IncrementDate ( CDateInfo &Date )
{
  static int TotalDays[12] =
          ( 31, 28, 31, 30, 31, 30, 31, 31, 30, 31, 30, 31 );
  Date.Day++;
  if (Date.Day > TotalDays[Month-1])
  {
    Date.Day = 1;
    Date.Month++;
    if  (Month > 12)
    {
      Date.Month = 1;
      Date.Year++;
    }; // if
  } // if
} // IncrementDate
```

Because the rules of type compatibility apply to parameter values too, either a CDateInfo or a CDateInfo-derived object can be passed to the procedure. You learn about deriving new objects from existing objects in Chapter 9, "The Power of Inheritance." The ability to create a new class of objects that resembles an existing class of objects, but with a few twists, is one of the most important features of C++ programming.

Static Class Data Members

The data members of a class are private to each instance of the class. If you define three instances of the CDateInfo object by declaring

```
CDateInfo Date1, Date2, Date3;
```

then each object—Date1, Date2, and Date3—has its own private copy of the Month, Day, and Year members. But what if you want your object instances to share data? For example, suppose that the CDateInfo class has a new data member named DateFormat which is set to 1 for U.S. format dates (*MM/DD/YY*) or 2 for the European date format (*DD-MM-YYYY*). When any member of the class sets the DateFormat, you want each object instance to display its date according to the common date format.

You could create a global variable outside the class to share data among the object instances; however, that approach does not enforce information hiding. The best solution is to declare the DateFormat data member as a static data member. (Static class data members, however, require the use of a little programming trick that you learn later in this chapter.) Static class data members behave in the same way that static local data behaves in a function—static data members are given permanent memory storage. Each object instance shares the same bit of memory allocated for the static data member, so static data members become global to a class.

To see how a static data member works in a class structure, look at CDateInfo, modified to include the DataFormat member and a new member function, SetFormat():

```
class CDateInfo {
public:
  CDateInfo(int MonthNum, int DayNum, int YearNum);
  void SetDate( int MonthNum, int DayNum, int YearNum );
  void GetDate( int &MonthNum, int &DayNum, int &YearNum );
  void GetStringDate ( string80 &DateStr );
  void GetMonth ( string80 &MonthName  );
  void SetFormat(int format);
private:
  int Month, Day, Year;
  static int DateFormat;
};
```

If you try to compile this class definition, the compiler issues an error message. The trick to implementing a static class data member is that you must define the data member in the class, as shown in the CDateInfo class declaration, but you also must define the static data member out of line. This technique means that in addition to the preceding CDateInfo declaration, you have to add the following outside the class definition:

```
int CDateInfo::DateFormat;
```

The separate definition for the DateFormat member provides the actual memory allocation for the shared DateFormat variable. The complete implementation of this class is shown in listing 8.3.

Listing 8.3 Sharing a Static Data Member between Object Instances

```
 1  // SHARED.CPP
 2  // Uses a static data member to share class data
 3  // between instances of the class.
 4  #include <iostream.h>
 5  #include <string.h>
 6  #include <stdio.h>
 7
 8  typedef char string80[80];
 9
10  // Constants used to select date formats.
```

(continues)

Listing 8.3 Continued

```
11   const int US_FORMAT = 1;
12   const int EU_FORMAT = 2;
13
14   class CDateInfo {
15   public:
16     CDateInfo( int MonthNum, int DayNum, int YearNum );
17     void SetDate( int MonthNum, int DayNum, int YearNum );
18     void GetDate( int &MonthNum, int &DayNum, int &YearNum );
19     void GetStringDate ( string80 &DateStr );
20     void GetMonth ( string80 &MonthName );
21     void SetFormat( int format );
22   private:
23     int Month, Day, Year;
24     static int DateFormat;
25   };
26
27   int CDateInfo::DateFormat; // static data member
28
29
30   void main(void)
31   {
32     CDateInfo Date1( 6, 30, 1993), Date2( 8, 13, 1993);
33     string80 DemoStr;
34
35     // Get and display dates in default date format.
36     cout << "U.S. Format:" << endl;
37     Date1.GetStringDate( DemoStr );
38     cout << "Date 1 = " << DemoStr << endl;
39     Date2.GetStringDate( DemoStr );
40     cout << "Date 2 = " << DemoStr << endl;
41
42     // Select European date format.
43     Date1.SetFormat( EU_FORMAT );
44
45     // Get and display dates. Even though the
46     // SetFormat() member is only called for Date1,
47     // because DateFormat is a shared data member,
48     // both of the following output lines will
49     // appear in European date format.
50     cout << endl << "European Format:" << endl;
51     Date1.GetStringDate( DemoStr );
52     cout << "Date 1 = " << DemoStr << endl;
53     Date2.GetStringDate( DemoStr );
54     cout << "Date 2 = " << DemoStr << endl;
55
56     cout << "Press Enter to continue.";
57     cin.get();
58   } // main
59
60
61   CDateInfo::CDateInfo( int MonthNum, int DayNum, int YearNum )
62   {
63     Month = MonthNum;
64     Day = DayNum;
65     Year = YearNum;
```

```
66    DateFormat = US_FORMAT;
67  }
68
69
70  void CDateInfo::SetDate( int MonthNum, int DayNum, int YearNum )
71  {
72    Month = MonthNum;
73    Day = DayNum;
74    Year = YearNum;
75  };
76
77
78  void CDateInfo::GetDate( int &MonthNum, int &DayNum, int &YearNum )
79  {
80    MonthNum = Month;
81    DayNum = Day;
82    YearNum = Year;
83  };
84
85
86  void CDateInfo::GetStringDate ( string80 &DateStr )
87  {
88    string80 TempStr;
89
90    switch (DateFormat) {
91      case US_FORMAT: { // Display U.S. Format
92                sprintf( DateStr, "%d", Month );
93                sprintf( TempStr, "%d", Day );
94                strcat( DateStr, "-" );
95                strcat( DateStr, TempStr );
96                strcat( DateStr, "-" );
97                sprintf( TempStr, "%d", Year % 100 );
98                strcat( DateStr, TempStr );
99                break;
100             } // case
101     case EU_FORMAT: { // Display European Format
102               sprintf( DateStr, "%d", Day );
103               sprintf( TempStr, "%d", Month );
104               strcat( DateStr, "-" );
105               strcat( DateStr, TempStr );
106               strcat( DateStr, "-" );
107               sprintf( TempStr, "%d", Year );
108               strcat( DateStr, TempStr );
109               break;
110             } // case
111    } // switch
112  }; // GetStringDate
113
114
115  void CDateInfo::GetMonth( string80 &MonthName )
116  {
117    static char *Months[] =
118      {"January", "February", "March", "April", "May", "June",
119       "July", "August", "September", "October", "November",
```

(continues)

Listing 8.3 Continued

```
120      "December"};
121    strcpy( MonthName, Months[Month-1] );
122  } // GetMonth
123
124
125  void CDateInfo::SetFormat( int format )
126  {
127    DateFormat = format;
128  }
```

In listing 8.3, lines 24 and 27 define the shared DateFormat member as a static member of class CDateInfo. To see how the DateFormat is shared between object instances, look at the code for the main() function in lines 30 through 58. Lines 36 through 40 output the value of Date1 and Date2 in *MM/DD/YY* format. Line 43 uses Date1.SetFormat() to change the DateFormat variable to European format. Thereafter, each time GetStringDate() is called, regardless of which object is used, the date is returned in the *DD-MM-YYYY* format. When you run this program, you see the output shown in figure 8.1.

Fig. 8.1
The output generated by listing 8.3.

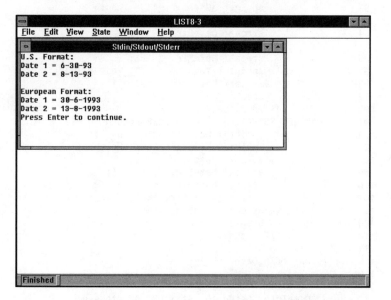

This example should convince you that the DateFormat member is indeed being shared between object instances of a single class. You can use shared data this way when your class needs a global-like data element having permanent storage, or when you want to have objects of a class share data with each other.

Implementing the List Class

Chapter 6, "Functions and Macros," introduced a set of routines written as a pseudoclass (using the `struct` definition) to implement a doubly linked list of elements. You can modify the original program in listing 6.15 (LIST.CPP) so that the `struct` definition is changed to a true class definition. Listing 8.4 shows the changes necessary to make this conversion. Just place the `list_type` and `list_element` declarations into a class definition and add `public` and `private` keywords in the appropriate places. After making these changes to listing 6.15, you can recompile the program and use your new `list_type` class.

Listing 8.4 Modifying LIST.CPP to Use a True Class Structure

```
// The only changes required to implement the list
// as a true class are those shown here: placing the
// list_type and list_element into a true class.
class list_type {
private:
struct list_element
{
  char name[MAXNAMESIZE];
  // The following point to the next entry in
  // the list and the previous entry in the
  // list, respectively.
  list_element *next;
  list_element *prev;
};
public:
  void Initialize_List(void);  // Initializes head and tail.
  void Add_to_Tail(char name_to_add[]);
  void Display_List(int Direction);
  void Destroy_List(void);
private:
  list_element *head;  // Points to the front of the list.
  list_element *tail;  // Points to the end of the list.
};
```

The *this* Pointer

The *this pointer is a special pointer to the current object instance. A member function, for example, is often used to copy the data from a parameter object to the current object instance. Consider the following `TimeClass` definition:

```
class TimeClass {
private:
```

```
    int hours;
    int minutes;
public:
    TimeClass( int new_hours, int new_minutes )
      { hours = new_hours; minutes = new_minutes; };
    void SetTime( int new_hours, int new_minutes )
      { hours = new_hours; minutes = new_minutes; };
    void GetTime( int &current_hours, int &current_minutes )
      { current_hours = hours; current_minutes = minutes; };
    void CopyTime ( TimeClass &Time2 );
};
```

The member function CopyTime copies the value of one TimeClass object
to another. For example, suppose that you have two TimeClass objects
declared as

```
TimeClass Time1(10, 30), Time2(12, 15);
```

This line initializes Time1 to 10:30 and Time2 to 12:15. Now suppose that you
want to copy Time2 to Time1, effectively setting Time1 to 12:15. To perform the
copy, write

```
Time1.CopyTime( Time2 );
```

The CopyTime() member function copies the data fields of Time2 to Time1. The
easiest way to implement CopyTime() is to use the *this pointer as shown
here:

```
void TimeClass::CopyTime ( TimeClass &Time2 )
{
  // Use *this so that all the class data is copied
  // with a single assignment statement.
  *this = Time2;
  // This is easier than individually copying each
  // member data element, one element at a time.
};
```

When the function call

```
Time1.CopyTime( Time2 );
```

is executed, *this is set to point at Time1. Hence, the assignment statement

```
*this = Time2;
```

causes Time2's member data to be copied to Time1's member data. The complete program to demonstrate the use of *this is shown in listing 8.5. You
can also use the *this pointer in a copy constructor to ease the copying of
member data from one object to the other (see the section "The Copy Constructor" earlier in this chapter). Because *this is a pointer to the current

object instance, you can also use *this with the -> pointer member-of operator to access individual data members of the object:

```
this->hours = Time2.hours;
```

Listing 8.5 Using the *this* Pointer

```
 1  // TIMECLAS.CPP
 2  // Demonstrates the use of the *this pointer.
 3  #include <iostream.h>
 4
 5  class TimeClass {
 6  private:
 7    int hours;
 8    int minutes;
 9  public:
10    TimeClass( int new_hours, int new_minutes )
11      { hours = new_hours; minutes = new_minutes; };
12    void SetTime( int new_hours, int new_minutes )
13      { hours = new_hours; minutes = new_minutes; };
14    void GetTime( int &current_hours, int &current_minutes )
15      { current_hours = hours; current_minutes = minutes; };
16    void CopyTime ( TimeClass &Time2 );
17  };
18
19  void TimeClass::CopyTime ( TimeClass &Time2 )
20  {
21    // Use *this so that all the class data is copied
22    // with a single assignment statement.
23    *this = Time2;
24    // This is easier than individually copying each
25    // member data element, one element at a time.
26  };
27
28  void main(void)
29  {
30    TimeClass Time1 (10,30), Time2(12,15);
31    int hrs, mins;
32
33    Time1.GetTime(hrs, mins);
34    cout << "Time is: " << hrs << ":" << mins << endl;
35
36    Time1.CopyTime(Time2);
37
38    cout << "After copying Time2 to Time1, the time is: "
39        << hrs << ":" << mins << endl;
40
41    cout << "Press Enter to continue.";
42    cin.get();
43  } // main
```

Friend Functions

As you know, only member functions of a class can access private members of that class. Sometimes, however, it is convenient for nonmember functions to access the private class members. You can make such members public, but doing so defeats the purpose of the encapsulation and information hiding made possible by the class structure. Instead of making these private members public, you can define a set of *friend functions* that are given access to the private members. Friend functions are normal (outside of classes) functions that are given access to the private members of the class.

Suppose that you have two functions, named Time12() and Time24(), which display the time in 12- and 24-hour formats, respectively. Suppose also that for some reason unique to your application, you do not want to have Time12() and Time24() be member functions of the TimeClass. Instead, Time12() and Time24() should be implemented as normal functions that access the member data of TimeClass directly. So that these functions can access private member data, you declare the functions as a friend of the class. You declare a friend function by specifying the function's prototype header inside the class. Following is an example showing how to define Time12() and Time24() as friends:

```
class TimeClass {
private:
  int hours;
  int minutes;
public:
  TimeClass( int new_hours, int new_minutes )
    { hours = new_hours; minutes = new_minutes; };
  void SetTime( int new_hours, int new_minutes )
    { hours = new_hours; minutes = new_minutes; };
  void GetTime( int &current_hours, int &current_minutes )
    { current_hours = hours; current_minutes = minutes; };
  void CopyTime ( TimeClass &Time2 );
  friend void Time12( TimeClass TheTime );
  friend void Time24( TimeClass TheTime );
};
```

The actual implementation of the friend function is just like any other function except that the friend function can access the private member data of the class. The object whose private data you want to access must be passed as a function parameter. You can see the implementation of the friend functions in FRIEND.CPP, shown in listing 8.6.

When Should You Use Friend Functions?

You may want to use friend functions to access the private members of a class for several reasons. One reason was suggested regarding the Time12() and Time24() functions: sometimes your application may require that the functions be implemented outside the class. This can occur, for example, if you must write your function in a language other than C++ (such as assembly language, C, or other programming languages). The only way to access such a routine is to declare the external function as a friend of the class.

C++ enables you to provide overloaded operator definitions—in other words, the ability to overload the +, -, *,/, and other arithmetic operators (see the next section, "Overloaded Operator Functions") just as you are able to overload the functions you write. In certain situations involving binary operators (which have two operands), the use of friend functions to implement overloaded operators provides greater flexibility.

Listing 8.6 Using Friend Functions

```
1   // FRIEND.CPP
2   // Illustrates the use of friend functions.
3   #include <iostream.h>
4
5   class TimeClass {
6   private:
7     int hours;
8     int minutes;
9   public:
10    TimeClass( int new_hours, int new_minutes )
11      { hours = new_hours; minutes = new_minutes; };
12    void SetTime( int new_hours, int new_minutes )
13      { hours = new_hours; minutes = new_minutes; };
14    void GetTime( int &current_hours, int &current_minutes )
15      { current_hours = hours; current_minutes = minutes; };
16    void CopyTime ( TimeClass &Time2 ) { *this = Time2; };
17    friend void Time12( TimeClass TheTime );
18    friend void Time24( TimeClass TheTime );
19  };
20
21  void Time12( TimeClass TheTime )
22  {
23    int PMFlag;
24
25    if (TheTime.hours > 12)
26      {
27        TheTime.hours -= 12;
28        PMFlag = 1;
29      }
30    else
```

(continues)

Listing 8.6 Continued

```
31       PMFlag = 0;
32
33    cout << TheTime.hours << ":" << TheTime.minutes;
34    if (PMFlag) cout << " PM" << endl;
35    else
36       endl;
37  } // Time12
38
39  void Time24( TimeClass TheTime )
40  {
41    cout << TheTime.hours << ":" << TheTime.minutes
42          << endl;
43  } // Time24
44
45  void main(void)
46  {
47    TimeClass Time1 (14, 30);
48
49    Time12( Time1 );
50    Time24( Time1 );
51
52    cout << "Press Enter to continue.";
53    cin.get();
54  } // main
```

In listing 8.6, line 49 calls Time12(), and line 50 calls Time24(). Because Time12() and Time24() are ordinary functions, they are not themselves members of any class; therefore, you do not need to use the scope resolution operator (::) to access friend functions. You can also implement friends, as with all other C++ functions, as inline—either by placing the implementation of the friend function inside the class definition or by using the inline keyword. You can also write friend functions in assembly language or other programming languages that produce compatible .OBJ files for linking to C++.

Overloaded Operator Functions

You learned in Chapter 6, "Functions and Macros," how to write an overloaded function. Overloaded functions enable you to reuse the function name for multiple functions, provided that each function has a different set of parameter types. In C++, you also can overload the standard arithmetic operators, such as +, -, *, /, and other operators. Overloaded operators are implemented similarly to basic overloaded functions and are most often used as member functions of a class.

Using overloaded operators enables you to create new data types in C++. Just as you can perform addition or subtraction on the standard data types, such as int or float, you can define such operations for your own classes. Given the CDateInfo type, for example, you can provide + and - operators to add or subtract two dates, respectively. Consider two date objects defined as the following:

```
CDateInfo Date1(1, 1, 1993), ChangeOfDate( 1, 15, 0 );
```

Date1 is set to January 1, 1994. ChangeOfDate is not really set to a true date at all; instead, it uses the Month, Day, and Year fields to record a duration of time beginning January 1. Here, ChangeOfDate records 1 month, 15 days, and 0 years. By overloading the addition operator, you can write expressions such as the following:

```
Date1 = Date1 + ChangeOfDate;
```

This expression produces the new date of February 16, 1994.

You define an overloaded operator function by using the keyword operator followed by the operator symbol. Here is an example of a function header for overloading the addition operator to add two dates:

```
CDateInfo operator +(CDateInfo ChangeOfDate);
```

You can see that the result of the + operation is to return a result of the CDateInfo result type. Exactly how the addition operator performs its function on two operands is not immediately apparent. The key to this operation is that in the expression

```
Date1 + ChangeOfDate
```

the compiler translates this expression into the following equivalent code:

```
Date1.+(ChangeOfDate)
```

Essentially, ChangeOfDate is an argument to Date1's addition member function. Therefore, Date1 is the other operand. Inside the implementation of the overloaded + function, you reference Date1 with the *this pointer. You can see this process in action in line 113 of listing 8.7, where *this accesses the member data of the object performing the calculation. Listing 8.7 also overloads the subtraction (-) operator so that you can subtract one date value from another (see lines 130 through 154).

Listing 8.7 Using Overloaded + and - in the *CDateInfo* Class

```
1   // OVERLOAD.CPP
2   // Overloads the + and - operators to implement
3   // addition and subtraction of dates. I'm not exactly
4   // sure what it means to add or subtract a date
5   // like this, but it's fun!
6   #include <iostream.h>
7   #include <string.h>
8   #include <stdio.h>
9
10  typedef char string80[80];
11
12  class CDateInfo {
13  public:
14    CDateInfo() {};
15    CDateInfo( int MonthNum, int DayNum, int YearNum);
16    void SetDate( int MonthNum, int DayNum, int YearNum );
17    void GetDate( int &MonthNum, int &DayNum, int &YearNum );
18    void GetStringDate ( string80 &DateStr );
19    void GetMonth ( string80 &MonthName );
20    CDateInfo operator +(CDateInfo ChangeOfDate);
21    CDateInfo operator -(CDateInfo ChangeOfDate);
22  private:
23    long Convert_to_Days( CDateInfo ADate );
24    CDateInfo Convert_to_Date( long Num_Days);
25    int Month, Day, Year;
26  };
27
28  static int DaysInYear[] =
29      { 0, 31, 59, 90, 120, 151, 181, 212, 243, 273, 304, 334, 365 };
30
31
32
33  void main(void)
34  {
35    CDateInfo Date1 (1, 1, 1993), ChangeOfDate (1, 15, 0);
36    string80 DemoStr;
37
38    // Add ChangeOfDate to Date1.
39    Date1 = Date1 + ChangeOfDate;
40    Date1.GetStringDate ( DemoStr );
41    cout << "Date1 + ChangeOfDate is:  " << DemoStr
42        << endl;
43
44    // Subtracting ChangeOfDate from Date1 gets us
45    // back to the date we started with.
46    Date1 = Date1 - ChangeOfDate;
47    Date1.GetStringDate ( DemoStr );
48    cout << "Date1 - ChangeOfDate is:  " << DemoStr
49        << endl;
50
51    cout << "Press Enter to continue.";
52    cin.get();
53  } // main
54
55
```

```
56   long CDateInfo::Convert_to_Days( CDateInfo ADate )
57   {
58     // Convert the date to the number of days since
59     // 1/1/0000. This calculation is performed by
60     // multiplying Year * 365, then adding the number
61     // of days in the year up to the current month,
62     // and then adding the day of the month. This
63     // calculation does not accommodate leap years.
64     return ADate.Year * 365L + DaysInYear[ADate.Month-1] + ADate.Day;
65     // Note the use of a long constant, 365L. Without
66     // the L, the calculation Year * 365 is done with the
67     // int type. As you can see, 1993 * 365 is much larger
68     // than can be represented using int. Therefore, the
69     // use of the long constant forces the compiler to
70     // multiply the values as the long type.
71   } // convert_to_days
72
73
74   CDateInfo CDateInfo::Convert_to_Date( long Num_Days)
75   {
76     // This function translates a number of days back
77     // into a Month, Day, Year formatted date.
78     CDateInfo ADate;
79     int Days_Left, Which_Month;
80
81     // Convert the number of days back to number of years.
82     ADate.Year = Num_Days / 365;
83     // And extract the number of days in the current year.
84     Days_Left = Num_Days % 365;
85
86     // Determine which month to use.
87     for(Which_Month=0;
88         Days_Left > DaysInYear[Which_Month];
89         Which_Month++);
90
91     // Convert the Which_Month zero-based array index
92     // into a Month value in the range of 1 to 12.
93     ADate.Month = Which_Month;
94
95     // Calculate the Day within the month.
96     ADate.Day = Days_Left - DaysInYear[Which_Month-1];
97
98     // And return the result.
99     return ADate;
100  } // convert_to_date
101
102
103  CDateInfo CDateInfo::operator +(CDateInfo ChangeOfDate)
104  {
105    // This is the overloaded + operator for the
106    // CDateInfo type.
107
108    long converted_date1, converted_date2;
109    CDateInfo TempDate;
```

(continues)

Listing 8.7 Continued

```
110
111     // Convert the left operand (this object) into
112     // a number of days measurement.
113     converted_date1 = Convert_to_Days(*this);
114
115     ChangeOfDate.Month++;
116     converted_date2 = Convert_to_Days(ChangeOfDate);
117
118     // Add the two day measurements together.
119     converted_date1 = converted_date1 + converted_date2;
120
121     // And convert the number of days back to a
122     // Month, Day, Year date.
123     TempDate = Convert_to_Date( converted_date1);
124
125     // Return the result.
126     return TempDate;
127 }; // operator +
128
129
130 CDateInfo CDateInfo::operator -(CDateInfo ChangeOfDate)
131 {
132     // This is the overloaded - operator for
133     // the CDateInfo type.
134
135     long converted_date1, converted_date2;
136     CDateInfo TempDate;
137
138     // Convert the left operand (this object) into
139     // a number of days measurement.
140     converted_date1 = Convert_to_Days(*this);
141
142     ChangeOfDate.Month++;
143     converted_date2 = Convert_to_Days(ChangeOfDate);
144
145     // Add the two day measurements together.
146     converted_date1 = converted_date1 - converted_date2;
147
148     // And convert the number of days back to a
149     // Month, Day, Year date.
150     TempDate = Convert_to_Date( converted_date1);
151
152     // Return the result.
153     return TempDate;
154 } // operator -
155
156
157 CDateInfo::CDateInfo( int MonthNum, int DayNum, int YearNum)
158 {
159     Month = MonthNum;
160     Day = DayNum;
161     Year = YearNum;
162 };
163
```

```
164
165   void CDateInfo::SetDate( int MonthNum, int DayNum, int YearNum )
166   {
167     Month = MonthNum;
168     Day = DayNum;
169     Year = YearNum;
170   };
171
172
173   void CDateInfo::GetDate( int &MonthNum, int &DayNum, int &YearNum )
174   {
175     MonthNum = Month;
176     DayNum = Day;
177     YearNum = Year;
178   };
179
180
181   void CDateInfo::GetStringDate ( string80 &DateStr )
182   {
183     string80 TempStr;
184     sprintf( DateStr, "%d", Month );
185     sprintf( TempStr, "%d", Day );
186     strcat( DateStr, "-" );
187     strcat( DateStr, TempStr );
188     strcat( DateStr, "-" );
189     sprintf( TempStr, "%d", Year );
190     strcat( DateStr, TempStr );
191   };
192
193
194   void CDateInfo::GetMonth( string80 &MonthName )
195   {
196     static char *Months[] =
197       {"January", "February", "March", "April", "May", "June",
198        "July", "August", "September", "October", "November",
199        "December"};
200     strcpy( MonthName, Months[Month-1] );
201   } // GetMonth
```

To understand the OVERLOAD.CPP program, first look at the class definition in lines 12 through 26. The overloaded + and - function prototypes are in lines 20 and 21. Two new and private functions, Convert_to_Days() and Convert_to_Date(), have been added to assist in the date arithmetic operation.

You can follow the program's operation by starting at the main() function (lines 33 through 53). Two instances of CDateInfo are declared and initialized in line 35. Line 39 uses the overloaded addition operator to add Date1 to ChangeOfDate, storing the result in Date1. (The = operator for CDateInfo is not defined; the compiler has created a default assignment operator.) The program displays the result of the addition and then performs subtraction, executing

```
Date1 = Date1 - ChangeOfDate;
```

which produces the original date of 1/1/1993. Remember that when the compiler sees the overloaded + or - operator, it translates the arithmetic expression into a function call resembling either

```
Date1.+(ChangeOfDate)
```

or

```
Date1.-(ChangeOfDate)
```

depending on which operation is performed.

Because the actual implementation of + and - is nearly identical, only the + operation is explained in detail. The easiest way to add two dates (or more commonly, to add a number of days to an existing date in the *MM/DD/YYYY* format) is to convert all the dates to a common format. For this program, I wrote the function named Convert_to_Days() to convert the *MM/DD/YYYY* format into a total number of days since 1/1/0000. This calculation is performed by multiplying the number of years by 365 and then adding the number of days in the year up to the current month plus the day of the month. For example, to convert March 17 to the number of days since the beginning of the year, add 31 days for January, 28 days for February, plus 17 days for the date in March. This calculation is simplified in the program in two ways:

- To keep things simple for this illustration of overloaded operators, the program ignores leap years.

- An array, DaysInYear[] (see lines 28 and 29), contains the precalculated cumulative days since the beginning of the year. DaysInYear[0] corresponds to January and, therefore, has the value 0 because there are no days prior to January. DaysInYear[1] has the value 31; DaysInYear[2] has the value 59 for the cumulative days in both January and February; and so on.

Line 64 performs the calculation and returns the result, all in a single statement.

In line 113, the conversion routine is called to convert the current object instance's Month, Day, and Year fields to a cumulative number of days. The same conversion is applied to ChangeOfDate (see line 116), with the addition of a little trick. The date being added, for example, 1/15/93, is intended to be treated as 1 month and 15 days. The conversion routine, however, correctly calculates 1/15 as 15 days since the beginning of the year. For the purpose of performing the addition, you really want this number to be calculated as 46 (which is 31 + 15). The solution is to increment the Month member of ChangeOfDate before the conversion. For the sample date of 1/15/93, this trick produces 2/15/93, and the conversion routine now correctly calculates this value as 46 days.

Line 119 performs the actual operation of adding the two cumulative day measures. The second new function, Convert_to_Date(), is called in line 123 to convert the cumulative number of days back into a standard *MM/DD/YYYY* formatted date.

The subtraction operator function is identical to the addition operator function except for the use of the subtraction operator, -, in line 146 instead of the + operator.

Overloading Unary and Binary Operators

Because some operators are unary (having a single argument, such as the negative operator, -*x*) and some are binary (such as *x* * *y*), you must give special attention to how you use each type. Not all C++ operators can be overloaded; refer to table 8.1 for a list of the operators that can be overloaded.

Table 8.1 Operators That Can Be Overloaded

+	-	*	/	%
-	+	++	- -	=
*=	/=	%=	+=	-=
==	!=	<	>	<=
>=	<<	>>	&	^
!	&&	||	<<=	>>=
&=	^=	|=	new	delete
[]	()			

When you overload a binary member operator function, the operator function has one parameter, as shown in lines 20-21 of listing 8.7:

```
20      CDateInfo operator +(CDateInfo ChangeOfDate);
21      CDateInfo operator -(CDateInfo ChangeOfDate);
```

In other words, to implement an operator function for the expression *a* + *b*, you write

```
operator +(classtype b);
```

The object that is executing corresponds to the *a* object in the expression, and the parameter it receives is substituted for *b*. Consequently, *a* + *b* is roughly equivalent to this pseudo-C++ code:

```
a.+(b);
```

The preceding code means that the + member function of *a* is to be invoked with the single parameter *b*.

For unary operators, you implement the unary operator member function with arguments. To implement the negative of *a* (or -*a*), for example, you define

```
operator -();
```

When you write -*a*, this line is translated to the following equivalent code:

```
a.-();
```

Special care must be taken when overloading the ++ increment and the -- decrement operators. As you know, when these operators appear before the operand as a prefix operator, the value of the operand is incremented or decremented before taking the value of the operand; when these operators appear after the operand as a postfix operator, the value of the operand is taken before incrementing or decrementing the operand. When you overload the ++ or -- operators, you have to indicate to the compiler whether you are overloading the prefix or the postfix form of the operator.

To distinguish between the prefix and postfix forms of these operators, you must follow these guidelines when you implement overloaded operator functions:

- When the ++ or -- operator is overloaded as a member function having no parameters, or as a nonmember function having one parameter, the compiler assumes that you have overloaded only the prefix form of the operator.

- To overload the postfix form of these operators, you should declare either an overloaded member function having a single `int` parameter, or a nonmember function having a class parameter (the parameter that the operator modifies) and an `int` parameter (which your function ignores). For example, to implement an overloaded ++ postfix operator as a member function, you should write

  ```
  operator++(int) { ... ;}
  ```

- When you reference the ++ operator as a postfix operator in an expression, the compiler matches the postfix operator to your postfix definition. When you use the ++ operator as a prefix operator, the compiler matches the prefix operator to your prefix definition (the definition not having an `int` parameter).

Using Friends for Overloaded Operators

You can also implement overloaded operators as friend functions, outside the class definition. In these cases, a binary operator must have two arguments, and a unary operator must have one argument. To overload + as a friend, for example, you must write

```
classtype overload +(classtype a, classtype b)
{
  classtype result;
  a.x = a.x + b.x;
    // Implement addition of a data member of
    // a to a data member of b, and store
    // the answer in result;
  return result;
}
```

Here, *a* corresponds to the first operand, and *b* corresponds to the second operand.

For the unary operator friend function, such as -, you must write

```
classtype overload -(classtype a)
{
  a.x = -a.x  // Calculate -a and return result.
  return a;
}
```

Implementing Fixed-Point Arithmetic by Using Overloaded Operators

C++ provides three data types for representing numbers that contain a decimal point: `float`, `double`, and `long double`. Another way to represent decimal numbers is to use *fixed-point notation*. A fixed-point number is one that places the decimal point at a known position. For example, a fixed-point number containing two digits to the right of the decimal point is ideal for calculations involving dollars, such as $6.50 + $113.75. Because the decimal point is positioned at a specific location, you can use an integer type such as `long` (which supports up to 10-digit accuracy) to store fixed-point values. You can store the value 6.75 as 675, provided you always remember that the decimal point is positioned 2 digits from the right.

Because C++ does not provide fixed-point numbers, you can implement a `fixedpoint` class by using the `long` data type to store the values and then overload the various operators to provide `fixedpoint` addition, subtraction, multiplication, and so on. You can also overload the various math functions. Listings 8.8 through 8.10 show how to write the `fixedpoint` class, and provide additional examples of operator overloading, both within a class and as friend functions. To compile this sample program, create a project file as described in Chapter 7, "Projects," and add FIXEDPT.CPP and TEST-FIX.CPP to the project. Then choose either **B**uild or **R**ebuild All from the Visual C++ **P**roject menu to compile and link the program. You can also use the Build or Rebuild All toolbar button.

Listing 8.8 Defining the *fixedpoint* Class

```
1   // FIXEDPT.H
2   // Defines the fixedpoint class.
3   class fixedpoint {
4   public:
5     fixedpoint() { value = 0; };
6     fixedpoint(double x);
7     fixedpoint( fixedpoint &other);
8     fixedpoint operator+(fixedpoint &b);
9     fixedpoint operator-(fixedpoint &b);
10    fixedpoint operator*(fixedpoint &b);
11    fixedpoint operator/(fixedpoint &b);
12    fixedpoint& operator=(double x);
13    friend double Double( fixedpoint &x);
14    friend fixedpoint Fixedpt( double x );
15    friend fixedpoint abs(fixedpoint &x);
16    friend fixedpoint sin(fixedpoint &x);
17  private:
18    long value;
19  };
```

Listing 8.9 Implementing the *fixedpoint* Class

```
1   // FIXEDPT.CPP
2   // Implements the fixedpoint class.
3   #include <stdlib.h>
```

```
 4  #include <math.h>
 5  #include "fixedpt.h"
 6
 7  const int ACCURACY = 100; // 10^Number of Digits
 8
 9  fixedpoint::fixedpoint( double x )
10  {
11    // The use of the ceil() function for rounding up is needed
12    // because the translation from double to long suffers from
13    // a conversion error, which can cause value to be off by a
14    // slight amount.
15    value = ceil(x * ACCURACY);
16  };
17
18  fixedpoint:: fixedpoint( fixedpoint &other)
19  {
20    value = other.value;
21  };
22
23  fixedpoint fixedpoint::operator+(fixedpoint &b)
24  {
25    fixedpoint temp;
26    temp = *this;
27    temp.value = temp.value + b.value;
28    return temp;
29  }
30
31  fixedpoint fixedpoint::operator-(fixedpoint &b)
32  {
33    fixedpoint temp;
34    temp = *this;
35    temp.value = temp.value - b.value;
36    return temp;
37  }
38
39  fixedpoint fixedpoint::operator*(fixedpoint &b)
40  {
41    fixedpoint temp;
42    temp = *this;
43    temp.value = (temp.value * b.value) / ACCURACY;
44    return temp;
45  }
46
47  fixedpoint fixedpoint::operator/(fixedpoint &b)
48  {
49    fixedpoint temp;
50    temp = *this;
51    temp.value = (ACCURACY * temp.value) / b.value;
52    return temp;
53  }
54
55  fixedpoint& fixedpoint::operator=(double x)
56  {
57    *this = Fixedpt( x );
58    return *this;
59  };
```

(continues)

Listing 8.9 Continued

```
60
61
62   //==========================================
63   // Implementation of friend functions follows:
64
65   double Double( fixedpoint &x)
66   // Convert a fixed-point value to a floating-point value
67   {
68     ldiv_t converted;
69     converted = ldiv( x.value, ACCURACY );
70     return converted.quot + (converted.rem+0.0) / ACCURACY;
71   }
72
73   fixedpoint Fixedpt( double x )
74   {
75     fixedpoint temp;
76     temp.value = x * ACCURACY;
77     return temp;
78   };
79
80   fixedpoint abs(fixedpoint &x)
81   {
82     if (x.value<0)
83       x.value = -x.value;
84     return x;
85   };
86
87   fixedpoint sin(fixedpoint &x)
88   {
89     return Fixedpt( sin( Double( x ) ) );
90   };
```

Listing 8.10 Demonstrating the Use of the *fixedpoint* Class

```
1    // TEST-FIX.CPP
2    // Demonstration of how a fixedpoint data class
3    // might be implemented.
4    #include <iostream.h>
5    #include "fixedpt.h"
6
7    // Demonstration of how the class is used.
8    void main(void)
9    {
10     fixedpoint a(1.52), b(3.88), c, d;
11
12     cout << "a=" << Double(a) << "  b=" << Double(b) << "\n";
13     cout << "Arithmetic:  a + b= " << Double( a + b ) << "\n";
14     cout << "              (a*b)/b=" << Double( (a*b)/b) << "\n";
15
16     // demo assignment statements
17     c=7.5;
18     d=-3.0;
19
```

```
20     // demo overloaded function
21     cout << "abs( c * d )=" << Double( abs( c * d )) << "\n";
22
23   };
```

The `main()` function demonstrates a few examples of how you can use the `fixedpoint` class. The `fixedpoint` type executes basic arithmetic functions about 12 times faster than using the `double` data type. If limited precision is all that you need in your calculations, you should consider using fixed-point representation to improve your program's performance. Depending on the needs of your application, you may want to overload more operators and functions.

Summary

This chapter introduced C++ classes. Through classes, you create a template for making many objects that are each an instance of a particular class. You learned about the following tasks in the class definition process:

■ Using the `class` keyword to define a C++ class

■ Using inline versus out-of-line member functions

■ Creating constructor and destructor functions

■ Declaring public and private sections in class definitions

■ Using pointers to objects

■ Passing objects as function parameters

■ Using static member data for classes

■ Using the `*this` pointer to access the current object instance

■ Declaring and using friend functions for accessing private data within objects

■ Overloading operators and implementing unary and binary overloaded operator functions as member functions and as friend functions

In Chapter 9, "The Power of Inheritance," you learn how to derive new classes from existing classes. Your programs can then get a head start by inheriting functionality from existing classes. Inheriting functionality frees you from reinventing code that has already been written—in a way that is far more useful than a mere library of functions.

Chapter 10, "Virtual Functions and Polymorphism," completes the discussion on the implementation of C++ classes and explains the mysterious world of virtual functions and polymorphic programming—techniques that unlock surprising programming capabilities.

Review Questions

1. What are the advantages of combining functions and data into a single object?

2. Can you think of one reason why using a true C++ class provides more capabilities than using the struct type?

3. Functions implemented as part of a class definition are called _____ functions.

4. In a C++ class, how do you label some parts of the class as public and other parts as private?

5. What is the fundamental difference between an inline function and a normal function?

6. Name two reasons why you should use a constructor function for your classes.

7. How do you implement multiple constructor functions in the same class?

8. Can you implement multiple destructor functions for a single class?

9. What is the special notation you should use for the delete operator when disposing of a pointer to an array of objects?

10. Why would you use a static class member?

11. What does *this point to?

12. What is a friend function? How do you define a friend function? What must it have as a parameter?

13. What is an overloaded operator function? How might you write an overloaded operator function header for multiplication?

Exercises

1. Use Visual C++'s on-line help to learn more about the `sprintf()` function.

2. As described in this chapter, modify listing 6.15 so that the program uses a true C++ class to implement a doubly linked list data structure. Separate the class definition into a separate .H file and place the implementation of the `list_type` class into a separate .CPP file so that you can reuse the class in other projects.

3. Using the class developed in exercise 2, develop a program to implement a telephone-logging program. You might use this program to track the time spent conferring with clients, for example. The program should accept entry of the following information:

   A name

   A telephone number

   The time the telephone call began

   The total duration of the call

   Implement the program as a class and be sure to include separate commands for adding new entries and listing the current entries.

4. Using the technique described in listing 8.2 for the `CFieldEdit` class, develop a new class, named `LineClass`, for storing variable-length lines. Use your program to prompt for and accept entry of several lines from the keyboard. Create an array of pointers to instances of your new object type and use this array to allocate memory storage for each line that is entered. Be sure to use `delete[]` to discard the line objects when your program has finished executing.

5. Develop a friend function for the class implemented in exercise 4. The friend function should access the stored text, character by character. To do this requires that the friend function have direct access to the private data members of the class.

6. Implement an overloaded + operator to perform addition of `LineClass` objects. Where a and b are instances of the `LineClass`, you should be able to write c = a + b to append b to the end of a.

7. Modify `TimeClass` described in TIMECLAS.CPP (listing 8.5) to add a seconds field to the member data. Implement the copy constructor for this class so that it uses the `*this` pointer.

Chapter 9

The Power of Inheritance

The C++ class, described in Chapter 8, "Classes," gives you a better way to enforce information hiding and data encapsulation in your C++ programs. In that chapter, you learned how to overload the C++ operator functions to manipulate new data types in C++. But the real power of OOP comes from the capability of one class to *inherit* functionality from existing ones. When you need to create a new class, you can often find an existing object that resembles the one you need. Then you *derive* the new object, which inherits the existing object's member functions and data fields. By overriding some of the inherited functions and adding some new functions, you can mold your new object into a unique and distinct class without rewriting the member functions that stay the same.

How Inheritance Works

To see how inheritance works, consider a program that uses the CDate class (equivalent to the CDateInfo class you used in Chapter 8) to represent U.S. format dates (MM-DD-YY). You now must modify the GetStringDate() function so that date objects can be displayed in European format (DD-MM-YYYY). If you have the source code for the CDate class, you can duplicate the entire class, modify GetStringDate() to return dates as DD-MM-YYYY, and then continue. This approach presents two problems:

- If the class comes from a library or a precompiled .OBJ module, you might not have access to the source.

■ Duplicating CDate results in copying code that might be the same between U.S. and European date formats. This approach can waste memory.

Instead of duplicating any code, you can use C++'s inheritance feature to define a new class, called CEuropeDate, derived from CDate. The CDate class presented in the preceding chapter is as follows:

```
class CDate {
public:
  CDate(int MonthNum, int DayNum, int YearNum);
  CDate( CDate &Other_Object); // Copy constructor
  void SetDate( int MonthNum, int DayNum, int YearNum );
  void GetDate( int &MonthNum, int &DayNum, int &YearNum );
  void GetStringDate( string80 &DateStr );
  void GetMonth( string80 &MonthName  );
private:
  int Month, Day, Year;
};
```

To derive a new class named CEuropeDate from the existing CDate class, you write

```
class CEuropeDate : public CDate {
  void GetStringDate( string80 &DateStr );
};
```

CEuropeDate resembles CDate, except the inherited GetStringDate method is overridden and replaced with a new GetStringDate method. The difference between the two date objects is that CDate returns the date in the standard U.S. format of MM-DD-YY, whereas CEuropeDate returns a European-style date format DD-MM-YYYY. All other functionality in CEuropeDate is inherited from CDate, including the fields Month, Day, and Year. You do not need to rewrite the other functions for the new date format—they are all inherited.

The first listing in this chapter, listing 9.1, shows a completed implementation of CEuropeDate. Look at this listing very carefully. Run the sample program. You might try overriding one of the other inherited methods. Experiment with this short program until you feel comfortable with the concept of inheritance. This program also demonstrates several new features, each of which is explained in the sections that follow the program listing:

■ Use of the protected keyword in the class declaration (line 25)

■ Use of the public keyword as part of the specification showing that CEuropeDate is derived from CDate (line 30)

■ Calling an ancestor's constructor method (lines 38 through 39)

The power of object-oriented programming lies in inheritance and the capability to derive a new class from the declaration of an existing base class. A new class derived from an existing one is a *derived class* (or a *descendant*); the original class is called the *base class* (or the *ancestor* class). A derived class can have descendants, creating a hierarchy of relationships. Figure 9.1 illustrates the concept of a hierarchy. In this drawing, the object type `CButton` is derived from `CWnd`, which is derived from `CCmdTarget`, which is derived from `CObject`.

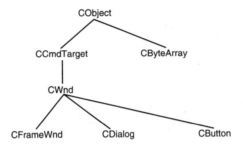

Fig. 9.1
An illustration of inheritance, showing the hierarchical relationships among derived object types.

The only methods that you must write in the derived class are the features that uniquely define it. The compiler efficiently reuses the older object's code. The only new code generated for `CEuropeDate` is the code for the `GetStringDate` method; the code for the other methods is shared among the objects.

Listing 9.1 A Demonstration of Inheritance

```
1   // OBJECT3.CPP
2   // Demonstrates inheritance and the derivation of a new
3   // object from an existing object.
4
5   // CEuropeDate is a new object type, inheriting its
6   // functionality from CDate. CEuropeDate overrides
7   // CDate's GetStringDate procedure so that it returns
8   // a European-formatted date (DD-MM-YYYY) rather than
9   // CDate's U.S. formatted date (MM-DD-YY).
10
11  #include <iostream.h>
12  #include <string.h>
13  #include <stdio.h>
14
15  typedef char string80[80];
16
17  class CDate
18  {
19  public:
```

(continues)

Listing 9.1 Continued

```
20    CDate( int MonthNum, int DayNum, int YearNum );
21    void SetDate( int MonthNum, int DayNum, int YearNum );
22    void GetDate( int &MonthNum, int &DayNum, int &YearNum );
23    void GetStringDate( string80 &DateStr);
24    void GetMonth( string80 &MonthName );
25  protected:
26    int Month, Day, Year;
27  };
28
29
30  class CEuropeDate : public CDate
31  {
32  // Is derived from CDate and inherits those
33  // fields and methods but overrides the
34  // GetStringDate method.
35  public:
36    // Define a constructor function; it just calls
37    // the ancestor's constructor function.
38    CEuropeDate(int DayNum, int MonthNum, int YearNum ) :
39      CDate( MonthNum, DayNum, YearNum ) { };
40    void GetStringDate( string80 &DateStr );
41  };
42
43
44  //=========================================================
45  // Implementation of CDate member functions.
46  CDate::CDate(int MonthNum, int DayNum,
47                     int YearNum )
48  {
49    SetDate( MonthNum, DayNum, YearNum );
50  };
51
52  void CDate::SetDate( int MonthNum, int DayNum,
53                       int YearNum )
54  {
55    Month = MonthNum;
56    Day   = DayNum;
57    Year  = YearNum;
58  };
59
60  void CDate::GetDate( int &MonthNum, int &DayNum,
61                       int &YearNum )
62  {
63    MonthNum = Month;
64    DayNum   = Day;
65    YearNum  = Year;
```

```
66  };
67
68  void CDate::GetStringDate ( string80 &DateStr )
69  {
70    sprintf( DateStr, "%d-%d-%d", Month, Day, Year % 100 );
71  };
72
73  void CDate::GetMonth( string80 &MonthName )
74  {
75    static char *Months[] =
76      {"January", "February", "March", "April", "May",
77       "June", "July", "August", "September", "October",
78       "November", "December"};
79    strcpy( MonthName, Months[Month-1] );
80  } // GetMonth
81
82
83  //====================================================
84  // Implementation of CEuropeDate member functions.
85
86  void CEuropeDate::GetStringDate ( string80 &DateStr )
87  {
88    sprintf( DateStr, "%d-%d-%d", Day, Month, Year );
89  } // CEuropeDate::GetStringDate
90
91
92  //====================================================
93  // A main() function to demonstrate use of the two
94  // classes.
95  void main(void)
96  {
97    CDate        USDate(8, 29, 1993);
98    CEuropeDate     EuropeDate(1, 10, 1993);
99    string80        DemoStr;
100
101   USDate.GetStringDate( DemoStr );
102   cout << DemoStr << endl;
103   USDate.GetMonth( DemoStr );
104   cout << DemoStr << endl;
105
106   EuropeDate.GetStringDate( DemoStr );
107   cout << DemoStr << endl;
108   EuropeDate.GetMonth( DemoStr );
109   cout << DemoStr << endl;
110
111   cout << "Press Enter to continue.";
112   cin.get();
113  } // main
```

Classes, Objects, and Inheritance

To better understand how inheritance works, think of object types as describing a *class* or group of similar objects, much as biologists use classifications to note the similarities and differences among animals. For example, dogs and cats are different species, yet both descended from the class of animals known as mammals. From this information, we know both dogs and cats have a certain set of common mammalian characteristics inherited from the mammalian animal type, just as methods and fields are inherited from ancestor objects.

The following shows an ordering for the derivation of the cat, *Felis catus*:

Kingdom Animalia

Subkingdom Metazoa

Phylum Chordata

Subphylum Vertebrata

Superclass Tetrapoda

Class Mammalia

Order Carnivora

Family Felidae

Species Felis catus

Consider two cats, Elvis and Waffles. Both cats are instances of the class cat (or in C++ parlance, instances of the class CCat). Cat (or CCat) is derived from the class of mammals (or CMammal).

This association indicates that both cats behave as generic ones because they are members of the cat family. Furthermore, Elvis and Waffles are members of the mammal family, so they have inherited characteristics of both cats and mammals. Without knowing the cats personally, you are already generally familiar with Elvis and Waffles. They have inherited their catlike, mammalian behavior from predefined animal classifications (classes). Yet each cat is also a unique individual: although each belongs to the class cat (C++ class CCat), each has a unique personality among other attributes—for example, one is big and orange, and the other is small and gray. These two cats are different instances of the same class. Note this distinction between a class and an instance of an object.

The *protected* Keyword

Line 25 of listing 9.1 introduces the protected keyword. Like public and private, protected specifies the right to access the members of the class.

To understand the need for protected members, consider the effect of inheritance on the members of the class. In the example class, CDate, the member data was previously marked as `private`. When `CEuropeDate` inherits the features of `CDate`, the compiler enforces the `private` access restriction even on `CEuropeDate`. This means that the member functions of `CEuropeDate`, tightly coupled with `CDate` by inheritance, are prohibited from using the `private` member data of `CDate`. You can mark the `CDate` members as `public`, but this defeats the purpose of encapsulating the data within an object. To solve this problem, a third category of protection is provided: `protected` members.

The `protected` members are available to derived classes, yet remain `private` to all other users of the class. The use of `protected` members is quite common in class definitions. Using `protected` members ensures that derived classes have direct access to necessary members of the ancestor class, yet remain `private` to all other functions.

The following list highlights the features of each of the access rights keywords that you can use in the class declaration:

- `public` members are visible and accessible to all users of the class.

- `private` members are visible and accessible only to members and friends of the class.

- `protected` members are visible and accessible only to members and friends of the class, and to members and friends of derived classes. `protected` members are neither visible nor accessible to all other users of the class.

Derived Classes and Access Specifiers

When you derive one class from another, you have the option of choosing an *access specifier* for the new class. The access specifier tells future derived classes which parts of the ancestor class they can access. In listing 9.1, members of the new class `CEuropeDate` have access to `protected` members of the base ancestor `CDate`, because `CEuropeDate` is derived from it. If you define `CEuropeDate` by using the notation

```
class CEuropeDate : CDate
```

and later decide to derive a third class from `CEuropeDate`, as in

```
class CCanadaDate : CEuropeDate
```

the new descendant class, `CCanadaDate`, does not have access to the inherited `private` or `protected` members of the base ancestor `CDate`. By default, `CEuropeDate` makes any inherited `public` or `protected` members `private` and inaccessible to future descendants. New classes you derive from `CEuropeDate` do not have access to the original `CDate` protected members.

To enable `CEuropeDate` to pass its inherited members to future descendants, you must use the `public` or `private` keyword in the class declaration header. For example, to enable `CEuropeDate` to provide `public` access to the original, inherited `public` members of `CDate`, you must define `CEuropeDate` by using this class declaration statement:

```
class CEuropeDate : public CDate
```

This form is used in line 30 of listing 9.1. The `public` keyword says `CEuropeDate` passes all inherited public features of `CDate` to future descendants as `public` members.

The `public`, `private`, or `protected` keywords used in the class declaration header indicate to future descendants the type of access they have to `protected` or `public` members of the parent classes. If you do not specify either the `public` or `private` keywords in the class declaration, the default makes the inherited members private for all descendants. The following is a summary of the keywords:

- *No keyword*: The default access specifier is `private`.

- `public`: Both `public` and `protected` members of the base class retain the same status when they are made members of derived classes. `private` members in the base class remain `private`.

- `private`: `public` and `protected` members of the base class become `private` members of the derived class, and are not available to future descendants of this class.

- `protected`: Both `public` and `protected` members of the base class become `protected` members of the derived class, and are available only to the member functions of derived classes and their friends. `private` members in the base class remain `private`.

If you find this issue confusing, simply insert the `public` keyword in the class declaration each time you derive a new class from an existing one. This provides full access to the `public` and `protected` members of the base class. As you become more comfortable with this concept, you can use the `protected` or `private` keywords to tailor each new class to your specific requirements.

Calling the Ancestor's Constructor

When a class is descended from others, you should have the constructor of your new class call the ancestor's constructor. In many cases, the compiler can generate a default call to the base class's constructor for you. But coding the call directly is best. This ensures that the ancestor's fields and other attributes of the object are correctly initialized. Lines 38 and 39 of listing 9.1 show the CDate constructor call from the CEuropeDate:

```
38    CEuropeDate( int DayNum, int MonthNum, int YearNum ) :
39        CDate( MonthNum, DayNum, YearNum ) { };
```

Line 38 defines the constructor function for CEuropeDate. Although a constructor is not essential for CEuropeDate, providing one enables the user of CEuropeDate to initialize the object instance and specify the parameters in the order, European style, of Day, Month, and Year.

When the constructor for any CEuropeDate object is invoked, the first behind-the-scenes action is to call the CDate() constructor. This action is the first invoked because of the colon at the end of the line, followed by the reference to the CDate() constructor. Until CDate() is called, no other code is executed for the CEuropeDate constructor.

Next, the CEuropeDate constructor acts on any of its own requirements. Line 39 provides the inline definition of the CEuropeDate constructor. Because the definition contains only empty braces ({ }), the constructor is not functional here.

You can, however, place code here to initialize member fields of CEuropeDate (if CEuropeDate had any). In this particular example, CEuropeDate inherits its member data fields from CDate, and this constructor initializes those fields.

Regardless of how many ancestors a particular class has, each ancestor constructor calls its ancestor's constructor.

The *sprintf()* Function

In lines 70 and 88, the sprintf() function converts the integer numbers into a string representation. The sprintf() function can process multiple values in one function call, as line 70 demonstrates:

```
sprintf( DateStr, "%d-%d-%d", Month, Day, Year % 100 );
```

The formatting string tells sprintf() to expect three integer values (the %d symbolizes a decimal conversion). The three variables specifying the time then follow the formatting specification. sprintf() substitutes the value of Month for the first %d, the value of Day for the second, and the remainder of

Year divided by 100 for the third. The hyphens (-) are inserted directly into the string. Therefore, if Month is 2, Day is 15, and Year is 1993, then the call to sprintf() produces the text string 2-15-93. (In Chapter 11, "C++ Input and Output," you learn how to use the strstream type to provide string formatting as an alternative to the sprintf() function.)

Inherited Member Data

Like member functions, the data fields of a class are also inherited from ancestor to descendant. Another similarity to functions is that the descendant class can define its own fields. The new descendant class then contains fields and memory allocations for both the inherited and new data fields. For example, a new class, CDateAndTime, can be derived from CDate to contain both date and time information. This descendant class looks like this:

```
class CDateAndTime : CDate {
public:
   void SetTime( int NewHour, int NewMinute, int NewSecond );
   void GetTime( int &Hour, int &Minute, int &Second );
   void GetStringTime ( string80 &TimeStr );
private:
   int Hours, Minutes, Seconds;
};
```

If you have two objects declared as

```
CDate : ADate;
```

and

```
CDateAndTime ADateAndTime;
```

memory is allocated for ADate containing three fields, as shown in figure 9.2.

Fig. 9.2
The three fields allocated for ADate.

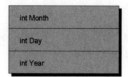

ADateAndTime contains six fields: three inherited fields and three of its own. These fields are shown in figure 9.3.

Unused fields in an object definition are not stripped out by the compiler or linker. If the new class CDateAndTime does not use the inherited Month, Day, and Year fields, those fields and their memory allocations remain. This does not usually incur a substantial memory penalty and is not a problem for most applications, but be aware that memory is allocated whether or not you use it.

Fig. 9.3
The six fields of
the ADateAndTime
class.

Listing 9.2 shows a sample implementation of the CDateAndTime class. As you look at the listing, notice how objects of the derived class call members in both CDateAndTime and CDate, particularly in the main() function.

Listing 9.2 A Sample Implementation of the *CDateAndTime* Class

```
1   // OBJECT3A.CPP
2   // Implements the CDateAndTime class.
3
4   #include <iostream.h>
5   #include <string.h>
6   #include <stdio.h>
7
8   typedef char string80[80];
9
10  class CDate
11  {
12  public:
13    CDate() {};
14    CDate( int MonthNum, int DayNum, int YearNum );
15    void SetDate( int MonthNum, int DayNum, int YearNum );
16    void GetDate( int &MonthNum, int &DayNum, int &YearNum );
17    void GetStringDate( string80 &DateStr);
18    void GetMonth( string80 &MonthName );
19  protected:
20    int Month, Day, Year;
21  };
22
23  class CDateAndTime : public CDate {
24  public:
25    void SetTime( int NewHour, int NewMinute, int NewSecond );
26    void GetTime( int &Hour, int &Minute, int &Second );
27    void GetStringTime ( string80 &TimeStr );
28  private:
29    int Hours, Minutes, Seconds;
30  };
31
32
33  //=========================================================
34  // Implementation of CDate member functions.
```

(continues)

Listing 9.2 Continued

```
35  CDate::CDate(int MonthNum, int DayNum,
36                       int YearNum )
37  {
38    SetDate ( MonthNum, DayNum, YearNum );
39  };
40
41  void CDate::SetDate( int MonthNum, int DayNum,
42                           int YearNum )
43  {
44    Month = MonthNum;
45    Day = DayNum;
46    Year = YearNum;
47  };
48
49  void CDate::GetDate( int &MonthNum, int &DayNum,
50                           int &YearNum )
51  {
52    MonthNum = Month;
53    DayNum = Day;
54    YearNum = Year;
55  };
56
57  void CDate::GetStringDate ( string80 &DateStr )
58  {
59    sprintf( DateStr, "%d-%d-%d", Month, Day, Year % 100 );
60  };
61
62  void CDate::GetMonth( string80 &MonthName )
63  {
64    static char *Months[] =
65      {"January", "February", "March", "April", "May",
66        "June", "July", "August", "September", "October",
67        "November", "December"};
68    strcpy( MonthName, Months[Month-1] );
69  } // GetMonth
70
71  //===================================================
72  void CDateAndTime::SetTime( int NewHour, int NewMinute, int NewSecond )
73  {
74    Hours = NewHour;
75    Minutes = NewMinute;
76    Seconds = NewSecond;
77  };
78
79  void CDateAndTime::GetTime( int &Hour, int &Minute, int &Second )
80  {
81    Hour = Hours;
82    Minute = Minutes;
83    Second = Seconds;
84  };
85
86  void CDateAndTime::GetStringTime ( string80 &TimeStr )
87  {
88    sprintf( TimeStr, "%d:%d:%d", Hours, Minutes, Seconds );
89  };
```

```
90
91   //===================================================
92   // A main() function to demonstrate use of the two
93   // classes.
94   void main(void)
95   {
96     CDate        USDate(8, 29, 1993);
97     CDateAndTime   LogEntry;
98     string80       DemoStr;
99
100    USDate.GetStringDate( DemoStr );
101    cout << DemoStr << endl;
102    USDate.GetMonth( DemoStr );
103    cout << DemoStr << endl;
104
105    LogEntry.SetDate( 7, 4, 1993 );
106    LogEntry.SetTime( 10, 15, 30 );
107    LogEntry.GetStringDate( DemoStr );
108    cout << "The date is " << DemoStr << endl;
109    LogEntry.GetStringTime( DemoStr );
110    cout << "The time is " << DemoStr << endl;
111
112    cout << "Press Enter to continue.";
113    cin.get();
114  } // main
```

Lines 23 through 30 define CDateAndTime as derived from CDate. Therefore, CDateAndTime inherits the member data and functions from CDate. CDateAndTime also defines three additional functions of its own and adds three private data members: Hours, Minutes, and Seconds. In effect, CDateAndTime is extending the features of CDate by adding new functions and data.

The implementation of CDate members is the same as in listing 9.1. The new members of the derived class, CDateAndTime, are implemented in lines 72 to 89. These new member functions provide routines to set and get the time data values to the CDateAndTime class.

Line 97 declares an instance of CDateAndTime, named LogEntry. A class that can track date and time might be useful in a program to log information, such as a telephone log.

Lines 105 through 110 show the CDateAndTime class at work. Note that in line 105, the SetDate() member function is called. However, no SetDate() member function appears in the definition for CDateAndTime. So where did this function come from? The answer is that SetDate() is inherited from CDate and is now a part of the CDateAndTime class. All public functions in CDate are now member functions for the CDateAndTime class.

The compiler handles the sharing of member functions internally to prevent duplication of code. Only one SetDate() member function exists. When objects derived from CDateAndTime use SetDate(), the compiler efficiently maps those calls to the ancestor object.

Classes and Type Compatibility

As with other data types in C++, type compatibility rules determine how one object can be assigned to another. A descendant class must be type-compatible with all ancestors. Therefore, given the previous definitions of CDate and CEuropeDate, if you have two object instances declared as

```
CDate Object1;
```

and

```
CEuropeDate Object2;
```

you can write

```
Object1 = Object2;
```

Paradoxically, you cannot write

```
Object2 = Object1;
```

The compatibility rules let you assign objects of a descendant class to an ancestor, but not the reverse. The reason is that the descendant has the same or more fields as the ancestor. When you assign the descendant to an ancestor, all its fields can be completely filled in from the inherited fields of the descendant. However, if you try to assign an ancestor to a descendant, you might face the problem of uninitialized fields: the descendant can define additional fields not present in the ancestor.

This type of compatibility extends upward through the entire object type hierarchy. When CObject4 is derived from CObject3, CObject3 from CObject2, and CObject2 from CObject1, and you declare objects as

```
CObject1 Object1;
CObject2 Object2;
CObject3 Object3;
CObject4 Object4;
```

the following assignments are legal:

```
Object1 = Object4;
Object2 = Object3;
Object1 = Object2;
```

These assignments are not legal, however:

```
Object4 = Object1;
Object3 = Object2;
```

How Multiple Inheritance Works

In C++, you can derive a new class from more than one class at the same time by using *multiple inheritance*. You derive a class from multiple existing ones by specifying multiple base classes in the class header line. Suppose that you have a class CDate for tracking date information, and a class named CTime for holding a time value. You want to create a new, unique class to keep track of both time and date in European format (DD-MM-YYYY). For this simple example, you could modify the previously created CEuropeDate format to add the time information. However, multiple inheritance offers another way to implement this new class.

To implement a new class containing both time and date information, you can create a new class named CEuropeTimeDate derived from both CDate and CTime. The definition of this new class is

```
class CEuropeTimeDate : public CDate, public CTime
{
public:
  CEuropeTimeDate() : CDate() {};
  CEuropeTimeDate(int DayNum, int MonthNum, int YearNum ) :
    CDate( MonthNum, DayNum, YearNum ) { };
  void GetStringDateTime( string80 &DateStr );
};
```

The key feature of this class definition appears in the first line. CEuropeDate is derived from both CDate and CTime. The two base classes are separated by a comma. When using multiple inheritance, you can have any number of base classes. Write the list of base classes, separating each one with a comma. Then add the public, private, or protected keywords as needed to each class identifier in the list.

When you use multiple inheritance, you may need to call both of the ancestor's constructor functions. The compiler will issue an error message if you need to call one of the ancestor's constructors and have failed to do so. To call more than one constructor, separate the calls to the ancestor's constructors with a comma, like this:

```
CEuropeTimeDate() : CDate(), CTime() {};
```

The new class CEuropeTimeDate inherits the member functions of both CDate and CTime, as well as the sets of member data. In effect, multiple inheritance causes the base classes to merge together, producing the new class. Listing 9.3 is an example of multiple inheritance. The CEuropeTimeDate object, named ADate (declared in line 121), accesses inherited members from both parent classes in lines 124 and 127.

Listing 9.3 A Program That Uses Multiple Inheritance

```
1   // OBJECT3B.CPP
2   // Demonstrates multiple inheritance by deriving
3   // CEuropeTimeDate from both CDate and
4   // CTime.
5
6   #include <iostream.h>
7   #include <string.h>
8   #include <stdio.h>
9
10  typedef char string80[80];
11
12  class CDate
13  {
14  public:
15    CDate() {};
16    CDate( int MonthNum, int DayNum, int YearNum );
17    void SetDate( int MonthNum, int DayNum, int YearNum );
18    void GetDate( int &MonthNum, int &DayNum, int &YearNum );
19    void GetStringDate( string80 &DateStr);
20    void GetMonth( string80 &MonthName );
21  protected:
22    int Month, Day, Year;
23  };
24
25  class CTime {
26  public:
27    void SetTime( int NewHour, int NewMinute, int NewSecond );
28    void GetTime( int &Hour, int &Minute, int &Second );
29    void GetStringTime( string80 &TimeStr );
30  protected:
31    int Hours, Minutes, Seconds;
32  };
33
34  // Demonstration of multiple inheritance:
35  // Class CEuropeTimeDate is derived from both
36  // CDate and CTime. This means that
37  // CEuropeTimeDate incorporates the members of
38  // both of its parents.
39  class CEuropeTimeDate : public CDate, public CTime
40  {
41  public:
42    CEuropeTimeDate() : CDate() {};
43    CEuropeTimeDate( int DayNum, int MonthNum, int YearNum ) :
44      CDate( MonthNum, DayNum, YearNum ) { };
```

```
45    void GetStringDateTime( string80 &DateStr );
46  };
47
48  //=========================================================
49  // Implementation of CDate member functions.
50  CDate::CDate( int MonthNum, int DayNum,
51                       int YearNum )
52  {
53    SetDate( MonthNum, DayNum, YearNum );
54  };
55
56  void CDate::SetDate( int MonthNum, int DayNum,
57                          int YearNum )
58  {
59    Month = MonthNum;
60    Day = DayNum;
61    Year = YearNum;
62  };
63
64  void CDate::GetDate( int &MonthNum, int &DayNum,
65                          int &YearNum )
66  {
67    MonthNum = Month;
68    DayNum = Day;
69    YearNum = Year;
70  };
71
72  void CDate::GetStringDate( string80 &DateStr )
73  {
74    sprintf( DateStr, "%d-%d-%d", Month, Day, Year % 100 );
75  };
76
77  void CDate::GetMonth( string80 &MonthName )
78  {
79    static char *Months[] =
80      {"January", "February", "March", "April", "May",
81        "June", "July", "August", "September", "October",
82        "November", "December"};
83    strcpy( MonthName, Months[Month-1] );
84  } // GetMonth
85
86  //===============================================
87  void CTime::SetTime( int NewHour, int NewMinute,
88                          int NewSecond )
89  {
90    Hours = NewHour;
91    Minutes = NewMinute;
92    Seconds = NewSecond;
93  };
94
95  void CTime::GetTime( int &Hour, int &Minute, int &Second )
96  {
97    Hour = Hours;
98    Minute = Minutes;
99    Second = Seconds;
100  };
```

(continues)

Listing 9.3 Continued

```
101
102    void CTime::GetStringTime ( string80 &TimeStr )
103    {
104      sprintf( TimeStr, "%d:%d:%d", Hours, Minutes, Seconds );
105    };
106
107    //=================================================
108    void CEuropeTimeDate::GetStringDateTime
109                              ( string80 &DateStr )
110    {
111      sprintf( DateStr, "%d-%d-%d   %d:%d:%d",
112              Day, Month, Year, Hours, Minutes, Seconds );
113    };
114
115
116    //=================================================
117    // A main() function to demonstrate use of the two
118    // classes.
119    void main(void)
120    {
121      CEuropeTimeDate  ADate;
122      string80         DemoStr;
123
124      // Call SetDate(), inherited from CDate.
125      ADate.SetDate( 1, 31, 1993 );
126      // Call SetTime(), inherited from CTime.
127      ADate.SetTime( 14, 30, 45 );
128      ADate.GetStringDateTime( DemoStr );
129      cout << "The date and time is:  " << DemoStr << endl;
130
131      // Demonstrate calling the inherited GetStringDate()
132      // member (from CDate ancestor).
133      ADate.GetStringDate( DemoStr );
134      cout << "The date is: " << DemoStr << endl;
135
136      // Demonstrate calling the inherited GetStringTime()
137      // member (from CTime).
138      ADate.GetStringTime( DemoStr );
139      cout << "The time is: " << DemoStr << endl;
140
141      cout << "Press Enter to continue.";
142      cin.get();
143    } // main
```

In listing 9.3, class CDate (lines 12 through 23) and class CTime (lines 25 through 32) are ordinary C++ classes. Lines 39 through 46 derive from both CDate and CTime to produce the new class CEuropeTimeDate. This class adds a new member function, GetStringDateTime(), which returns a string containing both the date (in European format) and the time.

You can obtain the individual components by calling the inherited `GetStringTime()` or `GetStringDate()`. The latter returns the U.S. format date string.

With multiple inheritance, as with single inheritance, the compiler links the code together so that it is not duplicated across these classes.

Even though `CEuropeTimeDate` objects are derived from both `CDate` and `CTime`, the compiler efficiently calls the base class function, so code is never duplicated.

Summary

You can add functionality to existing code with inheritance—even if you do not have access to the source code. You can adapt an existing class to new uses by inheriting from the class and adding new member data or functions. Because your derived class is based on presumably completed and tested code, you begin your coding chore from a reliable starting point. This helps to improve the overall reliability of your programs while helping you to build programs more efficiently.

In this chapter, you learned the following about C++:

- How to derive a new class from an existing base class

- How to use the `protected` keyword to share a base class's access to `private` member data with a derived class

- How to use the `public`, `protected`, and `private` keywords in the class definition process for specifying access rights to derived classes

- How to use multiple inheritance to derive a new class from two or more parent classes

Chapter 10, "Virtual Functions and Polymorphism," completes the discussion of the C++ class. With virtual functions, you can create object-oriented programs that can work with classes to be defined in the future. You can create programs that are extensible well into the future, and support future requirements without modifying original code.

Chapters 14 and 15 cover the Microsoft Foundation Class (MFC) library that comes with Visual C++. MFC contains ready-to-use classes such as collection classes, general-purpose string classes, and graphical user interface classes for writing Windows programs. These libraries rely on object-oriented programming and your ability to derive new classes from those available in the library. Deriving your applications from prewritten classes saves time and enables you to put pretested routines to work.

Review Questions

1. What is a major benefit of inheritance?

2. What is the purpose of the `protected` keyword when used in a class definition?

3. What is the purpose of the `public`, `private`, and `protected` keywords when used as part of the first line in a class definition?

4. What is multiple inheritance?

5. What does "a member function is overridden in a derived class" mean?

Exercises

1. Modify OBJECT3B.CPP in listing 9.3 to override the inherited `GetStringDate()` function for the `CEuropeTimeDate` class so that the new function returns a string representation in the European date format.

2. In OBJECT3B.CPP, change the `protected` members to `private` members and try to compile the program. What happens and why? Then change the `protected` members to `public` and recompile the program. Make sure that you understand the distinction among the `public`, `protected`, and `private` keywords as they apply to derived classes.

3. Design a simple class and implement it. Then derive a new class from your base class. Override at least one of the inherited member functions.

4. Modify the OBJECT3B.CPP program to use `new` to allocate an instance of the `CEuropeTimeDate` class dynamically. Your example should call at least two member functions.

5. Design two simple classes (one might be the class you created for exercise 3). Use both these classes as the base classes for a new class derived using multiple inheritance.

Chapter 10
Virtual Functions and Polymorphism

In Chapter 9, "The Power of Inheritance," you saw that inheritance and the capability to extend an object's inherited functionality by adding new member functions or overriding existing member functions are the keys to the power of object-oriented programming (OOP). In some situations, however, overriding an inherited member function can produce the wrong result. Understanding how inheritance can lead to problems and understanding the solution—virtual functions—are the topics of this chapter. Using virtual functions today enables you to develop code that is compatible with future classes you develop tomorrow; that is, the code you write today can be reused tomorrow to support new object types without even requiring that you recompile.

The Problem with Overridden Functions

The basic problem with plain-vanilla inherited functions is that, in certain situations, calls to an overridden function can be directed to the wrong function. Understanding how this error can occur can be a difficult concept to master. But once you understand the scenario, you will understand how *virtual functions* can create enormously flexible class libraries that you can use in new applications to perform functions the class's original author never dreamed of. With that in mind, take some time to understand and master virtual functions. Read (and reread if necessary) the following material and experiment with the sample programs until the information makes sense. If you find it confusing at first—that's because it is! But persevere, because virtual functions are an important, powerful, and essential feature of OOP.

By default, object instances and their member functions are linked together at compile time. This type of linkage is often referred to as *static linkage* because it occurs when the program is static—or not running—such as when the program is compiled or linked. (This use of the word *static* has nothing to do with the C++ static keyword you use when declaring variables.) Historically, member functions used in this way have been referred to as *static methods* (where the word *method* is equivalent to *function*).

Virtual functions are dynamically linked at runtime as the program executes. A limitation of statically linked member functions becomes apparent when a derived class overrides one of the parent's members, and the parent's member functions mistakenly call the parent function, not the overridden version in the child. The problem is rather abstract and may be difficult to understand. To help you understand the problem better (before looking at the solution), take a look at listing 10.1.

Listing 10.1 Demonstrating Why Virtual Methods Are Needed

```
1   // OBJECT4.CPP
2   /* Demonstrates a problem that cannot be solved using
3      static methods.
4
5      Object4 adds DisplayDate as a member of CDate.
6      The goal of DisplayDate is to display the date in the
7      appropriate date format.
8
9      However, when you run this program, you will see the
10     date displayed in U.S. format only. The inherited
11     CEuropeDate.DisplayDate method calls the static
12     method CDate.GetStringDate. Yet, because
13     CEuropeDate overrides GetStringDate,
14     CDate.GetStringDate is the wrong member function
15     to call! The solution is to use a virtual method, which
16     is shown in Object5.
17  */
18
19  #include <iostream.h>
20  #include <stdio.h>
21  #include <string.h>
22
23  typedef char string80[80];
24
25  class CDate
26  {
27  public:
28    CDate() {};
```

```
29    CDate( int MonthNum, int DayNum, int YearNum );
30    void SetDate( int MonthNum, int DayNum, int YearNum );
31    void GetDate( int &MonthNum, int &DayNum, int &YearNum );
32    void GetStringDate( string80 &DateStr);
33    void GetMonth( string80 &MonthName );
34    void DisplayDate( void );
35  protected:
36    int Month, Day, Year;
37  };
38
39
40  class CEuropeDate : public CDate
41  {
42  public:
43    CEuropeDate() : CDate() {};
44    CEuropeDate(int DayNum, int MonthNum, int YearNum ) :
45      CDate( MonthNum, DayNum, YearNum ) { };
46    void GetStringDate( string80 &DateStr );
47  };
48
49
50  //===================================================
51  void main(void)
52  {
53    string80        DemoStr;
54    CDate           USDate (8, 29, 1993);
55    CEuropeDate     EUDate (30, 10, 1993);
56
57    // This will display in U.S. format.
58    USDate.DisplayDate();
59    // This should display in European format
60    // but instead it appears in U.S. format
61    // because internally the wrong GetStringDate()
62    // member function is called.
63    EUDate.DisplayDate();
64
65    cout << "Press Enter to continue.";
66    cin.get();
67  } // main
68
69
70  //=======================================================
71  // Implementation of CDate member functions.
72  CDate::CDate(int MonthNum, int DayNum,
73                      int YearNum )
74  {
75    SetDate ( MonthNum, DayNum, YearNum );
76  } // CDate
77
78  void CDate::SetDate( int MonthNum, int DayNum,
79                         int YearNum )
80  {
81    Month = MonthNum;
82    Day = DayNum;
83    Year = YearNum;
84  } // SetDate
```

(continues)

Listing 10.1 Continued

```
85
86   void CDate::GetDate( int &MonthNum, int &DayNum,
87                             int &YearNum )
88   {
89     MonthNum = Month;
90     DayNum = Day;
91     YearNum = Year;
92   } // GetDate
93
94   void CDate::GetStringDate ( string80 &DateStr )
95   {
96     sprintf( DateStr, "%d-%d-%d", Month, Day, Year % 100 );
97   } // GetStringDate
98
99   void CDate::GetMonth( string80 &MonthName )
100  {
101    static char *Months[] =
102      {"January", "February", "March", "April", "May",
103       "June", "July", "August", "September", "October",
104       "November", "December"};
105    strcpy( MonthName, Months[Month-1] );
106  } // GetMonth
107
108  // Here's the new member function:
109  void CDate::DisplayDate(void)
110  {
111    string80 DateStr;
112    GetStringDate ( DateStr );
113    cout << "The date is " << DateStr << endl;
114  } // DisplayDate
115
116
117  //==================================================
118  void CEuropeDate::GetStringDate
119                             ( string80 &DateStr )
120  {
121    sprintf( DateStr, "%d-%d-%d",
122             Day, Month, Year );
123  } // GetStringDate
```

Why Virtual Functions Are Needed

Consider what happens when a new member function, DisplayDate(), is added to the base object, CDate. Calling CDate.DisplayDate() outputs the stored date information by calling the GetStringDate() member function to return the text representation of the date. In the case of calling CDate.DisplayDate() after initializing a CDate object instance to 8-29-1993, you see the following printed on the display:

8-29-93

Now consider the case of a derived class, CEuropeDate. CEuropeDate inherits the new member function DisplayDate(). The problem occurs when you call CEuropeDate.DisplayDate() and you see

    10-30-93

instead of

    30-10-1993

Even though you have implemented a CEuropeDate.DisplayDate() function (as in listing 10.1), the result is always the U.S. format rather than the European format. What happened?

When the compiler generated the code for CDate.DisplayDate(), it compiled a call directly to CDate.GetStringDate(), which is the only version of GetStringDate() that it knows about at this point in the compilation. When you call CEuropeDate.DisplayDate(), you really are making your call to the inherited CDate.DisplayDate(), which calls the original CDate.GetStringDate(); the overridden CEuropeDate.GetStringDate() never gets called at all.

How do you get the inherited CEuropeDate.DisplayDate() function to call CEuropeDate.GetStringDate() correctly? One approach is to override DisplayDate() also and implement a new CEuropeDate.DisplayDate() to call CEuropeDate.GetStringDate() explicitly. Note this example:

```
void CEuropeDate::DisplayDate(void)
{
  string80 DateStr;
  GetStringDate( DateStr );
  cout << "The Date is " << DateStr << endl;
}; // DisplayDate
```

This example solves the problem, but at the expense of duplicating a lot of code (especially if DisplayDate() is a large function). This approach assumes that you have access to the original source code, so that you know how to implement GetStringDate() correctly. If you are using a class library provided by someone else, you may have access only to the interface; reimplementing the overridden method may be quite difficult, or even impossible.

The right solution is to make GetStringDate() a virtual function by placing the keyword virtual after the definition header for GetStringDate() in both CDate and CEuropeDate. OBJECT5.CPP, shown in listing 10.2, solves the problem by implementing GetStringDate() as a virtual function.

Listing 10.2 Implementing *GetStringDate()* as a Virtual Function

```
1    // OBJECT5.CPP
2    /* Solves the problem presented in Object4 by making
3       GetStringDate() a virtual function. Now when the program
4       is run, CDate.DisplayDate() calls the virtual function
5       GetStringDate(). Because GetStringDate() is a virtual
6       function, the determination of which method to call,
7       CDate.GetStringDate() or CEuropeDate.GetStringDate(), is
8       made at execution time. And because GetStringDate is
9       overridden in CEuropeDate, the runtime system causes
10      CDisplayDate.DisplayDate() to call the overridden method,
11      CEuropeDate.DisplayDate().
12   */
13
14   #include <iostream.h>
15   #include <stdio.h>
16   #include <string.h>
17
18   typedef char string80[80];
19
20   class CDate
21   {
22   public:
23     CDate() {};
24     CDate( int MonthNum, int DayNum, int YearNum );
25     void SetDate( int MonthNum, int DayNum, int YearNum );
26     void GetDate( int &MonthNum, int &DayNum, int &YearNum );
27     virtual void GetStringDate( string80 &DateStr);
28     void GetMonth( string80 &MonthName );
29     void DisplayDate( void );
30   protected:
31     int Month, Day, Year;
32   };
33
34
35   class CEuropeDate : public CDate
36   {
37   public:
38     CEuropeDate() : CDate() {};
39     CEuropeDate(int DayNum, int MonthNum, int YearNum ) :
40       CDate( MonthNum, DayNum, YearNum ) { };
41     void GetStringDate( string80 &DateStr );
42   };
43
44
45
46   //================================================
47   void main(void)
48   {
49     string80        DemoStr;
50     CDate           USDate (8, 29, 1991);
51     CEuropeDate     EUDate (30, 10, 1991);
52
53     // This will display in U.S. format.
54     USDate.DisplayDate();
55     // This should display in European format,
```

```
56    // but instead it appears in U.S. format
57    // because internally the wrong GetStringDate()
58    // member function is called.
59    EUDate.DisplayDate();
60
61    cout << "Press Enter to continue.";
62    cin.get();
63  } // main
64
65
66  //=========================================================
67  // Implementation of CDate member functions.
68  CDate::CDate(int MonthNum, int DayNum,
69                       int YearNum )
70  {
71    SetDate ( MonthNum, DayNum, YearNum );
72  } // CDate
73
74  void CDate::SetDate( int MonthNum, int DayNum,
75                       int YearNum )
76  {
77    Month = MonthNum;
78    Day = DayNum;
79    Year = YearNum;
80  } // SetDate
81
82  void CDate::GetDate( int &MonthNum, int &DayNum,
83                       int &YearNum )
84  {
85    MonthNum = Month;
86    DayNum = Day;
87    YearNum = Year;
88  } // GetDate
89
90  void CDate::GetStringDate ( string80 &DateStr )
91  {
92    sprintf( DateStr, "%d-%d-%d", Month, Day, Year % 100 );
93  } // GetStringDate
94
95  void CDate::GetMonth( string80 &MonthName )
96  {
97    static char *Months[] =
98      {"January", "February", "March", "April", "May",
99       "June", "July", "August", "September", "October",
100       "November", "December"};
101    strcpy( MonthName, Months[Month-1] );
102  } // GetMonth
103
104 // Here's the new member function:
105 void CDate::DisplayDate(void)
106 {
107   string80 DateStr;
108   GetStringDate ( DateStr );
109   cout << "The date is " << DateStr << endl;
110 } // DisplayDate
```

(continues)

Listing 10.2 Continued

```
111
112
113  //=================================================
114  void CEuropeDate::GetStringDate
115                             ( string80 &DateStr )
116  {
117    sprintf( DateStr, "%d-%d-%d",
118            Day, Month, Year );
119  } // GetStringDate
```

How Virtual Functions Work

When the compiler generates code for CDate.DisplayDate(), it sees that CDate.GetStringDate() is a virtual function, rather than a statically linked member function. Instead of inserting code to call the CDate.DisplayDate() function directly, the compiler generates a virtual function call that figures out during program execution which version of GetStringDate() to call.

To implement this feature, the compiler adds an internal *virtual function table* to both CDate and CEuropeDate. When the program issues a call to GetStringDate(), it inserts code to look up the location of GetStringDate() in the class's virtual function table. In this way, CEuropeDate's inherited DisplayDate() knows to call CEuropeDate's GetStringDate().

The virtual table for each class contains a table of addresses specifying the location of each method in that object. The constructor function sets up the virtual table so that each table looks something like the following (the & symbol denotes *address-of*):

Virtual Table for CDate	Virtual Table for CEuropeDate
1) &CDate.SetDate	&CDate.SetDate
2) &CDate.GetDate	&CDate.GetDate
3) &CDate.GetStringDate	&CEuropeDate.GetStringDate
4) &CDate.GetMonth	&CDate.GetMonth
5) &CDate.DisplayDate	&CDate.DisplayDate

Because the virtual table is required for all classes that have virtual functions, you must have a constructor for such classes. The constructor initializes the virtual table.

CDate is a base class having no ancestors, so all the virtual table entries for CDate point directly to the corresponding method in CDate. For CEuropeDate, four of the five methods are inherited in their entirety, including SetDate(),

GetDate(), GetMonth(), and DisplayDate(). For these entries, the table points directly to the ancestor's implementation. But for the fifth method, GetStringDate(), CEuropeDate has overridden the inherited definition and provided its own implementation. Consequently, this entry in CEuropeDate's virtual table points directly to CEuropeDate.GetStringDate().

The virtual table is referenced each time a virtual function is called. Special code inserted by the compiler maps the virtual function call to the current object's virtual table, where the computer can find the actual location of the correct function to run. Look at what happens. When you write

```
CEuropeDate.DisplayDate();
```

(where CEuropeDate is the name of a CEuropeDate object), to display the European format date, this line is translated directly to the inherited method, CDate.DisplayDate(). CDate.DisplayDate() executes a virtual call to GetStringDate(), looking up the address in the current object's virtual table—and that points to CEuropeDate.GetStringDate(). This process results in the expected output in *DD-MM-YYYY* format:

```
1-10-1993
```

Objects Containing Virtual Functions Must Have a Constructor

Any object that contains one or more virtual functions should define a constructor function. The compiler will create one for you automatically, but you should define your own instead of accepting the default constructor. The constructor automatically performs critical initialization of the virtual function table.

Static versus Virtual: Which Do You Choose?

A class's functions can be either static (the default) or virtual. The following are the trade-offs between choosing to make your member functions static versus virtual:

- A virtual function takes slightly longer to execute, because the procedure call must be mapped as an index into the virtual function table to find the address of the function to call.

- A class that contains one or more virtual functions requires extra memory for the virtual table. The virtual tables are allocated in the data segment for each object type (or optionally, they may be placed in the code segment). Only one virtual table exists for each class, not for each instance of an object.

- A class containing one or more virtual functions must have at least one constructor. The constructor must be called before calling any of the class's member functions.

- Virtual functions permit more flexibility to descendant classes, because the ancestor can use the overridden descendant. The ancestor cannot use an overridden statically linked member function; the ancestor will continue to use the original method.

- Like static functions, virtual functions implemented in the base class need not be reimplemented in a derived class. The derived class or classes inherit the functionality of all member functions, except for pure functions.

- A virtual member function whose prototype is set to = 0 is a *pure function*. Such a function is not implemented in the base class but must be implemented in all derived classes. A class containing one or more pure functions is an abstract class. An abstract class cannot have any object instances created from it; the class exists solely as a base class for future descendants. The OBJECT8.CPP program (presented later in listing 10.5) shows an example of the use of a pure function.

- After a function is declared virtual, the function is virtual in all future descendants. You do not need to mark the function as virtual in descendants, because the compiler automatically marks the function as virtual.

- Derived objects can override and change the parameter list of an inherited, statically linked member function.

- In a derived class, you can redefine the virtual function, if you maintain the same parameter list as in the base class. If you overload the virtual function in a derived class—say, by creating a new function that has different parameter types—then C++ treats this new function as a different function. Because both the function name and the parameters determine a C++ function name, the redefined function is merely treated as another C++ member function, and the virtual status of the similarly named function is ignored.

Virtual functions provide maximum flexibility for future reuse and are fairly efficient in their implementation. Consequently, you probably should declare your member functions as virtual whenever there is any possibility that a descendant could override the method. When the extendibility of future derived classes is not an issue, or where time-critical issues require optimized function calling, choose the faster statically linked member functions.

Polymorphism

Virtual methods make possible another feature of object-oriented programming: *polymorphism*. Polymorphism allows related classes to have a function with the same name that produces different results depending on the class. For example, a car and a boat, both derived from a vehicle base class, can both have a MoveForward function that moves the vehicles forward, but does so in a different manner for each (because a car moves on land and a boat moves on water). Through polymorphic programming, you can write and compile code to handle object parameters that are not known when the code is compiled. This capability means that you can produce a class library for manipulating future objects, and the compiled code will work with those future objects even though they are not defined until much later. The CDate and CEuropeDate objects shown earlier in this chapter used this concept to call the derived object's GetStringDate() method correctly.

Like virtual functions, this concept may be difficult for you to understand. Because this topic is complex, you should read through all of this section's examples, even if the first one does not make sense to you.

Designing a Class to Support Polymorphism

To understand polymorphic objects, return to the concept of adding dates together, as demonstrated in the OVERLOAD.CPP program in listing 8.7 in Chapter 8, "Classes." To simplify the example, replace the original overload + operator with a function named AddDate(). The result is the following class declaration:

```
class CDate {
public:
  CDate() {};
  CDate( int MonthNum, int DayNum, int YearNum);
  void SetDate( int MonthNum, int DayNum, int YearNum );
  void GetDate( int &MonthNum, int &DayNum, int &YearNum );
  void GetStringDate ( string80 &DateStr );
  void GetMonth ( string80 &MonthName );
  void AddDate( CDate Date2 );
```

```
        long Convert_to_Days( CDate ADate );
        CDate Convert_to_Date( long Num_Days);
    private:
        int Month, Day, Year;
    };
```

AddDate() is a new method that adds the date specified by its parameter to the date contained in the current object instance. If ADate contains a specification for 1 month and 3 days, for example, and the year field is set to 0, when ADate is added to the current object's fields, the result is a new date 1 month and 3 days into the future.

AddDate() works by converting a traditional month, day, and year date specification into a cumulative number of days since 1/1/0000. For example, you can convert the date February 2, 1994, into a cumulative number of days by computing

$$2 + 31 + 1994 * 365$$

where 31 is the cumulative number of days up to February 1, and 2 is the number of days from the beginning of February. Multiplying 1994 by 365 gives you a total number of days since the year 0000; then adding 33 gives you a total of 727,810 days. (As implemented in the sample program later in this section, the algorithm does not accommodate leap years; you can, however, modify the algorithm to do so.)

To add one month and three days to this result, convert this value to 31 + 3, or 34, days. Then add this number to the base address:

727,810 + 34

giving the result

727,844

This number then is the cumulative number of days computed by adding one month and three days to the base date, February 2, 1994.

AddDate uses the Convert_to_Days() member function to convert a date into a cumulative number of days. After the addition is completed, AddDate uses the Convert_to_Date() function to convert the result back to a date. Listing 10.3 presents OBJECT6.CPP, which details both the modified class declaration for CDate and an example of the addition of two dates. Nothing is particularly special about this program (it is similar to the OVERLOAD.CPP program in listing 8.7 in Chapter 8). OBJECT7.CPP, presented in listing 10.4, modifies the program to demonstrate the properties of polymorphism.

Listing 10.3 Demonstrating the Modified Class Declaration for *CDate*

```
1   // OBJECT6.CPP
2   // This is a modified version of the OVERLOAD.CPP
3   // program used in Chapter 8.
4   // Here, for clarity, the overloaded operator +
5   // is rewritten as a normal function named AddDate().
6   // AddDate() adds the contents of its single parameter
7   // to the current object's date. This base program
8   // will be modified in OBJECT7.CPP to demonstrate
9   // polymorphism.
10  #include <iostream.h>
11  #include <string.h>
12  #include <stdio.h>
13
14  typedef char string80[80];
15
16  class CDate {
17  public:
18    CDate() {};
19    CDate( int MonthNum, int DayNum, int YearNum);
20    void SetDate( int MonthNum, int DayNum, int YearNum );
21    void GetDate( int &MonthNum, int &DayNum, int &YearNum );
22    void GetStringDate ( string80 &DateStr );
23    void GetMonth ( string80 &MonthName );
24    void AddDate( CDate Date2 );
25    long Convert_to_Days( CDate ADate );
26    CDate Convert_to_Date( long Num_Days);
27  private:
28    int Month, Day, Year;
29  };
30
31  static int DaysInYear[] =
32      { 0, 31, 59, 90, 120, 151, 181, 212, 243, 273,
33        304, 334, 365 };
34  /* This array contains a cumulative number of days since
35     the beginning of the year, indexed by month.
36     As implemented, this array does not account for
37     leap year.
38  */
39
40
41  void main(void)
42  {
43    CDate Date1 (1, 1, 1993), Date2 (1, 15, 0);
44    string80 DemoStr;
45
46    // Add Date2 to Date1.
47    Date1.AddDate( Date2 );
48    Date1.GetStringDate ( DemoStr );
49    cout << "Date1 + Date2 is:  " << DemoStr
```

(continues)

Listing 10.3 Continued

```
50          << endl;
51
52    cout << "Press Enter to continue.";
53    cin.get();
54  } // main
55
56
57  long CDate::Convert_to_Days( CDate ADate )
58  {
59      // Convert the date to the number of days since
60      // 1/1/0000. This calculation is performed by
61      // multiplying Year * 365, then adding the number
62      // of days in the year up to the current month,
63      // and then adding the day of the month. This
64      // calculation does not accommodate leap years.
65      return ADate.Year * 365L + DaysInYear[ADate.Month-1] + ADate.Day;
66      // Note the use of a long constant, 365L. Without
67      // the L, the calculation Year * 365 is done with the
68      // int type. As you can see, 1993 * 365 is much larger
69      // than can be represented using int. Therefore, the
70      // use of the long constant forces the compiler to
71      // multiply the values as the long type.
72  } // convert_to_days
73
74
75  CDate CDate::Convert_to_Date( long Num_Days)
76  {
77      // This function translates a number of days back
78      // into a Month, Day, Year formatted date.
79      CDate ADate;
80      int Days_Left, Which_Month;
81
82      // Convert the number of days back to number of years.
83      ADate.Year = Num_Days / 365;
84      // And extract the number of days in the current year.
85      Days_Left = Num_Days % 365;
86
87      // Determine which month to use.
88      for(Which_Month=0;
89          Days_Left > DaysInYear[Which_Month];
90          Which_Month++);
91
92      // Convert the Which_Month zero-based array index
93      // into a Month value in the range of 1 to 12.
94      ADate.Month = Which_Month;
95
96      // Calculate the Day within the month.
97      ADate.Day = Days_Left - DaysInYear[Which_Month-1];
98
99      // And return the result.
100     return ADate;
101 } // convert_to_date
102
103
```

```
104   void CDate::AddDate( CDate Date2 )
105   {
106     long converted_date1, converted_date2;
107
108     // Convert the left operand (this object) into
109     // a number of days measurement.
110     converted_date1 = Convert_to_Days(*this);
111
112     Date2.Month++;
113     converted_date2 = Convert_to_Days(Date2);
114
115     // Add the two day measurements together.
116     converted_date1 = converted_date1 + converted_date2;
117
118     // And convert the number of days back to a
119     // Month, Day, Year date.
120     *this = Convert_to_Date( converted_date1 );
121
122   }; // operator +
123
124
125
126   CDate::CDate( int MonthNum, int DayNum, int YearNum)
127   {
128     Month = MonthNum;
129     Day = DayNum;
130     Year = YearNum;
131   };
132
133
134   void CDate::SetDate( int MonthNum, int DayNum, int YearNum )
135   {
136     Month = MonthNum;
137     Day = DayNum;
138     Year = YearNum;
139   };
140
141
142   void CDate::GetDate( int &MonthNum, int &DayNum, int &YearNum )
143   {
144     MonthNum = Month;
145     DayNum = Day;
146     YearNum = Year;
147   };
148
149
150   void CDate::GetStringDate ( string80 &DateStr )
151   {
152     string80 TempStr;
153     sprintf( DateStr, "%d", Month );
154     sprintf( TempStr, "%d", Day );
155     strcat( DateStr, "-" );
156     strcat( DateStr, TempStr );
157     strcat( DateStr, "-" );
158     sprintf( TempStr, "%d", Year );
```

(continues)

Listing 10.3 Continued

```
159    strcat( DateStr, TempStr );
160  };
161
162
163  void CDate::GetMonth( string80 &MonthName )
164  {
165    static char *Months[] =
166      {"January", "February", "March", "April", "May", "June",
167       "July", "August", "September", "October", "November",
168       "December"};
169    strcpy( MonthName, Months[Month-1] );
170  } // GetMonth
```

Using Virtual Functions to Implement Polymorphism

To demonstrate polymorphism, derive a new object named CDayOfYear, which stores and represents dates in the form *DDD-YYYY*. This means that instead of storing February 2, 1994, as 2-2-1994, the object stores 33-1994 or the number of days from the beginning of the year. Interestingly, you can use the original AddDate() routine to add CDayOfYear object dates without making a single change to the original AddDate() function, even though the dates stored in CDayOfYear and CDate are in incompatible formats. In fact, you inherit and use the original AddDate() code with no modifications.

The trick that makes the calling of the correction function possible is the virtual methods Convert_to_Days() and Convert_to_Date(). For any CDate-derived object passed to AddDate(), the AddDate() routine calls that object's Convert_to_Days() member function to convert its internal date format into a number-of-days representation, performs the addition, and then calls the object's Convert_to_Date() method to translate the number of days back into its internal representation.

Listing 10.4 shows the new CDayOfYear class, derived from CDate. Note that CDayOfYear defines new statically linked member functions for the constructor, SetDate(), and GetDate(), with parameter lists containing only the day and year values. CDayOfYear also overrides Convert_to_Days() and Convert_to_Date() to perform the appropriate conversions for this class. An explanation of how the program operates follows the listing.

Listing 10.4 Modifying OBJECT6 to Demonstrate Polymorphism

```
1   // OBJECT7.CPP
2   /* Creates a new object type CDayOfYear, derived from
3      CDate. CDayOfYear stores dates in the form,
4      day of the year (from 1 to 365), and the year itself.
5
6      CDayOfYear overrides several of the static
7      and virtual members of its ancestor, CDate.
8      However, CDayOfYear inherits and uses AddDate directly,
9      even though the original AddDate knows nothing about this
10     new type CDayOfYear. This works because AddDate calls
11     the Convert_to_Days() and Convert_to_Date() member
12     functions provided by the parameter object. Hence,
13     AddDate is able to operate on different kinds of objects
14     provided that each object provides its own implementation
15     of Convert_to_Days() and Convert_to_Date().
16  */
17  #include <iostream.h>
18  #include <string.h>
19  #include <stdio.h>
20
21  typedef char string80[80];
22
23  class CDate {
24  public:
25    CDate() { };
26    CDate( int MonthNum, int DayNum, int YearNum);
27    void SetDate( int MonthNum, int DayNum, int YearNum );
28    void GetDate( int &MonthNum, int &DayNum, int &YearNum );
29    virtual void GetStringDate( string80 &DateStr );
30    virtual void GetMonth( string80 &MonthName );
31    virtual void AddDate( CDate Date2 );
32    virtual long Convert_to_Days( CDate ADate );
33    virtual CDate Convert_to_Date( long Num_Days);
34  protected:
35    int Month, Day, Year;
36  };
37
38
39  class CDayOfYear : public CDate {
40  public:
41    CDayOfYear() : CDate() { };
42    CDayOfYear( int DayNum, int YearNum ) :
43      CDate( 0, DayNum, YearNum ) { };
44    void SetDate( int DayNum, int YearNum );
45    void GetDate( int &DayNum, int &YearNum );
46    virtual void GetStringDate( string80 &DateStr );
47    virtual long Convert_to_Days( CDate ADate );
48    virtual CDate Convert_to_Date( long Num_Days);
49  }; // CDayOfYear
50
51
52  static int DaysInYear[] =
53      { 0, 31, 59, 90, 120, 151, 181, 212, 243, 273,
54        304, 334, 365 };
```

(continues)

Listing 10.4 Continued

```
55    /* This array contains a cumulative number of days since
56       the beginning of the year, indexed by month.
57       As implemented, this array does not account for
58       leap year.
59    */
60
61
62    // ===============================================
63    void main(void)
64    {
65       string80    DemoStr;
66       CDate       Date1(8, 29, 1993), Date2(0, 5, 1);
67       // Date2 is initialized "5 days, 1 year."
68       CDayOfYear  Date3, Date4;
69
70       // Add Date2 to Date1.
71       Date1.AddDate ( Date2 );
72       // This will produce 9/3/1994.
73       Date1.GetStringDate ( DemoStr );
74       cout << "Date1 + Date2=" << DemoStr << endl;
75
76       // Now, let us use the CDayOfYear class, which
77       // stores its dates in a different format. First,
78       // initialize Date3 to day number 10 of 1991.
79       Date3.SetDate( 10, 1991 );
80       // Display the starting date.
81       Date3.GetStringDate( DemoStr );
82       cout << "Date3=" << DemoStr << endl;
83
84       // Now add 1 day to day number 10.
85       Date4.SetDate( 1, 0 );
86       Date3.AddDate( Date4 );
87
88       // This will produce 11-1991.
89       Date3.GetStringDate( DemoStr );
90       cout << "Date3=" << DemoStr << endl;
91
92       cout << "Press Enter to continue.";
93       cin.get();
94       /* The important feature to notice is that
95       the inherited AddDate() function is called for both
96       CDate and CDayOfYear objects. Yet, because of
97       virtual functions and polymorphism, the AddDate()
98       function works correctly for both classes, even
99       though the classes are different. AddDate() works
100      because AddDate() calls the appropriate date
101      conversion routines provided by the parameter
102      object.
103      */
104   } // main
105
106
107   // ===============================================
108   long CDate::Convert_to_Days( CDate ADate )
109   {
```

```
110      return ADate.Year * 365L + DaysInYear[ADate.Month-1]
111           + ADate.Day;
112  } // convert_to_days
113
114
115  CDate CDate::Convert_to_Date( long Num_Days)
116  {
117     // This function translates a number of days back
118     // into a Month, Day, Year formatted date.
119     CDate ADate;
120     int Days_Left, Which_Month;
121
122     // Convert the number of days back to number of years.
123     ADate.Year = Num_Days / 365;
124     // And extract the number of days in the current year.
125     Days_Left = Num_Days % 365;
126
127     // Determine which month to use.
128     for(Which_Month=0;
129         Days_Left > DaysInYear[Which_Month];
130         Which_Month++);
131
132     // Convert the Which_Month zero-based array index
133     // into a Month value in the range of 1 to 12.
134     ADate.Month = Which_Month;
135
136     // Calculate the Day within the month.
137     ADate.Day = Days_Left - DaysInYear[Which_Month-1];
138
139     // And return the result.
140     return ADate;
141  } // convert_to_date
142
143
144  void CDate::AddDate( CDate Date2 )
145  {
146     long converted_date1, converted_date2;
147
148     // Convert the left operand (this object) into
149     // a number-of-days measurement.
150     converted_date1 = Convert_to_Days(*this);
151
152     Date2.Month++;
153     converted_date2 = Convert_to_Days(Date2);
154
155     // Add the two day measurements together.
156     converted_date1 = converted_date1 + converted_date2;
157
158     // And convert the number of days back to a
159     // Month, Day, Year date.
160     *this = Convert_to_Date( converted_date1);
161
162  }; // operator +
163
164
165  CDate::CDate( int MonthNum, int DayNum, int YearNum)
166  {
```

(continues)

Listing 10.4 Continued

```
167    Month = MonthNum;
168    Day = DayNum;
169    Year = YearNum;
170  };
171
172
173  void CDate::SetDate( int MonthNum, int DayNum, int YearNum )
174  {
175    Month = MonthNum;
176    Day = DayNum;
177    Year = YearNum;
178  };
179
180
181  void CDate::GetDate( int &MonthNum, int &DayNum, int &YearNum )
182  {
183    MonthNum = Month;
184    DayNum = Day;
185    YearNum = Year;
186  };
187
188
189  void CDate::GetStringDate ( string80 &DateStr )
190  {
191    sprintf( DateStr, "%d-%d-%d", Month, Day, Year % 100 );
192  };
193
194
195  void CDate::GetMonth( string80 &MonthName )
196  {
197    static char *Months[] =
198      {"January", "February", "March", "April", "May", "June",
199       "July", "August", "September", "October", "November",
200       "December"};
201    strcpy( MonthName, Months[Month-1] );
202  } // GetMonth
203
204
205  // =============================================
206  void CDayOfYear::SetDate( int DayNum, int YearNum )
207  {
208    Month = 0;
209    Day = DayNum;
210    Year = YearNum;
211  } // SetDate
212
213
214  void CDayOfYear::GetDate( int &DayNum, int &YearNum )
215  {
216    DayNum = Day;
217    YearNum = YearNum;
218  } // GetDate
219
```

```
220
221   void CDayOfYear::GetStringDate( string80 &DateStr )
222
223   {
224     sprintf( DateStr, "%d-%d", Day, Year );
225   };
226
227
228   long CDayOfYear::Convert_to_Days( CDate ADate )
229   {
230     int Months, Days, Years;
231     ADate.GetDate( Months, Days, Years );
232     return Years * 365L + Days;
233   } // convert_to_days
234
235
236   CDate CDayOfYear::Convert_to_Date( long Num_Days)
237   {
238     // This function translates a number of days back
239     // into a Month, Day, Year formatted date.
240     CDate ADate;
241
242     ADate.SetDate( 0, Num_Days % 365, Num_Days / 365 );
243
244     return ADate;
245   } // convert_to_date
```

In the main() function of OBJECT7.CPP, some sample code shows how these routines are called. As in OBJECT6.CPP, the first few statements create two date objects—Date1 and Date2—and then add Date2 to Date1 and print the result. Next, two objects of CDayOfYear type, Date3 and Date4, are initialized. The program adds the contents of Date4 to Date3 by calling AddDate(). AddDate(), in turn, calls the Convert_to_Days() conversion of its parameter object. Through the virtual function mechanism, these calls map to CDayOfYear.Convert_to_Days() and CDayOfYear.Convert_to_Date(). In effect, the same method name selects different tasks, depending on the object passed as a parameter. This capability is made possible by the virtual function mechanism, which in turn makes polymorphic programming possible. Polymorphic programming uses a single method name to refer to different functions, depending on the object that is used—hence, the term *polymorphic*, meaning roughly "having many forms."

Using Polymorphic Functions in a Graphics Application

For another demonstration of polymorphism, consider a painting program containing a function defined as follows:

```
void MoveTo( int NewX, int NewY, CGraphic &AnObject );
```

NewX and NewY are coordinates for a new location for the graphics element
AnObject. The graphics element could be a box, a circle, a line, or whatever is
appropriate for the application. The MoveTo() routine might resemble the
following code:

```
void MoveTo( int NewX, int NewY, CGraphic &AnObject )
{
  AnObject.MakeInvisible();
  X = NewX;
  Y = NewY;
  AnObject.MakeVisible();
};
```

This simple routine can handle any type of CGraphic object, as long as each
object provides a virtual method for MakeInvisible() and MakeVisible(). As
before, the names MakeInvisible() and MakeVisible() perform different tasks,
depending on the object involved. Therefore, a single name provides multiple
functions, which is the essence of polymorphic functions.

Using Polymorphic Functions to Implement a List Box

Now look at one last example. Using polymorphic programming, you can
write a list box display routine that handles any type of data, even data types
that have not yet been invented. Listing 10.5 shows a complete program for
writing these routines. An explanation of the program follows the listing.

**Listing 10.5 Using Polymorphism to Implement a List-Box Display
of Any Type of Data**

```
1   // OBJECT8.CPP
2   /* An additional demonstration of polymorphism. This
3      program creates a list of objects, such as might be
4      used in a list box display. The special feature of
5      this list box is that it's polymorphic - it can
6      display any type of objects within it, provided that each
7      object is descended from the CListBoxData base class.
8      For each descendant class, you must define
9      one or more data fields, as appropriate, and override
10     the GetText virtual function to return a
11     string representation of the data.
12   */
13
14   #include <iostream.h>
15   #include <string.h>
16   #include <stdio.h>
17
18   typedef char string80[80];
19
20   const int MaxListSize = 50;
21
22   class CListBoxData {
23   public:
```

```
24    CListBoxData() {};
25    // Adding =0 to next prototype makes this an
26    // abstract or "pure" function that must be
27    // overridden in derived classes.
28    virtual void GetText (string80 &Text) = 0;
29    // Because this is a "pure" function, there
30    // is no implementation for this class.
31  };// MaxListSize
32
33  class CListBox {
34  public:
35    CListBox();
36    void AddItem ( CListBoxData * AnObject );
37    void DisplayListBox(void);
38  private:
39    int TotalItems;
40    int CursorLocation;
41    CListBoxData * ListBoxData[MaxListSize];
42  }; // CListBox
43
44
45  // ============================================
46  // The following classes are derived from the abstract
47  // base class, CListBoxData. You can add more data
48  // types if you wish; be sure to override the GetText()
49  // member function for each type that you add.
50  class CListInteger : public CListBoxData {
51  // This class stores an int value.
52  public:
53    CListInteger(int X) : CListBoxData()
54        { intValue = X;};
55    virtual void GetText( string80 &Text);
56  private:
57   int intValue;
58  };
59
60
61  class CListString : public CListBoxData {
62  // This class stores a string value.
63  public:
64    CListString(string80 X) : CListBoxData()
65        { strcpy( strValue, X );};
66    virtual void GetText( string80 &Text);
67  private:
68   string80 strValue;
69  };
70
71
72  class CListFloat : public CListBoxData {
73  // This class stores a float value.
74  public:
75    CListFloat(float X) : CListBoxData()
76        { fltValue = X;};
77    virtual void GetText( string80 &Text);
78  private:
79   float fltValue;
80  };
```

(continues)

Listing 10.5 Continued

```
81
82   // ===================================================
83   void main(void) {
84     CListBox AListBox;
85
86     // Fill up the list box with three different kinds
87     // of data.
88     AListBox.AddItem( new CListInteger( 57 ) );
89     AListBox.AddItem( new CListInteger( 99 ) );
90     AListBox.AddItem( new CListString( "Hello 'dare!" ) );
91     AListBox.AddItem( new CListFloat( 3.14159 ) );
92     AListBox.AddItem( new CListString( "I'm a string too" ) );
93     AListBox.AddItem( new CListInteger( 1 ) );
94     AListBox.AddItem( new CListFloat( 2.718 ) );
95
96     // Display the content of the list box.
97     AListBox.DisplayListBox();
98   } // main
99
100
101  // ===================================================
102  CListBox::CListBox()
103  {
104    TotalItems = 0;
105  };
106
107
108  void CListBox::AddItem ( CListBoxData * AnObject )
109  {
110  /* Adds objects into the list. For simplicity in this
111     example, the "list" is really just an array, and no
112     error result is returned if you try to add too many
113     items to the "list."
114  */
115    if  (TotalItems <= MaxListSize)
116      ListBoxData [TotalItems++] = AnObject;
117  }; // AddItem
118
119
120  void CListBox::DisplayListBox(void) {
121  /* This could be modified to display an actual list
122     box, and perhaps allow cursor movements to scroll
123     through the list box. For now, it just writes the
124     returned string for each object.
125  */
126    int i;
127    string80 DemoStr;
128
129    // Display each object in the list box; use the
130    // object's own GetText() member function to
131    // convert its internal format into generic text.
132    for (i = 0; i< TotalItems; i++) {
133      ListBoxData[i]->GetText( DemoStr );
134      cout << DemoStr << endl;
```

```
135    };
136  };
137
138
139  // ============================================
140  void CListInteger::GetText (string80 &Text)
141  {
142    sprintf(Text, "%d", intValue );
143  }; // GetText
144
145
146  // ============================================
147  void CListString::GetText (string80 &Text)
148  {
149    strcpy( Text, strValue );
150  }; // GetText
151
152
153  // ============================================
154  void CListFloat::GetText (string80 &Text)
155  {
156    sprintf( Text, "%d", fltValue );
157  }; // GetText
```

Creating Pure Functions

The trick to implementing a generic list-box class is to create a common base class, CListBoxData, from which each type of object stored in the list box is derived. CListBoxData contains a constructor to initialize the virtual function table, and an abstract GetText() function, as shown in line 28 of listing 10.5:

```
28    virtual void GetText (string80 &Text) = 0;
```

Recall that you can create a pure member function by writing the function's prototype so that it ends in = 0;. When a class contains a pure function, it is an *abstract* class. An abstract class exists solely as a base from which to derive other classes. You cannot create an instance of an abstract class; you must first derive a new class and provide a definition for the pure function or functions declared in the base class.

Deriving a Descendant Class from an Abstract Class

Because CListBoxData is an abstract class, you must first create descendant classes. Listing 10.5 creates three derived classes: CListInteger (lines 50 through 58), CListString (lines 61 through 69), and CListFloat (lines 72 through 80). CListInteger adds a new field, intValue, to hold an integer value. CListString adds a new field, strValue, to hold a string value. And CListFloat adds a new field, fltValue, to hold a float value. Each of these descendant objects defines a constructor to set up its respective fields (each derived class also calls the base class's constructor).

Each descendant overrides GetText() to return a text representation of itself. Lines 140 through 157 implement the various GetText() functions. For CListInteger, GetText() converts the integer value intValue to a string. For CListString, the strValue field is used directly. And for CListFloat, the fltValue is converted to a text string.

The main() function (lines 83 to 98) initializes a list box object, AListBox, and adds objects to it, one after the other, by calling the AddItem() member function. The new operator instantiates new instances of the respective classes and passes the resulting pointer to AddItem(). In lines 88 through 94, note how each of the three different types of objects is added to the list box through the AddItem() function. AddItem(), in turn, stuffs the object pointer into the list box's internal array for keeping track of what objects are in the list; this is shown in lines 108 through 117 and repeated here:

```
108  void CListBox::AddItem ( CListBoxData * AnObject )
109  {
110  /* Adds objects into the list. For simplicity in this
111     example, the "list" is really just an array, and no
112     error result is returned if you try to add too many
113     items to the "list."
114  */
115    if  (TotalItems <= MaxListSize)
116      ListBoxData [TotalItems++] = AnObject;
117  }; // AddItem
```

For simplicity, this example uses an array instead of a list.

The DisplayListBox routine (lines 120 to 136) uses the object pointer stored in the ListBoxData array to access each object's GetText() member function. Each object is then responsible for producing a text representation of itself. Through this mechanism, the list box can store and display many different types of data, if each data element is derived from the CListBoxData base class (see lines 108 through 117). Because a different conversion is performed for the same function, GetText(), depending on the class of the object involved, this example uses polymorphism.

Using a polymorphic programming solution results in a list box that can handle data types which have not yet been invented. As long as future data types are derived from CListBoxData and implement a GetText() function, they can be stored in the list box. You won't even need to recompile the CListBox class if you've placed the class into a separate module. Now *that's* programming flexibility.

If you are having difficulty mastering the concept of polymorphic programming, try modifying this program to add more data types. Try adding `long` and `double` data types, or even a structure that holds multiple values, such as a point coordinate (X,Y). Through hands-on experimentation, you will eventually master this difficult concept.

Object Libraries

Your ability to create new classes from existing classes helps you develop software much more efficiently. You no longer need to rewrite software from scratch. Instead, consult a class library. You can then assemble software rather than write it, by putting together predefined objects. A software designer looks in a class library—as a hardware designer might refer to an integrated circuit manual—to find a software part that best matches his or her requirements. You add a few changes to the object, much like a hardware designer adding external circuitry to an integrated circuit, to enable the object to meet the unique needs of the project.

A class library has more flexibility than a typical subroutine library. A subroutine library gives you what it has, no more and no less. If you need a function that is similar to but not exactly like one in the library, you have a problem. The traditional approaches for solving such problems are to recode a new function from scratch, to obtain the original source code and modify it to suit your needs, or to add a special case flag to the original source.

The first approach, rewriting a routine from scratch, is both time-consuming and error-prone. You must first debug all the new programming to get it up and running, and then you must rigorously test it to ensure reliability.

The second approach, modifying the original source code, is fairly quick and requires less debugging than the first approach. However, you must now maintain two copies of the original source code. As you change the software, your ability to keep these copies synchronized becomes more difficult. Ultimately, when you make the same change to both copies, you must still thoroughly test both program routines.

The third approach, adding a special case flag, is no better than the second. This approach requires you to pass control information downward to the called routine by passing a flag value, or worse, by depending on the value of global variables. You should not use this technique of passing a flag or other control information downward to a set of function calls; splitting the functionality into two functions is usually better. Splitting yields two general-purpose, reusable subroutines rather than a single, specialized routine.

Although these last two approaches are quick and easy, they may take extra effort in the long run and increase the likelihood of future errors. In addition, you create a very specialized routine that you are unlikely to reuse efficiently in a future project.

The solution, of course, is to use object-oriented programming and class libraries that you can extend to suit your specific application. Using OOP's inheritance features, you define your new class as being like one of the classes in the class library. Then you add whatever customization you need. The Visual C++ Collection classes and the Microsoft Foundation class libraries described later in this book are examples of class libraries that you will use with increasing frequency as your C++ programming experience expands.

Designing Object-Oriented Programs

After you master object-oriented programming, you must also develop object-oriented design skills. The traditional approach to PC software design is a top-down refinement of a program's detail. Top-down design begins with a high-level functional description, such as "this program is a text editor," and proceeds to refine each function of the program into several smaller functions. In this model, a text editor becomes a collection of routines to perform cursor movement, text insertion and deletion, and file saving and loading. Each of these routines represents an action or function that the program performs. In many instances, each of these tasks is further refined into smaller and smaller subtasks.

In top-down design, the highest level provides an abstract description of the program's purpose. Through refinement, the design progresses downward, enumerating each program function and subfunction until eventually it gets down to individual program procedures.

Most designs following the top-down approach focus on the program's functions, and thus its user interface, rather than on the internal structure needed to build a given application. This approach results in a program design that follows the typical execution of program features. For example, such a program waits in a loop for keyboard input, looks at the input data, and then calls a routine such as DoSaveFile(), based on the entered command. Although this approach certainly works, the result is an application with an internal design tightly coupled to the overlying user interface. Changing the functions of such a program can be difficult, requiring a significant amount of rework.

Object-oriented design reverses the design priorities and focuses on the objects the software manipulates rather than the functions the software accomplishes. In an object-oriented approach, the designer tries to identify objects, where objects, in a sense, correspond to the program's data structures. The next step is to identify what services these objects make available to others.

One approach to finding objects is to look at the problem's description. Items that are described with *nouns* might be considered as objects; those described with *verbs* are probably actions or methods. In the text editor example, each of the following words corresponds to a noun: a document, a block of text, a line of text, or a word. Words like *insert* or *delete* correspond to action verbs.

This approach only approximately identifies objects because it does not identify classes or groups of objects that become a single object type. Spotting every noun in an application's design specification results in several potential objects but not necessarily their object types. Furthermore, the program's description probably has so many nouns that you will be overwhelmed with potential objects.

To refine the list, identify those potential objects that appear to have a number of functions performed on them. This process filters out the frivolous objects that noun-identification tends to create, because frivolous objects have few meaningful functions performed on them, and as such, do not deserve to be identified as a class. What's left should be a set of classes whose methods can then be enumerated.

Some programmers take an ad hoc approach to class design by grunting through several iterations of class creation. When these programmers then attempt to flesh out the design, the object model is revisited and modified as needed. Other programmers believe that major data structures are a good starting point for object recognition. Methods become the operations that are performed to or on the data within those objects. Object-oriented design methodologies are a new field and, unfortunately, an in-depth discussion is beyond the scope of this book.

Summary

Virtual functions, together with inheritance, are the heart of object-oriented programming. Because your programs can inherit functionality from previously compiled classes, and because of the extensibility provided by virtual functions, you can create powerful, reusable software components. Ultimately, as you build your own library of reusable classes (either by writing your own classes or by purchasing third-party-supplied class libraries), your own past programming experience becomes enhanced with the new technology; this knowledge will help you build new applications faster and with greater reliability.

In this chapter, you learned about the following topics:

- How statically linked member functions differ from dynamically linked or virtual member functions.

- How problems can occur when you override inherited member functions that are called by the base class.

- How the use of virtual functions can solve the problem of overriding an inherited member function that is called by the base class.

- How to use virtual functions to implement polymorphic programming solutions. Polymorphic programming enables you to assign one name to a common function available in several classes. You can use the common member function to provide similar functionality for several different classes.

- That pure functions are member functions left unimplemented in the base class and assigned the value =0, as in this example:

  ```
  virtual void GetText(string80 &Text) = 0;
  ```

- That a class containing one or more pure functions is an abstract class. Abstract classes exist solely as base classes from which to derive new classes. You cannot declare an instance of an abstract class—you must first derive a new class and implement the pure functions.

Review Questions

1. Describe a problem that can occur when you override statically linked member functions.

2. What is a virtual function?

3. Give an example, such as the list box example described in this chapter, of a situation in which you can use polymorphic programming to solve a programming problem.

4. What is a pure function?

5. What is an abstract class?

6. What is a virtual table, and how is it initialized?

7. Describe at least three differences between statically linked and dynamically linked member functions.

8. Define polymorphic programming.

Exercises

1. Modify OBJECT8.CPP (listing 10.5) to add several additional data types to the list box. Your modifications should include adding other standard C++ data types as well as at least one structure type.

2. Modify OBJECT8.CPP to add a type that contains a class. That is, modify the program so that it stores an entire class rather than, for example, `intValue` or `strValue`.

3. Implement an application of your choice that requires the use of one or more virtual functions. To implement the application, your base class must call one or more member functions that are overridden in the derived class.

Chapter 11

C++ Input and Output

In C++, input and output operations are handled through C++ streams. The name *stream* comes from the notion that data is flowing from one place to another, just as meltwater flows from a mountain glacier to a river. In a C++ program, the data flows from your program to the screen or disk file, or from the keyboard to your program.

In Chapter 1, "The Fundamentals of C++ Programming," you learned to send program output to the screen using the cout (short for *console output*) stream and the insertion operator <<. You learned to read input from the keyboard using the cin (short for *console input*) stream, and you learned how to use the extraction operator >>. In addition, you learned about the getline() and get() functions.

This chapter explores all aspects of C++ streams and covers the following topics:

- Output to the display

- Input from the keyboard

- Output formatting

- Using stream manipulators

- Input to and output from disk files

If you have programmed in the C language, you know that C++ streams replace the C functions used for input and output, such as printf(), fprintf(), and scanf(). The advantage in using streams is that each class you create might need to be processed for stream input and output. For example, if you have a class named CDate and have created an instance named

Today_Date, you can use streams to output Today_Date to the screen by using the standard stream notation, as shown in the following:

```
cout << Today_Date << endl;
```

You don't have to write a new function, such as PrintDate(CDate &DateObject). With inheritance and operator overloading, you can instead convince C++ that your new XDate type is similar to any other type. When you have done this, your new type uses the standard C++ notation for all input and output operations.

Output to the Screen

You use the insertion operator << to put data into the output stream. You have seen the insertion operator used in many examples in this book to display text on the computer display:

```
cout << "Press Enter to continue.";
```

The cout identifier is the name of a predefined stream that has been derived for you (in the IOSTREAM.H file). The stream system is fairly complex and uses multiple inheritance extensively. A basic understanding of the internal stream structure is helpful, but not necessary, for using streams in your programs.

If the indirection operator is cascaded, you can output several items in a single C++ statement, which looks like this:

```
cout << "Total = " << Sum << endl;
```

The insertion operator can process all standard C++ types: char, short, int, long, char * (a pointer to a string), float, double, long double, and void *. In the preceding C++ statement, the indirection operator inserts the string "Total =", followed by the value of Sum (converted to a textual representation), followed by an end-of-line marker. The endl symbol causes the output stream to advance to the next line. You can place endl anywhere in the stream. It doesn't have to appear at the end of the line as it does in the following code:

```
cout << "Results are as follows:" << endl
     << "January  " << Total_Jan << endl
     << "February " << Total_Feb << endl
     << "March    " << Total_Mar << endl;
```

As used in the preceding statement, `endl` advances to the next line, so the output produced resembles the following:

```
Results are as follows:
January    20
February   35
March      47
```

Adjusting the output is discussed in the section "Output Formatting" later in this chapter. Methods of adjusting the output help you to display values in hexadecimal (base 16) numeric representation, insert blank spaces, and perform other types of output formatting.

Another method of writing to an output stream is to call the stream's member functions. For example, to output a single character, use

```
cout.put( '?' );
```

The `put()` member function outputs its single character to the stream. You also can write a block of characters by using the `write()` member function, as in this example:

```
char Prompt[] = "Please enter your name: ";
cout.write( Prompt, sizeof(Prompt) );
```

The second parameter to `write()` specifies the number of characters to copy from the first parameter. `write()` copies the number specified, including null characters, if they appear in the text.

Although not shown in these examples, both the `put()` and `write()` member functions return a reference to the stream object. In these examples, the return value is ignored, but you can use it to test for error conditions. Testing return values for error conditions is discussed in the section "Handling Stream Errors" later in this chapter.

Input from the Keyboard

You use the extraction operator >> to handle input from a stream. The operator gets data from the stream and places it in a variable. You use the extraction operator with the stream variable in this way:

```
int Age;
cout << "Enter Person's age:";
cin >> Age;
```

As with the insertion operator, you can cascade the extraction operator, as shown in this example:

```
int Age, Height;
cout << "Enter Age and Height (in inches):";
cin << Age << Height;
```

When multiple items are processed for input, you must type at least one blank space between the input items. Blank spaces are known as *whitespace* characters and usually are passed over by the input operations. Following is the input for the previous prompt:

```
Enter Age and Height (in inches):  34 71
```

You can input all the standard C++ types by using the extraction operator. Adding your own user-defined types to the stream input system is covered in another section of this chapter, "Input and Output of User-Defined Classes."

Text and Character Input

The extraction operator does not always produce the desired results with input from the keyboard. Faulty results are even more likely when the extraction operator is reading character or string input from the keyboard. Consequently, the underlying cin stream has several member functions to directly process character and string input without using the extraction operator. The following sections are a partial list of the available member functions.

get(char&). The get() member function reads a single character from the input stream and places the character in the char variable passed to get(). The following is an example of this function:

```
char ch;
cin.get(ch);  // Read one character into ch.
```

get(). When no argument is passed to get(), it reads a single input character and discards it. Many sample programs use this input method after prompting the user to press Enter to continue, as in the following:

```
cout << "Press Enter to continue.";
cin.get();
```

getline(char *buffer, int, char = '\n'). When you want to read an entire line of text input, you should use the getline() function. You usually write the input function in this way:

```
char input_line[80];
cin.getline( input_line, sizeof(input_line) );
```

The int parameter specifies the maximum number of characters to process for input. (This helps prevent overflowing the char array.) You can ignore the last char parameter to getline() because the final parameter has a default value. It specifies the stopping character—`getline()` reads all the input text until it reaches the delimiter character. The default setting for the delimiter character is a newline character, which corresponds to the input character produced by pressing the Enter key.

eatwhite(). When you type text in response to an input prompt, the blank characters you enter are called *whitespace*. Notice the blank characters in the response to this input prompt:

```
cout << "Enter Month number and Total: ";
cin >> Month >> Total;
```

The following is the output from the preceding two lines:

```
Enter Month number and Total:  12  3
```

The spaces you type between the input values are called whitespace. At any time, you can scan over the whitespace that might be sitting in the input stream by calling eatwhite():

```
cin.eatwhite();
```

ignore(int n=1, int delim = EOF). You might want to ignore and discard actual input characters. Use the `ignore()` member function to skip over the next *n* input characters. By default, *n* is 1, so the statement

```
cin.ignore();
```

skips the next input character. When you set *n* to a value greater than 1, the `ignore()` function stops when it reaches the delimiter character.

Output Formatting

You can modify some of the formatting provided by the C++ input and output streams. The formatting information for each stream is in a set of flag bits that you can set directly by calling member functions of the respective stream class. Perhaps an easier way to use flag bits is through a function-like operator called a *manipulator*. By placing a manipulator in line with the insertion or extraction operator, you can modify the behavior of the output or input operation. You have seen one of the manipulators used in many program examples throughout this book: `endl`. The `endl` identifier is a manipulator that modifies the format of the output stream.

You can format also by calling member functions of the stream. The use of the member functions is described in the section "Output Formatting

Functions" later in this chapter. You can accomplish the same formatting option in several ways: by using a manipulator, setting a flag bit, or calling a member function.

Using Manipulators

Only a few of the stream manipulators are defined in IOSTREAM.H. You must include IOMANIP.H to obtain access to the full set of manipulators. You use a manipulator by placing it in the sequence of cascaded insertion operators. The individual manipulators are described in the next several sections.

You can use most of the manipulators for both output and input streams, although the examples that follow illustrate only output. When you use the manipulator on an input stream, it controls the processing of the input.

dec. dec is placed in the insertion list to select base 10 conversion of numbers. The default numeric conversion you use in C++ streams is base 10, or decimal. You use the dec manipulator in this way:

```
cout << dec << Total << endl;
```

This causes the value Total to be displayed in base 10. dec is important when it is used to reselect base 10 output after switching to one of the other bases. Some of them, such as hex and oct, are discussed in the following sections.

endl. endl inserts a newline character into the stream, causing it to be flushed to the output device.

ends. ends inserts a null-terminator ('\0') into the string.

flush. Some streams store the output in a temporary buffer area before writing to the output device. flush causes the buffer associated with the stream to be flushed to the output device.

hex. The use of hex is similar to the dec manipulator, but selects base 16 (hexadecimal) format instead of decimal. For example, if Total has the decimal value 255, the statement

```
cout << hex << Total << endl;
```

produces

```
ff
```

because ff is the hexadecimal representation of decimal 255. You can intermix the output formatting in a single statement by inserting an appropriate base selection manipulator in several places, as in this example:

```
cout << "Base 10=" << dec << Total
    << "  Base 16=" << hex << Total << endl;
```

You can use the hexadecimal manipulator to process hexadecimal input values, as shown in this example:

```
int input_value;
.
.
.
cin >> hex >> input_value;
```

If you type FF in response to this input prompt, `input_value` is assigned the decimal value 255.

oct. oct is similar to `dec` or `hex`, but selects base 8 (octal) format.

ws. You use `ws` for input only. It causes whitespace characters to be skipped.

setbase(int n). Use `setbase()` to set the numeric base to 8, 10, or 16. This parameterized manipulator works the same as the `oct`, `dec`, and `hex` manipulators.

setfill(int c). You use `setfill()` with `setw()`. When an item is output to a field whose size is larger than required, the excess space usually is filled with blank characters. You can select your own fill character by using the `setfill()` manipulator. You often use `setfill()` with `setw()` to set a specific field width. For example, if you write

```
cout << setw(10) << setfill('*') << 255 << endl;
```

you get this output:

```
*******255
```

The `setw()` manipulator sets the output field to 10 characters. `setfill('*')` sets the fill character to an asterisk. The value 255 occupies only three characters in the 10-character-wide field, so the excess spaces are filled with asterisks.

setprecision(int n). You use `setprecision()` to set the floating-point precision to n digits. The default precision is six digits to the right of the decimal point. If you set n to 2, only two digits appear to the right of the decimal point.

setw(int n). You use `setw()` to set the output field width to n bytes. For input, `setw()` applies only to character input.

Setting Stream Formatting Flags

You can set formatting options by directly setting the underlying formatting flag bits. You can set the bits by using two methods. You can use the setiosflags() or resetiosflags() manipulator, or you can use a member function to access the flag bits.

setiosflags() and resetiosflags(). The setiosflags() manipulator is defined as

```
setiosflags(long f)
```

This manipulator sets the formatting bits indicated by *f*. To select specific options, refer to the constants shown in table 11.1. You must preface each constant with ios::, as shown in the following example:

```
float pi =  3.14159;
cout << setiosflags( ios::fixed ) << pi << endl;
```

Fixed-point representation of floating-point values is selected here. This causes pi to print as

```
3.14159
```

You select scientific notation using the following statement:

```
cout << setiosflags( ios::scientific ) << pi << endl;
```

And you see the following output:

```
3.14159e+00
```

You can set multiple flag bits in a single operation by ORing them together. Note this example:

```
cout << setiosflags( ios::dec ¦ ios::showbase ) << Total << endl;
```

To clear a setting, use resetiosflags(). For example, to clear the showbase setting, type

```
cout << resetiosflags( ios:: showbase ) << Total << endl;
```

Table 11.1 The *ios* Flag Bits

Flag Bit	Purpose
skipws	Skips whitespace on input operations
left	Adjusts output to the left side of the field
right	Adjusts output to the right side of the field
internal	Pads the field after the sign or base symbol
dec	Selects decimal conversion

Flag Bit	Purpose
oct	Selects octal conversion
hex	Selects hexadecimal conversion
showbase	Displays the selected base next to the value on output
showpoint	For floating-point values; always shows the decimal point
uppercase	Displays hexadecimal values in uppercase
showpos	For all positive integers; displays a plus sign
scientific	Outputs floating-point numbers using exponential notation
fixed	Uses fixed-point notation for floating-point numbers
unitbuf	Flushes the stream after completing the insertion
stdio	Flushes the system stdout and stderr streams after insertion

setf( ) and unsetf( ). The second way to set the stream flags is to call the stream's member functions: setf() to set flag bits and unsetf() to clear flag bits. These functions are similar to the setiosflags() and resetiosflags() manipulators; however, setf() and unsetf() are true member functions. You access the member functions directly, as in

```
cout.setf( ios::scientific );
```

or

```
cout.unsetf( ios::scientific );
```

Output Formatting Functions

The input and output streams also have six member functions that enable you to adjust several formatting features. Some of these member functions duplicate the features found in the set of manipulators.

fill(char) and fill( ). To change the fill character, use the fill(char) member function. Note the following example:

```
cout.fill('*');
```

To learn the current fill character setting, use fill() without a parameter:

```
fillchar = cout.fill();
```

precision(int)* and *precision( ). Use the `precision(int)` member function to set the precision of floating-point values (the number of digits to the right of the decimal point). The example

```
cout.precision(2);
```

sets the precision to two decimal places. `precision(int)` is identical to the `setprecision()` manipulator. Use `precision()` without a parameter to obtain the current precision setting.

width(int)* and *width( ). Use the `width(int)` member function to change the field width. (The `width(int)` member function works the same way as the `setw()` manipulator in selecting a field width.) You use `width()` without any parameters to obtain the current field width.

Handling Stream Errors

When working with streams, particularly when using streams to read data to or from a disk file, you must have a mechanism to detect error conditions. For example, when your program opens a file, perhaps the operating system cannot find the file. Or when your program is reading data from a file, your program must read past the end of the file. Each of these situations represents an error condition.

You can detect an error condition and determine the specific error with several methods. Fortunately, you do not have to know each method in order to handle stream errors. After you have detected and processed the error, you must use the `clear()` member function to clear the error condition so that the stream can resume processing. The section "Clearing the Error Condition" later in this chapter describes how to use `clear()`.

Detecting a Stream Error

The simplest way to detect a stream error is to use the stream identifier in an `if()` conditional test, as in this example:

```
if (!cout)
{
    // Then an error has occurred.
    .
    .
    .
};
```

The stream identifier, when used by itself, returns true if an error has not occurred:

```
if (cout)
{
   // No errors have occurred. Continue processing.
   .
   .
   .
};
```

Another way to detect an error condition is through the member functions `good()` and `bad()`. `good()` returns a nonzero `int` value (or true) if no pending error conditions exist. `bad()` returns true if an error is present.

Detecting the End-of-File Condition

The `eof()` member function of input streams returns true when the system reaches the end of the input file. This function is covered in the section "Input and Output to Disk Files" later in this chapter.

Detecting Specific Error Conditions

So far, you have learned only to detect an error. You might want to learn more about the particular error. The stream system maintains a byte value whose bit settings indicate the general type of error that has occurred. To obtain the current error bit settings, call the `rdstate()` member function in this way:

```
int ErrorCode;
ErrorCode = cin.rdstate();
```

This section of code assigns the error settings to `ErrorCode`. Then you can test the individual bits in `ErrorCode` by ANDing one of the `ios` bit pattern constants. For example, you can detect whether the end of file bit is set by typing

```
if (ErrorCode & ios::eofbit) { ... };
```

Table 11.2 shows the bit constants and their meanings. To access these constants, you must preface each with `ios::`.

Table 11.2 The *ios* Stream Error Conditions

Constant	Meaning
goodbit	No bit is set; no error condition is present.
eofbit	The input stream is at the end-of-file position.
failbit	The last input or output operation failed.
badbit	You attempted an invalid operation of some type.

Clearing the Error Condition

When an error occurs, the stream suspends any activity until you explicitly clear or reset the error condition. To clear this condition, you must call the stream's `clear()` member function, like this:

```
cin.clear();
```

You can set individual bits in the error condition by passing a parameter to the `clear()` function. This action sets the stream's error condition to the bit pattern specified by the parameter. Note this example:

```
cin.clear( ios::goodbit );
```

Input and Output of User-Defined Classes

A remarkable feature of C++ streams is their capability to support output of new data types. Suppose that you have a class named CDate that stores date data, and you want to print the value of the date on the display. Using traditional programming, you might add a special function named PrintDate(CDate ADate) to print instances of the CDate type. With C++ streams, all you do is override the << insertion operator, and your new type becomes an integral part of the stream system.

The program in listing 11.1 overloads the insertion operator << and the extractor operator >> so that each operator properly supports the CDate type. After the insertion operator is overloaded, you can output CDate-derived objects or any other value, as illustrated by the following lines from listing 11.1:

```
85    CDate       USDate(8, 29, 1994);
86
87    // Demonstrates using the overload << operator
88    // to output an instance of type USDate.
89    cout << "Current date =" << USDate << endl;
```

Listing 11.1 Overloading Insertion and Extraction Operators to Provide I/O of User-Defined Types

```
1    // USERIO.CPP
2    // Demonstrates how to overload the << and >> operators
3    // for use with the ostream and istream derived streams
4    // (especially cout and cin).
5    #include <iostream.h>
6    #include <string.h>
```

```
 7  #include <stdio.h>
 8
 9  typedef char string80[80];
10
11  class CDate
12  {
13  public:
14    CDate( int MonthNum, int DayNum, int YearNum );
15    void SetDate( int MonthNum, int DayNum, int YearNum );
16    void GetDate( int &MonthNum, int &DayNum, int &YearNum );
17    void GetStringDate( string80 &DateStr);
18    void GetMonth( string80 &MonthName );
19    // The << and >> operators are declared as friends so
20    // that each function can access the protected members
21    // of the Date class.
22    friend ostream& operator <<(ostream& stream, CDate& ADate);
23    friend istream& operator >>(istream& stream, CDate& ADate);
24  protected:
25    int Month, Day, Year;
26  };
27
28  //=========================================================
29  // Overload the << operator to recognize the CDate type.
30  ostream& operator <<(ostream& stream, CDate& ADate)
31  {
32    stream << ADate.Month << "/" << ADate.Day
33            << "/" << ADate.Year << endl;
34    return stream;
35  }; // <<
36
37  // Overload the >> operator to recognize the CDate type.
38  istream& operator >>(istream& stream, CDate& ADate)
39  {
40    stream >> ADate.Month >> ADate.Day >> ADate.Year;
41    return stream;
42  }; // >>
43
44  //=========================================================
45  //Implementation of CDate member functions.
46  CDate::CDate(int MonthNum, int DayNum,
47                          int YearNum )
48  {
49    SetDate ( MonthNum, DayNum, YearNum );
50  };
51
52  void CDate::SetDate( int MonthNum, int DayNum,
53                          int YearNum )
54  {
55    Month = MonthNum;
56    Day = DayNum;
57    Year = YearNum;
58  };
59
60  void CDate::GetDate( int &MonthNum, int &DayNum,
61                          int &YearNum )
```

(continues)

Listing 11.1 Continued

```
62  {
63    MonthNum = Month;
64    DayNum = Day;
65    YearNum = Year;
66  };
67
68  void CDate::GetStringDate ( string80 &DateStr )
69  {
70    sprintf( DateStr, "%d-%d-%d", Month, Day, Year % 100 );
71  };
72
73  void CDate::GetMonth( string80 &MonthName )
74  {
75    static char *Months[] =
76      {"January", "February", "March", "April", "May",
77       "June", "July", "August", "September", "October",
78       "November", "December"};
79    strcpy( MonthName, Months[Month-1] );
80  } // GetMonth
81
82  //=================================================
83  void main(void)
84  {
85    CDate      USDate(8, 29, 1993);
86
87    // Demonstrates using the overload << operator
88    // to output an instance of type USDate.
89    cout << "Current date =" << USDate << endl;
90
91    cout << "Enter new date:  ";
92    // Use >> to input a new date value. For this
93    // prompt, you must enter the month, day, and year
94    // separated by spaces, such as 2 1 1994.
95    cin >> USDate;
96    cin.ignore(1); // Discard the trailing Enter key.
97    cout << "You entered:  " << USDate << endl;
98
99    cout << "Press Enter to continue.";
100   cin.get();
101 } // main
```

In listing 11.1, the overloaded function definitions are shown in lines 30-42 and are declared as friends of the CDate class in lines 22 and 23. The reason that both overloaded operator functions are made friends of the class is that they access protected member data of CDate to perform input and output operations.

Note that for output to the cout stream, you reference the ostream stream class. For input from cin, you reference the istream stream class. The reason for these references is that cout is derived indirectly from the ostream class, and cin is derived the same way from the istream class. Output is performed by writing the individual members of the CDate type to the stream parameter (see lines 32 and 33). Obviously, you must declare the overloaded operator function as a friend of CDate—to gain access to the Month, Day, and Year members. An alternative is to use the GetDate() (or SetDate()) member functions. Then you would not have to make these operator functions friends of the class.

String Stream Formatting

What steps do you take to convert a numeric value, such as the value

```
int LineNo = 1;
```

to a string representation? You have to convert the internal binary representation of the integer value 1 to the string value "1". Obviously, you cannot simply assign an integer to a character string and expect the computer to display the integer, as in this example:

```
char Text[80];
Text = LineNo;
```

C++ is a typed language that requires you to assign only compatible types to one another. Some of the program examples provided in earlier chapters showed how to use the sprintf() function to convert variables into string representation. Using sprintf() is certainly one way to convert the standard data types into a string. sprintf(), however, cannot support the overloading capabilities of the << insertion operator: with sprintf(), you cannot directly output a CDate-type object.

To meet this challenge, Visual C++ provides two streams: class ostrstream and class istrstream. They are known collectively as the string streams. ostrstream, which is derived from ostream, formats the items specified in the cascaded indirection list into a string. istrstream, derived from istream, converts textual items into the internal format required for variables. Both streams are declared in STRSTREA.H. You must #include this file in any program that uses the string streams.

Using *ostrstream*

Listing 11.2 shows how to put the ostrstream stream type to work. The listing shows two examples of formatting: the first formats a simple integer into the stream, and the second formats both text and a floating-point value.

Listing 11.2 A Sample Program That Uses the *ostrstream* Type to Place Formatted Text into a Character Array

```
1   // OUTSTR.CPP
2   // Shows how to use the ostrstream type to format
3   // output into a string variable.
4   #include <iostream.h>
5   #include <strstrea.h>
6
7   void main(void)
8   {
9     int Total = 55;        // A variable to output.
10    char buffer[40];       // A string to store the
11                           // formatted output.
12
13    // Use ostrstream to declare an output stream named os
14    // that is linked to the text string named buffer.
15    ostrstream os(buffer, 40);
16    // Use the indirection operator to write the value of
17    // Total to the os stream, which in turn copies its
18    // output to the buffer variable. Note the use of the ends
19    // manipulator to insert a null terminator into the
20    // string.
21    os << Total << ends;
22
23    // Display the result.
24    cout << "Buffer =" << buffer << endl;
25
26    // Next, demonstrate the conversion of a floating-
27    // point value to a string representation.
28    float pi = 3.14159;
29    // Select fixed-point, always display decimal point.
30    os.setf( ios::fixed | ios::showpoint );
31    os.seekp(0);  // Reset stream position to the beginning
32                  // of buffer.
33    os << "The value of pi=" << pi << ends;
34    // Note how the entire output string is formatted
35    // into buffer in line above.
36    cout << buffer << endl;
37
38    cout << "Press Enter to continue.";
39    cin.get();
40  } // main
```

The first example begins in line 10, which declares a character string variable called buffer. buffer is linked to the ostrstream stream, os, in line 15. After you make these declarations, you use the os stream identifier in the same way as the cout stream. However, when sent to os, the output is copied to the string named buffer. Line 21 outputs the variable Total to os, which internally transfers the data to buffer. The result, showing that buffer has the value 55, is displayed to cout in line 24. Note the use of the ends manipulator in line 21: `ends` inserts a null character into the output, causing `buffer` to become a null-terminated string.

When you write output through an `ostrstream` stream to a character string, the stream maintains its position using an internal position indicator. You can access the position indicator through the `tellg()` member function, as in this example:

```
cout << os.tellg() << endl;
```

The preceding statement displays the current position within the `os` stream. After decimal 55 is converted to the string `"55\0"`, the position indicator is set to the next unused character in the buffer variable—the character byte after the `'\0'` null terminator. Anything else written to the `os` stream is new data beginning at position 3. The new position poses a problem when `buffer` contains a null-terminated string, because the existing null character in `buffer[2]` remains in the string. For this reason, before you use the `os` stream to format data for the next formatting operation, you should call the `seekp(int streampos)` member function to reposition the stream to the beginning of the `buffer` character array. In listing 11.2, line 31 calls `os.seekp(0)` to perform the reset operation before continuing with the next formatting operation.

Line 30 in listing 11.2 uses the `setf()` member function to set some of the formatting flags. You can use any of the manipulators described in the section "Output Formatting" earlier in this chapter. Line 33 copies and formats both a text string and a floating-point value into the `os` stream (and then the buffer).

You can see that the use of the `ostrstream` is identical to any other stream type in C++. If you overload the indirection operator `<<` to support a new class type (such as the `CDate` class illustrated earlier), you can use the new class type in the `ostrstream` output as well. This is possible because `ostrstream` is derived from `ostream`. You do not have to overload any other operators. Remember that `ostrstream` is derived from `ostream` and inherits the capabilities that you add to `ostream`.

Using *istrstream*

Just as you can use `ostrstream` to convert internal data into textual representation, you can use `istrstream` to do the reverse. Listing 11.3 shows this process, which is analogous to the process used for `ostrstream`.

Listing 11.3 An Example That Uses the *istrstream* Data Type

```
1    // INSTR.CPP
2    // Shows how to use the istrstream process and
3    // separate a string of data into separate parts.
4    #include <iostream.h>
5    #include <strstrea.h>
6
7    void main(void)
8    {
9      int AnInt;
10     float AFloat;
11     char buffer[40];          // A string to store the input.
12
13     cout << "Enter an integer <space> floating point value: ";
14     cin.getline( buffer, sizeof(buffer) );
15
16     // Use istrstream to process the input.
17     istrstream is(buffer, 40);
18     // Extract the integer and the floating-point value.
19     is >> AnInt >> AFloat;
20
21     // Display the resulting values.
22     cout << "You entered the following: "
23          << AnInt << " and " << AFloat << endl;
24
25     cout << "Press Enter to continue.";
26     cin.get();
27   } // main
```

Line 17 declares is to be of type istream and associates the stream with the buffer character array. Lines 13-14 prompt and get a line of input from the display. If you type your input as

```
23 17.89
```

then buffer contains "23 17.89\0". Line 19 extracts an integer and a floating-point value from the is stream. Again, note the remarkable similarity between is and the use of the cin stream. The only difference is that, in the case of is, the data flows from buffer rather than the keyboard.

You can use the istrstream and ostrstream types whenever you want to convert text into data, or data into text. These streams are useful in many programming situations, including file operations (reading and writing text data to and from disk files), and in special program features, such as creating the text to fit in a list box.

Input and Output to Disk Files

When your program has to write data to or read data from a disk file, you use one of the special file-oriented streams. Because you already know how to use the insertion and extraction operators and the various manipulators, you know how to format your data for text file streams because they resemble any other C++ stream. File streams have other features you can use when you work with files. The capability to read and write binary data—and randomly select data from any place in the file—is especially useful.

Writing Text Output to a File

Before you can use a file stream, you must declare an instance of the `fstream` type (short for *file stream*). `fstream` is used for input and output of all file types (both text and binary data). After you declare a file using `fstream`, you open the file using the `open()` member function. The following example opens a file stream for output (or writes to the disk):

```
fstream outfile;
outfile.open( "test.dat", ios:: out );
```

The first parameter to `open()` is the name of the file you want to access. You can specify a full path name, including a disk drive letter, as in this example:

```
outfile.open( "c:\\logs\\test.dat", ios::out );
```

The second parameter indicates the access mode to the file. You can open a file for input, output, for both input and output, or in binary data mode. Table 11.3 shows the file access mode constants. You might combine the constants shown in this table by using the logical OR operator to select a variety of features. For example, the expression `ios::in ¦ ios::out ¦ ios::binary` opens the file in binary access mode so that your program can both read and write to it.

Table 11.3 *ios::* File Access Mode Constants

Enumerated Name	Use
in	Opens the file for input (reading).
out	Opens the file for output (writing).
app	Opens the file for output so that you can write new data at the end of the file.

(continues)

Table 11.3 Continued	
Enumerated Name	**Use**
`ate`	Opens the file and then scans until locating the end-of-file position.
`trunc`	If the file being opened already exists, this mode opens and truncates it to zero length. If the file does not exist, a new file is created.
`binary`	Opens the file in binary mode.
`nocreate`	Opens an existing file; if the file does not already exist, the open operation fails.
`noreplace`	If the file already exists, the open operation fails.
`ios::in ¦ ios::out`	Opens the file for both input and output.
`ios::out ¦ ios::binary`	Opens the file for binary output.
`ios::in ¦ ios::binary`	Opens the file for binary input.

You can write data to an open file by using standard stream output statements, as in

```
outfile << "Total = " << Total << endl;
```

When you finish using a file, close it by calling the `close()` member function, as in

```
outfile.close();
```

An Alternative Way to Open a File

In the examples of programs that access disk files, you learned to open each file by using the `open()` member function. You also can specify the file name and access modes as part of the file identifier's declaration, as in

```
fstream outfile( "test.dat", ios::out );
```

This declaration creates the `outfile` stream, opens the file, and connects the stream to the file.

Listing 11.4 shows a complete program designed to write text to a disk file.

Listing 11.4 A Demonstration of Text Being Written to a Disk File Stream

```
1    // TEXTOUT.CPP
2    // Demonstrates output of text data to a stream.
3    #include <iostream.h>
4    #include <fstream.h>
5    #include <stdlib.h>
6
7    void main(void)
8    {
9      fstream outfile;
10
11     // Open a new file named test.dat for output.
12     outfile.open("test.dat", ios::out);
13     if (!outfile) {
14       cout << "Error occurred while opening test.dat."
15             << endl;
16       abort();
17     };
18
19     outfile << "The quick brown fox jumped over the lazy "
20             << "brown dog." << endl;
21     outfile << "The quick brown fox jumped over the lazy "
22             << "brown dog." << endl;
23     outfile << "The quick brown fox jumped over the lazy "
24             << "brown dog." << endl;
25     outfile.close();
26   } // main
```

Reading Text Input from a File

You also can read text from a file by using the stream system. To open a file for reading, use the ios::in file mode. Listing 11.5 shows how the read process is performed. Because the program expects to read text lines (this program reads the text file produced by listing 11.5), you use the getline() member function to read each input line (see line 24).

When reading input from a file, the program must test for the end-of-file condition. In listing 11.5, the program tests for this condition by checking the eof() member function in line 22. If you do not check for the end-of-file condition, an attempt to read beyond the end of the file results in an error.

Listing 11.5 Reading Text Data from a Text File

```
1    // TEXTIN.CPP
2    // Demonstrates reading text data from an input
3    // stream.
4    #include <iostream.h>
```

(continues)

Listing 11.5 Continued

```
 5  #include <fstream.h>
 6  #include <stdlib.h>
 7
 8  void main(void)
 9  {
10    fstream infile;
11
12    // Open an existing file named test.dat for input.
13    infile.open("test.dat", ios::in);
14    if (!infile) {
15      cout << "Error occurred while opening test.dat."
16          << endl;
17      abort();
18    };
19
20    char textline[80];
21    // Repeat until the end of file is reached...
22    while (!infile.eof()) {
23      // Get a line from the file and...
24      infile.getline(textline, sizeof(textline));
25      // display the line to the screen.
26      cout << textline << endl;
27    };
28
29    infile.close();
30  } // main
```

get( ) and put( ). The TEXTOUT.CPP and TEXTIN.CPP programs (listings 11.5 and 11.6) showed you how to read and write text data from disk files by using the standard insertion and extraction operators. Most C++ file access is faster if you use member functions for input and output in place of the insertor and extractor operators. Another problem with the extractor operator is that you cannot always detect the end-of-file condition.

For single character input and output, you can use the get() and put() member functions. Listing 11.6 illustrates using the put() member function to output one character at a time to the file. Line 27 calls the put() function to output each individual character. The sample program in listing 11.7, TEXTGET.CPP, shows how to use the get() function to read character data from a file.

Listing 11.6 A Sample Program That Uses the *put( )* Member Function

```
1  // TEXTPUT.CPP
2  // Demonstrates output of text data to a stream
3  // using the put() member function.
```

```
 4  #include <iostream.h>
 5  #include <fstream.h>
 6  #include <stdlib.h>
 7  #include <string.h>
 8
 9  void main(void)
10  {
11    fstream outfile;
12
13    // Open a new file named test.dat for output.
14    outfile.open("test.dat", ios::out);
15    if (!outfile) {
16      cout << "Error occurred while opening test.dat."
17           << endl;
18      abort();
19    };
20
21    // Demonstrates writing text to the file.
22    char textline[] =
23      {"The quick brown fox jumped over the lazy brown dog.\n\0"};
24    // The following for loop uses the put() function
25    // to output a single character at a time.
26    for (int i=0; i<=strlen(textline); i++)
27      outfile.put( textline[i] );
28
29    outfile.close();
30  } // main
```

Listing 11.7 demonstrates use of the get() member function to read a disk file, character by character. The get() member function returns true as long as there are no errors and the end of the file has not been reached. Therefore, as you can see in line 23, you do not have to check the eof() function to test for the end-of-file condition. Instead, you can use get() to both read the next character and test the result—all in one statement. The statement in line 23 reads and displays on-screen each of the text characters of the file.

Listing 11.7 Using *get()* to Read Single Characters from a Disk File

```
 1  // TEXTGET.CPP
 2  // Demonstrates reading text data from an input
 3  // stream using the get() member function.
 4  #include <iostream.h>
 5  #include <fstream.h>
 6  #include <stdlib.h>
 7
 8  void main(void)
 9  {
10    fstream infile;
11
12    // Open an existing file named test.dat for input.
```

(continues)

Listing 11.7 Continued

```
13    infile.open("test.dat", ios::in);
14    if (!infile) {
15      cout << "Error occurred while opening test.dat."
16           << endl;
17      abort();
18    };
19
20    char ch;
21    // Read the file, character by character,
22    // and display the result on the screen.
23    while (infile.get(ch)) cout << ch;
24
25    infile.close();
26  } // main
```

Copying One File to Another. In line 23 of listing 11.7, you can see that a single while() statement and a call to get() could read through an entire file. If you combine the get() call with a put() function to another file, you have a very short program to copy one file to another. The COPYFILE.CPP program in listing 11.8 shows the results. Lines 13 through 19 open the existing file (the file being copied from), and lines 21 through 27 open the new file (the file being copied to). The entire file copy operation occurs in line 33. The while() statement reads a character and tests for the end of the file; if the end of the file has not been reached, the statement writes the character to the outfile stream.

Listing 11.8 A Program Demonstrating the Use of the *get( )* and *put( )* Member Functions to Copy an Entire File

```
1   // COPYFILE.CPP
2   // You can use the get() and put() member functions
3   // to perform a quick and easy file copy operation.
4   #include <iostream.h>
5   #include <fstream.h>
6   #include <stdlib.h>
7
8   void main(void)
9   {
10    fstream infile;
11    fstream outfile;
12
13    // Open an existing file named test.dat for input.
14    infile.open("test.dat", ios::in);
15    if (!infile) {
16      cout << "Error occurred while opening test.dat."
17           << endl;
```

```
18       abort();
19     };
20
21     // Open a new file for output.
22     outfile.open("test2.dat", ios::out);
23     if (!outfile) {
24       cout << "Error occurred while opening test.dat."
25            << endl;
26       abort();
27     };
28
29     char ch;
30     // Read the file, character by character,
31     // and send each character to the output
32     // file.
33     while (infile.get(ch)) outfile.put(ch);
34
35     infile.close();
36     outfile.close();
37   } // main
```

Using Binary Data Files

Most programs that read and write data to and from files do not perform a
conversion (or formatting) of data into textual representations. If a program
is to read a file's data only, it is not necessary to convert it into readable form
for a user. For example, if you want to store some information about a person, such as a value for floating-point height and a value for integer age, you
don't have to convert these values into their textual representation, such as
"70.75" or "33". The conversion of binary data to textual form is time-
consuming and inefficient. It is much faster to output the four-byte
floating-point value and the two-byte integer quantity, and leave them in
their binary formats.

To output binary data to a stream requires using the `write()` member function. `write()` takes two parameters: the first is a pointer to a character array,
and the second is the number of bytes to write from the array to the file.
Because `write()` expects a pointer to a character array, you can use the
`write()` function as a high-speed text output routine, as in this example:

```
char textline[80];
.
.
.
outfile.write( textline, strlen(textline) );
```

The preceding statement outputs the data stored in `textline`. `write()` always
outputs the number of bytes specified, regardless of whether the data contains a null terminator. Therefore, `write()` continues to write characters from

the specified data buffer to the file, even if write() detects a null character in the buffer. In fact, write() continues past null characters in the data buffer until it has written the requested number of bytes from the buffer to the file.

Writing arbitrary binary data requires some additional information. Because the write() function expects a char * parameter, you have to cast the data you really want to write into a char * type. For example, given the data record

```
struct person_info {
  char name[20];
  float height;
  unsigned short age;
} APerson;
```

you can write the APerson structure by using the write() member function:

```
outfile.write( (char *) &APerson, sizeof(APerson) );
```

The cast operation converts the address of APerson (which is properly person_info *) into a char * type. You specify the number of bytes to write to the file by using sizeof(). Given these parameters, write() copies all the bytes specified from APerson to the output file.

Listing 11.9 shows a complete program that writes several records into a binary file and reads them back. Line 38 outputs a small array of structures to the file. The data in each structure element is copied directly, with no formatting conversion. Note the use of the casting operator in line 39 to fool the compiler into thinking that the structure's address is just a char *. Line 51 reads each structure element back to memory and displays the values on-screen.

Listing 11.9 Reading and Writing Binary Data Files

```
1   // BINARYIO.CPP
2   // Demonstrates how to read and write binary data
3   // from and to disk files.
4   #include <iostream.h>
5   #include <fstream.h>
6   #include <stdlib.h>
7
8   // Declare a structure for holding
9   // some structured data.
10  struct person_info {
11    char name[20];
12    float height;
13    unsigned short age;
14  };
```

```
15
16   // Create an array of person_info structures
17   // and preinitialize the array.
18   person_info people[4] = {
19     "Worf", 22.5, 1,
20     "Dusty", 36.25, 3,
21     "Waffles", 42.0, 2,
22     "Elvis", 42.0, 1 };
23
24   void main(void)
25   {
26     fstream infile;
27     fstream outfile;
28
29     // Open a new data file for output.
30     outfile.open("data.dat", ios::out | ios::binary);
31     if (!outfile) {
32       cout << "Error occurred while opening data.dat."
33             << endl;
34       abort();
35     };
36
37     // Output each record to the file.
38     for(int i=0; i<4; i++)
39       outfile.write( (char *)&people[i], sizeof(people[i]) );
40     outfile.close();
41
42     // Open the existing file for input.
43     infile.open("data.dat", ios::in | ios::binary );
44     if (!infile) {
45       cout << "Error occurred while opening data.dat."
46             << endl;
47       abort();
48     };
49     // Read the records in the file, a record at a time.
50     for(i=0; i<4; i++) {
51       infile.read( (char *) &people[i], sizeof(people[i]) );
52       cout << people[i].name << " "
53             << people[i].height << " "
54             << people[i].age << endl;
55     };
56     // At exit from the preceding loop, the people[] array
57     // holds all the data read from the file.
58
59     infile.close();
60   } // main
```

Random-Access Data Files

An advantage of binary files is that most data you write to them is of fixed length. For example, each instance of the person_info structure is the same size. When data in the file consists of fixed-length records, you can go to the file and read any particular record you want. You do not have to read the records in sequential order. With random access, you can read the records in any order that makes sense for your application.

The C++ stream system keeps track of the current location within the stream, regardless of the type used. You can find the current stream position by calling the `tellp()` member function. This function returns the position of the stream as the number of bytes from the beginning of the stream. To position to a specific byte location in the stream, you call the `seekp()` member function in this way:

```
thefile.seekp( sizeof(data_record) * record_number );
```

`data_record` is usually the structure type you are using with the file, and `record_number` is the record number you want to locate (`record_number` begins at 0).

You can see random access in action in listing 11.10. This program is similar to listing 11.9 but writes a few more records to the file. Then the `seekp()` function positions the next file read operation to a specific location. You can see this in line 48:

```
thefile.seekp ( sizeof(person_info) * 3 );
```

Because `seekp()` positions to an absolute byte location from the beginning of the stream (or file), you calculate the location of a desired record by multiplying its size by its number. Because record numbers are counted beginning at zero, you access the fourth record (3 in the sequence 0, 1, 2, and 3) by multiplying the size by 3.

Listing 11.10 Using Random Access to Locate Any Record in a File

```
1   // RANDOM.CPP
2   // Demonstrates random access to binary data files.
3   #include <iostream.h>
4   #include <fstream.h>
5   #include <stdlib.h>
6
7   // Declare a structure for holding
8   // some structured data.
9   struct person_info {
10    char name[20];
11    float height;
12    unsigned short age;
13  };
14
15  // Create an array of person_info structures
16  // and preinitialize the array.
17  const num_people = 6;
```

```
18  person_info people[num_people] = {
19    "Worf", 22.5, 1,
20    "Dusty", 36.25, 3,
21    "Waffles", 42.0, 5,
22    "Elvis", 38.0, 4,
23    "Jack", 45.0, 5,
24    "Peggy", 31.5, 2 };
25
26  void main(void)
27  {
28    fstream thefile;
29    person_info APerson;
30
31    // Open a new data file for input and output in
32    // binary access mode.
33    thefile.open("data.dat",
34                 ios::out ¦ ios::in ¦ ios::binary);
35    if (!thefile) {
36      cout << "Error occurred while opening data.dat."
37           << endl;
38      abort();
39    };
40
41    // Output each record to the file.
42    for(int i=0; i<num_people; i++)
43      thefile.write( (char *)&people[i], sizeof(people[i]) );
44
45    // Locate record number 4. Remember that the file
46    // is zero-relative, so record number 4 uses the
47    // following multiplier of 3:
48    thefile.seekp ( sizeof(person_info) * 3 );
49
50    // And read the record.
51    thefile.read( (char *) &APerson, sizeof(people[i]) );
52    cout << APerson.name << " "
53         << APerson.height << " "
54         << APerson.age << endl;
55
56    // And read another record, this time record 2.
57    // (The * 1 is unnecessary, of course, but is used
58    // to emphasize the use of the record number.)
59    thefile.seekp ( sizeof(person_info) * 1 );
60
61    // And read the record.
62    thefile.read( (char *) &APerson, sizeof(people[i]) );
63    cout << APerson.name << " "
64         << APerson.height << " "
65         << APerson.age << endl;
66
67    thefile.close();
68  } // main
```

Printing

To send output from your program to a printer, you open the printer device as a file. Most computers have their printers connected to the DOS PRN or LPT1 devices, so you open the printer this way:

```
fstream printer;
printer.open( "PRN", ios::out );
```

The fstream type declares a stream identifier printer, which is opened for output to the PRN device. Listing 11.11 shows a program that sends its output to the printer. Line 7 defines a special newline character sequence that causes the printer to advance to the next line. If you use the endl manipulator when you send output to the printer, you don't get the results you expect—you have to send the appropriate command codes to the printer. All printers accept the ASCII 10 character as an "advance to next line" control command, and ASCII 13 as a "move the printhead to the left margin" command. Therefore, newline is set to contain these command codes. An ASCII 12 character is interpreted by printers as a "page eject" command. Line 8 initializes the pageeject constant to ASCII 12.

Listing 11.11 Opening and Using a Printer from Your C++ Programs

```
1   // PRINT.CPP
2   // Shows how to access the PRN printer device of
3   // your computer.
4   #include <iostream.h>
5   #include <fstream.h>
6   const char newline[3]= { '\xA', '\xD', '\0' }; // Hex values
7                   // for 10 and 13 are A and D, respectively.
8   const char pageeject[2] = { '\xC', '\0' };;; // Hex value for
9                               // 12 is C.
10  void main(void)
11  {
12    int age = 7;
13
14    fstream printer;
15    printer.open( "PRN", ios::out );
16    if (!printer)
17    {
18      cout << "Error while trying to print." << endl;
19    }
20    else
21    {
22      printer << "Person:  Kelsey" << newline;
23      printer << "Age: " << age << newline << newline;
```

```
24      printer << "Person:  To be determined" << newline;
25      printer << "Age:  unknown." << newline;
26      printer << pageeject;
27      printer.close();
28   };
29  }
```

Summary

In this chapter, you learned about C++ input and output operations. You learned how to use manipulators to adjust formatting options for output and to select input formats. You can read and write text and binary data to and from disk files. You learned the following:

- You display output to the screen using the cout stream identifier and the insertion operator <<.

- You receive input from the keyboard by referencing the cin stream identifier and using the extractor operator >>.

- You can use the get() member function to read single characters from the keyboard, and you can use put() to output single characters. These member functions work also for disk file stream I/O.

- When you need to read an entire line of input, you should use the getline() member function.

- Manipulators provide an easy way to modify the output or input stream. One example is the endl identifier used throughout this book to insert a new line or carriage return.

- You can check whether a stream error has occurred by referencing the stream identifier in an if() statement, as in

  ```
  if (!infile) { ... an error occurred };
  ```

- Through the power of overloaded functions, you can overload the insertion and extraction operator functions to provide direct support for user-defined data types. Once you write the appropriate functions, you can use your own data types as if they were a standard part of the stream I/O system.

- To format data into strings, you use the `ostrstream` type. To convert formatted text into internal variables, you use the `istrstream` type.

- All file I/O is handled through the `fstream` type. You use the `open()` member function to open a disk file and associate it with a stream identifier.

- You can perform disk file I/O by using ordinary insertion and extraction operators. But you can perhaps more easily use the `get()`, `put()`, `read()`, and `write()` member functions.

In Chapter 13, "Graphics Programming with QuickWin," you learn to incorporate the Microsoft Graphics library into your QuickWin programs and to display simple graphics on the screen, such as lines, circles, and boxes. First, however, Chapter 12, "Debugging Visual C++ Programs," teaches you how to find and fix errors that may appear in your programs.

Review Questions

1. Why is a stream called a *stream*?

2. Which stream identifier is predeclared for use in screen output?

3. Which stream identifier is predeclared for use in keyboard input?

4. How do you select scientific notation to display floating-point values?

5. When an error occurs during stream processing, what member function must you call before you resume using the stream?

6. When using the `ostrstream` type to output formatted data to a null-terminated character array, what manipulator should you place at the end of your insertion statement?

7. After you have placed data into an `ostrstream` type, what member function should you call before attempting to write new data to the stream?

8. What is the name of the file stream type?

9. Which stream do you use for extracting values from a text string into variables?

10. When you have finished processing a file stream, what member function should always be called?

11. When reading data from a text file, what member function must you be sure to check to ensure that the end of the file has not been reached?

12. How do you detect whether an error has occurred when a file is opened or stream data is processed?

13. You want to output a single floating-point variable named `Volts` to a binary data file. How do you write the call to the `write()` member function so that `Volts` is properly cast as the first acceptable parameter to `write()`?

Exercises

1. Write a program that uses `get()` to read individual keystrokes from the keyboard. Display the numeric representation of each keystroke entered.

2. Modify LISTDEMO.CPP and associated files from Chapter 7 to implement save-to-disk and load-from-disk commands. Use binary file I/O.

Chapter 12

Debugging Visual C++ Programs

No matter how careful you are in constructing your programs, errors creep into them. As your programs become larger and more complex, you can be assured that errors will occur. These errors can make your life as a programmer less than ideal. Errors in your program can also make the lives of your users less than ideal. Fortunately, Microsoft provides a tool in the Visual Workbench that aids in the prevention, search, and elimination of bugs. The tool is called, appropriately enough, the *integrated debugger*.

Some errors are the result of carelessness, such as mistyping a keyword in the C++ language. Some errors are caused by problems with physical resources, such as memory and disk space, which are outside the control of programmers or their programs. Other errors are caused by faulty logic coded by the programmer, such as multiplying a variable by the wrong value.

In this chapter, you learn the three types of errors you are likely to encounter as a programmer. You learn how to find and avert errors before your users find them, and how to prepare your programs for debugging. Finally, you examine the integrated tools included with Visual C++ to find and correct errors.

Note

All versions of Visual C++ contain the integrated debugger. You access the debugger with the **D**ebug option on the Visual Workbench main menu. However, both versions of the Professional Edition of MSVC contain a separate debugger called *Codeview*. This is a more powerful, stand-alone debugger that enables you to debug many different kinds of program files. Its use, although similar to that of the integrated debugger described here, is beyond the scope of this book.

Understanding the Three Types of Program Errors

Programmers encounter a myriad of errors during their careers, but most errors are one of three types: syntax errors, runtime errors, amd logic errors. Syntax errors are easy to catch and correct. Most compilers and linkers, including those found in the Visual Workbench, recognize such errors and report them to the programmer. Runtime errors occur while the program is executing and cause the program and its operating system to fail. These failures can be so catastrophic that the user is required to turn off the computer and start over again. When that happens, it is called a *lockup*. But even when a program compiles, links, and executes to completion, it may still have logic errors. The results reported may be in error—that is, the program may make mistakes while calculating or displaying the results. Actually, the preceding statement is itself in error, because programs do exactly what they are programmed to do. They do not make mistakes. Programmers make mistakes!

Syntax Errors

Syntax errors are the easiest errors to detect, and usually to correct. Most compilers and linkers detect syntax errors and provide an indication of each error's location within the source file, as well as the kind of syntax error detected. These errors range from misspelling C++ keywords (for example, whlie instead of while) to forgetting to place a semicolon at the end of a statement. Syntax errors can also include such actions as using a function name without providing a function definition. Listing 12.1 illustrates a program that contains several syntax errors. The results of attempting to build this project are shown in figure 12.1.

Listing 12.1 A Program Containing Syntax Errors

```
 1    #include <iostreams.h>
 2    void main()
 3    {
 4      int j = 0;
 5      k = 0;                // Error, K not declared.
 6      whiel( j < 10)        // while keyword misspelled!
 7      {
 8        my_undefined_function( j );         // Undefined function.
 9        cout << "j is = to " << j << eol;
10      }
11}
```

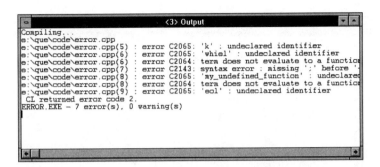

Fig. 12.1
Errors displayed in the Visual C++ Output window.

The following discussion recaps the information provided in the section "Compiler, Linker, and Runtime Errors" in Chapter 1, "The Fundamentals of C++ Programming." If you need to know what the error means, you can place the mouse cursor on the line containing the error and press F1. A help box is displayed, containing information specific to the error. If you want to edit the source file to correct the error, you can double-click the line containing the error. The Visual Workbench automatically reads the indicated file into the editor and positions the cursor on the offending line. You can then edit the source code to correct the error.

The Visual C++ editor also helps you detect possible syntax errors by color coding C and C++ keywords and data types. You learned how to use this feature in the section "Creating Your First C++ Program" in Chapter 1.

Runtime Errors

Runtime errors occur while your program is executing. An example of a runtime error is an attempt to allocate memory with the C++ new operator when insufficient memory is available. Another example is trying to open a file that does not exist.

Testing Function Return Values. Most C++ library functions return a value indicating the success or failure of the function call. You should get into the habit of checking these error codes after every function call. If you check for possible error conditions before continuing with the program, you have a chance to correct the condition, or at least to report the error to the user before exiting the application. Listing 12.2 illustrates this technique.

Listing 12.2 Testing Function Return Values for Success or Failure

```
1   #include <iostreams.h>
2
3   void main(void)
4   {
5     linkedlist * node;
6     node = new linkedlist();
7     if ( node == NULL )
8     {
9       // Report an error.
10      cout << "Error allocating a new node for linked list" << endl
11      cout << "Exiting application";
12    }
13    else
14    {
15      // All is well.
16      // Rest of main function goes here.
17    }
18  }
```

Line 6 attempts to allocate a node for a linked list, using the new operator. The test on line 7 checks the new operator's return value to see whether the operation has returned a NULL, or 0, value. If you check the on-line help entry for new, you see that it returns a 0 if enough memory is not available.

Line 6 has another potential problem. The new function not only allocates memory for a variable but also invokes the variable's constructor. An object's constructor is used to initialize member variables, as discussed in the section "Constructor Functions" in Chapter 8, "Classes." If the program cannot initialize the object, there is no way of indicating this problem because constructor functions do not return a value.

Exception Handling. One problem that you may encounter in C++ is an operation that does not generate an error, such as a division by 0 or insufficient resources to initialize a class's member functions in the constructor function. You cannot test such operations for success or failure because not all of them return a value, such as the division operation. The *Annotated Reference Manual* (ARM) and the proposed ANSI C++ standard handle such situations with exception handling. *Exceptions* are abnormal program errors, such as division by 0 or the failure to allocate sufficient memory. *Exception handling* is a mechanism for detecting and correcting such program errors. Exception handling allows programmers to handle such problems before they lead to a catastrophic failure. The syntax for this mechanism consists of what is called a try/catch block. You *try* an operation and then *catch* any exceptions thrown by the program.

The various versions of Visual C++ currently on the market do not support exception handling as defined by the proposed C++ standard. (As of February, 1994, these versions include the Standard and Professional Editions of MSVC 1.0, the Professional Edition of MSVC 1.5, and the 32-bit edition of MSVC for Windows NT.) Microsoft has stated that it will support exception handling in the next release of Visual C++ (Version 2.0). Microsoft currently emulates exception handling through a series of preprocessor macros and classes that are available only when you use the Microsoft Foundation Classes (MFC) class library. Chapter 14, "The MFC General-Purpose Classes and Collection Classes," provides general information on using the MFC class library.

Logic Errors

Logic errors occur whenever programmers instruct programs to perform incorrect actions. One type of logic error occurs when a program performs a calculation but yields an incorrect value. Another logic error occurs when a program takes an incorrect branch during execution. If you provide the wrong calculation or instruct your program to take the wrong path in an if statement, you have introduced an error in the program. Introducing such errors is referred to as GIGO, or "garbage in, garbage out." Remember that the program is simply following instructions you have provided.

One way to spot a logic error is to follow the program's execution path. You can use a debugger to follow each step in a program's execution, as discussed in the section "Using the Integrated Debugger" later in this chapter. A much simpler way is to print a statement to the screen, indicating that the program has reached a particular point in the source code. You can also print the value of any variables before and after their use in a calculation. Even though you are adding program code that provides little functionality to your eventual user, the extra code helps you, the developer, create bug-free code. Because this code is excess baggage, you should consider wrapping the code in preprocessor macros so that it is available for debugging but stripped out for the user. The following lines of code illustrate this technique:

```
#define DEBUG 1   // Include debugging code.
.
.
.
#ifdef DEBUG
cout << "Reached function X" << "value of var1 is " << var1 <<
endl;
#endif
```

In fact, Microsoft uses the same technique to include debugging code in its MFC class library, except that the symbol _DEBUG is used instead of DEBUG.

No matter how careful you are, errors are going to appear in your programs. When printing a variable's value no longer helps in your investigation of the problem, you must resort to the debugger. The easiest way to debug programs, though, is to write correct programs the first time. Unfortunately, perfect programs are found only in programmers' dreams and Upper Management Planning Offices. Errors are a fact of life, but you can still try to minimize them as much as possible.

Detecting Bugs Before Your Users Do

Listing 12.3 illustrates the METRIC12.CPP program, originally presented in Chapter 1, with several bugs added. Many of these errors could have been prevented by following the procedures outlined in the sections that follow.

Listing 12.3 A Simple C++ Program That Converts Miles into Kilometers

```
1   // METRIC12.CPP
2   // METRIC12.CPP shows a sample use of a function.
3   #include <iostream.h>
4
5   void convert_miles_to_km( float mileage )
6   {
7     const int KILOMETERS_PER_MILE = 1.069344;
8     const int METERS_PER_KILOMETER = 100;
9     // Display the calculated result.
10    cout << endl << mileage << " converts to "
11         << mileage * KILOMETERS_PER_MILE
12         << " kilometers." << endl << endl;
13
14    cout << "Or, "
15         << ( mileage * KILOMETERS_PER_MILE) / METERS_PER_KILOMETER
16         << " meters." << endl << endl;
17  );
18
19  void main(void) {
20    float miles;
21
22    cout << "English to metric conversion calculator."
23         << endl << endl;
24
25    // Display prompt for number of miles.
26    cout << "Enter number of miles:   ";
27
28    // Read keyboard input.
29    cin >> miles;
30
```

```
31    convert_miles_to_km ( miles );
32    cout << "Press Enter to continue." << endl;
33    cin.ignore(1);  // Ignore leftover Enter key.
34    cin.get();
35  } // main
```

Using Desk Checks and Code Previews

Programs typically operate on a vast quantity of data and display the results in many different formats. During program development, you should test each section of code to make certain that it operates correctly. For testing purposes, you can write a generic `main()` function that allows you to pass parameters to the function being tested. You can then analyze the results to make sure that the function is providing the correct answers. This technique is sometimes referred to as *unit testing* or a *desk check*. You create such a test by first calculating the results of the program on a set of test data. Then you should calculate, by hand or with a calculator, the expected results for the same set of input values. You should select input values to test the following types of conditions:

- Test the function with data you normally expect the user to enter. Make sure that the function provides the correct answer for the input value.

- Test the function with the minimum and maximum values it can handle or is designed to handle. These conditions are referred to as boundary conditions. An example is a function that operates on an array of N data types. Check to see what happens when the index is less than 0, 0, 1, $N-1$, N, and $N+1$, where N is the number of items in the array.

- Test the function for invalid inputs such as those values that may result in division by 0.

The process of calculating the desk check can also help you, as programmer, better understand the problem at hand. Then you can construct a correct and more efficient application. You can think of this process as a *code preview* or *design review*. The design review is done before you write a single line of code. Its purpose is to review the proposed variables, data structures, and algorithms you plan to use in solving the given problem. You should consider including a fellow programmer in the code preview because "two heads are better than one." Perhaps the second programmer can show you a more efficient algorithm to use to calculate the answer. Like a computer program, an *algorithm* is simply a series of steps used to solve a problem; an algorithm is presented in written descriptions and mathematics, however, rather than in a programming language. These descriptions are sometimes referred to as *pseudocode*.

After you review your algorithms and select the test data, you can code and test the program. Then you can run and check the results against the values you have calculated. If the calculated values match the desk check values, you can be confident that your program operates correctly. If the values do not match, you can be certain that your program contains errors in need of correction. Table 12.1 illustrates some test data for a desk check of METRIC12.CPP (listing 12.1).

Table 12.1 Test Data for METRIC12.CPP		
Input	**Expected Results (km)**	**Expected Results (Miles)**
0 miles		
1 mile	1.6 km	0.001609334 miles
5 miles	8.04672 km	.00804672 miles
10 miles	16.09344 km	.01609344 miles
23 miles	37.014912 km	.037014912 miles

After you have built METRIC12.CPP, run the program and enter each of the values listed in table 12.1, recording the results. Then compare the results with those listed in table 12.2, which shows the results of this test.

Table 12.2 Results of METRIC12.CPP When Run with the Test Data in Table 12.1		
Input	**Expected Results (km)**	**Expected Results (Miles)**
0 miles	0 km	0 miles
1 mile	24844 km	248.44 miles
5 miles	124220 km	1242.2 miles
10 miles	248440 km	2484.4 miles
23 miles	571412 km	5714.12 miles

Because the answers in table 12.2 are different from the expected answers in table 12.1, you should suspect that something is wrong with the program.

Using Code Reviews

In the last section, you learned that a code preview can help spot errors before you code your program, yet sometimes bugs make it pass such a test. Before spending hours, possibly days, tracking down a problem, you should have a fellow programmer take a look at the code you have written. The reason is that a programmer who has not been involved in writing a section of code is not accustomed to seeing the code day in and day out. Such a person might be able to spot an error you have inadvertently overlooked.

As you typed the METRIC12.CPP program in listing 12.3, you probably noticed a few of the errors yourself and could have corrected them before ever building and testing the program. Sometimes you can work on a section of code for so long and never spot the error; this is the programmer's version of the old expression "You can't see the forest for the trees." In that case, having a second programmer review your code can help you find and correct possible logic errors. A code review can also help you spot possible runtime error conditions you have not anticipated.

Preventing Future Problems

Programs do not spring into existence and then suddenly disappear overnight. They have a distinct "life cycle," as shown in the stages described here:

- The need for a program is determined.

- The problem to be solved is clearly defined.

- A software construction plan is created, including testing criteria.

- The program is designed.

- The program is constructed.

- The program is tested.

- The program is released to the users.

■ The program is used and updated as new features are required and bugs are discovered.

■ Finally, the program is no longer needed, because the problem it was originally designed to solve has changed, or newer technology has made the program obsolete.

As you can see, a program has a birth, a life, and a death. A program is not a static object frozen in place or time. Because a program evolves over its lifetime, you must keep track of how the program changes. You track changes with internal comments so that future modifications can be made. The technique most often used for tracking overall software modifications is to include a list of comments. The list is placed directly in the source code files, usually at the beginning. These comments typically identify the original author of the source code, as well as the date (and perhaps the time) of its creation. The comments also provide an indication of what the routines in the file perform and how they interact with the rest of the program.

As the program matures and modifications are made, either to correct bugs or provide new features, those who make changes add additional comments stating the changes made, who made the changes, and why the changes were needed. Sometimes the name of the person who authorized the change is added to the comments. These comments form a history of how and why the source code has evolved over time. Listing 12.4 illustrates a typical list of comments.

Listing 12.4 A Sample Source Code Comment Header and Modification History List

```
/******************************************************************/
// File: DBFUN1.CPP
// Current version: 1.2
// Author:  Jack Tackett, Jr.
// Date :   Dec. 7, 1993
// Purpose: To demonstrate debugging techniques.
// Revision History:
//          02/17/94 Fixed major problem with display function.
//                   Version 1.2 JT
//          12/31/93 Fixed problem of dividing by 0.
//                   Added several new functions.
//                   Version 1.1 JT
//          12/07/93 Created. JT
//                   Version 1.0
/
 ******************************************************************/
```

Placing comments at the beginning of the source file is inadequate. You must also comment your functions, describing what they do and any tricks you used to achieve the correct result. By providing internal comments, you help future programmers maintain the code, even if that future programmer is you. It is not unusual for programmers to revisit code written months before and not understand what they have written!

Preparing Your Program for Debugging

To use the integrated debugger, you must provide it with information inside your object code and inside the executable file. The debugger uses this information to do what is called *symbolic debugging*. Remember that a program is just a collection of bits in the computer's memory, representing instructions and data. Examining the program in this form, although possible, is tedious and is itself error-prone. A better approach is to follow the execution path of your program as if the computer were executing the program one instruction after the other. Instead of observing bits, however, you observe the lines of source code currently being executed, rather than the internal instructions they represent. The integrated debugger facilitates such an approach by controlling the execution of the program being debugged. The debugger executes all the instructions generated by each line of source code. The debugger can then pause after each line of code, allowing the user to examine the current state of the program.

Using Debug Builds versus Release Builds

To use the integrated debugger, you must instruct the Visual C++ compiler to place source code information in the executable file. You instruct the compiler to provide the necessary information by choosing which type of build your project creates: debug or release. By default, the project manager builds a debug version of your program. A debug version is much larger than a release version because of the extra source code debugging information inserted in the program. A debug version also executes more slowly because of all the extra information placed in the program.

Creating a Debug Build

To instruct the Workbench to build a debug version of your program, you choose the **P**roject command from the **O**ptions menu. The Project Options dialog box is displayed, as shown in figure 12.2. You can change the type of build your project creates by clicking the appropriate radio button, **D**ebug or **R**elease.

Fig. 12.2
The Project
Options dialog
box.

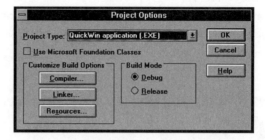

The Visual Workbench creates a debug build of your project by default. However, if you modify the project file, whether to build a release version from a debug version or to build a debug version from a release version, then you must rebuild the entire project. Rebuilding the program as a release build removes the extra information from the executable file. Rebuilding the program as a debug build places all the necessary information into the executable file for the integrated debugger's use.

Using the Integrated Debugger

Figure 12.3 shows the **D**ebug menu items, and figure 12.4 shows corresponding buttons located on the toolbar. To begin debugging a program, you must tell the debugger to load and execute your application. By default, the integrated debugger uses the executable file created by the current project.

Your computer's operating system (OS) normally loads a program into memory and then begins executing the program. Basically, the OS sets the instruction pointer (IP) to the first instruction in the program and then executes each instruction without pausing until the program terminates. The instruction pointer is a register, or pair of registers, that points to the next machine instruction to be executed by the CPU. The only time that a program pauses is to wait for user input.

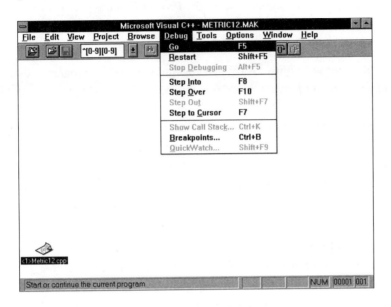

Fig. 12.3
The Visual
Workbench
Debug menu.

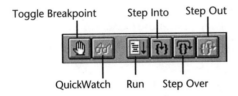

Fig. 12.4
The Visual
Workbench
toolbar buttons
used with the
integrated
debugger.

A program executed from within the integrated debugger, however, is under the control of the debugger, not the operating system. The execution sequence for a program being debugged is therefore different. When your program is debugged, the debugger is loaded and executed first, because the debugger is itself just another program. The debugger then loads the program into memory and begins its execution, but under your control. Thus, you can instruct the debugger to execute the program's instructions one at a time, pausing between instructions so that you can perform various diagnostic procedures. This procedure is called *single-stepping*—you are stepping through your program a single line of code at a time.

Controlling Program Execution

To tell the debugger to start, you use the **G**o command from the **D**ebug menu, the F5 shortcut key, or the Run toolbar button. Any of these executes the program just as if you had chosen the **P**roject E**x**ecute <project name> command, with one exception: the integrated debugger is in control of the program, and you are in control of the debugger.

One ability that you control is the starting and stopping of program execution at a variety of locations. You can command the debugger to step into a function call, step over a function call, or step out of a function call. You can command the debugger to execute every program instruction up to the current location of the mouse cursor in the source file. Or you can command the debugger to continue execution until it encounters a breakpoint you have set in the code, as discussed in the next section. A *breakpoint* is a command to the debugger to stop program execution at the specified place in the source code.

Setting Breakpoints

Setting a breakpoint at a specific source code line instructs the debugger to stop execution when it reaches the code generated by that line. To set a breakpoint in the Visual Workbench, you must open the source file in the Visual C++ editor. You then place the cursor on the line where you want to halt execution. After you have placed the cursor on that line, you can set the breakpoint by clicking the Toggle Breakpoint button on the toolbar or by using the F9 shortcut key. (The Toggle Breakpoint button resembles a hand.) The Workbench indicates that a breakpoint is set at this line by inverting the background color of the entire line. Figure 12.5 illustrates a breakpoint set on line 29 of listing 12.3.

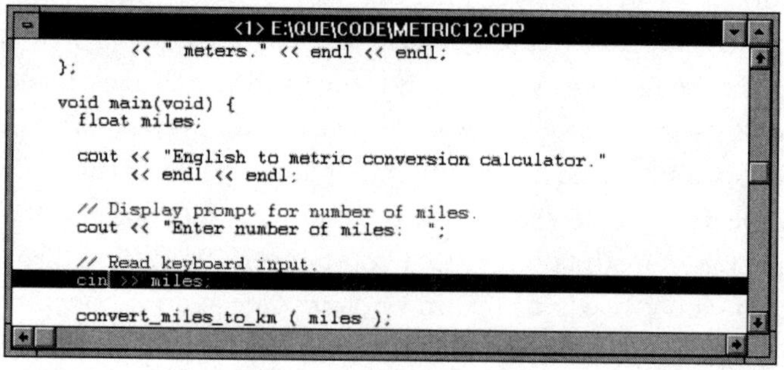

Fig. 12.5
Setting a breakpoint in METRIC12.CPP.

```
                     <1> E:\QUE\CODE\METRIC12.CPP
            << " meters." << endl << endl;
    };

    void main(void) {
      float miles;

      cout << "English to metric conversion calculator."
           << endl << endl;

      // Display prompt for number of miles.
      cout << "Enter number of miles:   ";

      // Read keyboard input.
      cin >> miles;

      convert_miles_to_km ( miles );
```

You can also control breakpoints with the **Debug B**reakpoints command. When you choose this option, the Breakpoints dialog box appears, as shown in figure 12.6.

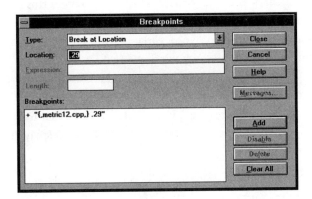

Fig. 12.6
The Breakpoints dialog box.

The Breakpoints dialog box provides an extensive list of options for controlling how the debugger sets breakpoints and decides to stop while stepping through your program.

Examining and Modifying Variables

As you step through the program, you would like to see the values of your variables displayed all the time, rather than using cout repeatedly to display the values. The integrated debugger provides two mechanisms for displaying the current value of any variable: the QuickWatch dialog box and the Watch window. The Watch window is discussed a bit later in this chapter, and the QuickWatch dialog box is shown in figure 12.7.

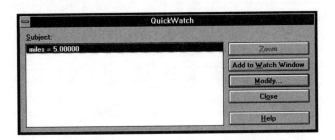

Fig. 12.7
The QuickWatch dialog box displaying variables.

Examining a Variable with the QuickWatch Dialog Box. You can examine a variable's current value by first placing the cursor on the variable and then clicking the QuickWatch button on the toolbar (refer to fig. 12.4).

Alternatively, you can use the shortcut Shift+F9 or the **Q**uickWatch command on the **D**ebug menu. The variable and its value are displayed only while the dialog box is open; once you close the QuickWatch dialog box, the watch information is lost. The Visual Workbench refers to this dialog box as the QuickWatch dialog because its use is meant for just a quick look at any given variable. If you want to track a variable while stepping through the program, you must use the Watch window. If you want to watch the value continuously, you need to add the variable to the Watch window. You can do so by first selecting the variable in the **S**ubject list box of the QuickWatch dialog box and then clicking the Add to **W**atch Window button. The debugger displays the values in hex if the He**x**adecimal Display check box is checked in the Debug dialog box.

The QuickWatch dialog box also enables you to display all the elements of arrays and all the fields located within a structure. If a variable is one of these aggregate data types, the dialog box displays a + next to the variable in the **S**ubject list box. You can expand such a variable in order to see all the data items, either by double-clicking the variable in the list box, or by selecting the variable and then clicking the **Z**oom button. To collapse the display so that only the variable is displayed, simply reverse the process.

Modifying a Variable. Examining a variable is useful because you can detect when a variable acquires an invalid value. Perhaps you would like to continue stepping through the program to make sure that the rest of the code is functioning correctly, but with an invalid value, the variable may cause further problems. What you need to do is change the variable to the proper value and continue stepping through the program, or continue until the next breakpoint. With the integrated debugger, you can modify a variable by clicking the **M**odify button in the QuickWatch dialog box. The Modify Variable dialog box then appears, as shown in figure 12.8.

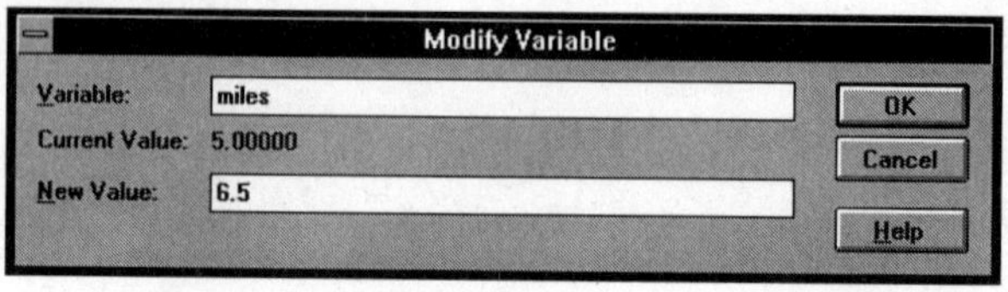

Fig. 12.8
The Modify
Variable dialog
box.

The first item in the Modify Variable dialog box, the **V**ariable edit box, displays the selected variable to be modified. The second item, Current Value, displays the variable's current value. The third item, the **N**ew Value edit box, is where you enter a new value for the variable. After you enter the new value, click the OK button to update the variable. Unfortunately, you cannot update the elements of an entire array or all the fields in a structure all at once. You must modify each element or field one at a time.

Miscellaneous Debugger Actions

Starting your application, controlling how the application steps through its code, and examining variables cover most of the debugging actions you need in order to debug your Visual C++ application successfully. However, the integrated debugger provides several other options to help you find and fix errors.

Using the Call Stack Dialog Box. If your program is encountering a runtime error that hangs the computer, you must locate the point in your code that causes the error. Because you do not know the exact source line, you cannot set a breakpoint. One technique you can use is to single-step through every line of code until your program stops working, but this can be tedious and time-consuming. A better technique is to start your program running in the debugger and just let your program crash. Then use the Show Call Stack command from the **D**ebug menu to access the Call Stack dialog box. It shows which function your program was executing when it crashed (see fig. 12.9). The **C**alls list box contains the functions the program has called, but from which it has not yet returned. Each listing displays the function parameters, if any, provided the **S**how Function Parameters check box is checked. You can then begin further investigation by placing a breakpoint at the beginning of the last function called.

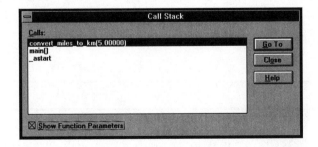

Fig. 12.9
The Call Stack dialog box displaying the functions into which the program has stepped.

Setting Debugger Options. With the Visual Workbench, you can set various debugger options with De**b**ug from the **O**ptions menu. Choosing De**b**ug displays the Debug dialog box, as shown in figure 12.10. The first edit box, **P**rogram Arguments, enables you to pass command-line arguments to the program you are debugging. Because you must execute the integrated debugger instead of your application, you have no way to specify command-line arguments, except through the Debug dialog box. Command-line arguments are parameters the user passes to the main() function. These parameters are normally entered on the command line, after the program's name.

Fig. 12.10
The Debug
dialog box.

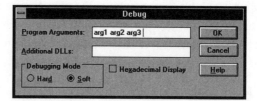

By convention, the first parameter is called argc and indicates how many command-line arguments follow. The second parameter is a pointer to a character array, which contains the command-line arguments. CMDARG.CPP, in listing 12.5, displays the command-line arguments passed to the main() function. Although not a standard, usually the first string in the argv array is the application's name. DOS programs make extensive use of command-line parameters.

Listing 12.5 The CMDARG.CPP Program for Displaying Command-Line Arguments

```
 1   #include <iostreams.h>
 2   void main( int argc, char *argv[])
 3   {
 4     cout << "number of arguments = " << argc << endl;
 5     for ( int i = 0; i < argc; i++)
 6     {
 7       cout << "argument #" << i;
 8       cout << " is " << argv[i] << endl;
 9     }
10   }
```

When CMDARG.CPP is run, it displays only the name of the application. The reason is that you have not specified command-line arguments. To pass command-line arguments to the program, open the Debug dialog box and enter the following strings in the **P**rogram Arguments edit box:

```
arg1 arg2 arg3
```

Now when the program is executed, it displays the name of the executable file and then the three strings specified as command-line arguments in the Debug dialog box.

The next edit box, **A**dditional DLLs, is specific to Windows programs and is not used for MS-DOS or QuickWin applications. DLLs are libraries that are linked at runtime rather that at build time. The Debugging Mode box, which contains two radio buttons, is also specific to Windows programming. Debugging Mode indicates how Windows responds to certain events while you are debugging a Windows program. The use of DLLs and Debugging Mode is beyond the scope of this book. The final item, the He**x**adecimal Display check box, determines how the Workbench displays information in various debugger windows. If this box is checked, a variable is displayed in hexadecimal, rather than decimal, notation.

Using the Debugging Windows

Figure 12.11 displays the **W**indow menu items for the windows used by the debugger: Watch, Locals, Registers, and Output. Each window provides you with information about the current debugging session as you step through the program.

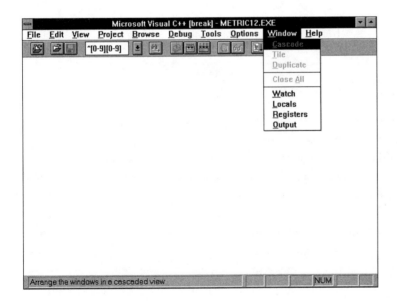

Fig. 12.11
The Watch, Locals, Registers, and Output commands on the Window menu.

The Watch Window

You can display in the Watch window, as you step through the code, the values of any variables. The Watch window provides the same functionality as the QuickWatch dialog box, except that the Watch window allows you to examine many variables at once, whereas the QuickWatch dialog box allows you to examine only a single variable at a time. Furthermore, any variable you place in the Watch window to observe is available in that window the next time you access it, even if you exit the Visual Workbench. However, any variable you examine in the QuickWatch dialog box is not available the next time the dialog box is opened. The debugger displays the values in hex if the Hexadecimal Display check box is checked in the Debug dialog box.

The values have valid data only when the variable is within current scope. Recall from the section "The Scope of Variables" in Chapter 7, "Projects," that a variable's scope depends on where in your source file you defined the variable. If you instruct the debugger to step out of the variable's scope, the Watch window indicates that it cannot "watch" the variable. Figure 12.12 shows some sample data in the Watch window.

Fig. 12.12
The Watch window displaying data.

Watching Structures, Classes, and Expressions. Variables are not the only items you can watch. You can enter any valid C/C++ expression in the Watch window and immediately see the results. Thus, you can use the indirection operator (*) to *dereference* pointers and display the pointer's contents. Use of the indirection operator was described in the section "Understanding Pointers" in Chapter 5, "Pointers." If the pointer referenced a structure or a class, the Watch window displays the variable with a + or - indicator. Any variable marked with a + means that the variable is an aggregate data type containing more fields. Just as in the QuickWatch dialog box, if you double-click one of these items, the Workbench expands the variable's display to include those fields. Each field in the variable is displayed on a separate line. When you no longer want to see the extra fields, another double-click collapses the display back to a single line containing the original variable.

Using the Watch Window to Modify Values. You've seen that you can add a variable by simply typing its name into the Watch window, and you can display the separate fields contained in aggregate data structures. It makes sense, therefore, that you can also modify their values. In the Watch window, as well as in the Locals window, you modify a variable by using the editing keys to erase the old value and then enter the new value. The variable is updated when you press the Enter key.

The Locals Window

In Chapter 2, "C++ Data Types and Expressions," you learned about local variables in the section "Duration of Variables." Local variables are available only within the scope of the current function. The Locals window aids in debugging by providing a quick way for you to display every local variable in a function without having to use the QuickWatch dialog box or Watch window. If you used the QuickWatch dialog box, then you must select and examine each variable one at a time, and thus you cannot examine all the local variables at once. With the Watch window, you can examine all the local variables at once, but you have to add each by hand. You must then delete each one by hand from the Watch window when you are done stepping through the function. The Locals Window allows you to observe all the current function's local variables (but only those of the current function) automatically without manually selecting each variable. Figure 12.13 displays the local variable `miles`, defined on line 20 of listing 12.3.

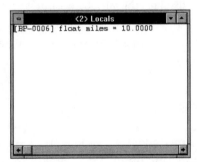

Fig. 12.13
The Locals window for METRIC12.CPP, displaying the local variable `miles`.

You can modify a local variable just as you modify a variable in the Watch window.

The Registers Window

In the section "Memory Addressing" in Chapter 7, "Projects," you learned about the various registers of the 80x86 family of CPUs, used in most IBM PC compatibles. While debugging, you may need to see what values are contained in these registers—for instance, to check a function's return value or to check the current value of the stack register. The values are displayed in the Registers window, as shown in figure 12.14. This window is one of four windows used by the integrated debugger to display information about the program currently being debugged. You access the Registers window with the **R**egisters option on the **W**indow menu. One helpful tip to know is that the AX register usually contains a function's return value. If the function returns a pointer, the AX register contains the address of the return value.

Fig. 12.14
The Registers window.

The Output Window

You are already familiar with the Output window. The Visual Workbench uses this window to display the results of compiling and linking your program. The Workbench displays the various warnings and errors generated by the current project as it is built. However, the Workbench uses this window also to display diagnostic messages from Windows programs built with MSVC and the MFC class library.

Summary

In this chapter, you learned about the various errors you can encounter while designing, implementing, and running your programs. You learned how to help prevent errors before they are coded in your programs, using such procedures as code reviews. You learned also how the integrated debugger can help you track down and correct the errors that invariably appear in computer programs.

This chapter covered the following topics:

- The three types of programming errors that programmers typically encounter (syntax, runtime, and logic errors)

- The different types of tests and procedures you can use in finding errors before your users find them

- How to include debugging information in a program

- How to use the integrated debugger to set breakpoints and step through a program

- How to examine variables and modify their values from within an executing program

Review Questions

1. Name three types of programming errors. Give a definition and an example of each type of error.

2. Line 10 in the following listing contains a syntax error. What is it?

```
 1  #include <iostreams.h>
 2
 3  void main(void)
 4  {
 5   linkedlist * node;
 6   node = new linkedlist();
 7   if ( node == NULL )
 8   {
 9     // Report an error.
10     cout << "Error allocating a new node for linked list" << eol;
11     cout << "Exiting application";
12   }
13   else
14   {
15     // All is well.
16     // Rest of main function goes here.
17   }
18  }
```

3. What is a desk check? Why do you need desk checks?

4. What is a code review? Why would you have a code review?

5. What are the three types of test conditions you should use in designing desk checks?

6. What are the stages in a program's life cycle?

7. How do you pass command-line parameters to a program in the debugger?

8. How do you prepare a program for debugging?

9. What are breakpoints? How do you set a breakpoint with the integrated debugger?

Chapter 13

Graphics Programming with QuickWin

Visual C++ provides extensive two-dimensional computer graphics support in an easy-to-use graphics library for all DOS applications. The library contains routines for basic drawing (lines, rectangles, circles, ellipses, polygons, and so on); multiple text fonts and text output routines; and special-purpose routines for creating ordinary bar charts, pie charts, and three-dimensional bar charts. This chapter introduces the drawing features of Visual C++ QuickWin applications.

Using Visual C++ Graphics

The graphics functions in Visual C++ are easy to use. To draw a line on the screen, for example, you move to a pixel by calling first _moveto() and then lineto(). You can use the graphics functions to draw common graphics elements, such as lines, circles, arcs, ellipses, boxes, rectangles, and pie slices. You can also display text in different fonts and text sizes.

To understand how the graphics operations are used, look at a complete but simple graphics program in listing 13.1. GRAPH1.CPP demonstrates some of the basic graphics features. It shows you how to initialize the graphics system and draw to the screen some graphics elements, a pie chart, and some text.

Listing 13.1 A Sample Visual C++ Graphics Program

```
1  //
2  // GRAPH1.CPP
3  // Introduces Visual C++ QuickWin Graphics.
```

(continues)

Listing 13.1 Continued

```
4   // Displays 6 concentric circles, some text, 5 rectangles, and a
5   // simple pie chart. This is followed by the prompt "Press Enter
6   // to continue."
7   //
8   // In the examples that follow, all drawings are relative
9   // to the current maximum X and maximum Y coordinates.
10  // These values vary depending on the graphics modes
11  // supported by the computer (e.g., CGA versus VGA). By making
12  // all drawing commands relative to the screen size, you
13  // enable this program to operate correctly on any monitor.
14  // Include the Microsoft graphics routines.
15  #include <graph.h>
16  #include <stdlib.h>
17  #include <stdio.h>
18  #include <string.h>
19  #include <conio.h>
20
21  // Global variables used for simplicity of demonstration.
22  //
23  struct _videoconfig video; // This gets the video configuration
24  // such as number of pixels, colors, etc.
25  int xmax,ymax; // max. # of horiz. & vertical pixels
26  //
27  // function prototypes
28  //
29  void StartGraphics(void); // Initializes video mode.
30  void DrawSomeCircles(int n);  // demo of ellipse() function
31  void DrawSomeText(const char *pText);  // demo of textout() function
32  void DrawPieChart(void); // demo of pie() function
33  void DrawFrame(int nThickness); // demo of rectangle()
34  void PromptAndWait(const char *pText); // Pauses the output.
35  void main()
36  {
37    StartGraphics(); // Initialize graphics system.
38    DrawSomeCircles(6); // Draw six circles using QuickWin calls.
39    DrawSomeText("Sample Text!");  // Pass text to show.
40    DrawFrame(5);  // Draw 5 rectangles.
41    DrawPieChart();  // Draw a pie chart.
42    PromptAndWait("Press any key to continue."); // Pause
43  }
44  //
45  // Initialize the graphics system
46  // to highest possible resolution.
47  //
48  void StartGraphics(void)
49  {
50    _getvideoconfig( &video ); // Get video configuration.
51    //
52    // Put video hardware into graphics mode.
53    //
54    if( !_setvideomode( _MAXRESMODE))
55        exit( 1 ); // FAILED TO SET ADAPTER CARD
56    //
57    // Get global information next.
```

```
58      //
59      xmax = video.numxpixels;   // Structure video has all info.
60      ymax = video.numypixels;   // Now have horiz. & vert. pixels.
61    }
62   //
63   // Draw some circles.
64   //
65   void DrawSomeCircles(int repCount)
66   {
67     int i, radius; // loop counter, radius of circle to draw
68     //
69     // Circles are described by a bounding rectangle. Define
70     // the rectangle using coordinates of upper-left and lower-
71     // right corners.
72     // Draw 'repCount' number of circles.
73     for(i=0; i < repCount; i++)
74     {
75       radius= i * 10; // Increase the radius each time...
76       ellipse( _GBORDER,100-radius,80-radius,150+radius, 130+radius );
77     }
78     PromptAndWait("Press any key to continue.");
79   }
80   //
81   // Draw some text in different colors.
82   //
83   void DrawSomeText(const char *pText)
84   {
85      short orig_txColor,left, top, right, bottom, k ;
86      long  orig_bkColor;
87      struct _rccoord orig_txPos;
88      orig_txColor = _gettextcolor();  // Save original text color.
89      orig_bkColor = _getbkcolor();  // Save original background color.
90      orig_txPos = _gettextposition(); // Save original text insertion pt.
91      clearscreen( _GCLEARSCREEN ); // Clear the screen.
92      //
93      // Center starting point for text in window.
94      // *** NOTE - Maximize window for best viewing.
95      //
96      gettextwindow( &top, &left, &bottom, &right ); // Get current window.
97      for(k=1; k < 16; k++)
98      {
99        settextposition((((bottom-top)/2)+k, (right-left)/2);
100       settextcolor(k);
101       outtext(pText);  // Display the text.
102     }
103     PromptAndWait("Press any key to continue.");
104     // Restore original foreground, background, and text position.
105     settextcolor( orig_txColor );
106     setbkcolor(orig_bkColor );
107     settextposition(orig_txPos.row, orig_txPos.col );
108     clearscreen( _GCLEARSCREEN );
109  } // End DrawSomeText().
110  //
111  //  Draw a frame around the entire screen.
112  //  nThickness is the thickness in pixels & number of
113  //  frames (rectangles) to draw.
114  //
```

(continues)

Listing 13.1 Continued

```
115  void DrawFrame(int nThickness)
116  {
117    int i;
118    for( i=0; i<nThickness; i++)
119      rectangle(_GBORDER, i+(i * 10), i+(i * 10),
120      xmax-(i * 10), ymax-(i * 10));
121    PromptAndWait("Press a key to continue");
122  }
123  //
124  // Display a prompt and wait for a keypress.
125  //
126  void PromptAndWait(const char *pText)
127  {
128    settextposition(0,0);
129    outtext(pText);
130    inchar(); // Wait for keystroke.
131    clearscreen( _GCLEARSCREEN );  // Erase screen.
132  }
133  //
134  // Draw a pie chart using different paint styles.
135  //
136  void DrawPieChart(void)
137  {
138    short origColor;
139    origColor = _getcolor();  // Save original color.
140    //
141    _setcolor(4);   // Draw using a RED pen/brush.
142    _pie(_GBORDER,80,50,240,150,240,12,0,150);
143    _setcolor(11);   // Draw using a CYAN pen/brush.
144    _pie(_GBORDER,80,50,240,150,0,150,240,150);
145    _setcolor(14);   // Draw using a yellow pen/brush.
146    _pie(_GFILLINTERIOR,80,50,240,150,240,150,240,12);
147    _setcolor(origColor);  // Restore original color.
148  }
```

Depending on the graphics adapter card and monitor that your PC uses, the picture can range from a white-on-black to a three-color pie chart. Figure 13.1 is a white-on-black screen shot of GRAPH1.CPP. The figure also illustrates the components of a typical QuickWin graphics display.

Using the QuickWin Graphics Library

The Microsoft graphics library is located in the file GRAPHICS.LIB. Programs that use the graphics library must place an #include <graph.h> directive at the top of the source file. GRAPH.H includes the function prototypes, constant symbols, and other elements that make up the graphics functionality in Visual C++.

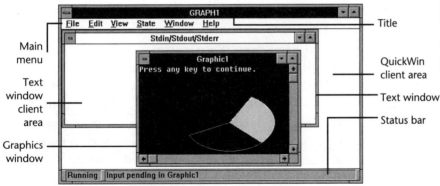

Fig. 13.1
The anatomy of a QuickWin graphics application.

To compile programs that use the graphics library, you must create a project file, as illustrated in previous chapters. To build the program in listing 13.1, choose **P**roject from the Visual C++ menu bar and then choose **N**ew. In the New Project dialog box, select QuickWin Application from the list box. Also remove the check mark in the **U**se Microsoft Foundation Classes box. Visual C++ automatically links GRAPHICS.LIB into your application because it is in your \MSVC\LIB directory.

The QuickWin Library Window

The QuickWin library provides a window for displaying graphics (refer to fig. 13.1). All graphics functions called from GRAPHICS.LIB are displayed in graphics windows. A QuickWin application has elements that are common to all QuickWin programs, as shown in figure 13.1. You are familiar with the first window displayed; it is the Stdin/Stdout/Stderr window seen in all previous programs in this book. The window emulates a DOS text screen for QuickWin applications so that they can run in the MS-Windows environment. This is the power of the QuickWin library—the capability to take a program written for DOS and then simply relink the application with the QuickWin library so that the application can run under Windows. This capability saves time and money when porting applications from the old DOS platform to the new Windows platform. In fact, Microsoft wrote the QuickWin library for this very reason.

The Stdin/Stdout/Stderr display window is meant for text output only, not graphics. In order for QuickWin to display DOS graphics, it must emulate the graphics hardware found on a typical DOS computer. MS-Windows provides the needed platform to perform this emulation.

Video Hardware Configuration for QuickWin

To use the graphics functions successfully, you must maintain independence across platforms with heterogenous video capabilities. Independence in a typical DOS-based application is maintained with the `getvideoconfig()` function. This function is called before `setvideomode()` is called. The return value from `getvideoconfig()`, a pointer to a `videoconfig` structure, is never hard-coded into a DOS program. The term *hard-coded* indicates that a programmer has provided, in the source code, the value of a parameter, such as the video system used by a program, instead of providing code to dynamically determine the value at runtime. Programmers can assure that an application will port seamlessly to different graphics hardware by not hard-coding the `videoconfig` structure into the application itself. QuickWin applications do not need to provide the same functionality because they run on top of Windows.

As mentioned in the preceding section, Windows provides emulation services to QuickWin applications. This means that you can set the video mode to any mode in a QuickWin program whether or not your computer hardware supports such a mode. An example is a CGA-based graphics program. Most computers running Windows have VGA or better graphic modes, but a QuickWin program can run in CGA mode because Windows can emulate a CGA system for the QuickWin library.

The `_videoconfig` structure is well documented in Visual C++'s help files but is of no concern to a QuickWin program. In fact, in a QuickWin program, several fields in the structure—such as the adapter, monitor, and memory fields representing the computer's video hardware—are set to 0. Windows provides all the "hardware" needed for your QuickWin graphics program.

The QuickWin User Interface

Figure 13.1, shown earlier, provides an overview of the QuickWin user interface. Like most Windows programs, a QuickWin application appears in a window complete with title bar, main menu, and status bar. Although most of your interaction occurs with the executing QuickWin application, you do have access to the framework's main menu. The menu provided by the QuickWin library contains **F**ile, **E**dit, **V**iew, **S**tate, **W**indow, and **H**elp menu items.

The File Menu. Unlike the **F**ile menu in typical Windows programs, the **F**ile menu here contains only one drop-down option, E**x**it. You can choose E**x**it to quit the application, or you can use the shortcut Ctrl+C. Ctrl+C is a typical key sequence that terminates a DOS program.

> **Note**
>
> Depending on the version of Visual C++ that you purchased, one of the smaller manuals contains a chapter on writing and using QuickWin applications. For the MSVC Professional Version 1.0 competitive upgrade, this manual is titled *C/C++ Version 7.0 Update*. For MSVC Professional Version 1.5, the manual is titled *Getting Started*.

The Edit Menu. The **E**dit menu provides several common editing functions found in most Windows programs. QuickWin allows you to **M**ark (select), **C**opy, and **P**aste information to and from the Windows Clipboard.

The View Menu. The **V**iew menu is important only to QuickWin graphics programs. The menu items **S**ize to Fit and **F**ull Screen enable you to control the size of your graphics window.

If you choose the **F**ull Screen option, the QuickWin user interface—including the main menu—will no longer be visible. You must press the Esc key or a mouse button to reactivate the user interface. If you choose the **S**ize to Fit option, QuickWin will try to fit your program's display into the available client area of the graphics window. If the client area is an inappropriate size, your graphics may appear distorted.

The State Menu. The **S**tate menu provides the **P**ause option, enabling you to suspend your application so that other Windows programs can execute. Later, you can return from the Windows program and choose **R**esume to continue your QuickWin program. The reason that you may want to suspend your application is that Windows shares resources, such as memory, with every application running under Windows. If too many applications are asking for the same resource, your computer can become sluggish or even stop working.

The Window Menu. The **W**indow menu options are similar to those in other Windows programs. Options enable you to cascade or tile your application's child windows, arrange iconized windows into a more aesthetic order, and hide such items as a toolbar or status bar. The **W**indow menu is similiar to the one found on the Visual Workbench's main menu.

The Help Menu. The **H**elp menu is another typical Windows menu. This choice allows you to activate the WinHelp program to seek help on a variety of QuickWin related topics.

Understanding the Graphics Coordinate System

Before understanding how graphics objects are drawn on-screen, you must briefly explore the coordinate system that describes how objects are placed. For all drawings, the upper-left corner of the screen is coordinate (0, 0), and the lower-right corner is coordinate (video.numxpixels, video.numypixels). For a 640 x 480 VGA display, the member numxpixels of the structure returned by getvideoconfig() is 640, and numypixels is 480. This tells you that the graphics screen is 640 pixels across by 480 pixels high. The word *pixel* is a peculiar contraction of *picture elements*. In practical terms, the screen's graphics resolution is 640 individual dots across by 480 dots high. Care must be taken when using these and other functions, as most are zero-based. In this example of a 640 x 480 screen, you would refer to the first line on the screen as pixels 0 through 639, not 1 through 640. Figure 13.2 shows the coordinates and their relationship to the screen.

Fig. 13.2
The Visual C++ graphics coordinate system places (0, 0) at the upper-left corner of the screen.

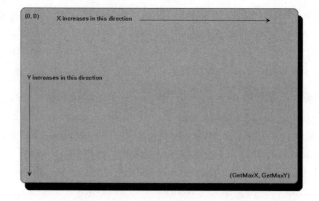

numxpixels and numypixels are structure members that contain the maximum x and maximum y values, respectively, of the graphics coordinates on-screen. The actual values vary depending on the screen resolution (CGA, EGA, or VGA). It is important that you refer to numxpixels and numypixels in your programs rather than writing the expected coordinate values as constants. The sample program in listing 13.1 cannot know the resolution of your computer's graphics screen. Therefore, you don't have to write a program that works only on Super VGA monitor, because all the x, y coordinate values are relative to numxpixels and numypixels. This way, the sample drawing is scaled to fit your computer screen.

Drawing Circles

Line 76 of listing 13.1 calls the GRAPHICS.LIB function _ellipse() to display a set of six overlapping circles (based on the constant 6 passed in line 38), centered in the top quarter of the screen. Other software packages that you may have used have a circle() function, but this is not the case in Visual C++. Mathematically speaking, a circle is just a special kind of ellipse, so circles and ellipses are drawn with the same function. The _ellipse() function is defined in GRAPH.H as follows:

```
short _far _ellipse(short control,short x1,short y1,short x2, short y2);
```

This prototype tells you that _ellipse() returns a *short* value and expects to be called with a far call. (You learned about near and far calls in the section "Memory Management" in Chapter 7, "Projects.") The prototype tells you also that the function has five parameters. The parameter control is a flag indicating whether the ellipse is to be filled. The parameters x1 and y1 are the upper-left coordinates of a bounding rectangle; x2 and y2 define the bottom-right corner. To draw a circle, you therefore define a *square* that surrounds the area in which the circle is drawn. Line 76 in listing 13.1 shows that the bounding rectangle of the first circle drawn is 50 pixels by 50 pixels. The radius of a circle is always half the size of the square. Here, the first circle has a radius of 25 pixels.

The sample program draws six circles by using a loop. Each time through the loop, the size of the bounding rectangle is increased, causing a larger circle to be drawn each time. This happens at line 75, which increases the size by 10 pixels.

Displaying Text

When you want to display text on the graphics screen, don't use cout; it does not work for displaying text in graphics mode. Instead, use combinations of the graphic text-output routines such as _settextposition(), _settextcolor(), and _outtext(). Another useful function is _gettextwindow(), which returns to you the current size of the window.

This is shown on line 96 of listing 13.1; the arguments are used in the call to _settextposition() on line 99 to move the text insertion point to the center of the screen. This sample program also saves the current text color, background color, and text position before drawing the text passed as the function parameter. Although saving these values is not actually necessary in this simple demonstration program, it is included to stimulate your thinking—you may need to save these values in a real production program. In fact, this is what has been done in the call to DrawSomeText(). After the text has been drawn 16 times (once for each primary color), the original text color, position, and so on, are restored at lines 105 through 107.

The sample program in listing 13.1 also draws a simple pie chart, a feat that is easy to do in Visual C++. The library function _pie() is used for this purpose. This function takes nine parameters. The first one is a flag indicating whether the pie chart is to be filled with the current color or left empty. For example, at line 146, the pie is drawn but not filled, as indicated by the first parameter's value of _GBORDER. But in line 146, a yellow pie is drawn *and* filled, as indicated by the _GFILLINTERIOR flag.

Now it gets tricky. The next four parameters define a bounding rectangle; the pie sections, like the circles described earlier, are drawn inside this rectangle. The center of the rectangle is the starting point of a vector, or line, that sweeps out an arc that draws the pie. The second point of the start vector is defined by the parameters x3 and y3. The end vector is at x4 and y4. The vector sweeps in a counterclockwise direction, and you must make sure that the end points meet if you want the pie chart to be contiguous. The pie-drawing function is illustrated in the sample program by the three pie sections created by the calls to the _pie() function:

```
141   _setcolor(4);    // Draw using a RED pen/brush.
142   _pie(_GBORDER,80,50,240,150,240,12,0,150);
143   _setcolor(11);   // Draw using a CYAN pen/brush.
144   _pie(_GBORDER,80,50,240,150,0,150,240,150);
145   _setcolor(14);   // Draw using a yellow pen/brush.
146   _pie(_GFILLINTERIOR,80,50,240,150,240,150,240,12 );
```

Line 142 draws the first pie, line 144 draws the second, and line 146 draws the last. Notice that the bounding rectangle does not change for each of these calls (80, 50, 240, and 150), but the last four parameters do change. Not only do they change, but the end point of the first is also the start point of the second, the end point of the second is the start point of the third, and so on. Thus, the pie chart is smoothly drawn and appears as intended.

The GRAPH1.CPP program has introduced several graphics library features. The following sections discuss additional concepts and elaborate on various procedures and functions found in the Visual C++ graphics interface.

Selecting Fonts and Character Sizes

You can use the `setfont()` function if you need to change the fonts or the point size used by your application. This function's prototype is as follows:

```
short __far _setfont( const char __far *options )
```

The *options* parameter describes the font—its name, size, and display characteristics (such as font height in pixels). A font must be registered before it can be used; you accomplish this with the function `_registerfont()`, which has as a parameter the directory containing available fonts. For example, if you want to register all fonts in the directory C:\MYFONTS, your call would look like this:

```
_registerfonts("C:\\MYFONTS\\*.FON");
```

The *options* parameter for `_setfont()` is somewhat involved. You should consult the Visual C++ help file for full details as well as a sample program. But, in essence, the parameter consists of the name of the typeface, its height and width, and a "best fit" flag. To set the font to Courier with a height of 30 pixels and a width of 24, you would use this call to `_setfont()`:

```
_setfont("t'Courier'h30w24b");
```

Detecting Graphics Errors

Errors encountered during the use of Visual C++ graphics should be processed when the routine is called. The most important error traps are the calls to `_getvideoconfig()` and `_setvideomode()`. All subsequent calls to graphics routines depend on success with these.

Assuming that your program has no difficulty with `_getvideoconfig()` and `_setvideomode()`, the next likely error traps are those dealing with pixel addressing, color, and attribute references. For example, trying to address a pixel at the point (-32, 350) is invalid because –32 is less than 0. Be sure to include checks in your programs that test for these conditions. These error checks can be easily added to a global function. The best way to handle graphics errors is through good, solid design. This goes a long way in preventing errors from ever occuring.

The *_grstatus( )* Error-Reporting Function

As part of your error checking, use the _grstatus() routine after each call to a graphics routine that could possibly generate an error. The function's prototype is as follows:

```
short __far _grstatus( void )
```

This function returns the status of the most recently used graphics routine. The return value should be tested. A value of less than 0 indicates an error, and a value greater than 0 indicates warnings. A return value of 0 indicates that the graphics routine request was successful. The following functions are the routines that cannot use _grstatus():

```
_displaycursor()

_getactivepage()

_getbkcolor()

_getgtextvector()

_gettextcolor()

_gettextposition()

_gettextwindow()

_getvideoconfig()

_getvisualpage()

_outmem()

_outtext()

_unregisterfonts()

_wrapon()
```

QuickWin Error Reporting

QuickWin applications provide two error messages in addition to the values returned by _grstatus(). The messages are displayed in either a QuickWin Error message box or a QuickWin Fatal Error message box. You can dismiss either message box by clicking the OK button.

The QuickWin Error message box displays an error number and a message indicating the general class of the error. The QuickWin system does not terminate your current application when you click the OK button, but allows the user to continue. This message is frequently seen as the result of not enough memory being available for the program to perform the current graphics routine.

The next error message displayed, QuickWin fatal error, does terminate your application after you click the OK button. The message indicates that a severe error occurred while QuickWin tried to execute your program and that no chance of reactivating the application exists. Insufficient memory to load and execute the application is a typical cause of this message.

Using Viewports

A viewport describes a window or region on-screen at which all drawing will take place. Initially, the viewport is set to encompass the entire screen. After you call _setviewport(), all subsequent drawing commands are mapped to screen positions relative to the location of the viewport region. Figure 13.3 shows a screen image containing a viewport region. By setting a _setviewport() option, you can restrict your drawings to appear only within the viewport. Any portion of an object that does not appear outside the viewport is clipped at the edge of the viewport and does not draw outside the region. In Visual C++, the prototype for _setviewport() is as follows:

```
void __far _setviewport( short x1, short y1, short x2, short y2 )
```

The parameters x1 and y1 define the upper-left corner of the viewport; x2 and y2 define the lower-right corner. Because the routine returns void, you will have to use _grstatus() to trap any errors.

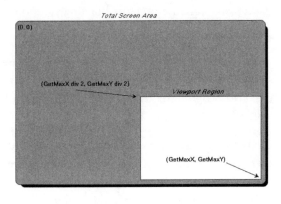

Fig. 13.3
The smaller box is a viewport region defined in the lower-right quarter of the screen.

For example, to set up a viewing portal that has an upper-left corner located at (100, 70) and that extends down to the lower-right corner of the screen, write

```
setviewport (100, 70, xmax, ymax);
```

where xmax and ymax represent the pixel resolution of the screen, obtained by calling _getvideoconfig(), as shown earlier.

If you now execute the drawing commands

```
_moveto(0, 0);
_lineto(50, 50);
```

the line's location is mapped to the viewport region, so that (0, 0) is at physical screen location (100, 70), and (50, 50) is at physical coordinate (150, 120). Figure 13.4 shows the result.

Fig. 13.4
How a line and other drawing commands are mapped to a viewport region.

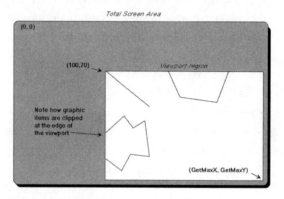

You can experiment with _setviewport() by placing calls to _setviewport() inside the GRAPH1.CPP program. As a first step, you might try placing the following statement just before the _ellipse drawing section in the loop:

```
_setviewport(20, 20, xmax, ymax/3 * 2);
```

Note that this slides the drawing down and over by 20 pixels and restricts the y coordinate to the top two-thirds of the screen. Give it a try and see what happens. Use _grstatus() right after the call to _setviewport() and examine its return value by using the Visual C++ debugger.

Viewports are often used to restrict new graphics from overrunning other graphics on the screen. For example, if your programs draw a rectangular border around the screen by calling rectangle(0, 0, xmax, ymax), you can protect the rectangle from being overwritten by calling

```
_setviewport(1,1, xmax - 1, ymax - 1);
```

This moves the viewport to one pixel inside the bounding rectangle and ensures that any items you subsequently draw are clipped at the edge of the viewport before they can overwrite the border.

Using the Current Pointer

When you type text in the Visual editor, your current location in the edit window is indicated with a flashing cursor. The graphics system maintains a similar entity, called the *current pointer*, which is never visible on-screen. The current pointer is used for drawing commands that draw relative to the viewport, and tracks the location at which the next drawing command will take place.

To position the current pointer (abbreviated CP) to a location on the screen, use the _moveto() function. To position the CP to the center of the screen, write

```
_moveto(xmax/2, ymax/2);
```

Next, you can draw an object relative to this starting point, as in

```
_lineto(0,0);
```

This results in a line drawn from the midpoint of the screen to the upper-left corner.

The following drawing commands use and set the position of the CP (all other commands have no effect on the CP):

```
_lineto(), _moveto(), _outtext()
```

You can find the current location of the current pointer by using the gettextposition() function, which returns the current pointer as an xycoord structure, defined in GRAPH.H.

Selecting Colors

Visual C++ graphics support 2, 4, 16, or 256 color choices, depending on the graphics mode you selected. Colors on the PC are handled in a manner similar to the way an artist mixes colors. The artist squeezes tubes of paint of various colors onto a palette board and mixes a selection of color choices to be used in a painting. Thereafter, the artist selects colors by choosing one of the paints from the palette.

On the PC, you draw a graphics object on-screen and select its color from a color palette. Instead of directly selecting, for example, red or purple, you select the palette entry that contains red or purple. Here are the standard color constants:

```
_BLACK

_BLUE

_GREEN

_CYAN

_RED

_MAGENTA

_BROWN

_WHITE

_GRAY

_LIGHTBLUE

_LIGHTGREEN

_LIGHTCYAN

_LIGHTRED

_LIGHTMAGENTA

_YELLOW

_BRIGHTWHITE
```

These color constants are used in calls to _setcolor(), and they apply to all video modes. Each of these constants selects a color from the corresponding standard 16-color palette.

Because the Visual C++ graphics system is optimized for 16-color VGA displays, it does not provide simultaneous 256-color support on Super VGA monitors. Through a programming trick, however, you can redefine each of the 16 entries in the basic color palette to be any color you want. That's because the VGA can display 16 or 256 different colors, each selected from a palette of 262,144 separate colors. See the section on the _remappalette() function later in this chapter for details.

Choosing Colors from the Color Palette

To make the next object that you draw appear in the color red, call
_setcolor() before drawing the object:

```
_setcolor(4);
_moveto(10,10);
_lineto(70,125);
```

This code selects the fourth entry in the color palette. (For 16-color palettes,
the palette is indexed with values from 0 to 15.) The result is a red line from
(10, 10) to (70, 125). _setcolor() changes the current or active drawing color
and affects all subsequent drawing commands until _setcolor() is called
again.

An interesting side effect of color palettes is that you can rearrange all the
screen's current colors by changing just the palette. You don't have to redraw
any of the objects—you just change the underlying palette. Two procedures
enable you to alter the palette entries: _remappalette() changes an individual
entry, and _remapallpalette() changes several or all of the entries in a single
procedure call. For example, to change the fifth entry to blue, type

```
_remappalette ( 5, BLUE );
```

Any objects previously drawn in color number 5 are instantly changed to
blue.

The actual set of colors available in the color palette depends on the type of
monitor in use, the graphics adapter, and the resolution of the screen, plus
the graphics mode in which Windows is currently running.

The _remappalette( ) Function. For VGA device drivers, the 16 basic palette
entries are programmable. By using _remappalette(), you can precisely
specify the amount of red, green, or blue for each index in the palette.

Each of the color values ranges from 0 to 63, with 0 being the lowest intensity and 63 being the brightest intensity. By mixing various intensities of red,
green, and blue, you can create custom colors, up to a maximum of 262,144
different combinations. _remappalette is defined as

```
long __far _remappalette( short index, long color );
```

Selecting Interior Colors and Patterns for Objects

Use _setcolor() to choose the active color for line-drawing and point-
plotting operations, including the drawing of the borders of circles and pie
charts. To color the interior of a bounded object (circles, pie slices, rectangles,

polygons, and so on), use the `_setfillmask()` function. With `_setfillmask()`, you can choose a variety of standard patterns to fill the interior of an object, including empty, solid, dotted, and cross-hatched patterns.

You can use `_setfillmask()` to establish a custom design pattern for filling the interior of all filled graphics objects (rectangles, circles, and so on). The object is filled with the current color as last set by `_setcolor()`. The prototype for the function is

```
void __far _setfillmask( unsigned char __far *mask );
```

Setting up the bit pattern that you need in order to use this function is difficult. However, it's a lot of fun to create new designs, so the CUSTOMPA.CPP program in listing 13.2 provides a custom design editor that makes it easy to create your own custom fill patterns.

Listing 13.2 A Demonstration of the Use of *setfillpattern( )* by Implementing a Custom Pattern Editor

```
 1   // CUSTOMPA.CPP
 2   // Use this program to help you design a custom fill
 3   // pattern. After the 8 x 8 grid displays, you can use
 4   // the arrow keys to navigate to a specific bit and set
 5   // it to a 1 by pressing the 1 key, or to clear the bit
 6   // by pressing the 0 key. Press the Esc key to terminate
 7   // data entry, and a sample filled circle is displayed on
 8   // the screen. Press Enter to return to pattern editing
 9   // or press Esc key again to terminate the program.
10   //
11   #include <graph.h>
12   #include <stdlib.h>
13   #include <conio.h>
14   #include <ctype.h>
15   #include <memory.h>        // for memset() call
16   #include <iostream.h>      // for cin, etc.
17   typedef int BOOL;          // boolean
18   struct _videoconfig video; // This gets the video configuration.
19
20   int xmax,ymax;             // max. number of pixels
21   //
22   // function prototypes
23   //
24   void DisplayPattern(const unsigned char *pPat);
25   void StartGraphics();
26   // keyboard values for extended keystrokes and '0' and '1'
27   const unsigned keyUpArrow    = '8'; // 72 << 8;
28   const unsigned keyLeftArrow  = '4'; // 75 << 8;
29   const unsigned keyRightArrow = '6'; // 77 << 8;
30   const unsigned keyDownArrow  = '2'; // 80 << 8;
31   const unsigned keyEscape     = 27;
32   const unsigned key0          = 48;
```

```
33  const unsigned key1          = 49;
34  unsigned char userPattern[8];
35  //
36  void main()
37  {
38    memset(userPattern, 0xff, 8); // initially all 1s
39  //
40  //
41    _clearscreen( _GCLEARSCREEN );
42  //
43  //  Set up graphics mode.
44  //
45    StartGraphics();
46    _settextposition(1,17);
47    _outtext( "Make sure NUM LOCK key is ON.");
48    _settextposition(2,17);
49    _outtext( "Use arrow keys ON NUMERICAL KEYPAD to navigate.");
50    _settextposition(3,17);
51    _outtext( "Press 1 to set a bit, 0 to clear a bit.");
52    _outtext( "Press Esc ONCE to see fillmask -- 2nd Esc ends program.");
53    int x = 1;
54    int y = 1;
55    unsigned keyPress = 0;
56    unsigned char tmp;        // for bit manipulations
57    do
58    {
59      _settextposition(x,y);
60      DisplayPattern(userPattern);
61      _settextposition(x,y); // Go to starting position.
62  //
63  //  Edit the pattern until user presses Esc.
64  //
65      int loop= 1;
66      while(loop)
67      {
68       keyPress= _inchar(); // Wait for key press.
69        switch(keyPress)
70        {
71          case keyEscape: // Escape, go draw ellipse.
72           loop= 0;
73          break;
74          case key0:        // Clear the bit.
75            _outtext("0");  // Draw a "0"
76          switch(y)
77            {
78              case 1:
79                tmp= 0x7f;
80              break;
81              case 2:
82                tmp= 0xbf;
83              break;
84              case 3:
85                tmp= 0xdf;
86              break;
87              case 4:
```

(continues)

Listing 13.2 Continued

```
 88              tmp= 0xef;
 89          break;
 90          case 5:
 91              tmp= 0xf7;
 92          break;
 93          case 6:
 94              tmp= 0xfb;
 95          break;
 96          case 7:
 97              tmp= 0xfd;
 98          break;
 99          case 8:
100              tmp= 0xfe;
101           break;
102           default:
103           tmp= 0xff;   // Don't change anything.
104           break;
105         }  // End test switch.
106         userPattern[x] = userPattern[x] & tmp;
107       break;
108       case key1: // Set the bit.
109         _outmem("1",1);
110          switch(y)
111          {
112             case 1:
113             tmp= 0x80;
114             break;
115             case 2:
116             tmp= 0x40;
117          break;
118          case 3:
119             tmp= 0x20;
120          break;
121          case 4:
122             tmp= 0x10;
123          break;
124          case 5:
125             tmp= 0x08;
126          break;
127          case 6:
128             tmp= 0x04;
129          break;
130          case 7:
131             tmp= 0x02;
132          break;
133          case 8:
134             tmp= 0x01;
135          break;
136          default:
137             tmp= 0xff;  // Don't change anything.
138          }  // End test switch.
139         userPattern[x] = userPattern[x] | tmp;;
140       break;
141       case keyUpArrow:     // Move "cursor" up a row.
142         if(x > 1) x--;
143       break;
```

```
144              case keyDownArrow:    // Move "cursor" down a row.
145                if(x < 8) x++;
146              break;
147              case keyLeftArrow:    // Move "cursor" to next column.
148                if(y > 1) y--;
149              break;
150              case keyRightArrow:   // Move cursor to previous column.
151                if(y < 8) y++;
152              break;
153            } // Switch key pressed.
154            _settextposition(x,y); // Go to new position.
155        }
156  //
157  // After editing the pattern, return to graphics mode
158  // and display an object containing the new pattern.
159  //
160        _setvideomode( _MAXRESMODE);
161        _setfillmask(userPattern);
162        _ellipse(_GFILLINTERIOR , xmax/2, ymax/2,xmax/3, ymax/3);
163    } while(_inchar() != keyEscape);
164    _setvideomode( _DEFAULTMODE);
165  //
166  }  // END MAIN
167  //
168  // Initialize the graphics system via auto detection.
169  //
170  //
171  void StartGraphics()
172  {
173  //
174  //  Determine the video resolution,
175  //  # of colors, pages, etc.
176    _getvideoconfig( &video ); // Get video configuration.
177  //
178  // Put video hardware into highest possible resolution mode.
179  //
180    if( !_setvideomode( _MAXRESMODE))
181      exit( 1 );        // FAILED TO SET ADAPTER CARD
182    xmax = video.numxpixels; // Structure 'video' has all info.
183    ymax = video.numypixels; // Now have horiz. & vert. pixels.
184  }
185  //
186  // Display the entire pattern on-screen.
187  //
188  void DisplayPattern(const unsigned char *pPat)
189  {
190    for(int x=1; x < 9; x++)
191    {
192      for(int y= 1; y < 9; y++)
193      {
194        _settextposition(x,y);
195        if(userPattern[x-1] )
196          _outtext("1");
197        else
198          _outtext("0");
199      } // y
200    } // x
201  }
```

CUSTOMPA.CPP illustrates a tool that you can use to create new custom fill patterns for your graphics applications. The function _setfillmask() is used when a drawing routine specifies that the object's interior is to be filled. This is indicated by the *control* parameter in calls such as _ellipse(), which has as its first parameter a flag indicating whether the ellipse should be painted. For example, the line

```
_ellipse(_GFILLINTERIOR, x1,y1,x2,y2);
```

would draw the ellipse within the given bounding rectangle and paint it with the current color. The parameter _GFILLINTERIOR would be replaced with _GBORDER if the ellipse were not to be painted.

Using and Filling Polygons

On occasion, the object that you want to draw may not be a conventional shape, such as a rectangle or circle. You can use _polygon() to draw simple or complex polygon shapes in which each vertex is specified with a flag to indicate painting, a pointer to an array of structures that hold the (x,y) coordinates of the vertices, and the total number of vertices. The routine is defined as

```
short __far _polygon( short control, const struct _xycoord __far
    *points, short numpoints );
```

The polygon is drawn in a "connect the dots" manner, moving from vertex 1 to vertex 2 to vertex 3, and so on. Figure 13.5 shows a house-shaped object drawn with _polygon().

Fig. 13.5
An example of an object that can be represented as a sequence of points.

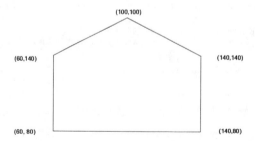

If the polygon encloses a region, you must specify one of the points at least twice. In figure 13.5, drawing the polygon requires *points* to list vertices 1, 2, 3, 4, and 5 and then to draw the final segment from vertex 5 back to 1. As a result, *points* must contain six sets of coordinates (1, 2, 3, 4, 5, and 1). Finally, *numpoints* must be 6, because there are 6 vertices. Listing 13.3 shows how to set up the point coordinates.

Listing 13.3 A Demonstration of the Use of the *drawpoly( )* Function

```
 1  // DRAWPOLY.CPP
 2  //
 3  main()
 4   {
 5    struct _xycoord polyside[6];   // Holds points of polygon.
 6    polyside[0].xcoord = 100;      // Initialize with vertices.
 7    polyside[0].ycoord = 100;
 8    polyside[1].xcoord = 60;
 9    polyside[1].ycoord = 140;
10    polyside[2].xcoord = 60;
11    polyside[2].ycoord = 180;
12    polyside[3].xcoord = 140;
13    polyside[3].ycoord = 180;
14    polyside[4].xcoord = 140;
15    polyside[4].ycoord = 140;
16    polyside[5].xcoord = 100;
17    polyside[5].ycoord = 100;
18    _polygon(_GBORDER,polyside,6); // Draw house-shaped polygon.
19    //
20    // _GBORDER draws but does not paint (fill) the polygon.
21    //
22  } // end of drawpoly.cpp
```

The _polygon() function draws the polygon by using the current _setcolor() color. In listing 13.3, replacing _GBORDER with _GFILLINTERIOR would draw the figure and fill it with the current color, the last color selected with _setcolor().

Drawing Charts in QuickWin Applications

Creating charts is the graphics subspecialty concerned with displaying data in the form of line, bar, pie, and other statistical charts. Visual C++ provides special routines to support the creation of these charts, although realistically they require a substantial amount of supplementary code to create useful general-purpose routines. This section shows you how to create a full-featured bar chart display program.

When you run the sample bar chart program presented in listing 13.4, enter sample data when prompted. For this demonstration program, you can type **999** to signify that you have entered the last data value. For the bar chart, the data value that you type corresponds to the y-axis. After entering each value, you are prompted for a label. This label becomes the x-axis label. For instance, if you draw a bar graph of sales per month, each bar or x-axis position is labeled with the month, and the height of the bar corresponds to the data or y-axis value.

The main program body prompts for the graph's title and the actual data values to be graphed. You can enter optional x-axis and y-axis titles for the chart. After the data is entered, the program calls DrawBarChart.

Drawing the actual bar in a bar chart is easy: Visual C++ provides a nifty bar() function specifically for drawing the bar portion of a bar chart. But there's more to drawing a bar chart than the bar itself. For one thing, if the chart is going to show more than relationships among data, you must add a y-axis and a grid to indicate the approximate value of each bar. Along the bottom or x-axis of the chart, you must add labels identifying what each bar represents. If your chart has negative values, you must ensure that positive values are drawn above the y-axis 0 line and that negative values are drawn below the 0 line. Listing 13.4 contains a complete bar chart drawing program.

Listing 13.4 A Program That Draws a Bar Chart

```
1   // BARCHART.CPP
2   //
3   // Demonstrates how to create a simple bar chart.
4   // Minimal error checking enforced--demo purposes only!
5   //
6   #include <graph.h>
7   #include <strstrea.h>
8   #include <iomanip.h>
9   #include <stdlib.h>
10  #include <string.h>
11  #include <conio.h>
12  #include <stdio.h>
13  #include <math.h>
14  #define RED 4  // colors to use
15  #define WHITE 15
16  #define GREEN 10
17  #define CYAN 11
18  typedef int BOOL;      // Boolean flag
19  //
20  // global constants
21  //
22  const int maxDataValues = 20;
23  const int maxTitleLen = 128;
24  const int maxLabelLen = 64;
25  struct _videoconfig video;  // This gets the video configuration
26  // such as number of pixels, colors, etc.
27  int xmax,ymax;     // max. # of horiz. & vertical pixels
28  short left, top, right, bottom; // text window coordinates
29  int nVals;  // number of data points entered
```

```
30   class CBarChart
31   {
32     public:
33     void CalcMinAndMax(float &min, float &max, BOOL &fThousands,
34     float *pData, int nVals);
35     void DrawBarChart(char *pMainTitle, char *pxAxisTitle,
36     char *pyAxisTitle,
37     char  pLabels[][maxLabelLen],
38     float *pData, int nVals);
39     void DrawBars(int xLeft, int yTop, int xRight, int yBottom,
40     float minVal, float maxVal,
41     float *pData, int nVals);
42     void DrawTitles(char *pMainTitle, char *pxAxisTitle,
43     char *pyAxisTitle,
44     int xLeft, int yTop,
45     int xRight, int yBottom,
46     long textColor = _WHITE);
47     void DrawXAxisLabels(int nVals,char pLabels[][maxLabelLen]);
48     void DrawYAxisInfo(int xLeft, int yTop,
49     int xRight,int yBottom,
50     float minVal, float maxVal, int nDivs,
51     long lineColor = _WHITE,
52     long textColor = _WHITE);
53     int GetGraphInfo(char *pMainTitle, char *pxAxisTitle,
54     char *pyAxisTitle,
55     char  pLabels[][maxLabelLen],float *pData);
56     void StartGraphics();
57     void PromptAndWait(const char *pText,
58                        long textColor= _WHITE);
59     inline void swap(int &a, int &b)
60     {
61       int t;
62       t = a; a = b; b = t;
63     }
64   }; // class CBarChart
65   void main()
66   {
67     char mainTitle[maxTitleLen];
68     char xAxisTitle[maxTitleLen];
69     char yAxisTitle[maxTitleLen];
70     char labels[maxDataValues][maxLabelLen];
71     float data[maxDataValues];
72     CBarChart BarChart;
73 // Get the title and data values.
74     nVals = BarChart.GetGraphInfo(mainTitle, xAxisTitle,
75                                   yAxisTitle, labels, data);
76     if(nVals == 0) {
77       cout << "No data entered!" << endl;
78       exit(1);
79     }
80     BarChart.StartGraphics();
81     BarChart.DrawBarChart(mainTitle, xAxisTitle, yAxisTitle,
82                           labels, data, nVals);
83     BarChart.PromptAndWait("Press Enter key to exit...");
84     setvideomode( _DEFAULTMODE);
85   } // end main()
86   //
```

(continues)

Listing 13.4 Continued

```
 87   // Initialize the graphics system via auto detection.
 88   //
 89   //
 90   void CBarChart::StartGraphics()
 91   {
 92    // Request auto detection of graphics capability.
 93    _getvideoconfig( &video );       // Get video configuration.
 94    //
 95    // Put video hardware into graphics mode.
 96    //
 97    if( !_setvideomode( _MAXRESMODE))
 98       exit( 1 );     // FAILED TO SET ADAPTER CARD
 99    //
100    // Get global information next.
101    //
102    xmax = video.numxpixels;       // Structure 'video' has all info.
103    ymax = video.numypixels;   // Now have horiz. & vert. pixels.
104    gettextwindow( &top, &left, &bottom, &right ); // Get current window.
105   }
106   //
107   // Display a prompt and wait for a keypress.
108   //
109   void CBarChart::PromptAndWait(const char *pText, long textColor)
110   {
111    _settextcolor(RED);
112    _settextposition(bottom-3,left);
113    _outtext(pText);
114    _inchar();
115   }
116   //
117   // Get the graph titles and data values.
118   // Return the number of values read.
119   //
120   int CBarChart::GetGraphInfo(char *pMainTitle,
121   char *pxAxisTitle, char *pyAxisTitle, char pLabels[][maxLabelLen],
122   float *pData)
123   {
124    _clearscreen( _GCLEARSCREEN );      // Erase screen.
125    // Use cin.getline() rather than >> to allow white space.
126    // Use getline() instead of get() to discard '\n'.
127    cout << "Enter main graph title: " << endl;
128    cin.getline(pMainTitle, maxTitleLen);
129    cout << "Enter x-axis title: " << endl;
130    cin.getline(pxAxisTitle, maxTitleLen);
131    cout << "Enter y-axis title: " << endl;
132    cin.getline(pyAxisTitle, maxTitleLen);
133    // Get all the data.
134    // Note that multiple values on one line are okay.
135    cout << "Enter data values (99999 when done): " << endl;
136    int nVals = 0;
137    float val;
138    while(1)
139    {
140       cin >> val;
141       if(val == 99999)
```

```
142          break;
143        pData[nVals++] = val;
144      }
145      // Discard any trailing characters.
146      cin.ignore(255, '\n');
147      // Get a label for each piece of data.
148      for(int i=0; i<nVals; i++)
149      {
150        cout << "Enter label #" << i << ": " << endl;
151        cin.getline(pLabels[i], maxLabelLen);
152      }
153      return nVals;
154    }
155    //
156    // Find the minimum and maximum values in a dataset.
157    // Set fThousands to TRUE if the absolute value of any entry
158    // is greater than 1000.
159    //
160    void CBarChart::CalcMinAndMax(float &min, float &max,
161              BOOL &fThousands, float *pData, int nVals)
162    {
163     min = max = 0.0;
164     for(int i=0; i<nVals; i++)
165     {
166       if(pData[i] > max)
167           max = pData[i];
168       if(pData[i] < min)
169           min = pData[i];
170     }
171     fThousands = ((fabs(min) > 1000) || (fabs(max) > 1000));
172    //
173    //
174    // Draw the y-axis divisions and value labels, given the
175    // pixel coordinates for the upper-left and lower-right
176    // corners of the display area, the range of values that
177    // the axis spans, the number of divisions to use, and
178    // the color for the lines and text.
179    //
180    void CBarChart::DrawYAxisInfo(int xLeft, int yTop,
181    int xRight,int yBottom, float minVal, float maxVal, int nDivs,
182    long lineColor, long textColor)
183    {
184    //
185    int tick= 0;  // value of each tick mark 100, 200, etc.
186    tick= (int)maxVal/nDivs;
187    //
188    float range = maxVal - minVal;
189    float dy = range / nDivs;
190    int dyPix = (yBottom - yTop) / nDivs;
191    // Calculate # of decimal places to show.
192    int ndigits;
193    if(fabs(dy) < 10/nDivs)
194        ndigits = 2;
195    else if(fabs(dy) < 100/nDivs)
196         ndigits = 1;
197    else
```

(continues)

Listing 13.4 Continued

```
198        ndigits = 0;
199  for(int i=0; i<=nDivs; i++)
200  {
201  // Pixel value for line and text output.
202  int yPix = yTop + i*dyPix;
203  // Don't want a dotted line on the edges!
204  if((i != 0) && (i != nDivs))
205  {
206   _setcolor((short)lineColor);
207   _moveto(xLeft, yPix );
208   _lineto( xRight, yPix);
209  }
210  // Draw the label to the left of the graph.
211  float label = maxVal - i*dy;
212  char buf[24];
213  memset(buf,0,sizeof(buf));
214  ostrstream os(buf, 24);
215  // Always use fixed point.
216  os.setf(ios::fixed, ios::floatfield);
217  // Display the decimal point, sometimes.
218  if(ndigits)
219  {
220    os.setf(ios::showpoint);
221    os << setprecision(ndigits);
222  }
223  // Display ndigits after the decimal.
224  os << setprecision(ndigits) << label << ends;
225  settextcolor(WHITE);
226  settextposition((top+20)- (i*3 ),12);
227  sprintf(buf,"%d",tick * i);
228  outtext(buf);
229  }
230  // Draw the 0 line if it's in the display area.
231  if((minVal < 0) && (maxVal > 0))
232  {
233    int pixRange = yBottom - yTop;
234    int yPix = yTop + (int)(maxVal/range * pixRange);
235    _setcolor(lineColor);
236    _moveto(xLeft, yPix );
237    _lineto( xRight, yPix);
238  }
239  }
240  //
241  // Draw the x-axis labels given the left and right pixel
242  // coordinates, the number of values, and the labels.
243  //
244  void CBarChart::DrawXAxisLabels(int nVals,char
pLabels[][maxLabelLen])
245  {
246    short nWidth= 60; // max. number of chars to go around for
labels
247    short nEach = nWidth/nVals; // what each item in graph gets
248    int plen, len;
249    for(int i=0; i < nVals; i++)
250    {
```

```
251    // Truncate each label if it's too long.
252    // Use a copy -- don't modify the original.
253     char copy[maxLabelLen];
254     strcpy(copy, pLabels[i]);
255 //
256      plen= strlen(copy);       // length of this label
257      if(plen > nEach)
258      {
259        strncpy(copy,copy,nEach);
260        copy[nEach]= '\0';
261      }
262      len= strlen(copy);  // Have true length of label, abrv. if nec.
263      // Write the label in the center of this division.
264     _settextcolor(WHITE);
265      // _settextposition(23,22+ (i*15));   // baseline
266     _settextposition(23,20+(i * nEach) );
267      _outtext(copy);
268   }
269 }
270 //
271 // Draw the bars themselves.
272 //
273 void CBarChart::DrawBars(int xLeft, int yTop,
274 int xRight, int yBottom, float minVal, float maxVal,
275 float *pData, int nVals)
276 {
277   // line style for each bar's bounding rectangle
278   // the width of each x division, in pixels
279   int dxPix = (xRight - xLeft) / nVals;
280   // the percent width of each bar in its pixel division
281   // 0.8 means 80 percent.
282   const float widthPct = 0.8;
283   const float barWidth = widthPct * dxPix;
284   const int maxColor = 16; // max colors
285   int color = 1;
286   //
287   // Calculate the base line. It will be 0 if 0 is on
288   // the graph, or the top or bottom edge otherwise.
289   //
290    float yrange = maxVal - minVal;
291    int ypixRange = yBottom - yTop;
292    int yBase = yTop + (int)(maxVal/yrange * ypixRange);
293    if(yBase < yTop)
294        yBase = yTop;
295    if(yBase > yBottom)
296        yBase = yBottom;
297    for(int i=0; i<nVals; i++)
298    {
299      // Calculate the left edge of the bar so that it
300      // will be centered in its division.
301      int x = xLeft + i*dxPix + (dxPix - barWidth)/2;
302      // Calculate the top and bottom edges of the bar.
303      float yPct = (maxVal - pData[i]) / yrange;
304      int yBarTop = yTop + (int)(yPct * ypixRange);
305      int yBarBottom = yBase;
306      // Ensure that yBarTop is always the top edge.
307      if(yBarTop > yBarBottom)
```

(continues)

Listing 13.4 Continued

```
308          swap(yBarTop, yBarBottom);
309      // Draw the bar and its bounding rectangle.
310      color= GREEN;
311      _setcolor(GREEN);
312      _rectangle(_GFILLINTERIOR,x, yBarTop, x+barWidth, yBarBottom);
313    }
314  }
315  //
316  // Draw the titles.
317  //
318  void CBarChart::DrawTitles(char *pMainTitle,char *pxAxisTitle,
319  char *pyAxisTitle, int xLeft, int yTop, int xRight, int yBottom,
320  long textColor)
321  {
322   // Use this to make string copies that you can modify.
323   char copy[maxTitleLen];
324   int xWidth = xRight - xLeft;
325   int xCenter = xLeft + xWidth / 2;
326   int yHeight = yBottom - yTop;
327   int yCenter = yTop + yHeight / 2;
328   settextcolor((short)textColor);
329   // main title
330   strcpy(copy, pMainTitle);
331   settextposition(2,(right-left)/2);
332   outtext(copy);
333   // x-axis title
334   strcpy(copy, pxAxisTitle);
335   settextposition(25,(right-left)/2);
336   outtext( copy);
337   // y-axis title
338   strcpy(copy, pyAxisTitle);
339   settextposition((bottom-top)/2,5 );
340   outtext( copy);
341  }
342  //
343  // Draw a bar chart, complete with bars, axes, and titles.
344  //
345  void CBarChart::DrawBarChart(char *pMainTitle,
346  char *pxAxisTitle, char *pyAxisTitle,
347  char  pLabels[][maxLabelLen], float *pData, int nVals)
348  {
349    float minVal;
350    float maxVal;
351    BOOL fThousands; // true if abs(any data) > 1000
352  //
353  // Find the minimum and maximum values. Then, if
354  // any of the data is in the thousands, scale it down.
355  //
356    CalcMinAndMax(minVal, maxVal, fThousands, pData, nVals);
357    if(fThousands)
358    {
359        for(int i=0; i<nVals; i++)
360          pData[i] /= 1000.0;
361        minVal /= 1000.0;
362        maxVal /= 1000.0;
```

```
363     }
364     //
365     // Scale the minimum and maximum values so that there's
366     // some space at the top and bottom of the graph.
367     //
368     const float minScaleVal = 0.1;
369     const float maxScaleVal = 0.1;
370     if(minVal > 0)
371         minVal *= (1.0 - minScaleVal);
372     else
373         minVal *= (1.0 + minScaleVal);
374     if(maxVal > 0)
375         maxVal *= (1.0 + maxScaleVal);
376     else
377         maxVal *= (1.0 - maxScaleVal);
378     //
379     // Draw the rectangle around the charting area.
380     //
381     float xLeft   = 0.20 * (float)xmax;
382     float xRight  = 0.95 * (float)xmax;
383     float yTop    = 0.20 * (float)ymax;
384     float yBottom = 0.85 * (float)ymax;
385     rectangle( _GBORDER,(short)xLeft, (short)yTop,
386                (short) xRight,(short) yBottom);
387     if(fThousands) // If using scaled data, say so!
388     {
389         _settextposition(top+4,left+15);
390         _settextcolor(WHITE);
391         _outtext("In 1,000's");
392     }
393     // Draw the titles.
394     DrawTitles(pMainTitle, pxAxisTitle, pyAxisTitle,
395                xLeft, yTop, xRight, yBottom, CYAN);
396     // Draw the y axis divisions and numerical labels.
397     const int nYDivs = 5;
398     DrawYAxisInfo(xLeft, yTop, xRight, yBottom,
399                  minVal, maxVal, nYDivs);
400     // Draw the x-axis labels.
401     DrawXAxisLabels(nVals, pLabels);
402     // Draw the data bars.
403     DrawBars(xLeft, yTop, xRight, yBottom, minVal, maxVal,
404              pData, nVals);
405 }
```

The main() function calls GetGraphInfo()—see lines 74 and 75—to prompt for the graph titles, the data, and the data labels. Next, StartGraphics() is called to initialize the graphics system. The code draws the actual chart by calling DrawBarChart() (see lines 81 and 82).

DrawBarChart() (lines 345 through 405) uses the CalcMinAndMax() function to determine the minimum and maximum data values and to set a flag, fThousands, if any value exceeds 1,000. If any values are over 1,000, all the data values are divided by 1,000, and a notation In 1,000s is placed on the chart. This way, the number of digits shown on the y-axis won't become so large that they do not fit.

The maximum value is adjusted upward slightly (see lines 365 through 377) so that the top of the grid is slightly higher than the highest data value entered. If you did not adjust this value, the bar representing the largest data value would push right up against the top of the chart and would not be aesthetically pleasing.

Lines 381 through 386 compute the location of the upper-left and lower-right corners of the bounding rectangle that will contain the bar chart. The size of the bounding rectangle is computed as a percentage of the total screen area, as determined by xmax and ymax. The Visual C++ graphics function _rectangle() (line 385) draws the bounding rectangle around the chart. The DrawYAxisInfo() function (lines 180 through 239) draws grid lines across the bounding rectangle, corresponding to various y values shown along the y-axis, and displays the y-axis labels. The grid helps the user interpret the bar chart. You can vary the number of grid lines by changing the constant nYDivs (see line 397), here set to 5. After the grid lines are drawn, a grid line marking the 0th value along the y-axis is added (see lines 230 through 238). This is particularly useful when the bar chart contains both positive and negative values.

The DrawBars() function (lines 273 through 314) displays the actual bars and their labels. The major part of the code appears within the loop at lines 297 through 313. Each bar is drawn using the same color, but you can easily modify this to suit your tastes.

Finally, you draw the bar itself by using the graphics library function _rectangle() (see line 312). If the bar represents a positive value, the code (in lines 307 and 308) handles proper placement of the bar above the 0 line. If the bar represents a negative value, however, the code places the bar below the 0 line.

DrawTitles() (lines 318 through 341) outputs the main title, the x-axis title, and the y-axis title. The main title is positioned above the bar chart, and the x-axis title is positioned along the bottom. Each of the title items is truncated, if necessary, to fit within the region allotted to it.

You might consider several options in modifying this code for your own use. The constant values used within DrawBarChart() (lines 345 through 405) can be set to reposition the top, bottom, left, and right sides of the charting area.

Because the code is written to work with various screen resolutions, these constants define a percentage of the screen rather than actual pixel locations. Therefore, 0.20 means that the leftmost edge of the chart appears 20 percent of the screen width from the left edge of the screen. The right edge is set to 95 percent (or 0.95) of the screen width to the right. The top of the chart is positioned with 20 percent of the pixels from the top of the screen, thus reserving the top 20 percent of the screen for the main title.

Summary

This chapter introduced Visual C++ graphics. You learned how to draw such graphics objects as circles, lines, and rectangles. You learned also how to display text in graphics mode, and you saw a complete graphics application, the BARCHART.CPP sample program.

This chapter covered the following topics:

- Using the QuickWin user interface.

- Using the coordinate system to place your drawings on the screen.

- Using some of the simple drawing functions, including `_ellipse()`, `lineto()`, `rectangle()`, and the polygon-drawing function `_polygon()`.

- Drawing text to the graphics display and selecting fonts and character sizes.

- Using a viewport and setting up a clipping boundary.

- Choosing colors for graphics objects.

- Choosing patterns and colors for the interior of graphics objects.

- Using charting to express data in a graphics format. You learned how to use the Visual C++ graphics routines to develop a program that displays data as colorful bar charts.

Review Questions

1. To access the graphics functions, which file must you include in your source? Which file must you link into your applications?

2. What routine can you use to output text to the graphics display?

3. What is a viewport?

4. What is a clipping region?

5. What function do you call to select a color for a graphics object?

6. What is the difference between a chart and a graph?

7. Draw a picture of a PC screen and identify the location of (0, 0) and (maximum x, maximum y).

Exercises

1. Write your own drawing program to display a simple object—a house. The house should include a rectangular door, a square window, and a round window. For fun, use _polygon() to draw a lawn area in front of the house.

2. Using the text-drawing functions, add a title to the drawing of the house.

3. Use _setcolor() to select different drawing colors (if your video display supports sufficient colors) for the house drawing.

4. Experiment with the different fonts available for text. Display text in each of the available fonts and also modify the character size.

5. Implement a line chart program. A line chart is similar to a bar chart, but instead of displaying a vertical bar for each data point, the line chart shows a line from left to right to connect each data point. Your line chart program should draw a small circle or square at each data point position. *Hint:* You can modify the existing BARCHART.CPP program to implement the line chart.

The MFC General-Purpose Classes and Collection Classes

Also: Message Box

The Microsoft Foundation Class (MFC) library is part of the MSVC package. MFC provides general-purpose classes that can be used with MS-DOS and Windows, and with some careful preparation, with QuickWin programs. These classes are discussed in the first half of this chapter. The second topic in this chapter is the use of the MFC collection classes. The collection classes provide support for a variety of data structures to track the information used by applications. By using the general-purpose and collection classes provided by MFC, you reduce greatly the time required to write your application. You also use pretested and optimized routines.

The use of prewritten classes such as the collection classes and the MFC Windows classes helps you become a more productive C++ programmer. This chapter and Chapter 15 cover the classes contained in the MFC library.

Introducing MFC

The classes in the Microsoft Foundation Class library form an *application framework* to aid Windows program development. Chapter 15, "Windows Programming with Visual C++," gives you a brief overview of Windows programming with MFC. Microsoft also provides within MFC several classes that can be used by both DOS and Windows applications. These classes are the following:

```
CString

CTime

CTimeSpan

CFile

CStdioFile

CMemFile

CFileStatus

CArchive

CException
```

You can also use these classes with the QuickWin programs presented in previous chapters. Some special preparations are needed, though, before QuickWin applications can use MFC general-purpose classes and collection classes.

Preparing QuickWin Applications to Use the MFC Library

Microsoft made the QuickWin library available as a quick and easy way to port existing DOS C programs to Windows. The QuickWin library was therefore never meant to be used with class libraries such as MFC. The Microsoft Foundation Class library is primarily intended for building Windows applications, not DOS or QuickWin programs. However, you can use the MFC general-purpose classes in QuickWin applications if you make some modifications to the project file used to build the program. The first step is to include the necessary header file containing the MFC class definitions. This header file is called AFX.H.

Including the AFX.H Header File in QuickWin Applications
To include the AFX.H header file in a QuickWin application, you must make sure that the Windows-specific definitions are not included in your program, because your application is not a Windows program. You must ensure that

the DOS-specific definitions are included in your program. Because these specific definitions are required in each QuickWin application that uses MFC, they are good candidates for inclusion in a header file. Using the Visual Workbench, create a new file and then type the code from listing 14.1. Save the file as QUICKWIN.H.

Listing 14.1 The QUICKWIN.H Header File for Using MFC Classes with QuickWin

```
1  #ifdef _WINDOWS        // Note the leading underscore.
2      #undef _WINDOWS
3          #define _DOS
4          #include <afx.h>        // MFC general classes.
5          #include <afxcoll.h>    // MFC collection classes.
6          #undef _DOS
7      #define _WINDOWS
8  #endif
9
```

Warning

Make sure that you place the extra line (line 9) at the end of your header file and, in fact, at the end of every header file. There is a bug in the Visual C++ compiler that will report

```
fatal error C1004: unexpected end of file found
```

if a blank line is not found at the end of an include file.

Note the header file AFXCOLL.H included in line 5. This file is needed for the collection class definitions used later in this chapter.

Project Options for QuickWin Applications That Use the MFC Library

After you have included the QUICKWIN.H header file, you are still not out of the woods. Before you can compile and link your application, you must change some of the linker options for your project to make certain that the appropriate MFC libraries are used. To ensure that the correct libraries are included, follow these steps:

- Create the project file for your application, as outlined in previous chapters.

- Activate the Project Options dialog box by choosing **P**roject from the **O**ptions pull-down menu.

- Select the **U**se Microsoft Foundation Classes check box (if it is already checked) in the Project Options dialog box.

- Click the **L**inker button to display the Linker Options dialog box, as shown in figure 14.1.

- Select the Prevent Use of Extended Dictionar**y** check box.

- In the **L**ibraries edit box, add to the beginning of the list the name of the appropriate MFC DOS library.

  The name of the MFC DOS library depends on the memory model you are using. The name depends also on the type of build, release or debug, that you are building. For a Medium memory model and a debug build, the name is mafxcrd. For a Medium memory model and a release build, the name is mafxcr. Make sure that you add the name to the *beginning* of the list; otherwise, the Workbench generates errors while linking your application!

Fig. 14.1
The Linker Options dialog box displaying the correct settings for a QuickWin application that uses the MFC library.

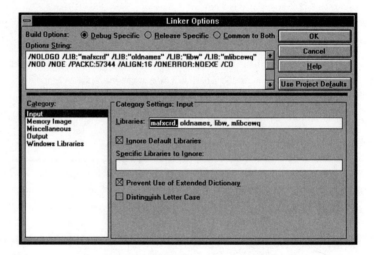

The libraries are located in the \MSVC\MFC\LIB directory, if you installed them during installation of MSVC. If the libraries are not there, you must install the missing libraries from the installation disks. If you are using the Standard Edition of MSVC, Version 1.0, you may have to build these libraries yourself. Instructions for building different versions of the MFC library can be found in a file named README.TXT in the \MSVC\MFC\SRC directory.

The next sections introduce you to CString, CTime, and CFile—the general-purpose classes offered by MFC.

The *CString* Class

Chapter 6, "Functions and Macros," provided a general overview of C/C++ strings. MFC provides a class called CString. CStrings support dynamic-length character strings in contrast to C's fixed-length arrays of characters. You manipulate CString objects much as you would a BASIC language string. The maximum size of a CString object is 32,767 characters. MFC supplies a variety of member functions that enable you to manipulate strings and convert from C-style strings to CStrings. Wherever you would normally use an array of characters, you can use a CString object. Listing 14.2 provides a sample program that uses CStrings. Following the listing is a complete explanation of the CString functions used.

Listing 14.2 A Sample QuickWin Application That Uses *CStrings*

```
 1   // STRINGS.CPP - A sample program using CString objects.
 2   #include "quickwin.h"
 3   #include <iostreams.h>
 4   const int STRSIZE = 80;
 5   void main()
 6   {
 7    int num;
 8    char c_string[STRSIZE];
 9    CString str1, str2, str3("Hello World");
10
11      cout << str3 << endl;
12
13      str1 = "Hello";         // str1 now contains "Hello".
14      str1 += " there ";      // str1 now contains "Hello there ".
15      str2 = str3.Right(5);   // str2 now contains "World".
16      str3.Empty();           // str3 now contains an empty string.
17      if ( str3.IsEmpty() )
18          cout << "String 3 is empty." << endl;
19      else
20          cout << "String 3 is NOT empty." << endl;
21
22      cout << str1 << str2 << endl;
23
24      str3 = str1 + str2;   // concatenation
25      cout << str3 << endl;
26
27      num = str1.GetLength();
28
29      cout << "The length of string 1 is " << num << endl;
30
31      str3.MakeUpper();       // Make all characters uppercase.
32
33      cout << str3 << endl;
34
```

(continues)

Listing 14.2 Continued

```
35      str3.MakeReverse();    // Reverse the characters in string 3.
36
37      cout << str3 << endl;
38
39      if ( str3 == "HELLO THERE WORLD" )
40      {
41          cout << str3 << " is equal to the constant string "
42                        << " HELLO THERE WORLD" << endl;
43      }
44      cout << "Press Enter to Continue. ";
45      cin.get();
46  } // main
```

In listing 14.2, line 9 declares three instances of the CString class: str1, str2, and str3. The str3 declaration invokes one of the many CString constructors to initialize str3 to the value "Hello World". Chapter 6 illustrated several of the library functions provided by C and C++ to manipulate strings. Functions such as strcpy(), strcmp(), and strcat() were introduced that manipulate null-terminated character arrays as strings. MFC supplies comparable functionality in CStrings through member functions and operators.

In Chapter 6, you had to pass two null-terminated character arrays to the strcat() function in order to concatenate the strings. Line 14 of listing 14.2 illustrates how a CString object can concatenate another string to itself with the use of the += operator. Line 13 shows you how to copy a string, "Hello", to the CString object str1 with the use of the = assignment operator. Assigning strings with the = operator instead of the strcpy() function is more intuitive and less error-prone. In Chapter 6, you learned to use the strcmp() function to compare two strings for equality. CStrings allow you to use the more familiar equality operator, ==, to test strings for equality, as shown in line 39.

Lines 31 and 35 illustrate some of the more esoteric member functions provided by the CString class. The MakeUpper() member function converts each character in the CString to uppercase. The MakeReverse() member function reverses the string represented by the CString object.

The *CTime* Class

A CTime object represents a time and date. You can use CTime objects to get the current system time, and then use member functions to display a variety of time- and date-related information. MFC uses a C runtime library data item called time_t, introduced in Chapter 6, to store a time value. MFC acts as a C++ friendly wrapper around the old C routines. One drawback to this approach is that you cannot derive a new object from the CTime class. Listing 14.3 illustrates a simple CTime program based on the GETTIME.CPP program presented in Chapter 6, "Functions and Macros."

Listing 14.3 A Program That Uses the MFC *CTime* Class

```
1    // GETTIME2.CPP
2    // Demonstrates using the library routines time() and ctime().
3    #include "quickwin.h"
4    #include <iostream.h
5
6    void main(void)
7    {
8      CTime ATime;
9
10     ATime = CTime::GetCurrentTime();
11     CString fmt("%A, %B %d, %Y");
12     cout << "Current date = "
13         << ATime.Format( (const char *)fmt )
14         << endl;
15         << "Current time = "
16         << ATime.Format( "%H:%M:%S %p")
17         << endl;
18
19     cout << "Press Enter to continue.";
20     cin.get();
21
22   } // main
```

In listing 14.3, line 8 declares a local CTime variable called ATime. Line 10 initializes ATime to your computer system's current time through the use of a static member function of CTime. Line 11 then constructs a format string to be used in line 13 to display the current date. Lines 13 and 16 use the CTime member function Format() to display the current date and current time, respectively. The format specifiers are similar to the specifiers used in the C runtime library function printf(). Table 14.1 lists some of the various CTime::Format() specifiers available. For a more detailed list of format specifiers, check the C/C++ Language Help file for the function strftime().

Table 14.1 *CTime* Format Specifiers	
Specifier	**Description**
%A	The full name of the current weekday, such as Monday
%B	The full name of the current month
%H	The current hour in 24-hour format
%M	The current minute
%p	The AM or PM indicator
%S	The current second
%Y	The current year including the century, such as 1994

The *CFile* Class

In Chapter 11, "C++ Input and Output," you learned how to use C++ streams for application input and output, especially to and from files. The MFC library provides several classes to help perform file I/O from an MFC application.

Listing 14.4 illustrates the COPYFILE.CPP program presented in Chapter 11 and rewritten here to make use of CFile objects. One aspect to notice is that CFile objects do not support insertion and extraction operators as do the C++ streams. In that sense, CFile objects are more like C file I/O library functions than like C++ I/O streams.

Listing 14.4 A Demonstration of the Use of *CFile* Objects to Copy a Binary File

```
 1   // CPYFILE2.CPP
 2   #include "quickwin.h"
 3   #include "iostream.h"
 4
 5   const int BUF_SIZE = 1024;
 6
 7   void main()
 8   {
 9     CFile from;        // input file  - file to copy from
10     CFile to;          // output file - file to copy to
11
12     CString iname;     // input file name
13     CString oname;     // output file name
14
```

```
15   char buffer[BUF_SIZE];
16   BOOL result;
17
18   long num_bytes;     // number of bytes in input file
19   long num_left;      // number of bytes left to copy
20   int  num_read;      // number of bytes read from input file
21   int  copy_size;     // number of bytes to copy in each chunk
22
23     copy_size = BUF_SIZE;
24
25     // Get input and output file names.
26     cout << "Enter input filename ";
27
28     cin >> iname.GetBuffer(80);
29     cin.ignore(1);
30     iname.ReleaseBuffer(-1);
31
32     cout << "Enter output filename ";
33
34     cin >> oname.GetBuffer(80);
35     cin.ignore(1);
36     oname.ReleaseBuffer(-1);
37
38     // Open the input file for reading.
39     result = from.Open( iname, CFile::modeRead );
40     if (FALSE == result)
41     {
42        cout << "error opening " << iname ;
43        return ;
44     }
45
46     // Open the output file for writing.
47     result = to.Open( oname, CFile::modeCreate | CFile::modeWrite);
48     if (FALSE == result)
49     {
50        cout << "error opening " << oname ;
51        return ;
52     }
53
54     num_left = num_bytes = from.GetLength();
55     cout << "Copying " << num_bytes << " bytes from "
56          << iname << " to " << oname << endl;
57
58     // Copy the file!
59     while( num_left )
60     {
61        num_read = from.Read( buffer, BUF_SIZE);
62        to.Write(buffer,num_read);
63        num_left -= num_read;
64
65     }
66
67     // Close the files.
68     from.Close();
69     to.Close();
70
71     cout << "Press Enter to continue ...";
72     cin.get();
73
74   }
```

The CPYFILE2.CPP program shown in listing 14.4 copies binary files. You can use the program to copy text files, but a small formatting problem would occur in the *to* file. The formatting problem occurs because of the way that DOS and C/C++ treat newline characters.

Text versus Binary Files

The newline character, \n, is represented as one character in C and C++ programs. When dealing with text files, however, DOS and Windows treat this character as two separate characters—the carriage-return (CR) and linefeed (LF) characters. MSVC and most other DOS-based compilers handle the conversion of these characters by specifying different types of files on which to operate. If a programmer specifies that a given file is to operate on text files with C/C++ routines, special handling code is provided to make sure that DOS processes the CR and LF characters appropriately. The special handling code translates the CR and LF characters to and from newline characters as needed.

Using the *CStdioFile* Class

Although you can process text files with CFile objects, the designers of the MFC library have provided another class specifically for text files. The CStdioFile class is an MFC class designed to handle text files and is derived from CFile. CStdioFile inherits much of its functionality from CFile and uses many of the base class's member functions to perform certain file operations. The CStdioFile class provides two member functions, ReadString() and WriteString(), specifically for processing text files.

Listing 14.5 provides a new version of CPYFILE2.CPP specific for copying text files. CPYTEXT.CPP uses the ReadString() and WriteString() member functions to copy one line of text at a time from the input file to the output file.

Listing 14.5 The Use of *CStdioFile* Objects to Copy Text Files

```
1   // CPYTEXT.CPP
2   #include "quickwin.h"
3   #include "iostream.h"
4
5   const int BUF_SIZE = 1024;
6
7   void main()
8   {
9     CStdioFile from;        // input file  - file to copy from
10    CStdioFile to;          // output file - file to copy to
11
12    CString iname;    // input file name
```

```
13   CString oname;     // output file name
14
15   char buffer[BUF_SIZE];
16   BOOL result;
17
18
19       // Get input and output file names.
20       cout << "Enter input filename ";
21
22       cin >> iname.GetBuffer(80);
23       cin.ignore(1);
33       iname.ReleaseBuffer(-1);
34
35       cout << "Enter output filename ";
36
37       cin >> oname.GetBuffer(80);
38       cin.ignore(1);
39       oname.ReleaseBuffer(-1);
40
41       // Open the input file for reading.
42       result = from.Open( iname, CFile::modeRead );
43       if (FALSE == result)
44       {
45           cout << "error opening " << iname ;
46           return ;
47       }
48
49       // Open the output file for writing.
50       result = to.Open( oname, CFile::modeCreate | CFile::modeWrite);
51       if (FALSE == result)
52       {
53           cout << "error opening " << oname ;
54           return ;
55       }
56
57       // Copy the file!
58       while( from.ReadString( buffer, BUF_SIZE ) )
59       {
60           to.WriteSting(buffer,num_read);
61       }
62
63       // Close the files.
64       from.Close();
65       to.Close();
66
67       cout << "Press Enter to continue ...";
68       cin.get();
69
70   }
```

Lines 58 through 61 perform the actual file copy in listing 14.5. The
CStdioFile member function, ReadString(), on line 58 is called from inside
the while statement to read characters from the file into the buffer. If the

function reaches the end of the file, a NULL value is returned. The NULL value then causes the program to exit the while loop and complete the program. ReadString() copies characters from the input file into the buffer until the function either encounters a newline character or copies BUF_SIZE characters into the buffer.

The Collection Classes

If you are an experienced C programmer, you might think that switching from C to C++ can immediately make you more productive. To set the record straight, switching from C to C++ does not make you a more productive programmer—at least not immediately. Most new C++ programmers probably take longer to reach their goals than if they had used a traditional language, such as C or Pascal. What happened?

The feature set of C++ is extensive and comes with a steep learning curve that new C++ programmers must climb. Learning C++ means learning not only new syntax but also new ways of thinking about software design and development. The power of C++ as a productivity enhancer does not come until after programmers cross the pinnacle of the learning curve, and when their applications are capable of inheriting from preexisting classes. For your first few applications, you might not have any classes from which you can inherit your application's features. Instead, you must write your classes from scratch. Writing those classes for the first time might take longer than if you had coded them by using non-OOP methods. The classes might initially take longer to build because of the tendency to make them complete, accurate, and useful for future projects.

So what can you do to make your initial use of C++ more productive? Borrow from existing class libraries, such as MFC. The collection classes provide support to programs that must keep track of data. Instead of writing your own routines, you can inherit data management routines directly from the collection classes.

Understanding the Collection Classes

The collection classes are usable in any C++ program. These classes provide generic data structure support for dynamically sized arrays, queues, lists, stacks, and such specialized structures as B-trees, sorted arrays, and maps. Member functions provide searching capabilities. By using the predefined classes, either directly or by deriving new classes from them, your application can put the power of C++ programming to work. When your program needs to keep track of information (such as a simple database application), you can use the collection classes.

Using the collection classes is not difficult, but when you are working with them the first time, a few traps can slow your progress. The programs in the following sections give you sample code that you can immediately put to work.

Learning about the Collection Classes

To learn more about the collection classes, you can do the following:

- Use the sample programs and descriptions presented in this chapter.

- Use the Visual Workbench's on-line help for access to reference information about the `CObject`-based collections.

- Look at the sample programs in the \MSVC\MFC\SAMPLES directory.

- Examine the collection library header file, AFXCOLL.H, located in the \MSVC\MFC\INCLUDE directory.

> **Note**
>
> If you have read Chapter 6, "Functions and Macros," you might suspect that collection classes are good candidates for C++ templates, and you would be correct. However, Microsoft does not yet support the emerging standard for C++ templates. Then how did Microsoft build the MFC collection classes? Microsoft built a DOS-based tool, called TEMPLDEF.EXE, to build template-like classes for MFC. You can also use the TEMPLDEF tool in situations where C++ templates are a great idea. Unfortunately, the use of such a tool is beyond the scope of this book.

This chapter provides program examples that use the MFC collection classes. The sample programs illustrate how to use some of the basic member functions provided by the collection classes. You can consult the Visual C++ on-line help to learn more about the basic member functions and the other member functions available to collection classes. Feel free to adapt the programs presented here for your own use.

Table 14.2 shows a list of the available collection classes. Space limitations do not allow a description of all these classes in detail. However, you can convert most of these examples into one of the other class types. Refer to the on-line help for information about the member functions available for each class. The AFXCOLL.H header file contains the prototypes for each collection class. MFC supplies three basic types of collection classes—arrays, lists, and maps—which Microsoft refers to as *shapes*.

Table 14.2 The MFC Collection Class Types	
Class	**Description**
Arrays	MFC provides classes for arrays of bytes, words, double words, CStrings, CObject pointers, and void pointers.
Lists	MFC provides classes for lists of CStrings, CObject pointers, and void pointers.
Maps	MFC provides a map collection (also known as a dictionary collection) that maps a key to a value.

Each collection is derived from a common ancestor, the CObject class. CObject is the "mother of all objects" (well, most anyway) in the MFC library. In fact, since MFC collections are derived from a common ancestor, most collection classes have the same member functions to perform the same activity. For example, most MFC collection classes have a SetAt() member function used to insert an object in the collection. Thus, when you use the on-line help or *Reference Volume 1: Class Library Reference for the Microsoft Foundation Class Library* to get information on a collection class, you may be instructed to see a reference to another collection class object. Take a look at the CPtrArray collection class for an example.

Using the Collection Classes

Among the same member functions available in the collection classes are functions to insert data items in the collection and to remove them from the collection. There are also functions to iterate through the collection, providing access to each item contained in the collection. Each type of collection also provides functions to delete every item in the list. Improper use of these functions can cause a problem for the collection classes that deal with pointers. The delete operations do not delete the data referenced by the pointers. The task of deleting the data object has been left to the programmer. The rest of this chapter contains information on the collection types. A simple program illustrates the use of each collection type.

The Array Collection Class

Array collection classes are available for bytes, words (that is, 16-bit integers or longs), double words, void pointers, CStrings, unsigned integers, and CObjects. Each array class provides a dynamically sized storage area for the data contained in the collection. The array classes allow you to access the data as if it were stored in a dynamic array. Thus, although a typical C/C++ array has a fixed size, usually determined at compile time, collection arrays can be dynamically sized at runtime to accommodate more storage slots. Just as in a typical array, a collection array can be indexed by an integer subscript. Array collections allow duplicate elements to be inserted into the array, but the insertion is relatively slow compared to, say, list and map collections. The contents of the collection are not sorted automatically, so searching for a specific item could take some time. Listing 14.6 illustrates the use of dynamic arrays.

Listing 14.6 A Sample Program That Illustrates Dynamic Arrays

```
1   // STRARRAY.CPP
2   // A simple program to illustrate the use of the MFC
3   // class Array shapes.
4   #include "quickwin.h"
5   #include "iostreams.h"
6
7   const int BUF_SIZE = 64;
8   const int ARRAY_SIZE = 2;
9
10  void main(void)
11  {
12    CStringArray  strings;
13    int index = 0;
14    int end;
15
16    strings.SetSize(ARRAY_SIZE);
17
18    end = strings.GetSize();
19    cout << "The size of the strings array is " << end << endl;
20
21    strings.Add("Hello");
22    strings.Add(" there ");
23    strings.Add("World!");
24
25    end = strings.GetSize();
26    cout << "The size of the strings array is " << end << endl;
27
28    for( index = 0; index < end; index++)
29    {
30        cout << "String located at index " << index
```

(continues)

Listing 14.6 Continued

```
31                << " is " << strings[index] << endl;
32   }
33
34   strings.RemoveAll();
35 }
```

Inserting an Item in an Array Collection

Lines 21 through 23 of listing 14.6 illustrate the use of the CStringArray member function Add(). You can use this function to insert new strings at the end of the array. Note that you have added three elements to the array. Note also that you set the size of the array to only two positions in line 16. If strings had been a typical C/C++ array, a runtime error would have occurred when you inserted the third element into the array on line 23. Why was there no runtime error? The function call on line 18 even confirms that the strings array has only two positions, yet the program inserted *three* strings.

The secret lies in the nature of MFC array collection classes. As mentioned earlier in this chapter, the array collections are dynamic—they can grow to accommodate new elements as they are inserted into the collection. The Add() member function specifically increases the size of the array, if an increase is needed, when it inserts a new string.

Iterating through the Array

Lines 28 through 32 of listing 14.6 show you how to iterate through an array collection class. The code looks the same as if you were using a normal C/C++ array. Because array collections are dynamic, the program determines the number of items in the strings array in line 25. The program calls the GetSize() member function, which returns the number of items—*not* the number of positions—in the collection. The program then uses the number as the ending condition for the for loop, as shown in line 28.

The List Collection Class

List collection classes are available for void pointers, CObject-derived objects, and CStrings. The list classes are implemented as a doubly linked list. Each has a head position and a tail position, allowing you to insert new elements in the list at each position and also within the middle of the list. It is possible to use the various member functions to implement both Stack and Queue data structures.

The list structure is maintained by the collection class, so you do not have to provide such items as next and previous in your structure or class, as was true for LIST.CPP in Chapter 6, "Functions and Macros." The list collection class provides all the list functions for you!

Inserting an Item in a List Collection

In LIST.CPP in Chapter 6, you defined a structure to hold your data and pointers to other list_elements so that you could build a list of such structures. A new version of that program is shown in listing 14.7. Note how much simpler the list collection class makes the program!

Listing 14.7 A Collection Class Implementation of List-Manipulation Routines

```
1   // LIST2.CPP
2   // This is a modified version of the LIST.CPP program
3   // from Chapter 6. Here, the program has been restructured
4   // to use CStringList to add, list, and destroy entries
5   // from the list.
6   #include "quickwin.h"
7   #include <iostream.h>
8
9
10  const int FORWARD = 0;
11  const int REVERSE = 1;
12  const int MAXNAMESIZE = 20;
13
14  struct list_type
15  {
16    CStringList list;    // The MFC self-contained link list
17                         // for strings.
18    Initialize_List();
19    void Display_List(int Direction);
20    void Destroy_List(void);
21  };
22
23  //================================================
24  void main(void) {
25    // Used to process keyboard command input.
26    char command_ch, direction_ch;
27    CString TheName;
28    list_type TheList;          // The list object.
29
30    TheList.Initialize_List();
31    do {
32      cout << "Select A)dd, L)ist or Q)uit? ";
33      cin.get(command_ch);
34      cin.ignore(1);
35
36      switch(command_ch) {
```

(continues)

Listing 14.7 Continued

```
37          // Add a new entry to the list.
38          case 'a': case 'A': {
39            cout << "Enter name:   ";
40            cin.getline(TheName.GetBuffer(MAXNAMESIZE),MAXNAMESIZE );
41            TheList.Add_to_Tail(TheName.ReleaseBuffer());
42            break;
43          } // case
44          // Display the contents of the list.
45          case 'l': case 'L': {
46            cout << "List in F)orward or R)everse direction? ";
47            cin.get(direction_ch);
48            cin.ignore(1);
49            switch (direction_ch) {
50              case 'f': case 'F' : {
51                TheList.Display_List(FORWARD);
52                break;
53              } // end case
54              case 'r': case 'R' : {
55                TheList.Display_List(REVERSE);
56                break;
57              } // end case
58              default: break;
59            } // end switch
60            break;
61          } // end case
62          // Quit running the program.
63          case 'q': case 'Q': {
64            TheList.Destroy_List();
65            break;
66          } // end case
67          default:
68            break;
69        } // end switch
70      } while ((command_ch != 'q') && (command_ch != 'Q'));
71
72      cout << "Press Enter to continue.";
73      cin.get();
74    } // end main
75
76    //===============================================
77    void list_type::Initialize_List(void)
78    {
89      list.RemoveAll();
90
91    }
92
93    //===============================================
94    void list_type::Add_to_Tail(CString name_to_add)
94    // Add new data to the tail of the list.
96    {
97          list.AddTail( name_to_add );
98
99    } // Add_to_Tail
100
```

```
101  //===================================================
102  void list_type::Display_List(int Direction)
103  // Display the content of the list in either
104  // the FORWARD or the REVERSE direction.
105  {
106    POSITION pos;
107
108    switch (Direction) {
109      case FORWARD: {
110        pos = list.GetHeadPosition();
111        while (pos != NULL) {
112          cout << list.GetNext( pos ) << endl;
113
114        } // end while
115        break;
116      } // end case
117      case REVERSE: {
118        pos = list.GetTailPosition();
119        while (pos != NULL) {
120          cout << list.GetPrev( pos ) << endl;
121;
122        } // end while
123      } // end case
124      default: break;
125    } // end switch
126  } // Display_List
127
128  //===================================================
129  void list_type::Destroy_List(void)
130  // Free up all memory used the list.
131  {
132          Initialize_List();   // Call our own member function.
133  } // end Destroy_List
```

Iterating through the List

Lines 110 through 113 of listing 14.7 illustrate iterating through the list. The first step is to get a pointer to the head of the list. All collection classes provide a generic type for the position pointer, called POSITION. A POSITION variable can be used with any collection class to represent the current location within the collection. In line 110, the POSITION variable pos is used to get the head of the CStringList.

The standard collection function GetNext() does double duty on line 112. It first updates the position pointer pos and then returns the CString located at that position. This value is then displayed to cout. This double duty shows the power of C++, but such coding styles can make debugging and program maintenance difficult. You should use such coding practices with caution.

Lines 118 through 122 illustrate iterating backward through the list, starting at the list's tail.

Deleting the List

Lines 77 through 91 of listing 14.7 illustrate deleting the list. Because the CStringList does not make use of pointers, you do not have to worry about deleting each data object contained in the list. Thus, you can call the generic collection class function RemoveAll() to remove all the CStrings stored in the list. In fact, the function call to destroy the list, Destroy_List() in lines 129 through 133, uses the object's own Initialize_List() member function to accomplish the same objective.

Searching the List

The MFC collection classes also provide member functions to search a collection for a given item. By using these built-in functions, you can easily add searching capabilities to LIST2.CPP. The first step is to add the command to the main function. Then you add the object's function to perform the command. The following lines of code provide the body of the search function:

```
BOOL list_type::Search( CString string_to_find )
{
  BOOL result(FALSE);
    result = list.Find( string_to_find );
  return result
}
```

As you can see, you do not have to write many lines of code in order to search the list for a given string; that functionality is already provided by the MFC collection classes.

The Map Collection Class

The map collection is a dictionary. You map objects associated with a key into the collection. Later, you use the key to locate items in the map. A good example of such a structure is a real-world dictionary: You look up a specific word (in which the word is the key), and the dictionary returns a definition. Listing 14.8 implements a short, five-word dictionary, using the CMapStringToString collection class.

Listing 14.8 A Program That Uses the *CMapStringToString* Collection Class

```
1  // DICTION.CPP
2  // Demonstrates the use of the CMapStringToString class.
3  // Stores a set of word definitions matched
4  // to a "key" (or the word that is defined).
```

```
 5  #include <iostream.h>
 6  #include "quickwin.h"
 7
 8  void Display( CMapStringToString & map, CString key )
 9  {
10    CString definition;
11
13    if ( map.Lookup( key, definition ) )
14      {
15        cout << "The definition of " << key << " is "
16             << definition << endl;
17      }
18    else
19      {
20        cout << "No definition for " << key
21             << " was found." << endl;
22      }
23  }
24
25  void main(void)
26  {
27    CMapStringToString dictionary;
28    CString key;
29    CString definition;
30
31    // Add a word "kick", and its matching definition.
32    key = "kick";
33    definition = "To strike out with the foot";
34    dictionary.SetAt( key, definition);
35
36    key = "cheat";
37    definition = "To use to deceive or deprive someone of something valuable";
38    dictionary.SetAt( key, definition);
39
40    key = "planetarium";
41    definition = "A model of the solar system";
42    dictionary[key] = definition;
43
44    key = "spunky";
45    definition = "One who is full of spunk";
46    dictionary[key] = definition;
47
48    key = "ghee",
49    definition = "Clarified butter";
50    dictionary[key] = definition;
51
52    // Look up each of the indicated words and
53    // display the result.
54    Display( dictionary, "kick" );
55    Display( dictionary, "ghee" );
56    Display( dictionary, "cheat");
57    Display( dictionary, "C++");
57
58    dictionary.RemoveAll();
59
60    cout << "Press Enter to continue.";
61    cin.get();
62  } // main
```

Associating a Key with a Value in a Map Collection

Lines 32 through 34 of listing 14.8 show you how to insert a key-value pair into the map collection. The generic map collection class member function is used to associate the string `"kick"`, referred to as the key, with the definition `"To strike out with the foot"`, known as the value. The MFC map collection classes also provide the bracket operators, `[]`, to accomplish the association, as illustrated in lines 42 and 46.

Searching the Map for a Definition

Lines 54 through 57 of listing 14.8 call the `Display()` function in order to search the map for the indicated key-value pair. The `Display()` function has been implemented as a stand-alone C++ function instead of as a member function—hence, the need to pass a reference to a `CMapStringToString` object.

The `Display()` function, defined in lines 8 through 23, uses the generic map function `Lookup()` to search the collection passed as a parameter. The function searches for an association between the key-value parameter and the values stored in the collection class. The `Lookup()` member function requires two parameters: a string representing the search key, and a `CString` to hold the results of the search, if successful. If the `Lookup()` function does find a value mapped to the key, it returns True, indicating success. The function then returns the value found in the `CString` parameter.

Summary

This chapter introduced you to the Visual C++ MFC general-purpose classes for use in MS-DOS, Windows, and QuickWin applications. The chapter also covered the collection classes. By using the collection classes, you can quickly incorporate data structure routines in your own applications. The use of these classes enables you to build your programs faster. Presumably, you can also build programs with fewer errors, because Microsoft has pretested the class libraries.

Chapter 15, "Windows Programming with Visual C++," discusses the tools and MFC classes that you can use to build Windows applications.

Review Questions

1. Use the Visual C++ on-line help to locate information about the collection classes. Pick a particular class, such as CObList, and examine the types of member functions provided for this class.

2. Why must you use the header file QUICKWIN.H for QuickWin applications that use the MFC library?

3. Name the three types of shapes in the MFC collection classes.

4. Which collection class provides the quickest way for checking whether a given item is located in the collection?

5. Which collection class would you use to implement a stack data structure?

6. Assume that you have a program which must maintain an address list consisting of names and related address information. You want to have the information presented in sorted order, based on the last name field. What type of collection class should you use for this application?

Exercises

1. Add the search command to LIST2.CPP.

2. Implement a Queue collection class, using a list-based collection class such as CPtrList.

3. Write a simple program to display the current date and time, using each of the CTime::Format specifiers.

4. Use the Queue collection class implemented in exercise 2 to simulate a bank teller line. For the purpose of the simulation, assume that three bank tellers are fed by one line. Use the time functions provided by CTime so that you can insert a new customer into the bank teller queue at a periodic interval (such as once every 10 seconds). Each "customer" should have an associated customer number so that you can track the location of each customer in the simulation. You might want to initialize the queue to contain perhaps five customers before starting the simulation.

5. Using the example in exercise 4, when a teller window is free, move the next customer from the queue to the teller. Experiment with customer processing times for each teller. For instance, set teller 1 to 5 seconds, teller 2 to 10 seconds, and teller 3 to 15 seconds. At periodic intervals (such as every 5 seconds), have your program display the current queue and the customer number of each customer currently being served by a teller. With the times suggested, the queue should be "in balance," so that customers arrive at the same rate at which they are processed. Experiment by varying the times for customer processing and new arrivals. What happens to the average processing time when one customer has a lengthy business transaction?

6. Implement a Stack collection class using the CPtrList class. Define the objects you put in the collection so that each object has several data fields.

7. Implement the address list application described in review question 6, using a collection class of your choice.

Chapter 15

Windows Programming with Visual C++

Programming an application for Microsoft Windows can be an intimidating task. Programs written for Microsoft Windows use the Windows Applications Programming Interface (API), which provides hundreds of functions and thousands of constants you can use to select messages and other operations. Each Windows program must call specific routines in the Windows API to perform such operations as displaying text, obtaining input, processing menus and dialog boxes, and drawing graphics.

Although Windows is an object-oriented programming environment, it is designed for use with the C programming language, which is not an object-oriented language. The side effect of this design is that Windows programs written in C must manage the object-oriented feature of Windows without the support of an object-oriented language. Now that C++ is becoming the language of choice for PC software development, you can program many aspects of Windows in a true object-oriented manner by using the class libraries that have been developed. The Microsoft Foundation Class (MFC) library is one of these libraries.

This chapter gives you a brief introduction to Windows programming with the Microsoft Foundation Class library. The following pages illustrate the power that these libraries and C++ can give you as a programmer. This chapter introduces you also to the AppWizard, ClassWizard, and App Studio tools provided with the Visual Workbench.

Writing Your First Windows Program with AppWizard

MFC is a collection of classes that provide you with an *application framework*. This framework is a complete—but skeletal—Windows application from which you derive your own application. By inheriting a complete yet skeletal application, you avoid having to write a traditional Windows application in C and with the Windows Software Development Kit (SDK). The result is a cleaner program, developed in less time, and definitely not as error-prone as it would have been had you written it in C. The best part of this process is that you do not have to write a single line of code to get a Windows program up and running, thanks to the Visual Workbench and the Application Wizard (AppWizard).

Using AppWizard

You develop an MFC application by starting with the Application Wizard, better known as AppWizard. This tool enables you to create a skeletal Windows application by simply checking a few items in several dialog boxes without having to type hundreds of lines of C-based SDK code. You access AppWizard by choosing App**W**izard from the **P**roject menu on the Visual Workbench's menu bar. The MFC AppWizard dialog box is displayed, as shown in figure 15.1.

Fig. 15.1
The MFC
AppWizard
dialog box.

You first enter a project name in the Project **N**ame edit box. You then choose a location for the files that AppWizard will create. Usually, this is a sub-directory with the same name as your project name. This subdirectory is located below your current working directory. You can select a new working directory in the **D**irectory list box. You can rename the subdirectory in the New **S**ubdirectory edit box. And you can select a new drive for these files in the Dri**v**e combo box. After you decide on the location for the project, you can set the various options by using the pushbuttons at the right of the dialog box. For your first Windows program, name the project FIRSTWIN.

Clicking the **O**ptions button displays the Options dialog box, as shown in figure 15.2. In this dialog box, you specify the Windows features to be included in your skeletal Windows application. Most of these options have check boxes, so you can select more than one option. Only the Memory Model group of radio buttons restricts you to one selection. For your first Windows program, accept the defaults set by AppWizard.

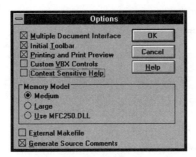

Fig. 15.2
The AppWizard Options dialog box.

Multiple Document Interface. There are two types of interfaces in a Windows program: Multiple Document Interface (MDI) and Single Document Interface (SDI). Microsoft Word is an example of a Multiple Document Interface program. MDI programs typically display different windows in the program's client area, each containing a different portion of the application's data. AppWizard generates an MDI application if you check the **M**ultiple Document Interface check box in the Options dialog box. If you uncheck this box, AppWizard generates an SDI application. An SDI application displays the application's data in the entire client area instead of in separate windows.

Initial Toolbar. The Initial **T**oolbar check box, when selected, instructs AppWizard to generate a toolbar below your application's main menu. Selecting this box also generates a simple status bar at the bottom of your application's window. If you select this option, your application also contains a main menu item called **V**iew, which enables you to hide and display the toolbar and status bar. Figure 15.3 shows the various components of your AppWizard-generated application.

Fig. 15.3
Components of an AppWizard-generated application.

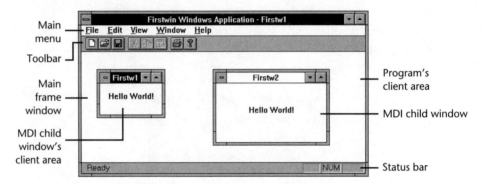

Printing and Print Preview. The **P**rinting and Print Preview check box provides you with the real power of application frameworks. When selected, this check box instructs AppWizard to provide simple printing and print preview operations to your skeletal program. These types of operations would require over 2,500 lines of C code if you used the Windows SDK! Yet all you need to do is select a single check box to get the same functionality without writing *one* line of code.

Custom VBX Controls. Selecting the Custom **V**BX Controls check box allows your application to take advantage of the thousands of custom Windows controls that have been developed for Microsoft's Visual Basic product.

Context-Sensitive Help. Selecting the Context Sensitive H**e**lp check box prepares your application for using the Windows help system. AppWizard generates a subdirectory containing various files to help build a Windows help system for your application. AppWizard also generates a batch file that you can use to generate the help file.

Memory Model. The Memory Model group of radio buttons allows you to pick only one type of memory model for your application. The first two items, Med**i**um and **L**arge, are identical in meaning to the Medium and Large memory models discussed in Chapter 7, "Projects." The final button, **U**se

MFC250.DLL, enables you to use a dynamic link library (DLL) version of MFC. DLLs are libraries that are attached to your executable file while it is running, rather than when it is built.

External Makefile. The External Makefile check box allows you to use a project file that was not created with the Visual Workbench. This advanced feature enables developers to use makefiles from older versions of Microsoft's languages, or to use different linkers and compilers from other vendors.

Generate Source Comments. The Generate Source Comments check box instructs AppWizard to add helpful comments and reminders to the source code that it generates. These comments help you identify areas in the skeletal application that need additional code for performing a complete function. The following code fragment illustrates AppWizard-generated comments:

```
CWinprogApp::CWinprogApp()
{
    // TODO: add construction code here,
    // Place all significant initialization in InitInstance
}
```

OLE and ODBC. After you select the appropriate options for your application, you can click the OK button in the Options dialog box to return to the MFC AppWizard dialog box. You can now build a fully functioning Windows program; however, you may want to define two other options, OLE 2.0 and OBDC, for your program. These options are new to MSVC++ Version 1.5. To define an OLE 2.0-aware application, you click the OLE Options button in the MFC AppWizard dialog box. To define an ODBC-aware application, you click the Database Options button. (ODBC stands for Open Database Connectivity.) Both of these options are advanced Windows topics and are not covered in this book. For more information on these topics, refer to *Using Visual C++* (Que, 1994).

AppWizard Defined Classes

Because MFC is a class library and AppWizard uses MFC to construct a Windows application, you can get a sneak preview of the classes that AppWizard will create for your program. Just click the Classes button in the MFC AppWizard dialog box, and the Classes dialog box appears (see fig. 15.4). The New Application Classes list box displays the classes that AppWizard will create for your Windows program. As you click each class name, the dialog box displays information about that class in the edit and combo boxes that appear below the list box. Click the OK button to exit the dialog box. You learn more about each class later in this chapter.

Fig. 15.4
The Classes
dialog box.

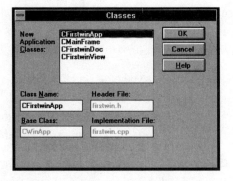

Generating Your Application

After you define the various options for your application, you can click the
OK button in the MFC AppWizard dialog box. The New Application Information dialog box appears, as shown in figure 15.5. This dialog box gives you a
capsule review of each class to be created and the features you have selected
for your application. Click the **C**reate button to have AppWizard generate
your Windows program. It is best to double-check the options you have selected for your application before clicking the **C**reate button. The reason is
that you can use AppWizard only once to create an application. You cannot
use this tool again to modify an application you have already created.

Fig. 15.5
The New
Application
Information
dialog box.

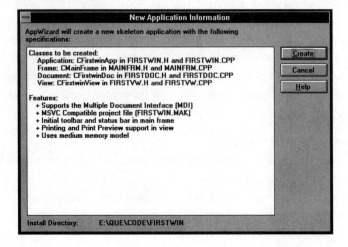

Running Your Application

When AppWizard finishes creating the various files needed by your program, you can use the Visual Workbench to build and run the application. This process is the same one you have used throughout this book to build your QuickWin application. You can choose the **R**ebuild All menu item from the **P**roject menu, or click the Rebuild All toolbar button, to have the Workbench build your application. You can then choose the E**x**ecute <project name> menu option from the **P**roject menu or use the shortcut Ctrl+F5 to run your program. Figure 15.6 shows the sample program created when you accept the AppWizard defaults. Go ahead and test the application. Pull down the menus and watch the status bar indicator. Click the toolbar buttons to see how they behave.

Fig. 15.6
FIRSTWIN—your first Windows program.

A Generic MFC Application

Congratulations, you have built and tested your first Windows program without typing a single line of C++ code! This is the power delivered by AppWizard and application frameworks like MFC—the ability to generate program code without ever typing a single line of source code. AppWizard generates several files that implement the program you designed. A complete list of files created, along with a brief explanation of each, is written to a file. This file is called README.TXT and is located in the project directory.

A generic MFC application contains five basic items:

■ An application object derived from the MFC CWinApp class. This object *is* your program (FIRSTWIN.CPP and FIRSTWIN.H).

■ A frame window object derived from CMainFrame. This is your program's main frame window (MAINFRM.CPP and MAINFRM.H).

■ A document class derived from the MFC CDocument class. This class holds your application-specific data (FIRSTDOC.CPP and FIRSTDOC.H).

■ A view class derived from one of several MFC view classes, such as CView and CEditView. This class displays your data in the frame window (FIRSTVW.CPP and FIRSTVW.H).

■ A resource file containing the definitions of your application's resources, such as dialog boxes, string constants, and menu items (FIRSTWIN.RC and RESOURCE.H).

The *WinMain()* Function

Every Windows program has a function named WinMain(). This function corresponds to the main() function your DOS applications use. When you start your Windows application, control is transferred to the WinMain() function. The most peculiar aspect of an MFC program is that the WinMain() function does not appear at all in the source code files. The reason is that the WinMain() function is hidden inside the implementation of CWinApp, which your application inherits. The application framework, MFC, calls this function as soon as you instantiate an instance of your derived class, as in line 44 of listing 15.1 (presented in the next section):

```
44  CFirstwinApp NEAR theApp;
```

Everything needed to run your Windows application is located in the CWinApp-derived class CFirstwinApp. Every MFC application requires one, and only one, application class. AppWizard generates a derived class and places the class definition in the FIRSTWIN.H header file.

Application Windows

Because you are developing a Windows application, it makes sense for the application to have a window. Every Windows application requires what is called a frame window. This window provides a framework for such items as the title bars, menu bars, and toolbars. The frame window also dictates the type of interface the program defines—either an SDI application or an MDI application. AppWizard generates a frame window class called CMainFrame and places the definition in the MAINFRM.CPP and MAINFRM.H source files. All windows generated by AppWizard, including dialog box controls (which are also Windows windows), are derived from a base class called CWnd. This MFC class encapsulates most of the functionality found in a Microsoft Windows' user interface window.

Closely tied to the frame window are classes that implement the new document/view architecture introduced in MFC 2.0. Documents, views, and resources are covered later in this chapter.

FIRSTWIN—Your First Application

Listing 15.1 shows the source code for the main FIRSTWIN.CPP file. An explanation of the key components of the program follows the listing.

Listing 15.1 The Main Application Source File for FIRSTWIN.CPP

```
 1  // firstwin.cpp : Defines the class behaviors for the application
 2  //
 3
 4  #include "stdafx.h"
 5  #include "firstwin.h"
 6
 7  #include "mainfrm.h"
 8  #include "firstdoc.h"
 9  #include "firstvw.h"
10
11  #ifdef _DEBUG
12  #undef THIS_FILE
13  static char BASED_CODE THIS_FILE[] = __FILE__;
14  #endif
15
16  /////////////////////////////////////////////////////////////////
17  // CFirstwinApp
18
19  BEGIN_MESSAGE_MAP(CFirstwinApp, CWinApp)
20  //{{AFX_MSG_MAP(CFirstwinApp)
21      ON_COMMAND(ID_APP_ABOUT, OnAppAbout)
22  // NOTE - the ClassWizard will add and remove mapping macros here.
23  //     DO NOT EDIT what you see in these blocks of generated code!
24  //}}AFX_MSG_MAP
25  // Standard file based document commands
26      ON_COMMAND(ID_FILE_NEW, CWinApp::OnFileNew)
27      ON_COMMAND(ID_FILE_OPEN, CWinApp::OnFileOpen)
28  // Standard print setup command
29      ON_COMMAND(ID_FILE_PRINT_SETUP, CWinApp::OnFilePrintSetup)
30  END_MESSAGE_MAP()
31
32  /////////////////////////////////////////////////////////////////
33  // CFirstwinApp construction
34
35  CFirstwinApp::CFirstwinApp()
36  {
37  // TODO: add construction code here,
38  // Place all significant initialization in InitInstance
39  }
```

(continues)

Listing 15.1 Continued

```
40
41  //////////////////////////////////////////////////////////////////
42  // The one and only CFirstwinApp object
43
44  CFirstwinApp NEAR theApp;
45
46  //////////////////////////////////////////////////////////////////
47  // CFirstwinApp initialization
48
49  BOOL CFirstwinApp::InitInstance()
50  {
51  // Standard initialization
52  // If you are not using these features and wish to reduce the size
53  //  of your final executable, you should remove from the following
54  //   the specific initialization routines you do not need.
55
56  SetDialogBkColor();        // Set dialog background color to gray
57  LoadStdProfileSettings(); // Load standard INI file options (including RU)
58
59  // Register the application's document templates.  Document templates
60  //   serve as the connection between documents, frame windows and views.
61
62  CMultiDocTemplate* pDocTemplate;
63  pDocTemplate = new CMultiDocTemplate(
64          IDR_FIRSTWTYPE,
65          RUNTIME_CLASS(CFirstwinDoc),
66          RUNTIME_CLASS(CMDIChildWnd), // standard MDI child frame
67          RUNTIME_CLASS(CFirstwinView));
68  AddDocTemplate(pDocTemplate);
69
70  // create main MDI Frame window
71  CMainFrame* pMainFrame = new CMainFrame;
72  if (!pMainFrame->LoadFrame(IDR_MAINFRAME))
73      return FALSE;
74  m_pMainWnd = pMainFrame;
75
76  // create a new (empty) document
77  OnFileNew();
78
79  if (m_lpCmdLine[0] != '\0')
80  {
81      // TODO: add command line processing here
82  }
83
84  // The main window has been initialized, so show and update it.
85  pMainFrame->ShowWindow(m_nCmdShow);
86  pMainFrame->UpdateWindow();
87
88  return TRUE;
89  }
90
91  //////////////////////////////////////////////////////////////////
92  // CAboutDlg dialog used for App About
93
```

```
 94  class CAboutDlg : public CDialog
 95  {
 96  public:
 97  CAboutDlg();
 98
 99  // Dialog Data
100  //{{AFX_DATA(CAboutDlg)
101     enum { IDD = IDD_ABOUTBOX };
102  //}}AFX_DATA
103
104  // Implementation
105  protected:
106  virtual void DoDataExchange(CDataExchange* pDX);   // DDX/DDV support
107  //{{AFX_MSG(CAboutDlg)
108  // No message handlers
109  //}}AFX_MSG
110  DECLARE_MESSAGE_MAP()
111  };
112
113  CAboutDlg::CAboutDlg() : CDialog(CAboutDlg::IDD)
114  {
115  //{{AFX_DATA_INIT(CAboutDlg)
116  //}}AFX_DATA_INIT
117  }
118
119  void CAboutDlg::DoDataExchange(CDataExchange* pDX)
120  {
121  CDialog::DoDataExchange(pDX);
122  //{{AFX_DATA_MAP(CAboutDlg)
123  //}}AFX_DATA_MAP
124  }
125
126  BEGIN_MESSAGE_MAP(CAboutDlg, CDialog)
127  //{{AFX_MSG_MAP(CAboutDlg)
128  // No message handlers
129  //}}AFX_MSG_MAP
130  END_MESSAGE_MAP()
131
132  // App command to run the dialog
133  void CFirstwinApp::OnAppAbout()
134  {
135  CAboutDlg aboutDlg;
136  aboutDlg.DoModal();
137  }
138
139  /////////////////////////////////////////////////////////////
140  // CFirstwinApp commands
```

The Initialization Step

The first action of a Windows program is to initialize itself for running under
the Windows operating environment. This is necessary because Windows
can allow multiple copies of the same application to run at the same time.

One-time application initialization is required the first time the program is loaded and executed. Instance initialization is done each time a copy of the program runs, including the first time.

The first program initialization is handled by a CWinApp virtual function called InitApplication(). FIRSTWIN does not override this virtual function, so the program uses the base class version found in CWinApp. The instance initialization portion of CFirstWinApp does call the virtual function InitInstance(). This function is defined in the FIRSTWIN.CPP program file (see lines 49 through 89 of listing 15.1).

The MFC Document/View Architecture

With the release of MSVC 1.0 and MFC 2.0, Microsoft introduced a new concept in MFC programming: documents and views. AppWizard generates one file for a basic document (FIRSTDOC.CPP) and one file for a basic view (FIRSTVW.CPP).

> **Note**
>
> The concept of documents and views may be hard to grasp, but an understanding is necessary for writing MFC-based Windows applications. AppWizard generates a basic system for you that can be used to create simple Windows applications, but advanced applications require a thorough understanding of the document/view architecture.
>
> You should find it helpful to complete the SCRIBBLE tutorial found in your MSVC package. Microsoft also provides several sample programs, located in the \MSVC\MFC\SAMPLES directory, which you can compile, run, and analyze. Exploring the sample programs provided by Microsoft can help you better understand the concept and use of MFC's document/view architecture.

You can think of a *document* as a container for your application's data. A document can track your data for modifications and also provide assistance in storing your data to disk. A *view* is a portal into your program's data. The framework allows you to interact with your data only through a view. MFC applications use a view to display data on printers and on the screen. MFC permits a program to have many views into its document's data. An MDI application can have several document types open at once, whereas an SDI application can have only one document type active at any given time.

A document template binds an application's documents and views together. This binding is shown in lines 62 through 68 of listing 15.1. Here FIRSTWIN.CPP registers with the application object its document and view. AppWizard generates only one document and only one view for an application. If you want to add additional types, you must do so by entering the code manually. You learn later in this chapter what kinds of actions you can perform in documents and views.

Creating the Main Frame Window

The InitInstance() function creates one document and view for FIRSTWIN.CPP. The next initialization needed by a Windows program is the creation of a main frame window. This window contains, among other items, the program's main menu. Figure 15.6, shown earlier in the chapter, indicates FIRSTWIN's main frame window. This window is created and initialized in lines 70 through 74 of listing 15.1:

```
70   // create main MDI Frame window
71   CMainFrame* pMainFrame = new CMainFrame;
72   if (!pMainFrame->LoadFrame(IDR_MAINFRAME))
73       return FALSE;
74   m_pMainWnd = pMainFrame;
```

AppWizard created a file named MAINFRM.CPP. This source file and its associated header, MAINFRM.H, contain the class for mainframe windows. Line 71 creates a new frame window based on the CMainFrame class defined in MAINFRM.H and implemented in MAINFRM.CPP. The framework then assigns this object to a pointer, pMainFrame. Within this object, the framework creates such items as the toolbar and status bar found in main frame windows. Another item contained by a mainframe window is the application's menu bar. Line 72 loads the menu bar, along with several other items, from the program's resource file into the object. (Resource files are covered later in this chapter.) The framework then assigns the pMainFrame pointer to m_pMainWnd. m_pMainWnd is a member variable inherited from CWinApp.

Displaying the Main Frame Window

Although the frame window is created in lines 70 through 74, the window does not appear until you specifically instruct Windows to display it. This is done in lines 85 and 86 of listing 15.1:

```
85   pMainFrame->ShowWindow(m_nCmdShow);
86   pMainFrame->UpdateWindow();
```

Line 85 instructs the frame window to display itself. How the main frame window is displayed is determined by the value passed to ShowWindow().

The valid values are listed in table 15.1. The display mode is stored in your application class member variable m_nCmdShow, which is a member variable inherited from CWinApp. To change the default display mode, assign a new value from table 15.1 to m_nCmdShow before calling ShowWindow().

Table 15.1 *ShowWindow()* **Parameters**

Parameter	Description
SW_HIDE	Hides the window
SW_MINIMIZE	Minimizes the window and activates the top-level window in the system's list
SW_RESTORE	Activates and displays the window in its original size, even if the window is minimized or maximized
SW_SHOWMAXIMIZED	Activates the window and displays it as a maximized window
SW_SHOWMINIMIZED	Activates the window and displays it as an icon
SW_SHOWNORMAL	Activates and displays the window in its original size and position

Finally, the application tells Windows to update the display by calling UpdateWindow(). By calling this member function, your application sends a message to the Windows operating environment telling it to redraw the application's main frame window.

The Message Loop

An overview of MFC's message processing is presented here. To understand the message loop processing, consider how you implement a typical program. For example, consider a program in which **F**ile, **E**dit, and **V**iew menu items are displayed. Perhaps this program accepts a few keystrokes for special processing. You would probably implement such a program inside a keystroke-wait loop, by waiting for a keystroke and then, depending on the keystroke entered, calling an appropriate function. A typical command-oriented program sits in a wait loop that resembles the following pseudocode:

```
do {
  wait for a keystroke
  switch (keystroke)
  {
```

```
      case <Alt+F>: handle the File menu
      case <Alt+E>: handle the Edit menu
      case <Alt+V>: handle the View menu
      case <PageUp>: handle paging upward
      case <PageDown>: handle paging downward
   }
   while (no exit command entered)
```

Each of the keystrokes represents an event. In Windows, events include keystrokes, mouse clicks, mouse movements, and so on. The Run() function, which is inherited from the CWinApp class, essentially performs the same function:

```
   do {
     get a message
     process the message
   } while (no quit message received)
```

Messages, or events, originate from many sources. When you click a menu item, a message that is internal to Windows is generated, and the Run() function dispatches the message to be processed to a function (such as a function in your application), which processes the message. Keystrokes, clock or timer interrupts, mouse movement, and many other aspects of your system are classified as events that must be processed, usually by your application or in Windows or MFC. The essence of writing Windows applications is to intercept the appropriate messages and implement the correct functionality.

Processing Command Messages

You can accept and process messages in Windows applications in a variety of ways. MFC makes message processing simple: you define a function for each message that you want to process by using a special macro. Each message entering your application has a specific numeric value, represented by such symbols as ID_FILE_NEW. Normally, programs do not embed numeric constants directly in the code (this makes the program hard to change), but programs use constant identifiers to identify each message. These identifiers, like ID_FILE_NEW, are contained in a header file called AFXRES.H, located in the \MSVC\MFC\INCLUDE directory. AppWizard includes this file in your program's .RC resource file.

For example, you can see a set of message map macros in lines 19 through 30 of listing 15.1. The first of these function definitions is

```
21    ON_COMMAND(ID_APP_ABOUT, OnAppAbout)
```

which provides a definition for the message identified by the `ID_APP_ABOUT` constant. Each of the functions shown in lines 19 through 30 corresponds to one of the messages identified using the constant symbols `ID_FILE_NEW`, `ID_FILE_OPEN`, and `ID_FILE_PRINT_SETUP`. Those lines are repeated here:

```
19  BEGIN_MESSAGE_MAP(CFirstwinApp, CWinApp)
20  //{{AFX_MSG_MAP(CFirstwinApp)
21    ON_COMMAND(ID_APP_ABOUT, OnAppAbout)
22  // NOTE - the ClassWizard will add and remove mapping macros here.
23  //    DO NOT EDIT what you see in these blocks of generated code!
24  //}}AFX_MSG_MAP
25  // Standard file based document commands
26    ON_COMMAND(ID_FILE_NEW, CWinApp::OnFileNew)
27    ON_COMMAND(ID_FILE_OPEN, CWinApp::OnFileOpen)
28  // Standard print setup command
29    ON_COMMAND(ID_FILE_PRINT_SETUP, CWinApp::OnFilePrintSetup)
30  END_MESSAGE_MAP()
```

When you design the program's menu (using the App Studio tool), the framework assigns a unique numeric value to each menu selection. When Windows processes your mouse click on the pull-down menu item, it translates the click into the message number you selected for the particular menu item. The framework then calls the function you have mapped to the ID through the message map entry.

Using ClassWizard

Windows has hundreds of messages to which it responds, and programmers can define new messages for their applications. MFC provides default handlers for most of the Windows-specific messages. If you want to provide a new functionality for a Windows message, or if you want to add your own message, you must add a new message map entry and a function. This operation can be tedious, but fortunately the Visual Workbench provides a tool to help map Windows messages to user-defined functions. This tool is called ClassWizard, and it is shown in figure 15.7.

> **Note**
>
> Remember, if your are using MSVC Version 1.0, this dialog box looks different.

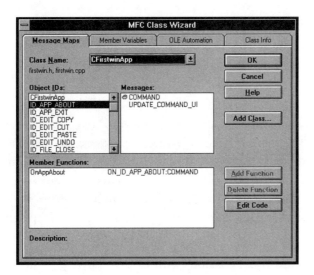

Fig. 15.7
The MFC
ClassWizard
dialog box.

The ClassWizard tool is implemented as a tabbed dialog box. Tabbed dialog boxes allow you to access different parts of the box by clicking the tabbed extenders along the top. The first tab in ClassWizard enables you to map a Windows message to a function you define. The next tab lets you add member variables to your class definition. Thus, you do not need to open the header file and manually type the variable definition. ClassWizard does this automatically for you! The next tab deals with OLE 2.0-aware applications. The final tab displays information about the class you are designing with ClassWizard. This part of the dialog box also enables you to change certain overall parameters for your class.

Adding a Message Map Entry with ClassWizard

To add a function to handle a Windows message, you must first specify which class will handle the message. You specify the class in the Class **N**ame combo box. This combo box contains all the classes defined in your project for which message map entries can be added. Unfortunately, not all classes are supported by ClassWizard. For those classes, you must manually enter the message maps and member variables.

After you select the appropriate class, ClassWizard displays the IDs to which you can map messages in the Object **I**Ds list box. As you click an object ID in this list box, the messages to which the ID can respond are listed in the Mes-sa**g**es list box. Double-click a message, and ClassWizard displays the Add Member Function dialog box, as shown in figure 15.8.

Fig. 15.8
Adding a
member func-
tion with
ClassWizard.

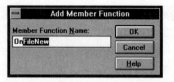

ClassWizard offers a name for this new function, but you can enter any name you want in the Member Function **N**ame edit box. ClassWizard then writes the function body to the source file and a function prototype to the header file. If you clicked the **G**enerate Source Comments check box in AppWizard's Options dialog box, ClassWizard adds a TODO reminder comment to the function body. ClassWizard adds also the appropriate message map entry to the source file.

Editing Message Map Functions with ClassWizard

If you want to edit the function body when you add the message map, you can click the **E**dit Code button in the MFC ClassWizard dialog box. This action places you in the Visual Workbench editor at the function's body section of code.

ClassWizard adds to the Member **F**unctions list box the function names you define. You can edit or delete functions by selecting the function in the list box and then clicking the appropriate button at the right of the MFC ClassWizard dialog box.

ClassWizard makes adding message maps easy for a variety of Windows messages, including the messages that Windows sends to and from dialog box controls. A list of controls is provided in table 1.2 in Chapter 1, "The Fundamentals of C++ Programming."

Resources

The user interface components of your application are stored as resources in a resource file. This file can also contain other portions of your applications, such as strings used in error messages, icons, bitmaps, and so on. As part of the compile-link step, the resource file is appended to the end of your .EXE application file. To load a resource, your program just needs to open its own .EXE file and read the resource from the end of the file.

Although several ways exist to design resources for your application, the easiest and most flexible way is to use Application Studio, or App Studio, provided by Microsoft. Figure 15.9 shows a typical view of the App Studio application, used here to design the About box. The illustration shows a set of drawing tools that you can use to draw the dialog box exactly as it will appear as part of your program. You can add text, edit fields, radio buttons, check boxes, pushbuttons, and all types of Windows user interface controls. You simply place the object in the drawing. When you double-click an item in this dialog box, you see a box of properties displayed (see fig. 15.10). You can use this properties box to set additional options.

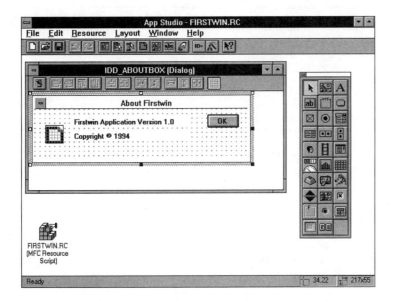

Fig. 15.9
App Studio showing how you draw the About dialog box.

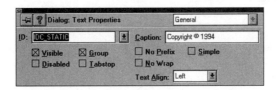

Fig. 15.10
A properties box for specifying a unique identifier for user interface controls.

When you have finished using App Studio to design the user interface for your application, you usually save the result as an .RC or resource script file. Listings 15.2 through 15.5 present some of the components of the FIRSTWIN.RC file that AppWizard generated for your application.

The necessary .RES file is created by compiling the resource script with a resource compiler named RC.EXE and is attached to the end of the .EXE file during the linking process. The project file created by AppWizard handles this compiling and binding as part of its build process.

Listing 15.2 illustrates the resource code generated by AppWizard for your application's main menu. You can use App Studio to add and delete menu items; thus, you do not need to edit the resource (.RC) file to add such items to your application. The IDR_MAINFRAME menu is the default menu displayed in an MDI application when no MDI child windows are visible. If an MDI child window is visible, the framework displays the menu represented by the IDR_FIRSTWTYPE menu.

Listing 15.2 The Menu Bar and Pull-Down Menus

```
IDR_MAINFRAME MENU PRELOAD DISCARDABLE
BEGIN
    POPUP "&File"
    BEGIN
        MENUITEM "&New\tCtrl+N",               ID_FILE_NEW
        MENUITEM "&Open...\tCtrl+O",            ID_FILE_OPEN
        MENUITEM SEPARATOR
        MENUITEM "P&rint Setup...",             ID_FILE_PRINT_SETUP
        MENUITEM SEPARATOR
        MENUITEM "Recent File",
ID_FILE_MRU_FILE1,GRAYED
        MENUITEM SEPARATOR
        MENUITEM "E&xit",                       ID_APP_EXIT
    END
    POPUP "&View"
    BEGIN
        MENUITEM "&Toolbar",                    ID_VIEW_TOOLBAR
        MENUITEM "&Status Bar",                 ID_VIEW_STATUS_BAR
    END
    POPUP "&Help"
    BEGIN
        MENUITEM "&About Firstwin...",          ID_APP_ABOUT
    END
END

IDR_FIRSTWTYPE MENU PRELOAD DISCARDABLE
BEGIN
    POPUP "&File"
    BEGIN
        MENUITEM "&New\tCtrl+N",               ID_FILE_NEW
        MENUITEM "&Open...\tCtrl+O",            ID_FILE_OPEN
        MENUITEM "&Close",                      ID_FILE_CLOSE
        MENUITEM "&Save\tCtrl+S",               ID_FILE_SAVE
        MENUITEM "Save &As...",                 ID_FILE_SAVE_AS
        MENUITEM SEPARATOR
        MENUITEM "&Print...\tCtrl+P",           ID_FILE_PRINT
        MENUITEM "Print Pre&view",
ID_FILE_PRINT_PREVIEW
        MENUITEM "P&rint Setup...",             ID_FILE_PRINT_SETUP
        MENUITEM SEPARATOR
        MENUITEM "Recent File",
ID_FILE_MRU_FILE1,GRAYED
```

```
            MENUITEM SEPARATOR
            MENUITEM "E&xit",                        ID_APP_EXIT
        END
        POPUP "&Edit"
        BEGIN
            MENUITEM "&Undo\tCtrl+Z",                ID_EDIT_UNDO
            MENUITEM SEPARATOR
            MENUITEM "Cu&t\tCtrl+X",                 ID_EDIT_CUT
            MENUITEM "&Copy\tCtrl+C",                ID_EDIT_COPY
            MENUITEM "&Paste\tCtrl+V",               ID_EDIT_PASTE
        END
        POPUP "&View"
        BEGIN
            MENUITEM "&Toolbar",                     ID_VIEW_TOOLBAR
            MENUITEM "&Status Bar",                  ID_VIEW_STATUS_BAR
        END
        POPUP "&Window"
        BEGIN
            MENUITEM "&New Window",                  ID_WINDOW_NEW
            MENUITEM "&Cascade",                     ID_WINDOW_CASCADE
            MENUITEM "&Tile",                        ID_WINDOW_TILE_HORZ
            MENUITEM "&Arrange Icons",               ID_WINDOW_ARRANGE
        END
        POPUP "&Help"
        BEGIN
            MENUITEM "&About Firstwin...",           ID_APP_ABOUT
        END
    END
```

Listing 15.3 represents the resource statements used to create the About dialog box. The About box displays four dialog controls: an icon indicated by the keyword ICON, two static text controls represented by the keyword LTEXT, and one default pushbutton indicated by the keyword DEFPUSHBUTTON. The DEFPUSHBUTTON is the button selected when the user presses the Enter key.

Listing 15.3 The About Dialog Box

```
    IDD_ABOUTBOX DIALOG DISCARDABLE  34, 22, 217, 55
    CAPTION "About Firstwin"
    STYLE DS_MODALFRAME ¦ WS_POPUP ¦ WS_CAPTION ¦ WS_SYSMENU
    FONT 8, "MS Sans Serif"
    BEGIN
        ICON            IDR_MAINFRAME,IDC_STATIC,11,17,20,20
        LTEXT           "Firstwin Application Version
                        1.0",IDC_STATIC,40,10,119,8
        LTEXT           "Copyright \251 1994",IDC_STATIC,40,25,119,8
        DEFPUSHBUTTON   "OK",IDOK,176,6,32,14,WS_GROUP
    END
```

Listing 15.4 shows the prompt strings that the framework displays in the status bar when the cursor is over a menu item. The framework knows which string to display because the ID for the prompt string is identical to the ID for the menu item.

Listing 15.4 String Table Entries for Status Bar Prompts

```
STRINGTABLE DISCARDABLE
BEGIN
    ID_FILE_NEW             "Create a new document"
    ID_FILE_OPEN            "Open an existing document"
    ID_FILE_CLOSE           "Close the active document"
    ID_FILE_SAVE            "Save the active document"
    ID_FILE_SAVE_AS         "Save the active document with a new name"
    ID_FILE_PAGE_SETUP      "Change the printing options"
    ID_FILE_PRINT_SETUP     "Change the printer and printing options"
    ID_FILE_PRINT           "Print the active document"
    ID_FILE_PRINT_PREVIEW   "Display full pages"
    ID_APP_ABOUT            "Display program information, version number and
                            copyright"
    ID_APP_EXIT             "Quit the application; prompts to save documents"
    ID_FILE_MRU_FILE1       "Open this document"
    ID_FILE_MRU_FILE2       "Open this document"
    ID_FILE_MRU_FILE3       "Open this document"
    ID_FILE_MRU_FILE4       "Open this document"
    ID_NEXT_PANE            "Switch to the next window pane"
    ID_PREV_PANE            "Switch back to the previous window pane"
    ID_WINDOW_NEW           "Open another window for the active document"
    ID_WINDOW_ARRANGE       "Arrange icons at the bottom of the window"
    ID_WINDOW_CASCADE       "Arrange windows so they overlap"
    ID_WINDOW_TILE_HORZ     "Arrange windows as non-overlapping tiles"
    ID_WINDOW_TILE_VERT     "Arrange windows as non-overlapping tiles"
    ID_WINDOW_SPLIT         "Split the active window into panes"
    ID_EDIT_CLEAR           "Erase the selection"
    ID_EDIT_CLEAR_ALL       "Erase everything"
    ID_EDIT_COPY            "Copy the selection and put it on the Clipboard"
    ID_EDIT_CUT             "Cut the selection and put it on the Clipboard"
    ID_EDIT_FIND            "Find the specified text"
    ID_EDIT_PASTE           "Insert Clipboard contents"
    ID_EDIT_REPEAT          "Repeat the last action"
    ID_EDIT_REPLACE         "Replace specific text with different text"
    ID_EDIT_SELECT_ALL      "Select the entire document"
    ID_EDIT_UNDO            "Undo the last action"
    ID_EDIT_REDO            "Redo the previously undone action"
    ID_VIEW_TOOLBAR         "Show or hide the toolbar"
    ID_VIEW_STATUS_BAR      "Show or hide the status bar"
END
```

Listing 15.5 illustrates the accelerator keys used in the application. Accelerators provide hot keys for often-used functions, such as opening a new file. The hot key combination for opening a file is Ctrl+N and is referenced by the ID given to the corresponding menu item ID_FILE_OPEN.

Listing 15.5 Accelerator Table Entries

```
IDR_MAINFRAME ACCELERATORS PRELOAD MOVEABLE
BEGIN
    "N",          ID_FILE_NEW,          VIRTKEY,CONTROL
    "O",          ID_FILE_OPEN,         VIRTKEY,CONTROL
    "S",          ID_FILE_SAVE,         VIRTKEY,CONTROL
    "P",          ID_FILE_PRINT,        VIRTKEY,CONTROL
    "Z",          ID_EDIT_UNDO,         VIRTKEY,CONTROL
    "X",          ID_EDIT_CUT,          VIRTKEY,CONTROL
    "C",          ID_EDIT_COPY,         VIRTKEY,CONTROL
    "V",          ID_EDIT_PASTE,        VIRTKEY,CONTROL
    VK_BACK,      ID_EDIT_UNDO,         VIRTKEY,ALT
    VK_DELETE,    ID_EDIT_CUT,          VIRTKEY,SHIFT
    VK_INSERT,    ID_EDIT_COPY,         VIRTKEY,CONTROL
    VK_INSERT,    ID_EDIT_PASTE,        VIRTKEY,SHIFT
    VK_F6,        ID_NEXT_PANE,         VIRTKEY
    VK_F6,        ID_PREV_PANE,         VIRTKEY,SHIFT
END
```

The MFC Class Hierarchy

MFC provides a set of prebuilt classes for implementing the user interface elements of a Microsoft Windows application. You can see the full inheritance hierarchy of these components in the MFC library hierarchy chart located on pages xvi and xvii of *Reference Volume 1: Class Library Reference for the Microsoft Foundation Class Library*. Figure 15.11 illustrates the basic hierarchy tree of MFC. You can see that most of the MFC Windows components descend from the CObject class.

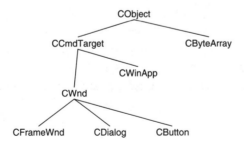

Fig. 15.11
The MFC class hierarchy.

The FIRSTWIN Application—Part 2

To complete this introduction to MFC, you add code to print Hello World! to the client area of the application. The following sections provide additional functionality to the FIRSTWIN program you generated with AppWizard. The application you generated is functional, but it does nothing specific. You must add this functionality yourself. A detailed explanation of the program appears following the various listings.

When studying the program in listing 15.1, keep in mind that a Windows program is processing Windows messages. To understand this concept, observe what happens when you click the **A**bout Firstwin option in the **H**elp menu. When Windows receives the click, it generates a WM_COMMAND Windows message with ID_APP_ABOUT as a parameter. This message then activates the OnAppAbout() member function of the CWinApp-derived class, CFirstWinApp. CFirstWinAPP::OnAppAbout() instantiates a new CAboutDlg (which is derived from the standard CDialog class), as defined in lines 91 through 130 of listing 15.1.

Line 136 calls the DoModal() function, which is the routine that displays the dialog box and processes your editing of its data. DoModal() exits when you choose either an OK button or a Cancel button, and returns the key you pressed as the result. The return value is ignored for the About dialog processed on line 136.

Documents Revisited

Earlier in this chapter, you learned of the new document/view architecture introduced with Visual C++ and MFC 2.0. You learned that a document is basically a storage area for an application's data. For the FIRSTWIN application, you need to add a CString member variable that holds the string "Hello World!". To add this member variable, first open the FIRSTDOC.H file. You can open this file by clicking the Project Files button (the first button on the Workbench's toolbar) and then selecting the file from the drop-down list that appears.

After the file is loaded into the Visual Workbench editor, you can add the following lines to the header file:

```
private:
   CString m_String;
```

This change is shown beginning on line 35 of listing 15.6, which contains the FIRSTDOC.H file.

Listing 15.6 The Definition File for the *CFirstWinDoc* Class

```
1   // firstdoc.h : interface of the CFirstwinDoc class
2   //
3   /////////////////////////////////////////////////////////////////
4
5   class CFirstwinDoc : public CDocument
6   {
7   protected: // create from serialization only
8       CFirstwinDoc();
9       DECLARE_DYNCREATE(CFirstwinDoc)
10
11  // Attributes
12  public:
13  // Operations
14  public:
15
16  // Implementation
17  public:
18      virtual ~CFirstwinDoc();
19      virtual void Serialize(CArchive& ar); // overridden for document i/o
20  #ifdef _DEBUG
21      virtual void AssertValid() const;
22      virtual void Dump(CDumpContext& dc) const;
23  #endif
24
25  protected:
26      virtual BOOL OnNewDocument();
27
28  // Generated message map functions
29  protected:
30      //{{AFX_MSG(CFirstwinDoc)
31      // NOTE - the ClassWizard will add and remove member functions here.
32      // DO NOT EDIT what you see in these blocks of generated code !
33      //}}AFX_MSG
34      DECLARE_MESSAGE_MAP()
35  private:
36    CString m_String;
37  public:
38    CString GetData() { return m_String };
39  };
40
41  /////////////////////////////////////////////////////////////////
```

You must also add an access function to the class definition. The access function allows other objects to retrieve this variable. The CFirstwinDoc class defines an inline access function, called GetData(), which returns the private data member m_String. You might also want to add a function to set the value of this data member so that other objects can assign a string value to this variable. For this example, you can give the string an initial value in the CFirstwinDoc's constructor.

To add the initialization code to the constructor, you need to load the FIRSTDOC.CPP file into the editor. You can follow the instructions given earlier for loading the FIRSTDOC.H file. Line 32 of listing 15.7 displays the initialization of the private data member m_String with the value "Hello World!".

Listing 15.7 The Document Implementation File

```
 1  // firstdoc.cpp : implementation of the CFirstwinDoc class
 2  //
 3
 4  #include "stdafx.h"
 5  #include "firstwin.h"
 6
 7  #include "firstdoc.h"
 8
 9  #ifdef _DEBUG
10  #undef THIS_FILE
11  static char BASED_CODE THIS_FILE[] = __FILE__;
12  #endif
13
14  /////////////////////////////////////////////////////////////////
15  // CFirstwinDoc
16
17  IMPLEMENT_DYNCREATE(CFirstwinDoc, CDocument)
18
19  BEGIN_MESSAGE_MAP(CFirstwinDoc, CDocument)
20      //{{AFX_MSG_MAP(CFirstwinDoc)
21      // NOTE - the ClassWizard will add and remove mapping macros here.
22      // DO NOT EDIT what you see in these blocks of generated code!
23          //}}AFX_MSG_MAP
24  END_MESSAGE_MAP()
25
26  /////////////////////////////////////////////////////////////////
27  // CFirstwinDoc construction/destruction
28
29  CFirstwinDoc::CFirstwinDoc()
30  {
31      // TODO: add one-time construction code here
32      m_String = "Hello World!";
33  }
34
35  CFirstwinDoc::~CFirstwinDoc()
36  {
37  }
38
39  BOOL CFirstwinDoc::OnNewDocument()
40  {
41      if (!CDocument::OnNewDocument())
42          return FALSE;
43
44      // TODO: add reinitialization code here
45      // (SDI documents will reuse this document)
```

```
46
47      return TRUE;
48  }
49
50  ////////////////////////////////////////////////////////////////
51  // CFirstwinDoc serialization
52
53  void CFirstwinDoc::Serialize(CArchive& ar)
54  {
55      if (ar.IsStoring())
56      {
57          // TODO: add storing code here
58
59      }
60      else
61      {
62          // TODO: add loading code here
63
64      }
65  }
66
67  ////////////////////////////////////////////////////////////////
68  // CFirstwinDoc diagnostics
69
70  #ifdef _DEBUG
71  void CFirstwinDoc::AssertValid() const
72  {
73      CDocument::AssertValid();
74  }
75
76  void CFirstwinDoc::Dump(CDumpContext& dc) const
77  {
78      CDocument::Dump(dc);
79  }
80  #endif //_DEBUG
81
82  ////////////////////////////////////////////////////////////////
83  // CFirstwinDoc commands
```

Lines 9 through 12 supply debug information to the integrated debugger, provided the macro _DEBUG is defined. If you have instructed the Workbench to create a debug build of your application (which is the default), this code is included in your executable file. Certain debug-specific functions are also included, as indicated by lines 70 through 80. For more information on debugging, see Chapter 12, "Debugging Visual C++ Programs."

You have now provided your program with a simple data element, a string, contained in the application's document class. Now you need a way to write this string to the client area of an MDI child window. This is a job for your program's view class.

Reviewing MFC Views

Documents hold data, but views allow a user to interact with the data. For this simple example, your program merely displays a string in the client area of an MDI child window. This is the type of window created by an MDI application. Listing 15.8 presents only the function you need to modify in order to display the text found in the document's data. A detailed explanation of the function, OnDraw(), appears following the listing. AppWizard generated the function body for OnDraw(), but you must supply the actual code to display the document's data. Load the FIRSTVW.CPP into the editor and enter the code shown in listing 15.8 into the OnDraw() function body after the TODO comment.

Listing 15.8 The Complete *OnDraw()* Member Function

```
1   ///////////////////////////////////////////////////////////////////
2   // CFirstwinView drawing
3
4   void CFirstwinView::OnDraw(CDC* pDC)
5   {
6       CFirstwinDoc* pDoc = GetDocument();
7       ASSERT_VALID(pDoc);
8
9       // TODO: add draw code for native data here
10      CString s;
11      CRect rect;
12
13      s = pDoc->GetData(); // retrieve the data from the document class
14
15      GetClientRect( rect );
16      pDC->SetTextAlign( TA_BASELINE | TA_CENTER );
17      pDC->SetTextColor( ::GetSysColor( COLOR_WINDOWTEXT ) );
18      pDC->SetBkMode(TRANSPARENT);
19      pDC->TextOut( ( rect.right / 2 ), ( rect.bottom / 2 ),
20                  s, s.GetLength() );
21
22  }
```

The first item to notice is the name of the function, OnDraw(). The body of this function was created by AppWizard in order for you to display information in your application. You do not display text characters to the screen as you do in MS-DOS or QuickWin applications. The reason is that Windows does not know how to handle text!

Windows is a graphical environment, and all it knows how to do is display graphics. Thus, all Windows' display functions paint graphics onto the screen, even text characters. One benefit of this technique is that Windows does not care whether the screen is a monitor or a printer. To accomplish this task, Windows uses what is called a *device context*, or DC. This data structure is internal to Windows and provides a hardware-independent "surface" on which to draw. In line 4, the framework passes to the OnDraw() function a pointer to an MFC class called CDC. This class encapsulates a device context and provides many member functions for drawing. Once you have such a pointer, you can use the CDC member functions to display text.

The first step in displaying the data string is to get a pointer to your application's document. Your document is where the data is stored. The function call on line 6, GetDocument(), provides such a pointer. You can now use this pointer to call the GetData() function you defined earlier in this chapter. The return value is stored in the local CString variable s. Line 13 illustrates this step.

Before you display a Windows graphic, you must tell the routines where on the device context to start and stop painting the image. This is why you need a rectangle—it provides a bounding area where you can start and stop drawing. Fortunately, MFC provides a class, called CRect, that represents a rectangle. Line 15 uses a Windows API function to get the rectangle containing the program's client area, and places this rectangle in the local CRect variable rect.

Lines 15 through 18 prepare the device context for displaying data as a text string. Line 19 then calls a CDC member function, TextOut(), to actually paint the text string onto the DC within the client rectangle. The function performs some calculations so that the text is always centered, no matter what the size of the MDI child window. Figure 15.12 displays the results from your modified FIRSTWIN program.

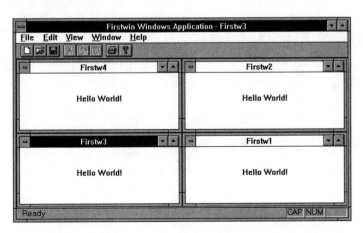

Fig. 15.12
Greetings from FIRSTWIN.

For one final example of the power provided by the MFC application framework, pull down FIRSTWIN's **F**ile menu and choose the **P**rint option. Your program prints the text string, although you have not written a single line of code for printing text! All this functionality, and more, has been provided by MFC.

Summary

Microsoft provides valuable tools and a class library to help you write Microsoft Windows applications. Using AppWizard and MFC, you can generate completely functional Windows applications and thus eliminate the complicated overhead inherent in writing Windows applications. All of this is handled for you by AppWizard and the MFC application framework. You can then concentrate on implementing the features that make your application unique.

MFC provides classes to support the common user interface elements, including windows, scroll bars, list boxes, and dialog boxes along with their controls (radio buttons, check boxes, edit fields, and pushbuttons). Each of these classes offers substantial functionality; you need only to extend the class to support your specific requirements.

The purpose of Windows programming is writing code to intercept and respond to messages. In Windows, messages come from events, such as mouse movements or clicks. Messages can originate also from other functions in the program (functions can "post" or send messages to other windows). The "guts" of Windows application programming are proper recognition and processing of Windows messages.

Review Questions

1. Which Visual Workbench tool do you use to generate an MFC-based Windows program?

2. From what class (object) do you derive your MFC application?

3. What is the purpose of the inherited InitInstance() function?

4. Which Visual Workbench tool do you use to write a function that handles Windows messages?

5. What is a resource? What programming tool is normally used to edit and create resources for use with MFC programs?

6. What is a resource script file?

7. When does the resource file get attached to your program?

8. What is a document?

9. What is a view?

10. What is a message? What are message maps?

11. What is the purpose of the `DoModal()` function?

Exercises

1. Use AppWizard to create an SDI application that displays `Hello World!` in the program's client area.

2. Provide a test in FIRSTWIN.CPP's `InitInstance()` function that checks for a previous instance of this program and then terminates if a copy is already running.

3. Create an application that has a dialog box as its main frame window. Use App Studio to design the dialog box and then use ClassWizard to create the member functions necessary for your controls.

Appendix A

ASCII and Extended ASCII Codes

ASCII (American Standard Code for Information Interchange) is a widely used standard that defines numeric values for a common set of alphabetic characters. The first 32 characters are reserved for formatting and hardware control codes. Following these codes are 96 "printable" characters. IBM defined symbols for the final 128 ASCII values when it released the IBM PC, and referred to the additional characters as *extended ASCII codes*. This entire set of 256 characters is often referred to as the PC-8 character set, or code page 437.

Dec X_{10}	Hex X_{16}	Binary X_2	ASCII Character	Ctrl	Key
000	00	0000 0000	null	NUL	^@
001	01	0000 0001	☺	SOH	^A
002	02	0000 0010	☻	STX	^B
003	03	0000 0011	♥	ETX	^C
004	04	0000 0100	♦	EOT	^D
005	05	0000 0101	♣	ENQ	^E
006	06	0000 0110	♠	ACK	^F
007	07	0000 0111	●	BEL	^G
008	08	0000 1000	■	BS	^H
009	09	0000 1001	○	HT	^I

Dec X_{10}	Hex X_{16}	Binary X_2	ASCII Character	Ctrl	Key
010	0A	0000 1010	■	LF	^J
011	0B	0000 1011	♂	VT	^K
012	0C	0000 1100	♀	FF	^L
013	0D	0000 1101	♪	CR	^M
014	0E	0000 1110	♪♪	SO	^N
015	0F	0000 1111	☼	SI	^O
016	10	0001 0000	►	DLE	^P
017	11	0001 0001	◄	DC1	^Q
018	12	0001 0010	↕	DC2	^R
019	13	0001 0011	‼	DC3	^S
020	14	0001 0100	¶	DC4	^T
021	15	0001 0101	§	NAK	^U
022	16	0001 0110	–	SYN	^V
023	17	0001 0111	↨	ETB	^W
024	18	0001 1000	↑	CAN	^X
025	19	0001 1001	↓	EM	^Y
026	1A	0001 1010	→	SUB	^Z
027	1B	0001 1011	←	ESC	^[
028	1C	0001 1100	∟	FS	^\
029	1D	0001 1101	↔	GS	^]
030	1E	0001 1110	▲	RS	^^
031	1F	0001 1111	▼	US	^_
032	20	0010 0000	Space		
033	21	0010 0001	!		
034	22	0010 0010	"		
035	23	0010 0011	#		
036	24	0010 0100	$		
037	25	0010 0101	%		
038	26	0010 0110	&		
039	27	0010 0111	'		
040	28	0010 1000	(		

Dec X_{10}	Hex X_{16}	Binary X_2	ASCII Character
041	29	0010 1001	)
042	2A	0010 1010	*
043	2B	0010 1011	+
044	2C	0010 1100	'
045	2D	0010 1101	-
046	2E	0010 1110	.
047	2F	0010 1111	/
048	30	0011 0000	0
049	31	0011 0001	1
050	32	0011 0010	2
051	33	0011 0011	3
052	34	0011 0100	4
053	35	0011 0101	5
054	36	0011 0110	6
055	37	0011 0111	7
056	38	0011 1000	8
057	39	0011 1001	9
058	3A	0011 1010	:
059	3B	0011 1011	;
060	3C	0011 1100	<
061	3D	0011 1101	=
062	3E	0011 1110	>
063	3F	0011 1111	?
064	40	0100 0000	@
065	41	0100 0001	A
066	42	0100 0010	B
067	43	0100 0011	C
068	44	0100 0100	D
069	45	0100 0101	E
070	46	0100 0110	F
071	47	0100 0111	G
072	48	0100 1000	H
073	49	0100 1001	I

Dec X_{10}	Hex X_{16}	Binary X_2	ASCII Character
074	4A	0100 1010	J
075	4B	0100 1011	K
076	4C	0100 1100	L
077	4D	0100 1101	M
078	4E	0100 1110	N
079	4F	0100 1111	O
080	50	0101 0000	P
081	51	0101 0001	Q
082	52	0101 0010	R
083	53	0101 0011	S
084	54	0101 0100	T
085	55	0101 0101	U
086	56	0101 0110	V
087	57	0101 0111	W
088	58	0101 1000	X
089	59	0101 1001	Y
090	5A	0101 1010	Z
091	5B	0101 1011	[
092	5C	0101 1100	\
093	5D	0101 1101	]
094	5E	0101 1110	^
095	5F	0101 1111	–
096	60	0110 0000	`
097	61	0110 0001	a
098	62	0110 0010	b
099	63	0110 0011	c
100	64	0110 0100	d
101	65	0110 0101	e
102	66	0110 0110	f
103	67	0110 0111	g
104	68	0110 1000	h
105	69	0110 1001	i

Dec X_{10}	Hex X_{16}	Binary X_2	ASCII Character
106	6A	0110 1010	j
107	6B	0110 1011	k
108	6C	0110 1100	l
109	6D	0110 1101	m
110	6E	0110 1110	n
111	6F	0110 1111	o
112	70	0111 0000	p
113	71	0111 0001	q
114	72	0111 0010	r
115	73	0111 0011	s
116	74	0111 0100	t
117	75	0111 0101	u
118	76	0111 0110	v
119	77	0111 0111	w
120	78	0111 1000	x
121	79	0111 1001	y
122	7A	0111 1010	z
123	7B	0111 1011	{
124	7C	0111 1100	¦
125	7D	0111 1101	}
126	7E	0111 1110	~
127	7F	0111 1111	Delete
128	80	1000 0000	Ç
129	81	1000 0001	ü
130	82	1000 0010	é
131	83	1000 0011	â
132	84	1000 0100	ä
133	85	1000 0101	à
134	86	1000 0110	å
135	87	1000 0111	ç
136	88	1000 1000	ê
137	89	1000 1001	ë

Dec X_{10}	Hex X_{16}	Binary X_2	ASCII Character
138	8A	1000 1010	è
139	8B	1000 1011	ï
140	8C	1000 1100	î
141	8D	1000 1101	ì
142	8E	1000 1110	Ä
143	8F	1000 1111	Å
144	90	1001 0000	É
145	91	1001 0001	æ
146	92	1001 0010	Æ
147	93	1001 0011	ô
148	94	1001 0100	ö
149	95	1001 0101	ò
150	96	1001 0110	û
151	97	1001 0111	ù
152	98	1001 1000	ÿ
153	99	1001 1001	Ö
154	9A	1001 1010	Ü
155	9B	1001 1011	¢
156	9C	1001 1100	£
157	9D	1001 1101	¥
158	9E	1001 1110	Pt
159	9F	1001 1111	*f*
160	A0	1010 0000	á
161	A1	1010 0001	í
162	A2	1010 0010	ó
163	A3	1010 0011	ú
164	A4	1010 0100	ñ
165	A5	1010 0101	Ñ
166	A6	1010 0110	a̲
167	A7	1010 0111	o̲
168	A8	1010 1000	¿
169	A9	1010 1001	⌐

Dec X$_{10}$	Hex X$_{16}$	Binary X$_2$	ASCII Character
170	AA	1010 1010	¬
171	AB	1010 1011	½
172	AC	1010 1100	¼
173	AD	1010 1101	¡
174	AE	1010 1110	«
175	AF	1010 1111	»
176	B0	1011 0000	▒
177	B1	1011 0001	▓
178	B2	1011 0010	█
179	B3	1011 0011	│
180	B4	1011 0100	┤
181	B5	1011 0101	╡
182	B6	1011 0110	╢
183	B7	1011 0111	╖
184	B8	1011 1000	╕
185	B9	1011 1001	╣
186	BA	1011 1010	║
187	BB	1011 1011	╗
188	BC	1011 1100	╝
189	BD	1011 1101	╜
190	BE	1011 1110	╛
191	BF	1011 1111	┐
192	C0	1100 0000	└
193	C1	1100 0001	┴
194	C2	1100 0010	┬
195	C3	1100 0011	├
196	C4	1100 0100	─
197	C5	1100 0101	+
198	C6	1100 0110	╞
199	C7	1100 0111	╟
200	C8	1100 1000	╚
201	C9	1100 1001	╔

Dec X_{10}	Hex X_{16}	Binary X_2	ASCII Character
202	CA	1100 1010	⊥
203	CB	1100 1011	╦
204	CC	1100 1100	╠
205	CD	1100 1101	=
206	CE	1100 1110	╬
207	CF	1100 1111	╧
208	D0	1101 0000	╨
209	D1	1101 0001	╤
210	D2	1101 0010	╥
211	D3	1101 0011	╙
212	D4	1101 0100	╘
213	D5	1101 0101	╒
214	D6	1101 0110	╓
215	D7	1101 0111	╫
216	D8	1101 1000	╪
217	D9	1101 1001	┘
218	DA	1101 1010	┌
219	DB	1101 1011	█
220	DC	1101 1100	▄
221	DD	1101 1101	▌
222	DE	1101 1110	▐
223	DF	1101 1111	▀
224	E0	1110 0000	α
225	E1	1110 0001	β
226	E2	1110 0010	Γ
227	E3	1110 0011	π
228	E4	1110 0100	Σ
229	E5	1110 0101	σ
230	E6	1110 0110	μ

Dec X_{10}	Hex X_{16}	Binary X_2	ASCII Character
231	E7	1110 0111	τ
232	E8	1110 1000	Φ
233	E9	1110 1001	θ
234	EA	1110 1010	Ω
235	EB	1110 1011	δ
236	EC	1110 1100	∞
237	ED	1110 1101	ø
238	EE	1110 1110	∈
239	EF	1110 1111	∩
240	F0	1111 0000	≡
241	F1	1111 0001	±
242	F2	1111 0010	≥
243	F3	1111 0011	≤
244	F4	1111 0100	⌠
245	F5	1111 0101	⌡
246	F6	1111 0110	÷
247	F7	1111 0111	≈
248	F8	1111 1000	°
249	F9	1111 1001	•
250	FA	1111 1010	·
251	FB	1111 1011	√
252	FC	1111 1100	η
253	FD	1111 1101	2
254	FE	1111 1110	■
255	FF	1111 1111	

Index

GO AHEAD. PLUG YOURSELF INTO
PRENTICE HALL COMPUTER PUBLISHING.

Introducing the PHCP Forum on CompuServe®

Yes, it's true. Now, you can have CompuServe access to the same professional, friendly folks who have made computers easier for years. On the PHCP Forum, you'll find additional information on the topics covered by every PHCP imprint—including Que, Sams Publishing, New Riders Publishing, Alpha Books, Brady Books, Hayden Books, and Adobe Press. In addition, you'll be able to receive technical support and disk updates for the software produced by Que Software and Paramount Interactive, a division of the Paramount Technology Group. It's a great way to supplement the best information in the business.

WHAT CAN YOU DO ON THE PHCP FORUM?

Play an important role in the publishing process—and make our books better while you make your work easier:

- Leave messages and ask questions about PHCP books and software—you're guaranteed a response within 24 hours

- Download helpful tips and software to help you get the most out of your computer

- Contact authors of your favorite PHCP books through electronic mail

- Present your own book ideas

- Keep up to date on all the latest books available from each of PHCP's exciting imprints

JOIN NOW AND GET A FREE COMPUSERVE STARTER KIT!

To receive your free CompuServe Introductory Membership, call toll-free, **1-800-848-8199** and ask for representative **#597**. The Starter Kit Includes:

- Personal ID number and password

- $15 credit on the system

- Subscription to CompuServe Magazine

HERE'S HOW TO PLUG INTO PHCP:

Once on the CompuServe System, type any of these phrases to access the PHCP Forum:

GO PHCP	**GO BRADY**
GO QUEBOOKS	**GO HAYDEN**
GO SAMS	**GO QUESOFT**
GO NEWRIDERS	**GO PARAMOUNTINTER**
GO ALPHA	

Once you're on the CompuServe Information Service, be sure to take advantage of all of CompuServe's resources. CompuServe is home to more than 1,700 products and services—plus it has over 1.5 million members worldwide. You'll find valuable online reference materials, travel and investor services, electronic mail, weather updates, leisure-time games and hassle-free shopping (no jam-packed parking lots or crowded stores).

Seek out the hundreds of other forums that populate CompuServe. Covering diverse topics such as pet care, rock music, cooking, and political issues, you're sure to find others with the sames concerns as you—and expand your knowledge at the same time.

Enhance Your Personal Computer System with Hardware and Networking Titles from Que!

Upgrading and Repairing PCs, 3rd Edition
Scott Mueller

This book is the ultimate resource for personal computer upgrade, maintenance, and troubleshooting information! It provides solutions to common PC problems and purchasing decisions and includes a glossary of terms, ASCII code charts, and expert recommendations.

IBM PCs and Compatibles
$34.95 USA
1-56529-467-X, 1,312 pp.

Introduction to Personal Computers, 4th Edition
White & Schafer

IBM, Macintosh, & Apple
$19.95 USA
1-56529-275-8, 512 pp.

Introduction to PC Communications
Phil Becker

IBM PCs
$24.95 USA
0-88022-747-8, 500 pp.

The CD-ROM Book
Sloman & Bosak

IBM, Macintosh, & Apple
$34.95 USA
1-56529-292-8, 480 pp.

Que's 1994 Computer Hardware Buyer's Guide
Bud Smith

IBM-compatibles, Macintosh, & Apple
$16.95 USA
1-56529-281-2, 480 pp.

Que's Speed Up Your Computer Book
David Reed

DOS 5
$29.95 USA
0-88022-761-3, 350 pp.

Using Novell NetWare 4, Special Edition
Que Development Group

Through Version 4
$35.00 USA
1-56529-069-0, 1,100 pp.

To Order, Call: (800) 428-5331
OR (317) 581-3500

Complete Computer Coverage

Que's 1994 Computer Hardware Buyer's Guide

Que Development Group

This absolute must-have guide packed with comparisons, recommendations, and tips for asking all the right questions familiarizes the reader with terms they will need to know. This book offers a complete analysis of both hardware and software products, and it's loaded with charts and tables of product comparisons.

IBM-compatibles, Apple, & Macintosh

$16.95 USA

1-56529-281-2, 480 pp., 8 x 10

Que's Computer User's Dictionary, 4th Edition

Bryan Pfaffenberger

This compact, practical reference contains hundreds of definitions, explanations, examples, and illustrations on topics from programming to desktop publishing. You can master the "language" of computers and learn how to make your personal computer more efficient and more powerful. Filled with tips and cautions, *Que's Computer User's Dictionary* is the perfect resource for anyone who uses a computer.

IBM, Macintosh, Apple, & Programming

$12.95 USA

1-56529-604-4, 650 pp., 4³/₄ x 8

To Order, Call: (800) 428-5331

Learn programming
By Example with Que!

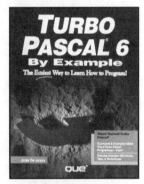

Que Has WordPerfect 6 Books
for All Types of Users!

Excel—Only from the Experts at Que

Order Your Program Disk Today

You can save yourself hours of tedious, error-prone typing by ordering the companion disk to *Object-Oriented Programming with Visual C++ 1.5*. The disk contains source code for all complete programs in the book, plus complete Visual C++ project files and executable files. You will also receive the list of answers to review questions and several of the sample programs.

For fastest service, order by phone (overnight delivery and electronic delivery are available at extra charge). Disks are available in both 5 1/4-inch and 3 1/2-inch format. The cost is $14.95 per disk, plus $1.50 for shipping and handling to U.S. addresses (outside U.S., add $5.00). North Carolina residents must add 5% sales tax. Allow 2-4 weeks for delivery.

To order by mail, complete the order form and mail to

Tristar Systems
2440 S. W. Cary Parkway
Suite #114
Cary, NC 27513

To order by phone, have your credit card information ready and call 1-800-229-5966.

Please specify the e-mail address if you would like your files delivered electronically.

Object-Oriented Programming with Visual C++ 1.5 Disk Order Form
Please PRINT

Product code: #100

Check desired disk size: 5 1/4" _____   3 1/2" _____

Check payment method: Check _____   Money order _____

For credit card holders: VISA _____   MasterCard _____

Credit card number: _____   Expiration: _____

Shipping preference: Regular UPS_____

UPS Next Day (extra charge)_____   FedEx Next Day_____

E-mail service: Compuserve _____   Internet _____

E-mail address: _____

Signature: _____
Name (please print): _____

Street Address: _____
City: _____   State: _____   ZIP: _____
Telephone: _____